A Theory of Criminal Justice

A Theory of
Criminal Justice

HYMAN GROSS

New York
Oxford University Press
1979

Second printing, 1979

Printed in the United States of America

Library of Congress Cataloging in Publication Data

Gross, Hyman.
A theory of criminal justice.

1. Criminal law—Philosophy. 2. Criminal
law. I. Title.
K5018.G7   345'.001   77-17049
ISBN 0-19-502349-8
ISBN 0-19-502350-1 pbk.

for
E.L.G., B.G., and J.M.G.

Contents

CHAPTER THREE
Conceiving Criminal Conduct: Culpability,
Intention, and Motive

CHAPTER FOUR
Conceiving Criminal Conduct: Harm and Attempts

Preface

When a crime is committed, justice must be done. Though it is easy to create an appearance of justice, mere appearance may turn out to be only an illusion. In this book I try to describe the real thing and examine its main features in detail. I do not invent a conception of criminal justice but discover it in the principles that are generally aimed at by the criminal law in every civilized society of a more or less liberal democratic complexion. Official deviations from these principles are abundant everywhere, but this need not embarrass the theorist so long as he remembers that he is not required to give an account of practices just as they are, any more than he is required to design an ideal jurisprudence for a utopian society. The theorist's job, I think, is to make clear the ideals that generally do guide practice and that make possible the very awareness of deviation. His job is also to show why those ideals are worthy of our acceptance, when indeed they are. The theorist thus provides the practitioner with guidance for sound practice and with a means of answering his critics when (but only when) they are not right.

In attempting to make a contribution along these lines I have found it necessary to deal critically with certain well-entrenched theoretical positions that seem to me wrong. In doing this I have tried wherever possible to avoid singling out particular authors or citing particular tracts—this in the belief that shoes anyway end up only on the feet they fit, and in the hope that what is controversial in this work may prompt better answers than I provide rather than intramural debates about other authors and their views. Similarly, I devote little time to the pedigree of the ideas I present, though in the entire book there can hardly be a single idea that does not have important antecedents elsewhere. I confess a lack of zeal for intellectual genealogy and offer as a penance a bibliography after the notes at the back of the book. This will allow the reader to rummage as I have through much that provides useful provocation and much that is a source of illumination—often both in a single piece. To avoid unnecessary interruptions, all the notes are collected at the back of the book. Nothing in the notes is necessary to follow the argument in the text, though on a few occasions the notes do provide some elaboration of the text that may ease one or another of the difficulties that linger on at the end of a section.

Two further bits of explanation are in order.

A volume embracing all the concerns of a truly comprehensive theory of criminal justice would extend into two great regions not explored here. It would take up the question of bounds beyond which the law ought not to go in establishing criminal liability for conduct. Discussions in this book of harm and danger do not define those limits, though I should like to think that what is said here could be put to good use in dealing with those other matters. That same all-embracing work would also have to deal with the problems of justice that are created by procedures of law enforcement, including matters of fairness both in and out of court. In the United States these problems have received far more attention as items of Constitutional law than have the more fundamental questions of criminal justice that are dealt with here. One hopes that, by reflecting on why we bother to enforce the law at all, we shall help to enlighten ourselves about what is and what is not the right way to go about it.

Finally, I must explain why some rather substantial topics are dealt with only superficially, while others are mined in depth. Defenses by way of justification, for example, only have their surfaces scratched even though rich veins lie beneath. Some neglect was made unavoidable by considerations of economy, and those topics that suffered least were those that seemed most important to understand our criminal jurisprudence as a whole and to reform the conceptual groundwork upon which it must stand.

I have profited much from discussion and criticism during the years of writing and rewriting, and find that my accumulated debts to friends and colleagues are far too numerous to be listed here. I should like, however, to acknowledge a general debt to the writing of H. L. A. Hart, since it drew me in a compelling fashion to the subject and then served to refresh even in the most tedious hours of my own work. There are two pieces of extended criticism that I cannot fail to acknowledge here with thanks. John Kleinig was kind enough to provide me with very useful comments on large portions of an earlier draft, and Don E. Scheid similarly commented with great care on the penultimate draft of the manuscript in its entirety. Both of them will of course recognize the many faults for which I alone am responsible and that remain in spite of their diligent efforts.

I am much indebted to Gertrude Schiller for long and faithful service at the typewriter, and to Patricia Rees for her very efficient help in proofreading and typing at the final stages. At Oxford University Press, James Anderson and Bethanie Alhadeff have been most helpful, and the role of manuscript editor has been performed by Mary Ellen Evans with consummate skill. Finally, I should like to thank the Bear Foundation for support of work that in one form or another found its way into parts of this book.

H. G.
Cambridge
June 1978

A Theory of Criminal Justice

CHAPTER ONE

Conceiving Criminal Justice

In the interest it arouses, little in life can compare with crime. Its appeal to the imagination is fresh and strong throughout literature, and in the world of everyday affairs the guilt or innocence of even an obscure stranger is a matter few people can turn away from with indifference. Through their crimes ordinary men become public figures and may even find a place in history, while a public figure accused of crime can expect a keener public than ever before in his illustrious career.

But crime is more than an absorbing preoccupation. Its presence as a social reality in every community gives rise first to anger and fear, then to an urgent concern about how crime ought to be dealt with. Ideas about the causes of crime and remedies rooted in these ideas succeed one another, reminding us as they pass out of fashion that explaining crime is an undertaking no less difficult than explaining law-abiding conduct, and that we are unlikely ever to see the kind of solution to the problem that our theories promise. All, however, is not change. One method of dealing with crime does endure through time. In a modern civilized society it is spoken of as criminal justice.

It is not hard to describe in a general way how the enterprise of criminal justice is supposed to be carried on. Crimes are defined and made punishable by the criminal law. Other laws designed to aid in the administration of the criminal law allow determinations of guilt or innocence and allow punishment to be imposed upon those found guilty. The criminal law itself consists of penal laws and principles of criminal jurisprudence. A penal law establishes a rule of conduct that most often prohibits (but sometimes requires) a designated act. In addition, a penal law prescribes a penal sanction that may be imposed for violation of the rule. Principles of criminal jurisprudence guide judgments as to whether a rule has been violated, whether there should be criminal liability if there has been violation, what the extent of such liability should be. Laws that aid in the administration of the criminal law establish procedures aiming at fair, accurate, and expeditious determinations of guilt or innocence that do not infringe upon the rights of citizens, and aim to provide an enlightened but effective system of punishment for those found guilty.

So far the account of criminal justice is a simple matter. But more is required, for any enterprise has a purpose, and it is necessary to understand what that purpose is if we are to judge the success of the enterprise, or if indeed we are to decide whether the enterprise is worthwhile. At this point there are serious difficulties, for everywhere criminal justice is strangely uncertain in its goals, and reasons that seem at first to be at odds are offered to explain what is going on. Sometimes it is said that the point is simply to pay the wicked for their wrongdoing; at other times, that correction of those who show themselves to be in need of it is the reason we determine criminal liability. One often hears the view that crimes are punished to show those who have broken the law and those who might be tempted to break it that the law has teeth that bite. And just as often one hears it suggested that the enterprise is carried on to make the community safer by identifying and then removing (or at least watching) those who have shown themselves to be dangerous.

It seems reasonable to suppose that each of these has a proper place somewhere among the aims and purposes of criminal justice, but there is little agreement about the proper place of each. This is distressing, for it is important to know what goal it is that causes this curious social pursuit to be carried on everywhere with such dedication that its abandonment is virtually unthinkable. A commercial enterprise similarly unenlightened could not long survive and certainly could not prosper.

Imagine if managers and stockholders disagreed among themselves about whether the company was in business to provide employment in the community, or to engage in profitable transactions, or to satisfy a need for certain products, or to provide a market for raw materials supplied by the parent company. Each of these purposes may well have a place in the enterprise, but what that place is must be known to enable those who control the enterprise to guide it toward success, as well as to enable those who judge it to tell whether it has succeeded and to decide whether, in any event, success is worth the effort and expense. The lesson for criminal justice is clear. Until we know what we aim at in punishing crimes we cannot know whether we are succeeding, how we might improve our performance, or even whether the game is worth the candle. Worse still, we are tempted to adopt barbarous measures out of disappointment, or foolish ones out of despair, simply because we fail to achieve what we have no right to hope for in the first place.

Three conceptions of criminal justice are presented in broad outline in this chapter. In each it is the *purposes* of the enterprise that are conceived differently; and while some ideas from all three are usually found in the body of opinions on criminal justice that most people hold, each conception

represents a distinctive point of view. The first of these conceptions is the one that makes sense of the criminal jurisprudence that guides the law in any modern legal system; what
follows in this book should make that clear. The second conception places stress on moral concerns, which are thought
by many philosophers and legal theorists to be of paramount
importance in criminal justice but in fact are not at all well
served by the criminal jurisprudence found in any modern
legal system. Even more popular is the third conception of
crime and punishment, which makes removal and correction
of dangerous persons the object of criminal justice. This
conception is encouraged by wishful thinking in which most
crime appears to be the exotic activity of certain alien beings
among us. It is truly remarkable that this view should be
such a great favorite, since principles of criminal law frustrate rather than advance what on this view are taken to be
the objectives of criminal justice. These three competing
conceptions are examined here only to understand the enterprise. Its justification is discussed in various connections in
other chapters throughout the book.

I. CRIMINAL JUSTICE AS SOCIAL CRITICISM

In any modern society criminal justice has three stages. In
the first there is an accusation that is critical of some act by
a person who is said to have thereby broken the law. But the
accusation itself must then be critically tested in order to
determine guilt or innocence, and this takes place in the second stage. If the accusation survives the test and proves to be
sound, there is a third stage to allow for condemnation of
what was done through punishment of the accused for what
he did. Since all three stages are occupied with critical activities that are governed by social rules of the highest authority

—the law—it seems apt to speak of criminal justice as social criticism.

No form of criticism is more dreaded than criminal justice, nor is any criticism more dreadful. The outcome can be loss of liberty without equal in the modern world, and even death. Yet criminal justice is everywhere pursued with unwavering determination and is supported by decent, sensitive, and thoughtful people who feel certain that society could not exist without prosecution and punishment for crime. But if criminal justice is to be accepted as the rational and morally enlightened response to crime that it is said to be, more than favorable and widespread sentiment is needed. An account is required which satisfies the demands of common sense and of morality. What follows in the remainder of this section is one such account.

The criminal law provides a set of rules to fix the limits of socially tolerable conduct and to prohibit those acts that are out of bounds. It also includes rules requiring that certain things of social importance be done. Without these rules the administration of criminal justice would be a dangerously arbitrary affair in which the personal views of those officials who happen to sit in judgment would determine whether the act of the accused is in fact against the law. Some rules— though only some—are important in another way as well. Certain acts we know to be criminal without the law's telling us, but other acts we know to be criminal only because the law says so.

At the core of any body of criminal law are rules that prohibit certain acts whose harm is plain, grave, and universally unwelcome. Personal safety and security of property mandate rules that are the criminal law's first order of business. But no one needs to consult the law to know that murder, rape, and theft are criminal acts. One need only consult common views in the community to find that out; and if somehow the penal code did not include these acts among its prohibitions, we should say it had left out some important crimes and was therefore incomplete. The rules for these crimes do provide more exact definition to allow a more discriminating application of the law, but that is necessary only to avoid arbitrary administration in marginal cases and not to identify as criminal the conduct of which there is then a marginal case.

In contrast to these common crimes, there are crimes in which conduct is generally thought to be wrong but not criminal unless the law says so. Common morality condemns much that the law may or may not regard as fit for inclusion in its catalog of crimes, among which are to be found such uncontroversial items as deception and promise breaking as well as the more controversial immoralities of sexual misconduct and gambling. The rules of the criminal law let us know that certain of these things that members of a community know to be against prevailing moral views are also against the law.

A third group of rules make certain acts criminal, though they would not even be thought wrong, much less criminal, except for the law. Willful destruction of one's draft card may have grave criminal consequences; yet apart from the law it is no more wrong and no more criminal than tearing up one's library card. Rules of this sort are found mainly in laws enacted in aid of some government activity or policy that is conceived to be necessary for the common welfare. The crime is essentially one of rule breaking, since apart from the rule the act that breaks the rule is in itself not wrong and certainly not criminal. Such crimes of rule breaking are not an unreasonable part of the criminal law, since enjoyment of the benefits of life in society depends upon copious regulation in the public interest, and certain rules must be observed if such regulation is to be effective.

Rules of these three kinds make possible life in society as we know it. It would be unthinkable to leave each member of society free to decide for himself whether the conduct he chooses to engage in is a tolerable imposition on the interests of others. Even men of good will often lack insight into harmful consequences and need rules to guide them, while less noble types if left without rules would pursue wicked or selfish ends heedless of the harm that others may suffer. With rules we have a common means of guiding ourselves and of judging objectively the acts of others. Through the institutions of a legal system that includes a legislature representing the people, rules have the further virtue of reflecting not a single person's judgment but the intelligence, will, and moral sense of the community at large.

But the criminal law does more than establish rules. It makes their violation *punishable*. This is necessary if the rules are to be taken seriously, for rules that can be broken without serious undesirable consequences for the rule breaker will often be ignored. When bound to observe the rules by nothing stronger than civic conscience, concern for the well-being of others, or personal conviction about right and wrong, it is true that a few exceptional people may be expected always to exercise self-restraint even in the face of strong temptation. Civilization, it has been said, is obedience to the unenforceable, and some among us are more civilized than the rest. But most of us could not be relied on in every situation to sacrifice our advantage and postpone our gratification simply because the law has prohibited as a crime what we wish to do. Without its being made punishable as well, even wise and morally superior persons who understand social necessities and respect the rights of others would sometimes find themselves compelled, if not tempted, to commit crimes. The very presence of strangers would often signal danger in a world in which these rules were commonly disregarded, and in order to protect what he valued the good man no less than the bad would have to threaten or attack those who approached him. In such a world he would also find himself at a most serious disadvantage in pursuing what he valued if he acted only in ways that respected the law while others flouted the rules when it suited their convenience.

The criminal law, then, establishes rules of conduct whose observance allows us to enjoy life in society, and in addition provides punishment for violation of these rules, for the rules would not be taken seriously enough by enough people to be generally effective if they could be broken with impunity. But an accusation of breaking the law results in liability to punishment only if the accusation survives the criticism mounted as a defense against it. There are two lines that this criticism may take: one denying that the rule has really and truly been broken, the other asserting that under the circumstances even if it has been there ought not to be liability for breaking it.

The first of these avenues of defense is especially obvious in those popular courtroom dramas in which "Did he or didn't he?" is the question. That question, however, turns out to be deceptively simple, for sometimes the issue is not the straightforward one of who did it, but a query about whether there really was an act at all, or whether the act was of the full-fledged sort that is required for a crime and not just some bit of involuntary behavior. If an accusation against Smith is to stand up, it must first be established that *he* acted in a way that violated the rule, and also that he *acted* in that way. It is necessary, further, that what Smith did be just the sort of act that is prohibited by the rule he is accused of breaking and not merely an act that could get included as a violation of that rule only by a mistaken interpretation of the rule. And it is necessary also (as later discussions of causation and attempts will show) that what was actually done be truly dangerous in the right way with respect to the harm that the rule is intended to protect against, for even if Smith's act can manage to qualify logically as a violation of the rule, his act will not be regarded as a violation that warrants liability unless its danger is of criminal proportions.

The other line that can be taken against an accusation emerges when a person truly violates a rule of conduct laid down in the criminal law and yet it would be wrong to make him liable to punishment for what he has done. This is the case when what he has done in violation of a rule is something for which he was not responsible or for which he is not to blame. He may have done it because he did not or could not know certain things, or because his life depended on it, or because he was out of his mind at the time, or because circumstances made it impossible for him to do otherwise. Similarly, he may have acted in self-defense or under other circumstances that justified him in acting contrary to the rule, or he may have been acting as a police officer or in some other special capacity that likewise gave him the right to act in violation of the rule. In all these cases the law provides an immunity which serves the rulebreaker as a defense to an accusation of breaking the law. Criminal liability in these cases would deeply offend our moral sense by disregarding the fact that the actor had a right to act as he did, or was unable to do otherwise.

But there is another reason for this grant of immunity. In cases such as these, punishment is needless. If persons who break the rules under such circumstances are not punished, the rules are not thereby diminished in stature and will not in consequence be taken less seriously. If the law is enforced only when a rule is broken by someone who is able to observe it, so that inability to observe it is a defense against enforcement, the law will not as a result be weakened in the eyes of others, nor in the future will it be less a restraint upon those who were for some reason unable to abide by the law on the present occasion. No one will be thought by others to have got away with a violation of the rules when he could not help violating them, and no one will be encouraged by his exemption from liability under such circumstances to engage in crime at another time when he is free to observe or to violate the rules as he chooses. Even more plainly, the law has no interest in ensuring that a rule is observed when a person has a right to break it. Nothing is lost in respect for the law when there is a rightful violation, without liability, of one of its rules of conduct.

Both of these lines of defense rest upon principles of criminal jurisprudence. If the accused has failed for any reason to break the rule that he is accused of breaking, he is innocent and it would be unjust to impose liability to punishment on him, since he does not deserve it. If there is no need to make him liable to punishment even though he has broken the rule, the suffering entailed by liability to punishment would be needless suffering and hence not justifiable. Punishment for what one has a right to do or what one cannot avoid doing also is intolerable not only as a cruelty, but as a tyranny as well. Though there is here an appeal to moral principles, expediency argues with equal force in favor of recognizing these defenses. If punishment of the innocent and needless infliction of suffering were allowed, an appropriate attitude of disrespect toward the law would soon replace the general allegiance to the rules which now prevails among the law-abiding in any community. For the law the likely consequence would be a loss of vitality so great that its rules of conduct no longer would serve effectively to make life in a social setting possible.

In essence, the aim of a system of criminal justice is only to keep a community on the whole law-abiding, and not to rid it of crime or reduce crime to a point where it is no longer a social problem. This objective may at first seem disappointingly modest. But there is nothing in our experience to justify more ambitious expectations though there is much, when criminal justice breaks down, that testifies in support of pursuing diligently this less dramatic goal.

.

II. CRIMINAL JUSTICE AS MORAL CRITICISM

"Crime is morally wrong, and punishment for it is morally right." Though it is altogether too simple and hides a nasty tangle of problems, this statement seems uncontroversial. But even the plainest truths are sometimes challenged, and it is not inconceivable that some skeptic may ask why crime is morally wrong and punishment of it morally right. We must then take a look first at our penal laws and show why it is morally wrong to violate the rules of conduct they establish. Criminal punishment itself must also be examined and shown to be more than simply an evil that we tolerate. Finally, we must look at those principles of criminal law upon which criminal liability turns and show if we can that these principles are the hinges of moral judgments as well.

RULES OF CONDUCT AND THEIR MORAL STATUS

It seems obvious that those crimes of violence, theft, and destruction that stand as paradigms of crime and comprise the core of any penal code are also moral wrongs. Everyone has a right to be free of such harm inflicted by others, and when murder, rape, arson, assault, or larceny is committed there is also a moral wrong since a moral duty to refrain from doing harm to others has been breached. The right to be free of such harm does not have its origin in law but in a general consensus on the rights enjoyed by any member of society, or even by any person, no matter how he lives. This consensus is a more fundamental element of society even than the law, and for that reason the violation of such a right is a moral wrong and not simply a legal wrong.

But beyond the most obvious crimes, legions of others are on the books for the reason that doing what is prohibited (or failing to do what is required) makes life hazardous or unpleasant. Members of the public are entitled to live and to work in safety, and to enjoy life in public places without fear, disgust, or embarrassment. Because acts violating these rights do not threaten a person's welfare as gravely as when a common crime is committed, these rights are not so important as the ones that are violated by common crimes. But these rights are also moral rights and not simply legal rights, since entitlement to the security and freedom that they represent is a matter of fundamental social consensus and not a matter simply of legal enactment.

Other crimes that are not common crimes are morally wrong for a different reason. Income tax fraud or draft evasion seem to place an unfair burden on others or deprive others of what is due them. Quite apart from any considerations of harm or offense, these acts have a bad moral odor because principles of fairness and entitlement that lie at the foundation of social life are transgressed by them.

Most crimes, then, seem independently to be moral wrongs as well. But there are two strong arguments for considering any criminal act to be morally wrong *on its face,* quite apart from our moral judgment of the particular act that happens to violate the law. Whenever a crime is committed, a social rule is broken. It is reasonable to insist that in a society in which general consent is necessary for the legitimate exercise of authority by government through law, there is as part of such consent a promise binding on each member of society to abide by the rules promulgated under legal authority. Criminal acts are violations of this solemn promise to live according to the rules and are morally wrong on that account.

The other reason for adverse moral judgment is the unfair advantage that is taken of the restraint exercised by others and the shirking of one's own social duty when one commits a crime. Principles of fair play seem to require that those who take benefits—and even those who merely receive benefits without objection—do their share to maintain the conditions of general benefit that they themselves enjoy; and certainly principles of fair play require that such persons not act in any way they may choose for their own advantage or gratification while others forego such an intolerably antisocial privilege.

Even when it is unclear that an act violating the criminal law is morally wrong in its own right, it seems clear, then, that according to either of two theories such an act is on its face morally wrong just because it is a violation of the law. In effect this makes morally wrong, at least *prima facie,* even those law-breaking acts that seem to many neither to cause real harm nor to furnish other grounds for genuine moral condemnation. Thus, even if one objects to regarding a certain offense as a genuine instance of morally wrong conduct, when one violates the law creating such an offense one still has the burden of meeting the *prima facie* case of moral wrong that is presented just because the law is on the books.

Even if all crime can confidently be said to be morally wrong, it is a serious mistake to suppose that conduct with which the criminal law concerns itself is prohibited and made punishable for the reason that it is morally wrong. Conduct is prohibited by rules with teeth only because it is thought of as some sort of peril. The point is not without consequence, for if we think that moral wrongs are the main concern, we are encouraged to adopt rules to prevent moral wrongs though no dangerous conduct is involved, and to prescribe punishment for crimes according to how wrong morally the criminal act *appears* to be instead of how serious it is as a danger or harm.

There are three separate reasons for concluding that it is not the moral wrongness of an act that prompts criminal liability for it.

In the first place there are many moral wrongs that the criminal law takes no notice of, though as moral wrongs they are much more serious than those involved when certain crimes—even serious ones—are committed. Betrayals of confidence, malicious gossip, and countless varieties of cruelty in personal relations are all outside the purview of the criminal law even when they have the stature of moral atrocity. The world's biggest burglary, viewed as a moral wrong, is a paltry affair compared to many moral wrongs committed every day in the name of greed and ambition but without criminal liability. There are good reasons why the criminal law ignores even these grave moral wrongs. The nature of the harm done, the social importance of its prevention, the wisdom and feasibility of attempting to regulate misconduct that is widespread no matter how reprehensible it may be, and the ability of people to protect themselves without the help of the law are the main considerations. But none of these considerations makes the morally wrong act a less urgent matter morally; and the refusal of the criminal law to take the act seriously even when it could do so without inconvenience is evidence that mere moral wrongs are regarded by the criminal law as none of its business.

A second point concerns crimes that are moral wrongs only because they violate a rule whose observance has been promised and whose violation is unfair to all who abide by the rules. In making these acts criminal the law is not creating criminal liability for the sake of punishing moral wrongs. Outside of Wonderland it would be odd indeed to have liability solely for the moral wrong in violating a rule when there would be no moral wrong except for such a rule. In such a case the moral wrong could be prevented by the simple expedient of doing away with the rule.

There is an even simpler and more direct answer to the suggestion that in such cases it is the moral wrong that prompts liability. There are many other contexts of promise breaking and of taking unfair advantage that are uncontroversial and plain for all to see, and the law does not create criminal liability for that morally wrong conduct, but at most provides civil remedies to redress the injuries flowing from it. True, promise keeping and fair play are also acts of civic virtue when they require us to desist from crime. But that adds nothing to the moralist's argument, since defections from civic virtue, though they occur in abundance as people selfishly place their own good ahead of the common good, appear to be in themselves no more a concern of the criminal law than promise breaking and taking unfair advantage.

Finally, the severity of punishment for crime makes it clear that punishment is not for the moral wrong that occurs. Though the gravity of the moral wrong and that of the crime do sometimes coincide, often they diverge so that a person who commits a crime carrying with it little or no moral opprobrium we think rightly punished with a truly sobering sentence; and in other cases we condemn a crime morally in the strongest terms while at the same time conceding that only a relatively light sentence is deserved for it. As we noted already, the biggest burglary in history is likely to be only a minor event in a pageant of moral wrongs, even though it is rightly punished as a serious crime. Stealing the coins of a blind beggar may fill us with a moral outrage stronger than those produced by most murders; and though our considered judgment of the moral wrong supports such feelings it will not support a measure of punishment that goes far beyond the range normally prescribed for minor thefts.

If we take the view that crimes are moral wrongs and are punished as such, we are forced to conclude on two accounts that in its design the criminal law is barbarously unjust. The punishment prescribed is in many cases disproportionate to the moral wrong, and so from a moral point of view punishment for many is undeservedly severe as well as unfairly heavy in comparison with the lighter punishment imposed on others whose crime, morally speaking, is no less wrong.

THE MORAL STANDING OF PUNISHMENT

"It is right to punish crime" can be understood in two ways. It might mean only that criminal punishment is a justifiable social practice. Or it might mean that a failure to punish crime is wrong and that a community that does not punish its criminals is derelict in its moral duty.

Only those who are indifferent to moral concerns can ignore the question of justifiability, for unless society is justified in making people suffer for their crimes, punishment is a morally wrong practice that must weigh on the conscience of society's members as a barbarism not yet discarded. One way to justify punishment is by establishing that we are morally bound to punish those who commit crimes, for if it is wrong not to do something, then doing it is, to say the least, justified. In such a case we are inclined to put it even more strongly by saying that no justification is needed, and by that route overcome in a summary way any suggestion that punishment is not justifiable.

Even if we are unwilling to endorse a moral requirement that crime be punished, we may still argue that criminal punishment is justifiable for other reasons. One might argue, for example, that punishment is an evil that is necessary in any community if even more crimes are not to be committed, and for that reason punishment is morally justifiable—while at the same time conceding that a community so unwise as to choose to leave crimes unpunished deserves not moral condemnation but only criticism for its folly. One might argue further that the evil of punishment is justifiable only so long as it is necessary and that, when it is not, punishment is morally wrong. But those claiming that there is a moral duty to punish crime will object to this, and will argue against its abandonment even when it is not a necessary social expedient, maintaining that it is morally wrong not to punish the guilty, even though reasons of utility no longer support the institution of punishment. It is at this point that those who view criminal justice as moral criticism part company from those who take a different view.

Two lines of argument support the claim that allowing impunity is morally wrong. The first looks to some source of moral authority and discerns what may be called a moral imperative to punish. If the law bears the authority of the deity or is in some other way a statement of the universal moral law binding on all men, it is plain enough that failure to carry out provisions for punishment would itself be a transgression of the moral imperative that the law represents. By failing to punish a crime as the law tells us we should, we would be accomplices after the fact in violation of the moral law; or, alternatively, we may be viewed as independent transgressors in shirking the moral duty laid down by the law.

The other line will be more congenial to modern thinking, though it too has its origins in the political thought of an earlier age. Before protection against crime was provided by the law, men were obliged to provide their own measures of protection. Without social rules enforced by the community, what they relied on was their own power of retaliation against those who did them harm. There was then a natural right to repay harm with harm, since without such a system of repayment everyone would generally be less restrained and more predatory, to the detriment of all. But society requires that this right be surrendered by its members, and in exchange undertakes to protect them by laws that can be effective only if violations are punished. The bargain that is struck, then, places a moral obligation on society to punish crime as it places a moral obligation on its members to refrain from breaking the law.

Looking at the first sort of argument, we find that it rests on a political ideology that is alien to any modern political society in which democratic ideals are professed. In such societies there are no universal moral laws imposed by divine authority. Nor does the voice of the people itself create such a moral imperative when that voice is enacted as law, for in every modern legal system the law itself allows great discretion to those who administer the law, and most especially when decisions about punishing crime have to be made. However it may have been (or still may be) in less developed societies or in modern authoritarian societies that appeal to transcendent moral authority, in modern societies of a democratic complexion there is no source of moral authority to command that crime must be punished.

A moral obligation to punish which rests on a commitment to protect against harm has better credentials. Having deprived each person of his right to retaliation as a condition of membership in society and so leaving people unable to take measures against those who endanger or harm them, the state is morally bound to provide the needed protection through rules of conduct whose effectiveness requires that violations be punished. The moral obligation may rest upon a promise-to-protect that is part of the social contract, or it may arise as a duty of the state to act on behalf of those whom the law has deprived of self-help and has left helpless as prey to predators except for the existence of effective laws. But on either theory the obligation is only to protect. Men may retaliate simply to avenge themselves against those who have harmed them, but, in the social transaction in which rights of retaliation are surrendered, no moral obligation arises to seek vengeance on behalf of a member of society who otherwise would be free to seek it himself. If this were not so and society were bound to avenge harm, society's obligation would then be an obstacle to the advancement of its moral ideals.

Limited in this way, the moral obligation to punish exists only so long as punishment is needed as part of a scheme of social protection. If some satisfactory alternative to this scheme were devised so that protection was provided without the need for punishment, that scheme might be put into operation and punishment discarded without a breach of moral obligation. This is important in considering objections to proposals for the elimination of punishment. It is important also in connection with the suggestion (to be advanced in Chapter Ten) that punishment less than deserved is proper whenever such lesser punishment does not in principle compromise the general scheme of protection. Though it would be wrong as a breach of moral obligation for the state not to punish crime under present circumstances—and perhaps under any circumstances that we can reasonably expect—still it is misleading to assert that crimes are punished because there is such an obligation. Imagining the moral constraint to be the reason for punishment makes criminal justice appear as an exceedingly strange social enterprise whose social purpose is less important than the moral rectitude of the state that is displayed by inflicting punishment.

MORALISM AND THE HINGES OF LIABILITY

In making determinations of criminal liability it is often necessary to invoke principles of criminal jurisprudence to decide whether the conduct of the accused was truly blameworthy. Sometimes those principles are themselves not well settled and are the subject of controversy in which those who see criminal justice as a moralistic enterprise argue that the accused ought to escape criminal liability by an exculpatory route only when it leads to the conclusion that what he did was not morally wrong. There are three characteristic features of this moralistic conception. *Mentalism, moral exclu-*

sivity, and *personalism* are terms we might use to identify them, and they can be illustrated by a few examples.

Often in life we feel called upon to say that we are sorry as we explain that we didn't intend what happened, that we thought things were different and did what we did by mistake, or that for some other reason we did what we did unintentionally. On these everyday occasions we mean to be kind to others and express our regret for what has caused someone else displeasure, but, no less important, we try to avoid censure or blame by pointing to certain facts that make us or make what we did appear in a different and kinder light. When there is a crime and someone is accused of committing it, he may also wish to avoid blame in this way by putting things in a better light. This is a very important matter, and the law in its doctrine of *mens rea* recognizes its importance. Perhaps we are to blame in spite of our excuses; perhaps we are even to blame precisely because of the very failures that our excuses rely upon; but often enough our excuses count in our favor and may even shield us completely from liability.

The moralist, however, looks at our excuses in an altogether different way. We point to our intentions and our beliefs to show that we did not in fact do what we are accused of doing. The moralist takes this to be an attempt by us to deny that we had a morally unsavory state of mind, and assumes that it is therefore our state of mind that is the true concern of those who accuse us. Our acts are thought to be significant mainly because they are the outward manifestations of wicked intentions. This external evidence is important because the law allows safe harbor to mere intentions and will not condemn even the most wicked of them unless they are acted on, thereby providing more room for a person to change his mind and at the same time insuring that mere surmise is not accepted in the place of the clear indication of intention that only conduct provides.

The doctrine of *mens rea* stands for the moralist as affirmation in the criminal law of the primacy of mind over act. True, the criminal law does furnish a few specimens of *mens rea* requirements that are distinctly mentalistic; but since these specimens are becoming scarcer and seem to be moving toward extinction, their presence provides scant support for the mentalist view. One important specimen is the traditional definition of murder that employs such mental terms as *deliberation, premeditation,* and *malice aforethought* to distinguish this most wicked form of homicide from less wicked ones; but this mode of definition in the law is increasingly rare and seems destined soon to disappear altogether.

In fashioning a doctrine of *mens rea,* the criminal law insists that conduct be blameworthy if there is to be criminal liability for it. The moralist, however, makes two mistakes in interpreting that doctrine. He assumes that judgments of culpability are always moral judgments, and he assumes that they are ultimately judgments of states of mind. The first of these errors can be illustrated by a bit of bridge table conversation.

N. With a hand like that your bid of three diamonds was utterly reckless.

S. No, I just got confused in reading my cards and in figuring out what bid to make.

E. It's no wonder with all the noise we have in this room.

W. I thought at first you might be getting back at your partner for his odd bidding the last hand. But I see now how three diamonds can be justified as a sound bid.

In the form of accusation, of excuse, and of justification seven claims bearing on the culpability of *S*'s bid are nested in this dialogue. But since inept bidding is not a moral wrong, no moral judgment is in the offing, as it would be if *S* were accused of cheating or of stealing the kitty.

The moralist's other assumption is that judgments of culpability are really judgments of states of mind. Once again, help can be obtained by turning to the bridge table. Thus, whether S's bid is blameworthy may well depend upon what he believed or intended in making it. But it need not, and often it will not. Consider, for example, these alternative replies to N's accusation.

> *E.* You know he's just learning the game and it's unfair to expect him not to make mistakes.
>
> *W.* The bidding has been erratic all evening and S's isn't any worse than the rest.

But there is more to be learned from this bit of dialogue. No reference is made to the actor's state of mind in either of these exculpatory moves; but, no less importantly, what is denied is not something that, if in fact it were the case, would then make the act blameworthy *because* it was the case.

It would make no sense to say that S was to blame for his bidding *for the very reason* that he was an experienced player or *for the very reason* that the bidding all evening had been impeccable. Similarly, it is not *for the very reason* that he read his cards correctly, was concentrating on his bidding, and intended to bid as he did that we judge his bidding culpable when the question of its culpability turns on his mental state. In either case it is simply a matter of the actor's being deprived of his exculpatory defense when the facts do not warrant it. In the case turning on his mental state the defense offered is an excuse denying the occurrence of the full-fledged act upon which a good accusation depends, and when that denial is rebutted the accusation is left standing.

Culpability, then, need not be a moral judgment, nor need it depend on mental affairs. In more ways than one, the criminal law is embarrassed when this is forgotten. Many theorists have qualms about mere negligent conduct's ever being made criminal, since the actor in such cases has only innocent intentions and what he does seems not to be morally wrong. On the other hand, beliefs and intentions that are part of a wicked design are, when acted upon, thought to support a case at least for a crime of attempt no matter how absurd the actor's expectation might have been, so that perfectly harmless acts that could never endanger anyone may nevertheless land a man in prison just because of what he meant to have happen. In determining criminal liability, however, neither the absence of moral fault in the case of negligence nor its presence in the case of a preposterous attempt ought to matter. Nor does our deliberation, premeditation, or malice aforethought have any proper place in determining our homicide liability, except insofar as their absence might be taken to indicate that our dangerous conduct was not so much of our choosing as might be thought but rather was heavily influenced by the circumstances in which we found ourselves or by the forces within us that operated independent of our choosing.

Moral exclusivity is a second feature of criminal justice when it is conceived moralistically. Sometimes there are hard cases when a rule of conduct laid down in a penal law has been violated under special circumstances that suggest that the violation might be defensible. Thus, one man might harm another because he is forced to by someone else, or because he has to in order to protect someone else from imminent harm at the hands of the person he harms. There are many situations in which a person seems to have had good reason for doing something that violates a rule, though he might have chosen otherwise; and the question then is whether his violation of the rule was justifiable. It is tempting to decide such a case by considering whether what he did was morally wrong, and then making the question of justifiability turn exclusively on that.

Two examples will suffice, the first a type of case in which the law has generally though uneasily taken such a moralistic course, the second a case in which the law is unsettled and its course uncertain. A man may find himself in a situation in which he must take the life of an innocent stranger if he does not want his own life taken by a third person, who threatens him with certain and instant death if he does not kill as directed. His choice to take that innocent life seems morally wrong, for what right does he have to cause the other man to assume his misfortune? Similarly, a person who is a complete stranger to the parties and to the situation might kill another person as the only means of ending the other person's deadly attack against a third person, though he knows that the attacker suffers mental aberration so extreme that it relieves him entirely from responsibility for what he does. There is then a strong case for judging the killing to be a morally wrong act since a person has no right to choose which of two innocent strangers shall die even when one or the other must surely die. Unless he can be persuaded that the act is not morally wrong, the moralist in cases such as these inclines to reject the claim that the act was justifiable.

Our criminal jurisprudence requires that conduct be culpable if there is to be criminal liability for it, and we have just seen that conduct may be culpable without being morally wrong. But it may also be morally wrong without being culpable under standards of culpability that suit the administration of criminal justice in a community of ordinary people. In cases like those we are considering, the act may be morally wrong, and yet an alternative course of action that avoids doing what is morally wrong can be expected only from a hero, a martyr, a paragon of self-restraint, or perhaps a prodigy of insight, inventiveness, and daring who devises on the spot still a third course of action that avoids any harm and so bypasses the moral dilemma. Since the law is designed to regulate affairs in a community of ordinary men and not on Olympus, it should regard the morally unworthy course as not deserving blame and therefore not criminally wrong.

If the law does not regard such acts as legally justifiable but chooses instead to condemn them from a higher moral plateau where ordinary human limitations do not count, the law will itself outrage a common sense of justice at the more mundane level at which life is normally lived. This will weaken the ties of allegiance to the law that are found in a community of ordinary men, for ordinary men would rightly regard the law then as assuming an arrogant and unbending posture of moral superiority.

"Good Samaritan" laws that impose criminal penalties for failure to help in situations of peril provide another example of moral exclusivity. In most societies people are generally privileged to mind their own business and ignore the distress of others when they are in no way connected with it; yet, in a situation in which one might safely and easily give aid, it is morally wrong simply to mind one's own business and do nothing in the face of danger or disaster. Although a stranger to the desperate situation who turns away or does no more than stand and watch may well be shirking his moral duty, in many countries he is free to do so without risk of being punished for it. The moralist wishes to extend the net to catch these moral derelicts and to create criminal liability for the neglect when there is a clear moral duty to act and when the harm in the offing is the sort that generally concerns the criminal law.

If looking out for one another in this way is part of our social commitment, it is eminently reasonable to include in the penal law rules of conduct that require us to do so. Laws properly rest on an agreement by members of society to recognize as binding on them the rules of conduct necessary to secure the benefits of society, and laws that do not have such support and exist without the consent of those whose lives are governed by them are despotic acts of legislation. Protection against harm is enhanced by Good Samaritan laws, and surely such protection is a benefit for whose sake society exists, but it is not at all clear that such laws are necessary to secure the benefit.

Another part of the arrangement that makes law possible is the reservation, by each member of society, of a right to mind his own business so long as his doing so does not interfere with or deprive others of the benefits of society. This right is very important, since in a social setting personal autonomy is uncertain without it and exists only interstitially where the law happens not to have chosen to regulate conduct. The right to mind one's own business is infringed not only when others intrude upon the management of one's affairs but also when one is forced to mind another's business. It is surely the case that in some societies the benefits for which its members have committed themselves to abide by the rules include helping one another whenever it is easy and safe to do so and the peril calling for intervention is great. Rules that are necessary to the enjoyment of this benefit are then proper, and at least the less controversial Good Samaritan laws are then properly part of the criminal law. But in other societies the benefits for which its members have committed themselves do not include being helped on such occasions, and there is then a right to mind one's own business that protects personal autonomy more broadly.

There is much room for reasonable disagreement as to just what the benefits are for which a social commitment has been made by members in a particular society, and about what rules are necessary to the enjoyment of those benefits. The controversy is complicated by the fact that such commitment is not permanently fixed in any society but is constantly changing—even if the rate of change is glacial. We need not enter this controversy here and may conveniently bypass the question of which Good Samaritan laws, if any, are warranted by social commitment. The point of importance here is that without a proper basis in social commitment, laws punishing morally wrong failures to intervene are a moralistic impertinence in the law, no matter how wrong morally the failure may be.

Persons rather than their acts often occupy the center of the stage when moral judgments are made, and a person's conduct then plays only the subordinate role of furnishing evidence of his good or bad character. The criminal law may at first appear to be mounting just such a production, for a person's conduct is judged according to its culpability in order to punish those who are found guilty. But this view would be misleading, since the criminal law is not designed to make judgments of persons but only of particular items of conduct, and then to impose liability for this conduct on the person whose conduct it is when the conduct warrants liability, without regard to the sort of person he appears to be when his conduct in general and other evidence of character are considered. In the administration of criminal justice, however, officials often allow themselves to be guided by their impressions of a person's moral worth in deciding what charges to make, what pleas to accept, and even whether to prosecute at all.

A person convicted of a crime or believed to have committed a crime is often treated as though he must stand moral scrutiny by the authorities and pay dearly for his moral unworthiness, even though such matters are everywhere else rejected as not a proper concern of the state in its dealings with its citizens. The result of these moralistic intrusions in the administration of criminal justice is a malignant encouragement to unequal treatment. Since there are no uniform standards by which a person's moral worth is to be judged and no set procedures for presenting evidence of moral character, each official is left to take into account or leave out of it whatever he may choose, and to exercise his discretion according to his own biases and idiosyncratic notions about who is good and who is bad. More serious, even, is the objection in principle to such judgments, for, in liberal societies of the modern world what good reason can there be for allowing the state to judge a person and then make him suffer according to his moral worth?

There is an important philosophical objection to punishment, one that rests heavily on the same mistaken assumption that the reason for punishing a person is his badness as evidenced by his crime. In fact we all change in our moral qualities from time to time throughout our lives, and many people who commit serious crimes undergo a radical change when the enormity of what they have done is brought home to them. No less dramatic are the changes that take place in prison when a person develops altogether new perspectives on his life over a period of time, so that by any reasonable measure of such matters, far from being morally unworthy, he has become a morally superior person. It then seems wicked to treat him as a criminal, for his crime no longer represents his moral worth, and punishment under such circumstances seems nothing more than suffering wantonly inflicted.

In this objection, once again, it is wrongly assumed that people are punished criminally for what they are, when in fact they are punished only for what they did. It does not matter that a wicked man is through conversion or reform now virtuous, since his character does not matter to begin with. What does matter, though, is the possession by a person of the ability to identify himself through his own sense of identity as the person who committed the crime. There are exceptional cases of an amnesia so complete that a person loses all touch with his former self, lacking even a sense of his own personal history and being cut off from the internal archives in which the events of that history are chronicled and stored. If we punish such a man for the crime he committed, we punish a person who is incapable of appreciating his crime as his own. To him it is as though another person had committed the crime and he is being punished for it, and this is true even though what he is told convinces him that he committed the crime. One might at first be tempted to think of such a person as the counterpart of someone who has completely lost touch with himself at the time of the crime and has in his own mind assumed another identity—perhaps that of Jack the Ripper.

Only responsible people deserve punishment for what they do, and, since for reasons to be discussed in Chapter Seven a person afflicted in this way is regarded as legally insane and not responsible, we exonerate and do not punish him. But in the case of total amnesia after the crime, the perpetrator was a responsible actor at the time of the crime and is still responsible even though afflicted with a loss of identity, and so he cannot claim lack of responsibility as an exemption from punishment. He does, however, have a claim akin to that available to a person who suffered severe mental abnormality after the crime and now has lost touch with reality. In such a case it is inhumane to punish, since the person punished cannot appreciate that his punishment is deserved. He experiences the misery of punishment without the sense of its justice that permits a normal person to accept his fate and reconcile himself to it. Though he has not lost touch with reality, the amnesiac, for his part, has lost all touch with his past and so is similarly unable to accept his fate and reconcile himself to it. To him it seems to be the fate of another man.

Since no one can think that such a person has got away with his crime if he is not punished, the law will not be taken less seriously when in such cases it is broken with impunity. For that reason, punishment in such cases is needless and therefore unjustifiable. We shall examine punishment and its justification more fully in the final two chapters of the book. Here the point of importance is simply that even though exoneration from punishment seems right for a person who is altogether out of touch with his past, it is not his utter disassociation *now* from the wicked self who committed the crime that makes such exoneration right.

MORALITY AND CRIMINAL JUSTICE

Although criminal justice as it is may not be the enterprise of moral criticism that some suppose, it could be altered either gradually or by radical measures to assume a posture that is mainly moralistic. Against such change the social and the political history of criminal justice stands as a formidable argument. Whenever the public force has been used to give teeth to morality, and the state has become an avenging angel bent on punishing moral wrongs, the state has done things in the name of morality that turn out to be far more serious than the wrongs that prompted them.

In any community there is a broad consensus about what is dangerous conduct. But in any complex modern community, judgments about moral wrongs are largely unsettled. Those in power regularly take advantage of this lack of agreement to enforce their own moral views or to enforce those moral views whose popularity appears at the time to give political benefit to those who enforce them. There is a broad community consensus about many moral matters, it is true, but when the law punishes those who do not share these views and act contrary to them, it places a restraint upon fresh moral insight and prevents those who wish to live according to their own lights from doing so even though they do not intrude upon the lives of others. The moralistic view of punishment similarly leads to morally wrong acts by the state, for needless or useless punishment is inhumane suffering, yet the moralist will not allow exemption even when punishment does not serve or is not needed to uphold the law.

The case against a moralistic conception of criminal justice is sometimes thought to be a case against moral criticism of the criminal law and its administration. Such a view is profoundly mistaken, for criminal justice must always remain under close and constant moral scrutiny, and must avoid whatever is morally wrong if it is not in one way or another to become official injustice. Rules of conduct may not curtail beyond what is morally justifiable the political liberties that citizens are entitled to enjoy in civil society, nor may such rules encroach needlessly upon rights that allow people to live their lives just as they see fit.

In deciding whether to impose criminal liability for the violation of a rule it is necessary to respect those fundamental principles of criminal jurisprudence that allow only persons whose acts were truly responsible and worthy of blame to be made liable to punishment. Punishment itself must be deserved, so that those who are not guilty are not punished, and those who are guilty are punished only within the limits of their guilt. Punishment must also be evenhanded, so that everyone who is guilty is made to answer for his crime under principles that are themselves just and that apply equally to everyone. And punishment must not be inhumane either as an excess beyond what is needed to meet the requirement that justifies it in the first place, nor inhumane as a transgression of those civilized standards that tell people how they ought to treat one another. Finally, the procedures followed by a system of criminal justice must be designed to find and then to respect the truth about matters bearing on liability, while at the same time conforming to principles of fair play and respect for human dignity when confronting individuals with the awesome machinery of the state.

Moral matters, then, are of the greatest importance in carrying on the business of criminal justice, though it is not for the sake of moral matters that it is carried on. And one may include among the many ironies of criminal justice that it is least likely to be morally sound when it is carried on most moralistically.

III. CRIMINAL JUSTICE AS A FEATURE
OF REMOVAL AND CORRECTION

THE POPULAR VIEW

Crime control has an important place among the major concerns of government in every country, and criminal justice is at times thought by almost everyone to be part of a large public enterprise that is carried on to reduce crime—to the vanishing point if possible. Law enforcement appears to play the most important part in this larger enterprise since it involves apprehending and taking out of circulation people who have shown themselves to be socially dangerous, both those who are already known to be criminals and those who have revealed their criminal tendencies for the first time. Seizing and removing dangerous people makes the social environment that much safer, at least for the time of their removal; and there is then opportunity to change those people who are dangerous so that when they are once again free their presence will no longer constitute a danger.

After the police apprehend criminals, those administering the law in courtrooms (and courthouse corridors) try to make sure that only those persons who really have shown themselves to be dangerous by committing a crime are deprived of their liberty. These officials also distinguish the more dangerous from the less dangerous among those who break the law, and exercise the discretion that they possess under the law to prosecute more readily and charge more heavily those who are more dangerous, and to pass heavier sentences upon those whose absence will benefit the community most. When a dangerous person is convicted he is sentenced to a custodial institution designed to prevent him from doing further harm, and he is supposed to be subjected there to a regime of correction intended to change him so that he is no longer a criminal danger. In all of this, criminal justice plays only an ancillary role—that of making sure that only the criminally dangerous are deprived of their liberty, and of measuring the deprivation imposed upon such people according to how criminally dangerous they have shown themselves to be.

This picture of removal and correction has one other crime-prevention feature. The enterprise is designed not only to correct those who have committed crimes, but also to correct inclinations to crime before a crime is committed, by holding up as a standing threat to everyone the unpleasant consequences that a criminal may expect.

THE INACCURACIES IN THIS VIEW

It is a serious mistake to assume that a person is dangerous simply because he has committed a crime. Because it rests on that assumption, the model of removal and correction provides an account of criminal justice that is very misleading. In one sense of the term *dangerous person,* of course, anyone who commits a crime is rightly described as a dangerous person. Criminal conduct may be spoken of as dangerous conduct since it threatens some sort of harm, and a person who engages in it is therefore a dangerous person not because he is inclined to engage in such conduct but simply because he has been its author on a particular occasion. Often when harm occurs or is only narrowly averted, we speak of its source as dangerous even though an examination beforehand would have disclosed no particular likelihood of the untoward occurrence. More is wanted, however, than license to call any author of dangerous conduct a dangerous person. If the model of removal and correction is to make sense, we must have grounds for inferring from a single instance of criminal conduct and nothing else the existence of a disposition to commit crimes, for under the law people may be taken out of circulation and put away on the basis of a single criminal act.

On the face of things such a standing inference from crime to criminal disposition seems extremely ill-considered, since almost any sort of crime is committed by many different kinds of people, in many different circumstances, for many different reasons, under many different constraints, and with many different motives. But there is still the possibility that the criminal behavior of anyone who commits a crime is evidence of some defect or abnormality that strongly disposes him to commit further crimes, and his crime would then indeed be evidence that such a person is dangerous in the requisite sense. That possibility seems safely regarded as a mere possibility, however. Lawmakers in deciding what crimes to have on the books consider only the undesirability of particular conduct and what scheme of prohibition and punishment is suitable to deal with it. They do not seek expert advice to identify the behavior that indicates a *disposition* to engage in such conduct, and they do not seek to create liability for such behavior, though surely they would if the dangerousness of dangerous persons were the true concern of the criminal law.

Nevertheless, there remains the bare possibility that by some extraordinary coincidence just those acts that are deemed undesirable and are prohibited by penal laws happen to be evidence of a continuing disposition to crime and can therefore be relied on to identify dangerous persons. Arguing against such a supposition, however, are the many widely different stories of crimes even of the same sort, making it abundantly clear that in some cases there is good reason to suspect a disposition to crime while in many others there are no grounds at all for such a suspicion. There are of course many people who suffer from defects or abnormalities that lead them to behave criminally and that make them dangerous if left at large. But removing these people from circulation to protect others and doing whatever can be done to help them is the business not of the criminal law but of legal proceedings directed to civil commitment.

Some people hold a slightly different view of the abnormality that makes a criminal dangerous. According to this view, there are persons in the community who simply do not have the disposition to abide by the law prevailing among the population generally but are disposed in an opposite direction, and these members of what might be called a criminal population would rightly be treated as dangerous when they commit crimes.

Organized crime, gang-style crime, terrorist activities, and ordinary street crime are surely carried on by people who regard the law as an enemy to be avoided and whose regular disposition is to operate outside the bounds and the reach of the law. Their attitude toward the law is in sharpest contrast to the law-abiding portion of the population and is a social fact of great importance to be taken into account in law enforcement activities as well as in designing programs and facilities in a correctional system. Yet a very large part of all crimes committed each year—including murder and other serious crimes—is committed by members of the law-abiding population to whom the law's prohibitions matter very much and who conduct their lives in a way that makes clear their general commitment to observing the law. Even though a person of this sort has committed a crime, he is no more disposed to commit crimes than his law-abiding neighbors, and he is no more dangerous than they are. The criminal law, however, does not distinguish between those who are dangerous and those who are not; and though it allows room for prosecutors and judges to exercise some discretion in this regard, it subjects equally to criminal liability those persons who are criminal hazards and those who are not.

The standard scheme of punishments to be found in penal codes also is at odds with isolation and correction as supposed objectives.

If correction of criminally dangerous proclivities were really the aim in imposing criminal liability, any legislature that wished to be regarded as rational would have to consider what period of corrective treatment would likely be necessary to correct the various different tendencies toward each different type of crime, and it would prescribe sentences accordingly. No doubt ample latitude would be allowed (as now) to make the finer adjustments that are called for in particular cases; and no doubt crimes would be defined somewhat differently, so that behavior indicating the need for a more or less lengthy program of correctional treatment would be taken into account in order to allow for a gradation of sentences better suited to correctional needs. Under such a scheme we should surely find that certain varieties of serious crimes are regularly committed by persons without dangerous tendencies or with dangerous tendencies that are particularly amenable to corrective treatment in very short time, while certain varieties of less serious crimes are regularly committed by people who for one reason or another are much inclined to repeat the crime and can only hope to become disinclined if subjected to a lengthy course of corrective treatment.

The striking contrast between such a scheme and the one provided by our penal laws speaks eloquently against the supposed correctional objective. It is not correctional needs that are considered at all in establishing sentences for crimes, but rather the culpability of the criminal conduct: How important are the interests threatened by such conduct? How serious a threat does this sort of conduct pose? Is the conduct in pursuit of some legitimate interest and therefore to be indulged as a more acceptable risk of harm? The answers to these questions guide decisions about how heavily to punish a particular crime, but they have no place in determining how much time is probably needed to correct dangerous criminal tendencies. Where they exist, of course, indeterminate sentences are intended to allow whatever time is required for correction. But indeterminate sentences represent a radical departure from the normal scheme of sentences, have never received more than marginal acceptance, and seem now to be in particular disfavor almost everywhere.

The protective version is equally implausible, and for much the same reasons. If those who committed more serious crimes had generally stronger and more persistent tendencies to repeat them, a rational program of social safety would mandate keeping such people out of circulation for a longer time on the theory that at any given time fewer dangerous people will then be at large in the community. But once again there is lacking the presumed correlation between dangerousness of perpetrator and seriousness of his crime, for many instances of murder, rape, arson, treason, and grand larceny can be said to be in all likelihood a once-in-a-lifetime occurrence, while the future petty larcenies of certain shoplifters are almost as certain as the sunrise.

In behalf of the protective view, it might be said that not only the strength and persistence of the criminal tendency must be considered but the seriousness of the harm as well; and so for some serious crimes longer imprisonment is warranted by the greater harm that is in the offing even if the likelihood of its occurring is no greater. But in the case of a great many serious crimes committed by otherwise law-abiding citizens, there is no more reason to believe that such a crime will again be committed by the perpetrator than there is to believe that it will be committed by one of his law-abiding neighbors who has not broken the law; and yet the law makes no provision for discharging, free of liability, persons who are guilty but not dangerous.

It might be objected also that the criminal law does recognize the needs of social safety in recidivist provisions allowing or even requiring longer terms of imprisonment (or other measures of incapacitation) for habitual offenders. Insofar as these provisions are based on undiscriminating and *a priori* notions of dangerousness they are very disturbing, for they often do not allow for explanations of a pattern of crime that might well be changed by providing opportunity for a decent life, and in other cases they cause persons whose needs are therapeutic to be committed as hopelessly hardened criminals under a penal regime that is single-mindedly concerned with custody of dangerous persons. At the same time, recidivist provisions are authentic attempts to take from circulation for a very long time people who are presumed to be incorrigibly dangerous; and, unlike indeterminate sentences, such provisions are widespread and deeply entrenched in the criminal law. They are nevertheless only extreme measures at the outer fringes of the criminal law, and are perhaps best viewed as crude counterparts of civil commitment carried on under the aegis of the criminal law, while differing in purpose from its main sentencing provisions.

The point about general deterrence is similarly misconceived. It is thought by some that punishing those who commit crimes corrects in others a tendency toward crime by providing an example of the consequences of breaking the law, and that more severe punishment for more serious crime provides a more fearful threat to prevent those crimes that are most unwanted. If, in general, temptation to all crime were of the same strength it would indeed be understandable that the law should make greater or lesser threats according to the seriousness of the crime being dealt with. But in fact temptations to engage in different forms of criminal conduct are of very different strength, and temptations to commit the most serious crimes are often far weaker than temptations to commit less serious crimes.

If indeed the aim of correcting in advance the inclination to crime were being pursued, it would be incumbent on a rational legislature to reserve the severest punishment not for the most serious crimes but for those most tempting in general. A scale of punishments would be attached to all crimes according to how tempting they are, crimes being redefined to allow more sensitive distinctions with respect to temptation. But the fact that grades of punishment are not assigned in this way makes clear the mistake of supposing that punishment is to correct in advance criminal tendencies among the population at large.

Admittedly, widespread criminal activity of a particular kind does sometimes cause public expression of fear and indignation carrying in its wake increased penalties in the hope of deterring further crime. But such sporadic attempts at eliminating crime through measures of intimidation are inconsistent with the principles of punishment (to be discussed in Chapter Ten) that prevail generally in a penal code, and are best regarded as draconian departures from principle that take place in times of stress when a particular crime seems out of control. To the extent that such increased penalties accord with general principles of criminal jurisprudence they are not designed to curb increased temptation, but are enacted in the belief that the crime is now a more serious one because of its prevalence.

A RADICAL CHANGE AND THE OBJECTIONS TO IT

Again, the possibility of a radically different system deserves consideration, for we might abandon much of criminal justice as we know it now and might instead adopt procedures designed to identify, sequester, and correct criminally dangerous persons. Just as the automotive industry calls back for correction models found to be defective and a danger on the road, we might require persons who have shown signs of being a threat to social safety to submit first to diagnostic examination and then to a regime of corrective therapy if the existence of dangerous tendencies is confirmed.

In such a system, rules of conduct in the law would be replaced by specifications of suspicious behavior indicating possible dangerous tendencies; facts offered to establish lack of responsibility or other grounds of blamelessness would be relevant only if they tended to show that the person under consideration was not really dangerous. There would no longer be room for excuses and other claims to avoid blame that would leave dangerous persons at large simply because they could establish that under the circumstances it would be unjust to condemn them. And since it is dangerousness and not wickedness that would provide grounds for removal and correction, only treatment directed to converting those who are now dangerous into safe members of the community would be justifiable.

The first objection to this radically new approach is that of diagnostic inadequacy. In general we have hardly a clue about how to identify personality tendencies that are *peculiarly* criminal. Some small part of all those who are criminally dangerous are abnormal in ways that have a definite and distinctive pathology permitting the peculiar cause of their dangerousness to be identified. But popular fancy preserves the myth of a criminal personality possessed in common by most criminals, with fresh pseudo-scientific speculations constantly advanced to keep the myth alive.

On the contrary, to people who come in contact with those who commit crimes, and whose notions are therefore less fanciful, it is plain enough that there are generally no distinctive personal traits to distinguish people who have broken the law from people who have not committed a crime, and that in most cases there is no reason even to suspect the existence of defects or abnormalities either to account for criminal conduct or to set the criminal apart. Perpetrators of crime display a range of motivations no narrower or more special than the motivations that prompt law-abiding activity—a truth nicely captured by the observation that a criminal is a person with pronounced predatory instincts but insufficient capital to form a corporation. The disappointing fact is that in most instances of crime there is no special dangerous tendency toward unlawfulness to be found and treated, though of course it is always possible to explain criminal behavior in the same way that analogous law-abiding behavior is explained.

Though examination of personal traits will generally prove disappointing, there is other information that is much more promising as a way of predicting crime and making its prevention possible. Social statistics make it clear that often there is a heavy concentration of crime among the part of the population that can be identified by reference to such things as education, race, occupational history, sex, economic status, and age. If a target group is defined with sufficient statistical precision, an astoundingly high proportion of its members can be expected to commit crimes, and often just the types of crime that concern other members of the community most urgently. People in this dangerous group are not possessed of peculiar personal traits that make them dangerous, yet a great many of them are dangerous nonetheless, and measures of a very different kind—measures restricting where they may go and what they may do—might be taken to prevent the crimes they are likely to commit.

Though such a program for control of dangerous persons would be based on a rational assessment of dangerousness, it would shock the conscience of a society committed to egalitarian ideals and to rights of individual self-determination. Citizens would be deprived of their liberty because of their statistical misfortunes. And even though a person chooses, despite the disadvantages of his background and present circumstances, to live a life no less law-abiding than his statistically fortunate neighbor, under this program of crime control he would not be allowed the opportunities that normally attend such a choice.

Proposals for radical change of a different kind claim support in certain existing practices. Criminal punishment as we know it now is thought to be a fulfillment of remote and very general threats to prospective lawbreakers. On this view punishment is a crude and inefficient form of behavioral control, one that reinforces the threat to everyone who might be tempted to break the law and, in addition, brings home the unpleasant consequences to the person who disregarded the threat and needs to experience its fulfillment if he is to take it more seriously in the future. Instead of continuing to use this primitive method, it is suggested that people exhibiting tendencies toward criminal behavior be conditioned through techniques of modern behavioral science that can create and reinforce aversions to what society deems undesirable. Replacing the existing scheme of threats with these quasi-therapeutic programs would result, it is believed, in far greater efficiency and economy, for untoward dispositions would be tracked down and rooted out in an intense and sharply focused procedure requiring only a fraction of the time and cost that sentences in correctional institutions now entail. But more than efficiency and economy recommend these new methods, for they are regarded as a morally superior alternative to punishment that spares years of prison misery to a person in need of correction and preserves his family from the hardship and shame that now is often their lot.

Though these proposals are truly amazing in the light of our general inability to isolate and identify a treatable cause of dangerousness, they are nothing less than astonishing in the light of our exceedingly meager ability to treat successfully even members of that small part of the population who truly are dangerous because of some specific, known abnormality or defect. There are indeed effective techniques of treatment that transform dangerous persons into quite harmless creatures, and these techniques can be applied just as well to make persons not dangerous to begin with into persons incapable of doing harm. There is nothing remarkable in this, for in either case measures that incapacitate a person are all that is required, and thoroughly effective means of doing that have been known since the dawn of mankind. Among civilized people, however, killing and maiming have long been unacceptable as official techniques of incapacitation, and modern science has filled the void not only with techniques of conditioned response that create aversions to certain modes of behavior, but with psychosurgery and drugs as well.

These methods are feasible as programs of incapacitation, but they are profoundly objectionable. For one thing, as a result of such interventions a person often suffers personality alterations that make him an altogether changed person; and while a person is free to undergo such changes if he wishes, no one else has a right to deprive him of his personality and make him into a person of a different sort. No less serious is the consequent loss of ability to meet life's challenges, and the pitifully sheltered life that this makes necessary; or the impairments that make impossible those things which bring with them life's greatest rewards. By contrast, our legal system now provides reasonable protection against dangerous persons, but it does not cast so broad a net or allow such great debilitation of those hauled in that we need be ashamed of what we do to maintain our security.

So long (and only so long) as he remains a menace, a person who can be responsibly identified as a serious danger if left at large in the community may be civilly committed to treatment and custody without regard to whether he has engaged in criminal conduct, although, as with any other kind of medical treatment, only when it is in the best interest of the patient may treatment be given. A person who might seem in some way dangerous but who does not menace us by his very presence may be punished if he is guilty of some crime, but otherwise we are bound to run the risk that his freedom presents to us. In life there are many dangerous things that we choose to tolerate, even though we could easily reduce such hazards to our health or safety if we wished. For the sake of our pleasures, our convenience, our economic prosperity, we run risks in eating, drinking, traveling, and even breathing. In the same way, for the sake of our liberty and our humanity we run certain risks by allowing to remain at large in our social environment certain people who are marginally dangerous and whose removal would indeed increase the margin of safety for those who continue to live in the community.

Among people who do commit crimes, some are dangerous either because they have chosen to live a life of crime or because some personal abnormality constrains them toward criminal behavior. Prosecutors, judges, and other officials either influence decisions or decide themselves how long within the prescribed range a person is to be kept out of circulation. The question then arises, of whether a person's dangerousness ought to be taken into consideration. In the many cases when bare impressions and biases decide the matter, this will be an invitation to abuse of official powers of discretion. In other cases a sound judgment that a person is dangerous will be feasible even though he could not be put away as in civil commitment merely for being dangerous. In principle there seems to be no justification for punishing more heavily the person who is more likely to commit another crime—and once again we must reconcile ourselves to running greater risks than we otherwise would. There are two reasons for this. For one thing, every person has a right to change his ways, either alone or with the help of others, and then to live a law-abiding life. Further, everyone is entitled to be judged in the same way for his crime, and to be punished only for his crime according to standards of punishment that apply equally to every crime.

One other method of dealing with dangerous persons is of an altogether different kind. Not a few who are dedicated to a life of crime and have no allegiance to the law might be brought inside the community of the law-abiding by education and by having made available to them attractive opportunities in society as a rational inducement to live by its rules. The removal and exclusion that is an incident of criminal justice would be abandoned, and instead a policy of greater inclusion would be adopted. Though admittedly such abandonment can only be partial, to the extent that it is feasible it offers far greater hope in the long run of reducing the incidence of crime among those who now are without allegiance to the law.

CHAPTER TWO

Conceiving Criminal Conduct: Acts

The picture of criminal justice sketched at the beginning of the first chapter gave prominence to rules of conduct whose violations the law makes punishable. Such rules are violated when a person acts contrary to the rule by engaging in conduct that the rule prohibits or by failing to engage in conduct that the rule requires.

But conduct is a slippery notion, and criminal conduct more slippery still. One thing about conduct can be grasped easily: it is attributable only to persons. Beyond that the important questions remain elusive. What is it about persons—their minds, their bodies, or something else—that uniquely qualifies them to engage in conduct? How do we tell when a person has done something, and distinguish that from the thing's simply happening? How do we distinguish a person's *doing* something from a person's *being* something? What must occur for there to be conduct at all, and how do we know whose conduct it is? How is an act marked off from its consequences, and from the circumstances under which it takes place? And finally—though certainly not least important—is the question of why conduct should be the principal concern of the law in deciding questions of criminal liability.

These matters have not been neglected by theorists of the criminal law in their attempts to formulate first principles of criminal liability, but their efforts seem often to end in quandaries that occupy other theorists and darken the path of those who administer the criminal law. Once again, these matters are looked into in this chapter and the two that follow, in order to provide a conceptual groundwork upon which the criminal law may safely rest.

I. ACTS AND BODILY MOVEMENTS

THE ORTHODOX VIEW AND ITS DIFFICULTIES

There are ideas about criminal liability that collectively might be called the orthodox or the official view, and in the course of a long and influential life this view has changed hardly at all. The Model Penal Code, a paradigm of penal legislation reflecting enlightened modern theory, relies on a conception of conduct that has persisted in Anglo-American criminal law theory for centuries and is no less prominent in Civil law than in Common law writings. According to the official view, conduct has a public aspect—the act, and a private aspect—the mental state accompanying the act. The public aspect consists of bodily movements, and certain bodily movements that arouse public concern constitute a criminal act. Whether the movements will result in criminal liability for the person making them will then depend upon the mental state that accompanied his act.

Efforts to make clear in this way what an act is are intended to serve two purposes. First, since it is *acts* and not mere intentions that concern the criminal law, it is necessary to know what an act is. Otherwise it may not be possible in difficult cases to tell whether an act has taken place and so not possible to tell whether this minimum condition for criminal liability has been met. The other purpose is to make clearer the complementary mental component of conduct. The mental part, though insufficient by itself, is thought nevertheless to be the essential stuff of liability, and what that mental part consists in becomes clear only when the physical part is separated off. A man starts a fire that does damage to an unoccupied building. Knowing that, we know his act. But the man's liability depends on his mental state. In New York, for example, if he recklessly damaged the building by intentionally starting the fire he may be punished by imprisonment for up to four years. If he intentionally damaged the building by starting the fire he is liable to imprisonment for up to fifteen years. If he damaged the building simply through negligence, he is not criminally liable at all. So, it is thought, by subtracting the overt elements, which are the same in all three cases, we become clearer about the hidden inner elements which are different in each case and which make the difference.

To make clear that this generally accepted view is misconceived, it is necessary to show in the first place that acts are not bodily movements. Those who talk as though they were do not reflect common sense, but simply resolve summarily by fiat an important problem that all of us in a more thoughtful moment perceive as difficult and obscure. "Between the motion and act falls the shadow," wrote T. S. Eliot. And even the conventional theorist is bound, in the spirit of this observation, to acknowledge that unsettled matters of theory raise doubts that acts are bodily movements. For one thing, bodily movements are distinguished from acts when involuntary bodily movements are spoken of and contrasted with involuntary acts. Consider the jabbing movements of an epileptic's arms during a seizure, or the flailing of a drowning man, or the movements of someone trying to recover his balance as he falls. There is a question in each case of whether there is an act or whether there is nothing more than bodily movements. Acts and bodily movements are different kinds of things, and the appropriate move to defend against a charge of doing harm is different for each.

Another unsettled matter that embarrasses the theorist is what to include among bodily movements when describing an act. The man who starts the fire holds a match, strikes it, and then tosses it onto a combustible substance. Are the movements of the match part of his bodily movements for purposes of defining the relevant act? If so, where do extensions of his body end? If not, how can the act so meagerly defined be useful for purposes of imposing criminal liability? As a final discomfort, there is the matter of *not* doing something and incurring criminal liability for that. Is failing to file a tax return a crime that involves a special sort of motionless act, or an act whose bodily movements are found in something that is done instead of the act required by the law, or are we in desperation to say that this crime simply does not require that there be an act at all?

Doubts stirred by these unsettled points are fully aroused when bodily movements necessary and sufficient for a particular criminal act are sought. A list of the many criminal acts that are thoroughly perplexing in this regard might begin with swearing falsely, causing death, engaging in conduct commonly called hazing, impersonating another, concealing a record, refusing to provide support. If the acts designated by these verb phrases are in any useful way to be understood as bodily movements, we must be able to tell that an act of that kind has occurred by looking at bodily movements. But even paying the closest attention to bodily movements, how are we to distinguish *swearing falsely* from *swearing truly,* or *swearing* from simply *affirming?* (One thinks here of the criminal law teacher who told his students that even he had trouble distinguishing an act of adultery from an act of fornication. "I've tried them both, and I still can't tell them apart.")

If we were really able to identify acts as bodily movements, we would be able to answer two questions. First, during what period of time did the act take place—that is, when did the first and the last bodily movements belonging to the act occur? Second, which bodily movements during that period are part of that act, and which are not? If these questions cannot be answered, then bodily movements certainly cannot be relied on to determine either the occurrence or the character of the act.

A simple experiment will show that these questions cannot be answered. Imagine a film in which a criminal act—say burglary—is portrayed. As in real life, the crime is part of a course of events in which many activities take place, some of them innocent and unrelated to the crime, others just the sort of activity that typically are part of the crime, still others associated in some way with the crime though perhaps not part of it. One views the film, noting the criminal act, and then sits through the film again (as many times as necessary) to observe the bodily movements that mark the beginning of the criminal act and those that mark the end of the criminal act in order to distinguish it from the many other acts that are depicted and so isolate a definite basis of criminal liability. Even the most meticulous observation will be disappointed, and the ensuing sense of futility will give way to recognition that what is being attempted is absurd.

Some movements, of course, are made before the act takes place, and some after. The burglar's movements in combing his hair before he sets off, for example, and in removing his coat when he returns, are outside the time span of his act of burglary. Moreover, while the act is being performed certain movements are related to the act in some important way, though others are not. His movements in breaking the lock are clearly important; his movements to brush off his clothes are not. Regarding many of the movements, there will be little doubt. But there is small consolation in this for traditional theory, since there are still bound to be unresolvable doubts about many other movements as one contemplates the numberless motions of the burglar's body in his various activities throughout the scenes portraying the burglary. The result is that neither the occurrence nor the character of the criminal act can be known simply by reference to bodily movements.

OBJECTIONS TO THE ORTHODOX VIEW

The objection to conceiving criminal acts as bodily movements may be stated briefly in a half-dozen points.

1. *Some criminal acts do not consist of bodily movements.* There is criminal liability for failure to act and for possession, and such crimes present a standing problem for legal theorists. Postponing special consideration of them to the next section, we might note here certain other items of conduct that qualify in a fairly straightforward way as acts, though they need involve no bodily movement. Benefiting from illegal proceeds, living as a spouse with a person then married to another, neglecting to care for a child, keeping a person unlawfully confined, maintaining unlawful premises, appearing in an intoxicated condition—all are examples of criminal acts requiring no movement. Their distinguishing feature is that a person's relation to a state of affairs rather than to an event is what is crucial for liability.

2. *Some criminal acts involve no bodily movements, and could not, since the actor has no body.* Corporations commit acts of pollution and unfair competition; nations, acts of aggression and genocide. There must be no misunderstanding here about who the actor is. Sometimes, of course, criminal liability is imposed vicariously on some bodiless entity within whose authority a wrongdoer has acted. Au-

thority implies responsibilities, and so even though the wrongdoing may not be an act of that entity, its scope of authority makes it responsible. But these are not instances of such vicarious liability by a bodiless entity for the acts of persons within its authority. Liability here is for the act of the corporation or of the state itself, and so it is liability solely for the act of a bodiless actor.

3. With very few exceptions, *no particular bodily movement or set of bodily movements is required for the occurrence of a criminal act.* Any set of bodily movements said to comprise an act causing death, for example, will contain not a single bodily movement that need be part of some other set that may with equal plausibility be said to comprise another instance of the same act. The only exception would be that rare species of criminal act whose definition entails certain bodily movements—such as making an obscene gesture known as the sign of the fig, striking a person with a closed fist, producing a noise known as the "Bronx cheer," and rape.

4. Except for criminal acts of the exceptional variety just mentioned, *no set of bodily movements is sufficient to constitute the act.* Breaking and entering is a criminal act. Suppose the activity involved in a paradigm performance of breaking and entering is specified in minute detail, and an expert is then employed who punctiliously acts out the scenario. Even though no movements were lacking, there will not have been an act of breaking and entering if the performance was commissioned by the owner of the house to test the burglar alarm system. In that case the act performed that most closely approximates breaking and entering is the act of simulated breaking and entering. Although bodily movements are identical, it is a different act for which there is no criminal liability. (This should not be confused with justifiable breaking and entering, which is the same act for which normally there is liability, but performed under special circumstances that exempt from liability. Breaking and entering could take

place when seeking shelter in a blizzard, and the peril to be avoided may then justify the prohibited act. In the case of testing the burglar alarm the permission would not be introduced to justify the act, since there is no prohibited act to be justified in the first place. The permission then would only be part of the explanation of why the act is the innocent one of simulated breaking and entering rather than the unlawful act of breaking and entering.)

5. *There is no way of telling what criminal act, if any, is constituted by a given set of bodily movements.* For one thing, no matter how intent and discriminating our observation of such movements, there is nothing to tell us whether breaking and entering or a simulation of it is being performed. There is no way of so distinguishing any act of pretense, such as playing, shamming, imitating, practicing, testing, from the act of which it is a pretense. And, more generally, there is no way of distinguishing by bodily movements different acts that consist of identical movements—as an example, striking a match from making a flame.

6. *There is nothing to fix any particular bodily movement (or combination of them) as part of one criminal act rather than of another, or as part of any act at all.* Consider a traditional favorite: the pull of a trigger finger. No coordinates in the physical world of bodily movements can mark a movement as part of an act of causing death rather than as part of an act of causing fright; yet both acts occur when a captured soldier who remains silent is shot to induce his comrade to give information. Nor can the finger's movement be described as part of any act at all if it simply took place as a momentary spasm much to the astonishment of all, including the man whose finger it is.

TOWARD A BETTER CONCEPTION

Since neither the occurrence nor the character of an act can be determined from bodily movements, conceiving acts as

bodily movements provides no help in dealing with problems of criminal law theory that require investigation of the
concept of an act in the first place. Most (though not all) acts
are usefully described in terms of events that include bodily
movements of the actor, and for that reason we should certainly not attempt to put bodily movements out of bounds in
speaking of acts, any more than we should try to limit our-
sclvcs to an account wholly or mainly in tcrms of thc actor's
movements. Banning talk of bodily movements in describing
conduct would be as foolish as not allowing talk of molecular
activity when cooking is the subject of conversation. Culi-
nary skills and gastronomic appreciation are little enhanced
by talk in terms of molecules; yet it is likely that some matters in the arts of cooking can be dealt with most conveniently by reference to them, and surely a trivial description
of a great deal that goes on in the kitchen can be provided in
terms of molecules if anyone wishes to take the trouble.

As a first step in determining criminal liability, to what
then—if not to bodily movements—should we turn our attention to discover whether an act has taken place and to discover what sort of act it might be? The answer to the first
and more difficult of these questions is postponed to the end of
Chapter Four so that discussion of the important conceptual
problems surrounding criminal conduct can precede it. The
answer makes principles of responsibility fundamental and
insists that acts are whatever satisfy certain basic requirements under these principles. It is an answer that in effect
turns orthodox theory upside down. More particularly, an act
consists of events or states of affairs for which a person might
be responsible according to the principles of responsibility that
guide such judgments; and so an act has taken place when
such events occur or when such states of affairs exist. Events
and conditions over which a person might have control in a
way required for responsibility is the key to an act's being
lone, and since these events and conditions are of every con-

ceivable type, bodily movements turn out to be only a small and not especially important part of the full range of events that comprise acts. The kinds of events and states of affairs there are will determine what kind of act has taken place; and in the case of any criminal act these events or states of affairs will augur some kind of harm that concerns the criminal law.

II. THE SCOPE OF AN ACT

AN ACT, ITS CONSEQUENCES, AND ITS ATTENDANT CIRCUMSTANCES

The concept of an act is only the first among several that the theorist needs as he labors to give account of what is required for criminal liability. What is spoken of as the mental element must be dealt with as well, and its many trying conceptual difficulties will occupy us in the chapter to follow. In the meantime we must look into two other concepts that are needed to account for requirements set by the law for many, though not all, crimes. It is often necessary that conduct take place under certain *circumstances* or have certain *consequences* if there is to be criminal liability for it. Though conduct is always a requirement, there is not in all crimes a requirement that the act be done under specified circumstances or with specified outcome. When there is such a requirement, which is often enough, it is sometimes difficult to distinguish the act from these other elements—to prize off conduct, as it were, from the rest of the world that is of interest. Yet it is important both for practice and for theory that such discrimination be made. A few illustrations will make the point.

Under a typical aggravated assault provision, injury must be inflicted with a dangerous instrument, and the injury must constitute serious bodily harm. Normally the dangerous instrument requirement is taken to be circumstantial, and the requirement of serious bodily harm is taken to be consequential, with reference in both cases to an act of assault. Accordingly, there would be liability only for *attempted* aggravated assault when the actor caused serious bodily harm with the butter knife he snatched up, believing it to be the steak knife he had reached for; or when his attack with a steak knife was meant to cause serious bodily harm, though it did not. It is possible, however, to regard as part of the *act* either or both of the elements that normally are not taken to be part of it. The act then would be assault with a dangerous instrument, or assault causing serious bodily harm, or assault with a dangerous instrument causing serious bodily harm. In that case (as we shall later see in Chapter Four) there might not be liability even for an attempt, either if serious bodily harm does not occur, or if the assault is not with a dangerous weapon, since the act that takes place in such a case might not be deemed sufficiently dangerous.

Though theory remains baffled, aggravated assault is ordinarily an offense whose different elements are readily delineated and can be separated by simple intuition. Other offenses, however, baffle even our intuitions and are genuinely troublesome in practice. Two examples will suffice.

Bribing an official of a labor union to influence him in his official activities is a crime. If a bribe is given for this purpose to an impostor posing as a union official, it is truly problematic whether criminal liability may be imposed for *attempting* to bribe a union official. If the prohibited act is *bribing*, and the person being a union official is only an attendant circumstance necessary for the harm of the completed crime, then the act that is interdicted has been done, and grounds for attempt liability have been supplied. But if *bribing a labor union official* is the prohibited act, grounds for attempt liability arguably do not exist, for the criminal act was not performed and was not even in progress, nor was it even in prospect as part of the course of activity that is now in question.

A second example poses the dilemma regarding an act and its consequence. If performed with intent to defraud, it is a crime to alter an object to make it appear to possess a rarity that it does not in fact possess. If *altering the object* is taken to be the prohibited act, and the deceptive appearance created by it is taken to be a consequence of the act, a hopelessly botched job (done with the requisite intent) would nonetheless furnish grounds for attempt liability, since the prohibited act was done. But if the criminal act is taken to be *altering an object so as to create an appearance of rarity* (perhaps more neatly expressed as "creating an appearance of rarity by altering an object"), then quite likely the bungler should not incur even attempt liability, since he neither did that act nor was he even on the way to doing it.

Official theory provides no help, even though on its own misconceived premise it makes easy work of these distinctions. If acts are bodily movements, when bodily movements are subtracted from what is necessary for a crime, what is left is either a consequence of the act or some circumstantial element. But when this premise is rejected a new solution is needed, and this is to be found first in the idea of a criminal act that has been suggested here already: the act can consist only of elements of a crime that are so thoroughly within the control of an accused person that under normal conditions he can prevent their occurrence or thwart their existence if he chooses. This will disqualify certain elements of a crime as possible parts of the criminal act, but it may still leave in the running other elements that are not properly part of the criminal act for this particular crime. There is a second condition to be met, one that disqualifies the remaining elements not properly included as part of the criminal act. An element is part of the act only if its presence is necessary for the existence of a threat of the harm that concerns the law, and not simply for the occurrence of that harm.

There are, in other words, two conditions that an element of a crime must meet to be part of the criminal act. The first places a premium on responsibility so that only things that a normal actor may prevent if he chooses are counted as part of his act; the second, by requiring dangerousness of the right sort ensures that liability is no more extensive than was intended by those who created and defined the crime. Thus, for example, the law prohibiting the bribing of union officials may not, after all, be dealing with the corrupt labor practices of management but only with the corrupt practices of union officials. It would then be unreasonable, in construing the law, to say that the very act of bribing someone mistakenly taken to be a union official is enough to pose a threat of the harm that concerns the law. The bribe taker's being a union official then becomes an element of the crime that is necessary for the harm that concerns the law to be threatened; it is not an element that is necessary only for the harm to *occur;* hence it is not an attendant circumstance but part of the criminal act, which may be designated as *bribing a labor union official.*

If, on the other hand, the corrupt practices of management is the evil with which the law has concerned itself, the very act of bribing an imposter believed to be a union official is an act of the kind the law has concerned itself with, even though the evil cannot occur unless the person bribed is actually a union official. Since the bribe taker's being a union official is then an element necessary only for the harm to occur but not for it to be threatened, it is only an attendant circumstance and not part of the criminal act.

An act can be distinguished from its consequences by following the same line. If the evil that concerns the law is deception of the buying public, the criminal act would be *alter-*

ing the object so as to create an appearance of rarity, since there would be a threat of harm only when such alteration was in progress. But if it is simply a matter of protecting the honest members of the business community from counter-feiters, every attempt at faking a rare piece would rightly be regarded as dangerous conduct, no matter how clumsy it was and no matter how unsuccessful in creating the desired appearance. In that event *altering the object* with the requisite intent would be enough for the criminal act to take place, and any appearances of rarity would be a consequence of it necessary only for the harm to occur.

These questions of just what evil it is that really concerns the law are not unfamiliar to lawyers, and customarily they decide such questions by arguments of legislative history that often include quite astonishing interpretations of the past in order to make its transactions seem responsive to present needs. Even so, defining the act in each crime by reference to supposed legislative concerns has much to recommend it, for criminal justice has as its aim liability only for acts that are criminal according to the accusations, and this means, among other things, liability only when what the accused did posed a threat of the particular harm that the law has made its business.

OMISSIONS

Finding the outer limits of an act is troublesome enough. Even more vexing to the theorist are the vanishing points beyond which no act can be found.

Those who hold that acts are to be understood as bodily movements are embarrassed first of all by criminal omissions. Since no bodily movements can be appropriated specifically to the omission, an omission to do something appears to them to be no act at all. Liability then is for something *not done* by the one made liable. Under such circumstances the justice of penalties is brought into question just as it is when another person and not the one made liable is in fact the person who broke the law.

Criminal omissions are uncongenial for two other reasons. One is that duties to act are created by such criminal prescriptions; and while such duties are familiar in the realm of moral demands when minding one's own business is not enough to keep one morally correct, as legal demands they seem an unwarranted public burden on persons who wish only to be let alone when they are doing nothing that harms others. The other objection to omissions derives once again from the official version of conduct. Some crimes of omission may be committed when all is quiet on the mental front. In such cases there simply is no mental activity that can be associated with the failure to act for which there is liability, and this is very disturbing to those who believe that, for punishment to be proper, a wicked mental element must always have been present within the actor at the time of the crime.

Punishment for *not* doing something is firmly established as part of the law, and this suggests that theorists' objections are better dealt with by reforming theory than by reforming the law. Failures to report, to register, to obtain a license are made offenses in order to facilitate government regulation that is thought desirable. Failures to take protective measures in the interest of health or safety comprise innumerable other offenses the credentials for which are deemed impeccable. Still other laws require that certain things be done by persons who occupy positions of special responsibility—in a family, as an employer, as an owner of property; and punishment for failing to do what these laws require is, once again, uncontroversial. Attempting to keep his theory afloat in a sea of offenses that are apparently actless, the official theorist suggests that omissions might be acts after all, to be contrasted with other acts that are commissions—perhaps to be captured, as one writer suggests, by the notion of a *negative act*. But as these suggestions provide not even a hint of why liability is justified without the bodily movement normally required by official theory, they are mere terminological evasions and hardly the enrichment of a theory of acts that they purport to be.

Offenses of omission and offenses of commission—requirements to do something and prohibitions against doing something—are in fact only variant forms of the same legal proscription, different in stress but not in what they provide as grounds for liability. When an activity not on its face legitimate is thought to qualify for being made criminal, a provision prohibiting it is appropriate. But when an activity on its face legitimate is thought to be in need of regulation, or when such activity is viewed as part of a larger social enterprise with which the government must concern itself for purposes other than regulation, it is usual for the law to set requirements that must be met by those who engage in such an activity, and to make failure to meet these requirements an offense. Criminal omissions, then, always prescribe what must be done (or how something must be done) *when something else is done or takes place.*

In this regard criminal omissions are similar to crimes of negligence, for to act negligently is normally to engage in legitimate activity in an unacceptable way. But unlike crimes of negligence, which consist of failure to meet more or less general standards of care, criminal omissions occur when there is a failure to do something specified by the law. It is this specification of what must be done that creates the illusion that liability for an omission, unlike negligence, is simply liability for failing to do what is required. In fact, however, liability for criminal omissions is complex, and can be understood only when the act required is seen in relation to the legitimate (though problematic) activity that prompted what the law requires. *That* legitimate activity is the conduct necessary for liability, and so in laws creating criminal omissions there is conduct required for liability, though liability is not for that conduct alone.

By considering whether the conduct that must take place is legitimate or not, one can decide whether a prohibition or a requirement is the more appropriate form of penal legislation. If a legislative body wishes to enact penal provisions for driving on highways at speeds of either less than 30 miles per hour or more than 60 miles per hour, it seems natural to impose liability for *failure to drive* at a speed of at least 30 miles per hour, and to *prohibit driving* at a speed in excess of 60. On its face, driving slowly is a legitimate activity that is being specially regulated when engaged in as part of highway travel, while driving at a high speed is not a legitimate activity and so is being prohibited. If in a country in which speed limits are previously unknown it is provided simply that all highway travel shall be at speeds not less than 30 nor more than 60 miles per hour, it may well be unclear with respect to both the lower and the upper limit whether violation should constitute an omission or a commission. Although the legitimacy of both types of conduct is indeterminate, it is perfectly clear in both cases that the same conduct could constitute either an omission or a commission.

What is more naturally formulated as a criminal omission may always be framed as a criminal prohibition, though usually not without awkwardness and a false stress that is misleading to citizens and officials who must always ascertain what is reasonably implied by the law in order to guide themselves in situations not covered explicitly by it. A state may wish to create criminal liability for residents who fail to file an income tax return. It seems natural then to create liability for an omission. But, alternatively, the law might formulate this as a prohibition that prohibits residence in the state without filing a return. What is then prohibited (though not unconditionally) is a legitimate activity, and this will cause reasonable men to scratch their heads and wonder what the legislature had in mind. Because the law in this form suggests that residence in the state is the thing of underlying concern, very strange issues of exculpation are likely to arise as those against whom such a law is enforced try to show that they did not reside in the state intentionally, or that they could not help themselves and were forced to live there, or that laws restricting residence in this way are in any case invalid.

We are left, then, with a view of criminal omissions that represents no departure from the general requirement that liability be for conduct. Crimes of omission are committed only when specified acts are done, just as is the case with straightforward prohibitions. The stress in omissions, however, is on what must be done additionally if there is not to be liability. Even though liability is imposed *because* something was not done, liability nevertheless is *for doing* certain things without doing certain other things.

POSSESSION

Crimes of possession similarly appear to be below the threshold of activity, and therefore to be also something of an embarrassment for criminal law theory. This rather large class of crimes is comprised by those provisions of the law that make illegal the possession of something or other. Liability then appears to attach to the possessor, even though no physical activity is identifiable as the act of possession. One solution proposed by the embarrassed theorist fixes on some antecedent or contemporaneous activity that is necessary for possession—such as acquiring or retaining—and then fixes on the physical activity assumed to constitute those acts as being the gist of the act of possession. There is a short reply to this proposal. The act made criminal on this account ought to be that of acquiring or retaining, rather than possessing; but this is not done for the simple and obvious reason that such acts are in certain important respects quite different from possessing.

Another proposed solution regards possession as the failure to relinquish, and then makes liability rest on whatever in general justifies liability for omissions. But this suggestion is disappointing if one looks at possessory offenses in the light of what has just been learned about omissions. Crimes of possession do not normally turn out to be a failure to do something when something else is done, as every omission should. Possession of burglar's tools is not a failure to get rid of them when one has acquired or retained them, and for this reason crimes of possession defy analysis in this way as crimes of omission.

Crimes of possession, like all other crimes, can be committed only when there is an act. An act of possession is, however, rather special and belongs to a class of acts already noticed in the first section of this chapter. The distinguishing feature of all these acts is that they all consist of a state of affairs, rather than an event, which is attributed to a person for purposes of ascribing responsibility. *Possessing* is in this regard an act of the same class as *appearing, benefiting from, neglecting, keeping, maintaining,* and the like. It is not a novel proposition but part of common sense that in general a person may be responsible for the way things stand no less than for what happens, and that acts include both these grounds of responsibility. Orthodox theory finds this most inconvenient, however, for on its account all acts are physical movements, and all physical movements are events and not states of affairs. Though crimes of possession are for this reason a sorry inconvenience to the orthodox theorist, his embarrassment disappears immediately once he forms a conception of an act that genuinely suits the purposes of his theory.

III. VOLUNTARY AND INVOLUNTARY ACTS

ANALYSIS OF THE VARIOUS CONCEPTS

The foundation of criminal liability is conduct, for without an act there can be no liability. But not any act will do. There are qualifications that an act must meet, and the first is that it be *voluntary*.

But stating simply that an act must be voluntary if there is to be liability can be quite misleading if one does not notice the different senses the term *involuntary* may have. For one thing, a person may still be liable for what he does when he does something against his will at the insistence of someone else. He may also be liable after putting himself in a condition in which he is not aware of what he is doing. In both cases the conduct is involuntary in some well-recognized sense. But it is not involuntary in the sense that interests us when we seek initially to qualify an act as the basis of liability. Worth noting also in this connection is liability for involuntary manslaughter. When "voluntary" is to be understood as (roughly) a paraphrase of "willful," the corresponding opposite term "involuntary" designates a lesser degree of blameworthiness, and conduct involuntary in that sense may still be fully voluntary in the sense that is of interest at this point. Obviously, then, acts may be voluntary or involuntary in different senses, and when these different senses are confused, as they often are, we may expect arguments at cross purposes resulting in unsound judgments about responsibility and culpability. To avoid this, we now must carefully examine and distinguish several different notions of voluntary and involuntary conduct.

An involuntary act of the kind that interests us as the first requirement for liability must be distinguished first from two other classes of personal events. Mere bodily motions are one class; involuntary movements are another. When a living human body is subjected to the forces of the physical world, it may respond in much the same way as an inanimate object, and we then have *bodily motion*. Though pushing a human limb and pushing the limb of a tree both result in motion, in neither case can the motion taking place be called either voluntary or involuntary. In the case of the tree the movement is not that of a person at all, and in the case of a human limb it is not the movement of a person *as a person*. *Involuntary movements,* on the other hand, are bodily movements of the sort that only animate creatures are capable of making. Persons (who are those animate creatures that are capable of acting) move involuntarily when they twitch, have muscle spasms, or react reflexively.

Involuntary acts stand in contrast to involuntary movements. Involuntary acts are episodes in a person's history for which it appears at first that he might be responsible, but which turn out not to be of that kind at all. An involuntary act is simply not an act, just as a movie set is not a village, or an art forgery an old master. After learning the truth about what happened, we no longer consider what took place to be an act, though originally we had reason to think otherwise. For acts as for objects it is important to have a way of referring to what is apparent so that appearance and reality may be reconciled. This allows us to say that an involuntary act of stabbing is what occurred when someone stumbled as he turned with a knife in his hand to greet his friend. There is then in truth no act at all, even though there is a setting of responsible activity (and not mere physical movements) that induces us to make a *prima facie* case for treating it as an act. If the stabbing occurred as arms jabbed back and forth during an epileptic fit, we would not even have an involuntary act, but only involuntary movements, for there would then be no setting to suggest responsible activity and so no *prima facie* case for treating as an act what went on.

The sense in which an act is involuntary when it is contrasted with involuntary *movements* is quite different from the sense in which an act is involuntary when it is contrasted with a voluntary *act*. When it is asserted that an act is involuntary in this latter sense, it is implied that there is an act, but for reasons having to do with freedom of choice the actor is not responsible for it. Instead of denying a *prima facie* imputation of conduct to some occurrence, we admit that the occurrence is an act—that is, an occurrence for which someone might be held responsible. But because the actor could choose only with inordinate difficulty to do otherwise—or could not choose to do otherwise at all—we deny that he is in fact fully responsible, or responsible at all. In this sense the following are not (or are not fully) voluntary acts: (1) acts done only because coerced by others; (2) acts done only because of one's own uncontrollable urges; (3) acts done only because circumstances left no choice; (4) acts done when one is in an abnormal mental state that leaves one unable to appreciate what he is doing. To avoid confusion, the use of two different terms is a sensible precaution. We might speak of an *involuntary act* when as it turns out there was no act, while reserving *not voluntary* for those occasions when the actor is not responsible for what he does because of factors affecting choice.

There are other senses of both *voluntary* and *involuntary* which are found in the language of obligation and in certain other contexts, but which are only distant relations of their homonyms in the language of responsibility. It is well to note this, for confusion is sometimes bred by postulating a common root in meaning to which all uses are traced and all senses assimilated. Though nothing is meant to be said about responsibility, court appearances, bankruptcies, enlistments, donations, and rescues, are examples of things commonly qualified by one or both of these terms to indicate something about duties, constraints, or origins. The senses of *voluntary* and *involuntary* that are then put into play do not interest us here, for they refer to what brought about some state of affairs or to what ought to occur, but not to whether someone is or might be accountable for it.

ORTHODOX THEORY AND ITS FLAWS

Official theory cares little for such nice distinctions, for it has no need of them. Instead of looking at the way these words are really used, official theory presumes that such terms as *voluntary* and *involuntary* refer to what is going on in the actor when he acts. In this view, the actor is a psychological complex whose mind is normally in charge of bodily movements, or at least in charge of those grand external movements that comprise acts. The mind plans, orders, and oversees, while the body carries out the mind's instructions. Bodily movements resulting from such happy collaborations are *voluntary acts*. Under unusual circumstances, however, the mind may not be in charge of what the body does, and bodily movements may take place independently. These bodily movements are *involuntary acts*. Only voluntary acts, however, can serve as the basis of ascription of responsibility, for the reason that, without a planning, directing, and controlling agent on the job, no one can be held responsible for what is done. The mind is such an agent, whereas the body alone is only a dumb brute—and, as everyone knows, it makes no sense at all to hold dumb brutes responsible.

This curious yet commonplace conception of mind-body relations, which orthodox theory appropriates as a foundation for responsibility, can be viewed as a metaphor. In relations among people it is not uncommon for a person under whose authority or at whose direction a thing is done to be held responsible. And it is common enough for one who is duped and simply used by others to be found free of any responsibility. It is therefore not unreasonable to suppose that when a person is conceived as an embodied mind he is being conceived along lines deriving from social relations among individuals. Giving priority to the social facts seems warranted if for no other reason than that they are certain. It is clear enough what claims are regularly made and accepted to avoid responsibility when one person harms another while acting innocently under the authority of a third person. It is far from clear, however, what is going on in the realm of the mind and the body when analogous claims are made about an individual's conduct.

Be that as it may, there are two reasons why the account of a voluntary act provided by official theory is unsatisfactory. In the first place, many unquestionably voluntary acts are engaged in without the mind's being any more in charge than when nonvoluntary acts are performed. Familiarity or preoccupation are the usual hallmarks of these acts. When an actor is inattentive to what he is doing or is engaged in some rote practice, he may still be acting voluntarily. Yet his mental participation is no greater or more influential than in such clear instances of nonvoluntary conduct as that of the compulsive voyeur, the epileptic, the person under hypnosis, or the man who causes injury to others when he falls down the stairs. Since the point of judging conduct voluntary or nonvoluntary is to designate it eligible or ineligible to serve as the basis of an ascription of responsibility, and since much conduct is generally recognized as eligible in this regard even though it is done without prompting or supervision of the mind, such mindlessness cannot serve to distinguish nonvoluntary from voluntary conduct.

The other reason for rejecting the account furnished by official theory will already be obvious, and requires only the briefest reminder of matters discussed in the first section of this chapter. Since acts are not bodily movements, a nonvoluntary act cannot be understood as bodily movements made without the mind in charge, nor can a voluntary act be understood as bodily movements made when the mind is in

charge. Since acts are not bodily movements, even if we were
to accept the proffered psychological model it would not be
acts that were being performed with or without the mind in
charge, but only bodily movements. Acceptance of the psychological model, then, would in any case afford a distinction
only between voluntary and involuntary bodily movements.

Here as elsewhere, official theory means to furnish support
for a doctrine of the criminal law; and even though the theory may be unsound, the doctrine is not. It is important that
there truly be conduct if there is to be liability, and so at the
very threshold of proceedings aimed at imposing liability,
anything that seems to be an act but isn't must be turned
away. This is accomplished by identifying an act as involuntary in the relevant sense and rejecting it. But official theory,
with its unneeded mind-body baggage, tends to weigh down
the doctrine in a way that leads finally to its breakdown. In
the first place, this theory makes it appear that a voluntary
act is one that has been willed. This opens the door to sup-
positions and proposals rooted in a philosophical psychology
that makes the *will* the main hinge of responsibility. But
whether a person willed what he did when he committed a
crime is not something upon which his liability depends. Assuming that a person has not been made to act against his
will, the fact that he does act against his will in committing a
crime will not relieve him of liability for it. Much against his
will, he may kill his closest friend because otherwise, so he
believes, the woman with whom he is hopelessly in love will
certainly leave him for the other man. He has searched fran-
tically for an alternative, but to no avail, and only then in
utter desperation and with the greatest reluctance does he
commit murder. The fact that he does so against his will does
not, however, provide him with a defense.

The other way in which official theory brings the law to
grief is when it confuses the initial question about whether
an act is voluntary with later questions about voluntary con-

duct. As we shall see in Chapter Seven, many important questions affecting determinations of responsibility ask in some way whether the actor could really have done otherwise as a matter of choice. Being free in this way when one acts means that one is engaging in conduct that is voluntary, though *voluntary* in that sense is different from *voluntary* in the sense applicable here. Official theory, once again, conceives these later questions about freedom as questions about relations between mind and body, this time as questions of whether an act was free of foreign influences and so truly determined by the mind of the actor. For this reason, those who rely on official theory often fail to distinguish the two very different kinds of questions about voluntariness, one asking whether what took place is even the sort of thing for which anyone might be held responsible, and the other asking whether the accused ought to be held responsible for something that admittedly is that sort of thing.

CHAPTER THREE

Conceiving Criminal Conduct: Culpability, Intention, and Motive

Both in law and in morals, judgments of blameworthiness seem to rest heavily on the intentions and motives of the actor, with intentions apparently bearing the weight far more when judgments are to be made for legal purposes. Culpability itself is a consideration of the greatest importance in deciding questions of criminal liability, both to determine whether there can be liability at all and to determine what should be the extent of liability. In this chapter attention is turned to the notion of culpability and to its companion notions of motive and intention, in order to lay a foundation for these most important of all judgments about conduct in the context of a criminal accusation.

I. CULPABILITY AND INTENTION

DESIGNATION OF CULPABILITY AND THE ROLE IT PLAYS

All talk about conduct abounds in phrases that are used to make what was done appear more or less blameworthy, but nowhere is the language of culpability more in evidence than when criminal conduct is the subject. The criminal law itself makes heavy use of these terms, and so does theoretical discussion aimed at illuminating its principles. But one can also turn to ordinary life, where fascination with crime never ends and where language is likewise abundantly rich in the vocabulary of blame and exculpation.

If one looks first in the law, there are express qualifications of conduct according to its culpability which are regularly made in statutory language by such terms as *maliciously, with premeditation, with intent, knowingly, willfully, purposely, recklessly, negligently.* Though there are less firm conventions to govern their use, other terms of similar import appear more often in judicial opinions than in legislation, and are prominent also in the literature of criminal law theory—*voluntarily, deliberately, mistakenly, accidentally, inadvertently, intentionally.* On the whole, precise use of these terms is less fixed by authoritative definitions, for usually only terms in statutory provisions suffer the rigors of express definition. For this reason terms less characteristically legislative are often more interesting for general theoretical work concerned with responsibility and culpability. They are shaped more by use in blaming and excusing than by authoritative stipulations of a legislature and by interpretations of a court that must be faithful to the text and intention of legislative enactment. Still other terms of this kind do not usually appear at all in contexts in which criminal liability is being prescribed or decided or explained. *Cold-blooded, wanton, well-meaning, vicious, merciful, atrocious, heinous, trivial,* and the like are seen in newspapers and heard at the dinner table; and even though such descriptive terms do not help in judging culpability, they reflect a conclusion about some aspect of culpability.

Often both administrators and theorists of criminal justice seem not to appreciate fully the extent to which the criminal law is occupied with matters of culpability. In the first place there is the question of liability itself. As we shall see, culpable conduct is always required for criminal liability. The requirement is often made explicit in the law itself, where language of the kind we have mentioned appears to tell us, for example, that an assault must be with intent to kill, or a life must be endangered recklessly. But sometimes the requirement is not explicit, so that, for example, we do not know simply by reading the text whether any taking of another's property creates liability for larceny under a particular statutory provision, or whether the taking must be done at least *negligently* or, even more likely, *knowingly*. Judicial interpretation based on legislative intent is then one way of making the requirement explicit. Another way is by invoking the general principle of justice imposed by any civilized jurisprudence as a constraint upon valid legislation, requiring—even when evidence in legislative intent is lacking—that any conduct for which the law provides punishment be culpable.

Beyond setting a minimum requirement for liability, in the administration of the criminal law culpability plays an important part in decisions about prosecution and about sentencing. A very broad discretion is enjoyed by police, prosecutors, and judges in deciding who shall be charged, what the charge shall be, and what punishment is fitting if the accused is found guilty; and nothing is more important in guiding that discretion than the blameworthiness of what was done. Clearly, then, for criminal justice it is an urgent matter to discover just what it is that makes conduct more or less culpable, and indeed what makes it culpable at all.

Throughout this voyage of discovery it is wise to remember that criminal justice requires us to determine the culpability of a person's conduct, not the culpability of a person. True enough, a person is rightly blamed for the culpable conduct he engages in, and in that sense he may be said to be blameworthy. But there is a quite different sense in which a person is sometimes said to be blameworthy, and in this sense the blameworthiness of a person falls outside the concerns of the criminal law. Judgments sometimes are rendered about what a person is rather than about what a person has done. At times it is a conclusion about him based on what he has done in the past. At other times it is a conclusion about him based on certain conduct he has engaged in that is assumed to be representative of what he is disposed to do. On still other occasions it is a judgment about the person that is based not on his conduct at all but on what is assumed to follow from certain facts about him, such as his ancestry, the shape of his head, or his political beliefs.

When determining criminal liability, the criminal law confines its concern with culpability to specific conduct that is alleged to constitute a crime, placing these other matters entirely out of bounds. But a certain discretion is necessary in order to keep criminal justice a sensible social practice that avoids needless suffering; and a person's general disposition to live a law-abiding life should not be lost sight of by those who must decide what charges to make, what sentence to pass, or whether a prosecution should be undertaken at all, any more than should his dedication to a life of crime. In this way a person's culpability and not simply the culpability of his criminal conduct enter into the administration of criminal justice when the question is not simply whether or not he is liable.

THE DIMENSIONS OF CULPABILITY

Culpability of conduct might be said to have four dimensions. The first (which we shall investigate in this section) can for convenience be called the dimension of *intentionality*. It is apparent that harm resulting from recklessness calls down blame upon the one who is responsible, but that if the harm is done deliberately even greater blame will often be in order. Just what it was that the actor meant to do matters

very much in this regard, and if he only did unintentionally
something that must be done intentionally for liability under the law, he can escape liability because of that. What
really matters here is whether conduct of a particular degree
of dangerousness was done intentionally. It is apparent here
that dangerousness and its degrees need further explanation,
and this will be provided when we reach the third dimension.

The second dimension is one of *harm*. Some harms are
more serious than others, and the conduct constituting or
threatening more serious harm is therefore more blameworthy. Taking a life is more serious than taking property; and
because the harm is greater, criminal homicides are in general more serious and more blameworthy than larcenies. Because culpability has more than one dimension, not all homicides are more culpable than all larcenies, just as (for the
same reason) not all deliberately harmful acts are more culpable than reckless acts that cause harm.

Two related points should be noted. First, the term
harm as we use it here, embraces everything that is regarded as an untoward state of affairs by the criminal law in
creating liability for the kind of conduct that can, or actually
does, bring about such a state of affairs. This terminological
stipulation leaves open the question of whether what is regarded as undesirable by the law really is some harm, and
even the question of whether it really is undesirable. A fuller
discussion of harm begins the next chapter, and more on
these matters is postponed until then. The second point is
that all provisions of the criminal law create criminal liability for conduct because that conduct is believed to bring
about or threaten some undesirable state of affairs. Much argument is needed in support of this proposition, and it will
be provided at several places in later portions of the book.

The third dimension of culpability is one in which the
dangerousness of conduct is measured. It is plain enough
that not all threats of harm posed by conduct are the same.

Conduct sometimes *merely* poses a threat of harm, so that there is a present danger of its occurring but nothing more threatening than that. Sometimes there is more, and the danger then seems imminent. Sometimes conduct is even more dangerous than that, and the occurrence of the harm itself can then be said to be imminent. These three degrees of dangerousness might be illustrated by three assassins, the first simply lying in wait for his victim, the second about to shoot at him, and the third actually shooting. It is natural to think first of difference in dangerousness as difference in likelihood of harm's occurring. But although the relative probability of harm is important, it cannot alone account for conduct's being more or less dangerous. Likelihood of harm does in a general way inform reasonable expectations about the occurrence of harm. But likelihood of harm on any particular occasion does not alone change what are in general to be regarded as reasonable expectations. Reasonable expectations are what the actor knows or should know about the consequences of what he does, and only these expectations determine how dangerous his act is insofar as its dangerousness matters for a judgment of its culpability. This, too, needs fuller explanation, and though extended discussion of reasonable expectations is undertaken in Chapter Six and again in Chapter Ten, a preliminary word is useful here.

Probabilities in general over an extended period of time are the source of common-sense expectations that we count as reasonable, but actual probability on a particular occasion also may affect reasonable expectations in special cases, and so may affect culpability as well. The actual probability of harm's occurring on a particular occasion is relevant for judgments of culpability only if the actor knows, or should know, what the actual probability is. If the danger is less than general expectations would indicate and he knows that when he acts, he may avail himself of this fact to avoid blame, for then he knew his act to be less dangerous than it would normally appear to be. If, on the other hand, it was less dangerous but the actor did not know that when he acted, he may not avail himself of its less dangerous character to avoid blame, for, by a parity of reasoning, it is the danger as it appeared to him (or should have) that affects culpability, and the danger appeared in this case to be what it normally would be. Conversely, if the actor knew (or should have known) when he acted that there was a greater likelihood of harm than normal expectations would indicate, according to the same principle the culpability of his conduct is greater. If the greater than normal likelihood of harm was unknown to him at the time, unless he should have known of the greater likelihood, once again culpability for what he did is determined simply according to normal expectations of harm.

The principle to be observed throughout is the same. Culpability is affected by what the actor knows (or should know) about the likelihood of harm on a particular occasion. In the absence of special knowledge or of a special duty to inform himself, the actor may rely on general expectations under the circumstances, which is what he normally knows and is in any case bound to know by conventions of common sense. These conventions, it is true, are shaped through time by experience of harm and what is likely to produce it; yet on any given occasion normal expectations may well be disappointed without impairing the credibility of common sense.

In our fourth and final dimension of culpability (which our subsequent discussions of motives and of justifications will bring into prominence), the *legitimacy* of conduct under the circumstances is appraised. This appraisal might be thought of as a weighing-on-balance of the harm that is done or threatened by the conduct in question, while the countervailing legitimate interests that are served by that conduct weigh against blame. Sometimes even the gravest harm may be completely justified by the interests that prompt it, as when an assailant is killed in self-defense. Almost always, some legitimating interest can be found to make conduct appear at least a bit less culpable than it otherwise would, and most commonly this is found in the motive. In this connection, too, many activities do not appear in need of justification at all, though much serious injury is occasioned by them. Automobile driving and tunnel construction, for example, are considered legitimate activities in spite of the fact that they claim many lives even when every precaution is taken. Since the interests they serve are considered very important, these activities are not regarded as blameworthy even *prima facie*.

For an act to be culpable at all it must be culpable in four dimensions. Just as there are no physical objects with only one dimension or two, so an act with only one, two, or three dimensions of culpability is not a culpable act at all. Culpable acts of less than four dimensions are like tables with length alone, or with length and width, but no height. If what is dangerous is done unintentionally; or if there is no harm in the offing when something is done; or if what is done does not really threaten harm; or if on balance what was done was legitimate; then in any of these cases, or in any combination of them, the act is not culpable. It seems clear enough that we cannot blame anyone at all when the questionable parts of what he did turn out not to have been anything he at all meant to do; or when it turns out that what was threatened (so to speak) was actually quite harmless; or when there was not enough done to threaten harm, really; or when, all things considered, it was right to do what at first seemed questionable.

Though describing culpability in terms of dimensions seems a useful device, it is well to confess a certain awkwardness in conceiving the matter this way. The first dimension and the fourth are complex in a way in which the second and the third are not. The first makes use of the third and in that way becomes itself susceptible of measurement in degrees. It is only because dangerousness admits of degrees that dangerous acts done intentionally admit of degrees; acts may be intentional or unintentional, but not more or less so. Similarly, the fourth dimension makes use of the second, and so likewise becomes susceptible of measurement by degrees. It is mainly because harms are greater or less that we can intelligibly regard some acts as more justifiable than others (though it is also because interests protected by the harmful acts are more or less important). But legitimacy does not admit of degrees, and a harmful act is simply legitimate or illegitimate.

Perhaps the chief virtue of recognizing dimensions of culpability is the comparison of two different acts that this permits. Just as the size of two physical objects may be compared by measuring them in each of their dimensions, so the culpability of two acts may be compared by seeing how extensive each act is in each dimension of its culpability. But comparisons of culpability among acts must remain a far cruder affair than comparisons of size among tables and oranges. We do not have common units of measure either for the four dimensions of culpability or for overall culpability, nor de we have ways of calculating overall culpability by computing culpability in each dimension. Nevertheless, we do make rough determinations as best we can, in order to assign a particular crime a place on the scale of punishments in the penal law, and in deciding how to sentence particular offenders under it. The question of whether taking life recklessly is more culpable than destroying property purposely may seem unmanageably abstract, and we may feel in need of more detailed information before we can answer it, but we are not in the dark about what sort of things will matter in arriving at an answer.

CULPABILITY IN THE FIRST DIMENSION

Much that goes on in the world is harmful or dangerous, and much of what is harmful or dangerous takes place without there being an act or an actor. The world often goes on about its business in ways and by means that do not involve humans, and, even though the events of the nonhuman world may profoundly affect human life, they take place heedless of our interests. Oceans, earthquakes, and wild animals pose dangers and do harm to us, but they are not capable of conduct, and only madness or superstition will lead us to blame them for what they do. Though the sea may turn dangerous and cause ships to sink, it cannot do so either intentionally or unintentionally. This suggests that among the first three dimensions of culpability distinguished here, the dimension of intentionality enjoys a special importance because it is associated exclusively with conduct, while harm and dangerousness serve to characterize the events that issue from nonhuman agencies as well.

This special importance of intentionality is reflected in criminal law theory, where, under the mysterious rubric of *mens rea,* questions of culpability are sometimes treated as though they were questions only of intentionality. Although the other facets of culpability all have a full complement of difficulties, none are so vexing as those of intentionality, and in the remainder of this section as well as in that to follow we shall examine and try to unravel the many tangles that present themselves. It is a job that requires patience as well as forbearance until the end is reached.

The principle of culpability in its first dimension has two parts. An act posing a threat of harm must be done intentionally if it is to be judged a culpable act; and the extent of culpability (in this dimension) depends upon the magnitude of the threat of harm that exists because of what was done intentionally. To test this suggestion we can consult a set of conventional terms that mark degrees of culpability. The Model Penal Code, among the most sophisticated and influential works of modern penal legislation, provides us with a fully equipped testing ground. Throughout, the Code makes use of four terms only—*purposely, knowing, recklessly,* and *negligently.* We shall not attempt to paraphrase here the definitions appearing in the Model Penal Code, for in some respects these definitions seem misleading. What is wanted is an explication that will facilitate the use intended for the terms in the Code while avoiding the misleading features.

Suppose that a sailor dies when his ship is fumigated while he is asleep in the hold. The medical examiner's report establishes that asphyxiation resulting from the fumes was the cause of death. We are interested now in determining whether those responsible for the fumigation are criminally liable for the sailor's death, and if so, to what extent. Under the law, that will depend upon the degree of their culpability in causing his death. If our investigation leads us to conclude that the fumigation activities were directed to bringing about his death, we say that it was caused *purposely,* and so on its face it is a case of murder.

The important features for judging the culpability of the activity can be described as follows. Those engaged in it will have exercised control over the things that can be expected to bring about the harm so that it will occur. More particularly, alternative courses of action that are thought to leave the outcome more to chance or make the harm less likely will not have been adopted. One way of describing such conduct is to say that it consisted of a *harmful* act engaged in *intentionally* (though we should keep in mind that the notion of a harmful act has its own complications, the examination of which we postpone for the final chapter). The point to be emphasized here is that this conduct is of the most dangerous sort.

Though not as dangerous as could be, the activity causing the sailor's death might still have been exceedingly dangerous. A routine fumigation might have been carried on for the purpose of ridding the ship of rats, with knowledge that a sailor was sleeping below, or at least with good reason to believe that he was. Death, we would then say, is caused *knowingly*, though not purposely. What the fumigators did *intentionally* was to fumigate the ship knowing or having good reason to believe that a sailor was below, and this conduct was *imminently dangerous;* for though the fumigators were not in hot pursuit of harm, what they did was notoriously likely to bring it about. Causing the sailor's death *knowingly* differs from causing it *purposely* only because in the case of *knowingly* the act is indifferent to the possibility of an escape from the harm, while in the case of *purposely* that is not so; the act is less dangerous because of that, and hence less culpable.

Since in both the first and the second case death has occurred, it may seem odd to describe the conduct as *harmful* in the first case, but in the second case as only *imminently dangerous.* Pacifying linguistic intuition on this point need not be postponed, though its full satisfaction requires the extended discussion presented in later chapters. In the sense of "harmful" relevant here, the term refers only to acts that leave nothing of the harmful outcome to chance. Whether harm occurs or not, if a course of activity consists of all that might reasonably be done to ensure that the harm will occur, the conduct is harmful. But if as in the second case there is indifference toward the harmful outcome that—theoretically at least—leaves some opportunity for harm to be avoided, the conduct is not harmful in the relevant sense of that term, even if the harm occurs.

The fumigation might have been performed in a manner indifferent to the extremely hazardous character of such an activity—and this presents a third case when the sailor is killed as a result of the fumigation. Suppose most of the crew were on shore leave and the ship appeared generally deserted, but no precautions were taken and no check was made to find out whether anyone was below. The fumigation would then be a very dangerous activity, though not so dangerous as in the second case. In that case there was a risk of death represented by the presence, or likely presence, of a sailor in the hold. In this third case the risk of death is represented by the chance of a sailor's presence in the hold—which is a lesser risk of death. *Recklessly* causing death is the way we would describe this act (though, speaking in a less elliptical way, we should say that the recklessly performed fumigation caused the death). Once again, the fumigation was performed intentionally, and that intentional act once again presented a very real danger to anyone who might be below. But the fumigation this time did not make death itself imminent, as in the first case. Nor did it make *the danger* of death imminent, as in the second case. In this third case the fumigation is conducted with indifference to the danger of death but not with indifference to the occurrence of death, and for that reason it is less dangerous than in the second case.

Many activities we engage in have dangers inherent in them. Indeed, little of importance that we do is altogether without risk, and as a step in most activities we take measures of precaution, or at least do things in a suitably circumspect and attentive way so as to avoid the risks. Failing that and ignoring the dangers in what we do, we are doing those things in a dangerous way when we could and should do them safely. Certainly a ship's fumigation has dangers inherent in it, and even though it is carried on with circumspection and a certain precaution, there still may be a deficiency of precaution when not enough is done to ensure that harm does not occur.

Suppose the sailor is lying in his bunk, sleeping off his night on shore, and is not roused by several loudspeaker warnings of the impending fumigation, with orders to anyone below to come up on deck immediately. If such announcements were the only precaution against someone's remaining below, we might well decide that the fumigation was carried out *negligently,* and (again speaking elliptically) that the sailor's death caused by the fumigation was caused *negligently.* The fumigation is again performed intentionally, and it is still a dangerous act, but less dangerous than in the previous case. In the case of reckless conduct, there is indifference to the dangers inherent in the fumigation of a ship. In the case of negligent conduct, those performing the fumigation do not do so in a manner indifferent to its inherent dangers, but only fail to take adequate precautions directed to those dangers so that it will be a dangerous activity safely performed.

Four different measures of culpability of conduct have been distinguished according to the difference in degree of danger posed by what is done intentionally. Together, these different degrees comprehend the full range of culpability in its first dimension. In order of decreasing culpability, the conduct in question may be described as intentionally doing what is harmful in that it is aimed at not allowing an escape from the harm; intentionally doing what creates imminent danger of harm; intentionally doing what creates a serious risk of the harm, though not imminent danger of it; and doing intentionally what bears a significant risk of the harm in the absence of adequate care and precaution. All terms of culpability in this area of the criminal law serve either to paraphrase the four adopted in the Model Penal Code, or else to mark some intermediate measure of culpability between the four major terminals; as when we speak, for example, of conduct that is *wantonly reckless,* or *grossly negligent,* or (with even more precision) conduct performed *under circumstances manifesting extreme indifference to the value of human life.*

Questions of terminology lead swiftly and almost imperceptibly to questions of substance, and the most important of them is why degrees of culpability are scaled as they are. Why, after all, should what is done *purposely* be more blameworthy than what is only done *knowingly?* The answer is that as the scale is ascended, conduct of each degree leaves succeedingly less room for chance to determine the occurrence of harm. Because of that the harm (whether actual or in prospect) is attributable to the actor more and more as the scale is ascended. It is then more within or under his control, and it is fair as well as reasonable to blame the actor more when the harm is more subject to his control and less a matter merely of chance. How dangerous his act was and the fact that it was done intentionally both play a part in this.

II. SOME CLARIFICATIONS
REGARDING INTENTION

WHAT IT MEANS TO ACT INTENTIONALLY

The analysis of culpability in its first dimension has placed stress on what is done intentionally, and that notion is itself in urgent need of clarification.

Acting, like much else in the world, has its standard and its substandard forms. When it is said *simpliciter* that a person has performed a particular act, it is implied that the act is standard. When the act is nonstandard we make use of an abnormality-designating term to note this. *Unintentionally* is such a term, and control of the actor is the respect in which an act qualified by this term is abnormal. When we say that an act is done *intentionally,* we simply make a countermove against that imputation of abnormality, which itself may be expressed or only implied, and which may have actually been made already or may only be in prospect.

Criticism of conduct by this imputation of abnormality is the warrant for the countering claim that it is *intentional,* and while critical controversies take place most often when blame is to be assigned, there are other reasons for critical appraisal of conduct. We may wish, for example, to give credit for what was done ("He intentionally avoided upsetting the sick old lady"). Or, quite apart from matters of condemnation or commendation, we may wish to assess skill ("He shot the six-ball into the side pocket intentionally"). Whatever the critical purpose, the actor's control in the events comprising what was done and what happened is the issue signaled by *intentionally* and *unintentionally*.

Control (and its failure or absence) is sometimes a mental matter, sometimes a physical matter, and sometimes a matter belonging to neither category. A letter one wishes to keep may be destroyed unintentionally when one takes it to be a different letter and because of that mistake destroys it; or it may be destroyed unintentionally when because of a palsied hand one spills acid on it; or it may be destroyed unintentionally when one places it on a stone that turns out, when the wind comes up, to be—alas—too close to the fire. A government may unintentionally cause interest rates to rise, and indeed may engage in numberless other acts that are *in a perfectly literal sense* unintentional or intentional, though the relevant control or lack of it is not in any of those acts either a mental or a physical matter.

Since what matters is the agent's control over the events in which he is implicated as agent, we should expect a dispute about whether or not something was done intentionally to be settled by evidence either that there was or was not control. In fact that is exactly what is deemed relevant, and the evidence is publicly available just as is the conduct itself. Our opponent makes an extraordinary shot and we think it luck. He claims it was done intentionally. To settle the matter, we consult others who have seen him play before, and we watch for a repetition. A person pays with counterfeit money and is accused of having passed it intentionally. He claims he had no idea the money was counterfeit and is a victim of circumstances. What we want to know then is where he got the money, how he acted when paying with it, whether there are things in his history that make it likely that he did what he is accused of. Someone speeds down a hill, and mishap results. Did he intentionally speed? or did his brakes not operate properly, as he claims? We consider how he was driving before, whether he was in a hurry, what evidence there is of mechanical defect, how he behaved after the accident.

These are the kinds of facts that in all cases are the grounds of inference to conclusions about what was intentional and what was not. The general rules that warrant inferences from the facts are presumptions that are part of our store of social intelligence—presumptions about how people normally act and what normally happens in given circumstances. The inference may be rebutted by further hard facts that under the same presumptions support a different conclusion; or by introduction of different presumptions, called for when the circumstances are shown to be different than originally supposed. The inference may also be undermined by arguing that general experience in fact leads to a different conclusion than what is now being offered as a presumptive truth, and that our presumption ought therefore to be amended.

CRITICISM OF THE ORTHODOX VIEW

According to the official view, *intentionally* and *unintentionally* do not speak to the relation of an actor to what happened, but rather to a relation within an actor between his mind and his body. It is not a matter of the extent to which he was in charge in acting, but rather the extent to which his mind was in charge of his body when it acted. An act done *intentionally* is done by the actor's body in accordance with the designs, instigations, and directions of the actor's mind, and a claim that an act is unintentional then becomes an assertion that the mind did not give the order or grant permission for it. To refute a claim that conduct was intentional, the appropriate procedure is thought to be an argument denying that what was done was ordered by the mind, or at least denying that the mind gave its consent.

A distinction is sometimes drawn between theories of intention said to be "subjective" and those said to be "objective," but in fact advocates of both theories adhere to this intrapersonal model. Those whose criteria are generally taken to be "objective" endorse the model and differ from those in the "subjective" camp only in insisting that nothing more than inferences from what is publicly available can furnish knowledge of the actor's mental state. On either the "subjective" or "objective" view, intention is the private inner workings that give significance to the physical activity on public display. When that public activity is criminal and lawyers are talking about it, it is called *actus reus,* and the private mental state is called *mens rea.* Both are required for the crime because a crime is held to consist of something done and something intended, with what is done made blameworthy by the fact that it is intended.

Assorted points compel the rejection of the mentalist view. We need first to remind ourselves only briefly that, since acts are not bodily movements, intentional (or unintentional) acts cannot be bodily movements made under (or not made under) certain related mental conditions. Quite apart from the question of what an act is, other points make it clear that whether an act is intentional is not determined by resort to the facts of the actor's mental life at the time.

When there is controversy about whether conduct was intentional, no attempt is made to determine what the actor's mental state was. Whether bills were known to be counterfeit counts in deciding whether they were intentionally passed as counterfeit. But the question of what was known cannot be answered by what the psychologist's probings may disclose or by the actor's introspective recollections. Evidence of thoughts, wishes, feelings, perceptions, moods, fantasies, and urges at the time is not what is sought, and any offer of such evidence would only be treated as evidence that the one offering it did not understand the meaning of the words "in-

tentional" and "unintentional." It is not that evidence of
mental states is deemed unobtainable or unreliable. When
the issue in controversy is one of responsibility—whether an
abnormal mental condition at the time made it difficult or
impossible for the actor to help doing what he did—precisely
such evidence is sought and eagerly received as part of expert
testimony on the question of abnormality. But it is deemed
irrelevant in deciding questions of culpability that turn on
whether a particular act was intentional.

There are other reasons for rejecting the mentalist view of
intentional acts. We might imagine a counterfeiter who takes
the law very seriously. In order to provide himself with a defense if he is caught, he consults some leading works on the
principles of the criminal law in the hope of finding one or
two items of criminal jurisprudence that might be useful.
Taking quite literally what he reads, he concludes that he will
have an alibi of sorts if his mind is occupied elsewhere at the
time he passes the money, for according to these authorities his
act will not be intentional unless an intention to do it accompanies the act and can be connected to the act as the mental design of which the act is an execution. Accordingly, he trains
himself either to be completely preoccupied or to imagine
himself engaged in a perfectly lawful transaction. He learns to
distract or to delude himself so thoroughly that his mental state
is exactly the same as that of a perfectly innocent passer of
counterfeit money at all times when his state of mind might be
thought relevant as accompaniment of criminal activity. After
passing the money and being caught he will of course be sadly
disappointed by the reception his mental alibi of unintentional conduct gets, even though he is entirely successful in
convincing everyone that not for a moment was he thinking
that the money was counterfeit.

Mentalist theory might first attempt to explain liability in
this case by pointing to the fact that the accused deliberately
deluded himself to make what he was doing appear innocent

to himself, and that because the appearance depended upon deliberate self-deception it was not an authentically innocent state of mind. But what reason can there be for requiring for innocence an authentically innocent state of mind not contrived for the occasion, when for guilt there is no requirement of an authentically guilty mind? If only by deliberate self-deception did he come to believe that he was committing a crime, that fact would afford him no defense if he was actually committing a crime after all. It does not matter in either case that his belief was not an honest one.

Another mentalist argument that might be advanced to explain liability is more formidable. Its line is that a state of mind earlier than the act is its causal accompaniment, so to speak, and because at an earlier time the accused intended to pass counterfeit bills and later fulfilled that intention, the act fulfilling it was done intentionally. This argument is unsatisfactory because having an intention fulfilled by an act is neither a necessary nor a sufficient condition for the act's being intentional. A person may at no time have had an intention to pass counterfeit bills but may still pass them intentionally if he knows what he is doing when he acts on the spur of the moment to gratify some wanton impulse—perhaps because as he stood at the cashier's window reaching into his wallet it suddenly seemed to be worth the risk. And when an intention to do something is fulfilled by the act, the act may nevertheless be unintentional—as when I have the intention of running you down the next chance I get, and by chance later that very day you dart out unexpectedly from between two parked cars just as I am driving by, and although I slam on my brakes I can't stop in time. Since having an intention fulfilled by an act is neither a necessary nor a sufficient condition for the act to be intentional, the previous intention of the deluded actor cannot be the key to his liability.

Two further points may be made against a mentalist account of intentional acts. On the mentalist view, the actor alone is in a position to know with certainty what he did intentionally because only he has direct access to the relevant states of mind. Others are remitted to mere probable inference from what is in the public domain, including what the actor says—if he chooses to say anything. In fact, however, the actor is often in a position no better than anyone else to know whether or not he has acted intentionally. He may indeed claim with perfect sincerity that his act was intentional. But after consideration of what he is normally capable of doing, exactly how he did what he did, the circumstances affecting what he could do, and what people normally do, we may come to a different conclusion than he does, even though we accept everything he tells us about his mental states.

The actor may know something about himself not known to anyone else. It may be relevant because it is about what he did or what he could do, or because it is something about what he was thinking or what he believed. This private information is no more important than what another person may independently know about him, or what he might in fact not know about himself. True, when one's acting intentionally depends only upon whether in acting one is fulfilling an intention, then the actor is in a position of special privilege in deciding the question, for he has a special knowledge of his intentions which we do not have. But as we saw already (and shall see again) acting intentionally is often not a matter of fulfilling an intention.

The other point is that certain acts are never (or hardly ever) said to be either intentional or unintentional, and yet actors performing these acts have mental states that are indistinguishable from persons performing acts that are commonly said to be intentional or unintentional. Only under the most unusual circumstances are such acts as singing, smoking, speaking, doubting, criticizing, arguing, praising, or blaming said to be done either intentionally or unintentionally; and under no circumstances are such acts as castleing and inferring spoken of in this way. This is because rarely if ever is there doubt about the actor's control over the immediate outcome of his effort when these acts take place, and so there is no question of whether the act was under or within the actor's control—a question to be cleared up by designating the act as intentional or unintentional. Still, in doing any of these things the actor may have his mind wholly occupied with them, or on the other hand he may be thoroughly preoccupied or deluded and be unaware of what he is doing.

In view of the objections to be made against it, one can hardly remain unimpressed by the vitality and long life of mentalist theory. Three reasons for this vigor can be found in the shadows of language. The first is a grammatical illusion. "He did it intentionally" looks to be of much the same form as "He did it delicately." It is assumed that the adverb in both sentences is meant to tell something about the performance—in one case something about an outer aspect and, in the other, something about an inner aspect. If doing it delicately can be explained in terms of characteristic physical activity, then doing it intentionally must be explained by what characteristically goes on in the mind, for even the closest scrutiny of physical activity never uncovers unambiguous marks of intentionality.

Statements about what the actor thought or knew or believed are a second source of misconception. If it is said by his accuser that the accused *knew* that the bills he was passing were counterfeit, it would be appropriate to claim in his behalf that he *thought* or *believed* them to be genuine. The issue is an important one, for a person cannot intentionally engage in the passing of counterfeit bills if he thinks that they are genuine, and intentionally engaging in the passing of counterfeit bills is required for liability. The mentalist assumes that the issue is one concerning goings-on in the mind of the actor, and particularly goings-on that account for the conduct in question.

But the statement "I knew the money was not genuine" does not even purport to give a report of what was going on in the mind of the speaker. As we already know, a person may at any relevant time be thinking that the money is genuine, and yet at the same time know that it is not. He will then say, "I knew the money was not genuine, though I was thinking it was." He will thereby confess having had an ability to judge, to choose, and to decide—an ability not possessed by others who do not know. He will also report as going on in his mind at the time something that would not normally take place if he were making use of that ability. The ability, and not the mental promptings of conduct, is what concerns the law. Those who do not know—who think (*not* who are thinking) otherwise, or who believe otherwise—lack an ability to choose to do otherwise, while those who do know have the ability. This defense of inability is not available if the accused knew; and commonly the law asserts this by requiring for liability what in criminal law theory is called "knowledge" or *scienter*. In the prescriptive contexts of legislation this requirement is commonly expressed by such phrases as "with knowledge that . . ." and "knowing it to be . . ." (which is not to be confused with the "knowingly" that measures culpability).

The point about knowing may be put briefly in this way. When it matters that one knows something, it matters only because not knowing it would matter. And what one does not know matters—when it does—because one then does not have the ability to choose (in order to obey the law) not to do what the law prohibits. Under such circumstances, according to well-established notions of responsibility one is not responsible for what one does.

Finally, the mentalist version of intentional acts is encouraged by confusion regarding intention as it appears in *having an intention* and in *acting intentionally*. Certainly we have intentions, and though having an intention is not so simple as having a toothache or even as having a wish, mental states are clearly what matter when one has an intention. One may say, "I intend to go tomorrow." This might at first seem to be a special kind of statement predicting what the actor will do, a statement that bears the special authority belonging to statements uttered by those who alone know what is going on in the mysterious region where acts originate. But the statement is not a prediction at all. One might without any strain in logic add to "I intend to go tomorrow" the further statement, "but I must admit it is unlikely that I will." This simply would not do as a prediction, as one can easily see by imagining that statement offered by the actor as a prediction of what he will do: "I will go tomorrow, though I must admit it is unlikely that I will." Nor is a statement of intention simply a report of one's mental state, for one cannot properly say, "I intend to go tomorrow, though of course going is impossible"; although one could say, for example, "I imagine myself going tomorrow, though of course going is impossible."

Something of anticipation and something of commitment are always elements of an assertion of having an intention. In fact such an assertion might be described as an avowal by a person of his own anticipation of what he will do. He commits himself thereby, at the very least, to being in a certain frame of mind. That we should have intentions and that they should be made known to others is very important for each of us individually as well as for our life together as social beings. If we had no intentions we should act only spontaneously, without plan, on impulse. And if our intentions were not known by others, advance accommodation and planned response to our acts, as well as reliance on them by others, would be impossible. Since response, accommodation, and reliance depend upon knowing another person's intentions, we naturally are very much interested in finding out what in fact another person's prevailing state of mind is, and even in holding him accountable for his stated intentions.

The mentalist, then, is not wrong in thinking that having an intention is largely a matter of mental state. His mistake lies in thinking that *acting intentionally* is the acting in fulfillment of his intentions by an actor. We have seen already that this is not the case, for many acts done intentionally are not in fulfillment of any intention, and many intentional acts are not even preceded by any intention to do them.

Some may complain that not enough attention has been given to the role of the mind in this account of intentional conduct. Surely, they will say, the states and processes of the actor's mind are different when his conduct is intentional rather than unintentional. Indeed, the presence or absence of control—which on our analysis is the crucial matter—may be shown to depend in no small measure upon matters of mind. The complaint is misconceived, nevertheless. Culpability in its first dimension is a matter of *control* by the actor. And how matters of control are in turn to be explained—by the mental or the physical condition of the actor, or by other conditions in the world—has no bearing on culpability. Mentalism is objectionable because it purports to give an account of intentional and unintentional acts—and thus of culpability—in terms of the mental affairs of the actor. The mentalist account is not always objectionable as a false account, but only as an irrelevant account. It may often be the case that a person's doing something unintentionally is best explained by his state of mind; but even then it is not because of his state of mind that his act is to be regarded as unintentional. And even though no doubt in a large proportion of cases of unintentional acts it is the actor's state of mind that explains what was wrong, it is certainly not always the case that when something is done unintentionally it is because there was some mental failing on the part of the actor.

In the previous section we saw that in assessing blame the most important questions concern the degree of dangerousness of what was done intentionally. But intention appears in yet another form to plague the theorist when it relates to the second, or harm, dimension of culpability. *Intention in doing something* is often a matter of importance in the criminal law. Provisions of the criminal law sometimes speak of doing something "with intent to . . ." (or some paraphrase of that expression). Lawyers refer to this as *specific intent,* and once again it is generally assumed that reference is being made to what is in the actor's mind. Informed and even thoughtful laymen no less than legal theorists are sometimes victims of this misconception. A notable illustration was produced by the *New York Times* columnist Tom Wicker when writing about the Chicago trial of those charged in connection with public disturbances at the time of the 1968 Democratic convention. One provision of law under which an indictment was obtained made it a crime to cross a state line *with intent to cause acts of violence,* and Wicker commented:

> The defendants here are the first to be tried under a provision of the 1968 Civil Rights Act that made it a Federal crime to cross a state line with the intent to cause a riot or a disturbance. The constitutionality of this statute has yet to be determined, but the Chicago trial clearly suggests—as, indeed, does the language of the act —that what it seeks to prohibit or penalize is a state of mind, not an overt act.
>
> Ironically, it is also pretty clear from this proceeding how difficult it is to prove a state of mind, long afterwards. It is probably more difficult for the prosecution, on whom rests the burden of proof, than for the defendants, which is why Mr. Schulz sounded so preposterous in

his efforts to show that Rennie Davies was saying one
thing to Roger Wilkins while "thinking other thoughts."

Nevertheless, if the issue of a trial actually comes down
to "other thoughts," rather than to actual words and
deeds, the deeper question may be whether even "the
burden of proof" any longer means anything.

It was of course not the object of the law to find what was
in the accused's mind at the time he crossed a state line, much
less to make him liable in some measure for it. Specific intent
is simply part of the description of the act required for the
offense to be committed. In doing what he does, the actor has
a purpose that makes the act an act of that kind rather than
of another kind—crossing a state line to incite a riot rather
than to sell ice cream. That purpose is the specific intent of
the act. But having a purpose as one acts does not mean that
one then has a purpose in mind. One *may* have a purpose in
mind, but that is a rather unusual case. It is normal to have a
purpose in mind when, as one acts, one must give attention
to what one is doing or to how one is doing it in order not to
have things go awry. If one travels unfamiliar roads, and
crossing the state line at one point rather than another will
affect one's ability to cause a riot as planned, then, naturally
enough, one has one's purpose in mind as one seeks out the
right crossing point and then crosses.

Even more extraordinary than having one's purpose in
mind is a case in which one is thinking about one's purposes
as one acts. This is normal when for some reason one's purpose is not entirely settled, as, for example, if one were still
undecided about whether to run the risk of causing a dis-
turbance in Chicago or whether simply to settle for a visit to
one's mother in the suburbs. But neither having the purpose
in mind nor thinking about it is necessary for the purpose to
be the specific intent of the act. Having boarded a bus in New
York, one may promptly fall into a deep and dreamless
slumber which lasts all the way to Chicago, and one may

still have crossed state lines with intent to cause acts of violence.

Evidence one way or another for the existence of a particular specific intent is publicly available, just as is evidence of any other feature of the act. Why one traveled to Chicago may call for inference and surmise from things said and done as well as from circumstances that would normally prompt a trip of one sort or another. The evidence is no different than that available to determine the purpose being pursued in any other act; and certainly determinations of purpose are commonly and confidently made when necessary in many kinds of legal proceedings, as well as everywhere else in life. States of mind, which admittedly are private, largely inaccessible, and a subject only of speculation much of the time, are not what we must know about to know about specific intent. Far from creating opportunities for abuse of prosecutorial power through intrusion and speculation, the requirement of specific intent provides protection against wrongful prosecution by describing in greater detail the act for which there is said to be liability so that it cannot be confounded with some other act which in other ways it resembles, though not in purpose.

Specific intent relates to the second dimension of culpability since it bears on the question of how serious is the harm threatened by the act. Assault with intent to kill, for example, threatens more serious harm than simple assault. Crossing a state line in itself threatens no harm, but when it is done with intent to incite a riot there is a prospect of harm in the act. Not always is specific intent expressed in the legal prescriptions appearing on the statute books, and, in assessing culpability in the second dimension, one must sometimes pay attention to what is only implicit until it is expressed through judicial interpretation. Larceny, for example, requires an intent to appropriate what is taken. If the accused meant only to examine and return what he took, his intent in taking it was not to appropriate it and he has not committed a larceny. Specific intent is most important for appreciating the precise harm that is being dealt with by the law, and even if unmentioned in the code provision that defines the crime, it is important whenever the relative culpability of the act is a matter of concern.

This conception of specific intent helps make sense of what is known in criminal law theory as "the doctrine of transferred intent." That doctrine supports liability in a case where, for example, the accused, intending to kill a certain person, shoots at him and, because of poor aim, causes instead the death of another person whom he had no intention of killing. In its most appealing version, conventional theory holds that there is liability for murder, since both the state of mind and the act of the accused satisfy the requirements for murder; and because, in addition, the act of the accused was the cause of the death. To those who object that his state of mind was not the required one, since a different victim was intended, conventional theory replies that the difference is immaterial, since what is required for the offense is simply an intention to kill some person.

The trouble with this is that in the case at hand the accused did not intend simply to kill someone—anyone at all. If he had, there would be no difficulty in holding him liable, since the law does not require that a particular person be intended as a victim. Wanton, indiscriminate killing that is indifferent to who the victims may be is readily accepted as full-fledged murder. In the case of the unintended victim, however, the accused did not intend to kill the person he did kill, nor did he intend to kill just anyone (which would include the victim), and so he did not have a "state of mind" that in relevant respects is the same as the one he would have if the victim were intended.

The difficulty here stems from the mentalist account of transferred intent upon which the analysis relies, and is remedied by a recasting that makes use of specific intent as we now understand it. The act of the accused in this case can be correctly described as shooting with intent to cause death, and that act satisfies the act requirement for murder. The offense of homicide (and not merely attempted homicide) requires further that the act cause the death, and this requirement is also satisfied in this case. Thus, the difficulty to be found in conventional theory vanishes once the accused is seen to be acting with an intent to kill; and once it is understood that the intent is part of the act and not some state of mind that may have accompanied it.

III. MOTIVES

HOW MOTIVES MATTER

When a crime is committed and the perpetrator is unknown, motive is often an important consideration. The police may first try to find out why the crime was committed in order to decide who is likely to have committed it. One sort of answer to this question offers a motive, and so persons who had a motive often become suspects. If they are charged, their motives are then presented as part of the prosecutor's case in seeking indictment or conviction. It is, however, hardly ever a requirement for criminal liability that the accused should have done what the law prohibits with a specified motive (or with any motive at all), nor hardly ever is it grounds for acquittal that the accused had a particular motive (or no motive at all) in doing what was prohibited. Hence it may be said that, in general, motives may play a role in deciding whether a particular person committed a crime but not in deciding whether a particular crime was committed.

It would be a mistake, however, to overlook the importance of motives in determining issues incidental to liability. Whether prosecution of someone believed guilty should be undertaken, what the particular offense to be prosecuted ought to be, and what penal consequences ought to follow upon conviction, are all discretionary matters that may with propriety be heavily influenced by considerations of motive. Indeed, criminal justice is seriously impoverished if motives are disregarded as mitigating and as aggravating factors. The point is well illustrated through a statement of the Vice-President of the United States in the closing days of the 1972 election campaign. Mr. Agnew (though mistaken at several points about the facts) compared the illicit and fateful quest for confidential information at the Watergate headquarters of the Democratic Party to illicit taking of secret papers from the Pentagon, which resulted in the celebrated Ellsberg affair. In the first case the purpose was apparently to gain underhanded political advantage in an election; in the second, the no less apparent purpose was to make public an illuminating study of the nation's Vietnam policy.

> What disturbs me greatly [Mr. Agnew observed] is the moral outrage of the same people who have in the past condoned this kind of conduct. . . . I also feel that whether a person steals Larry O'Brien's secret papers or steals the Pentagon papers he should be punished. I didn't see any of these cries of moral indignation against the person accused of stealing the Pentagon papers.

In order to give effect in the criminal process to justifiable moral indignation or to its exculpatory counterparts, it is sometimes necessary above all else to pay attention to motives—which is precisely what Mr. Agnew failed to do.

Motives are important for discretionary decisions about prosecution and punishment for the reason that motives may affect culpability. There are two ways in which this may happen. For one thing, the likelihood of harm may be affected by the actor's motive, and the same act done with one motive may be less dangerous than if done with another. This is an important consideration when criminal activity is still in its early stages and its dangers not yet apparent on its face. Two different people are apprehended with bombs that they intend to plant in a government building. One person wants to call attention to the immorality he sees in his country's foreign policy; the other wants to take revenge against a government that he thinks has denied him certain benefits to which he is entitled. The first man regrets what he is about to do and views it as a necessary evil; the second relishes the prospect of finally being able to show the world that it can't push him around. In important details—the place, the time, the concern for consequences—the two criminal acts may reasonably be assumed to present quite different dangers and therefore to be not equally blameworthy.

In this way motives have a bearing on culpability in its third dimension. But in another way motives may affect culpability in its fourth dimension as well. A legitimate interest may be pursued in an untoward way, and the reason for doing the apparently unlawful act then tends to justify it—entirely in the case of justifiable homicide and a few other exceptional situations, but more often only partly so as to moderate but not to exempt from blame. The converse is important as well, for the fact that the apparently unlawful acts are in pursuit of distinctly illegitimate interests tends to aggravate the offense. Fine examples of mitigating and aggravating motives of this kind are in the two cases referred to by Mr. Agnew, and one can ask for no better illustration of the unfortunate conclusions to be expected when motives are neglected.

MOTIVES REQUIRED EXPRESSLY FOR LIABILITY

Although for almost all crimes motive is irrelevant in determining liability, there are a few for which this is not the case.

In all these crimes there is either the absence of a legitimating interest in the face of something *prima facie* illegitimate, or the presence of an interest that renders illegitimate what otherwise would be legitimate conduct. Publication of material having a prurient appeal may be considered publication of obscenity and may give rise to criminal liability unless publication is for the sake of education, art, or some other legitimate social interest. When a public official engages for advancement of his personal interests in a transaction that otherwise is a proper function of his office, the improper motive may make the act an item of criminal misconduct. Similarly, an improper motive may make a criminal libel out of an otherwise noncriminal injury to reputation—for example, when the injurious statement is made for the very purpose of doing damage to the victim's reputation. There is, further, a general class of motive-regarding crimes that are marked by the term *malicious* when that term is used in a motive-regarding way. *Malicious destruction of property,* for example, may refer to conduct engaged in for the sake of destroying property, in which case the requirement of maliciousness is a requirement of motive. (Maliciousness is not a motive requirement, however, when it signifies only a purpose to harm but not necessarily for the sake of harming. Acts of civilized warfare, for example, consist of destroying *purposely,* but only for the sake of gaining a military objective.)

Motives, then, are very much a matter of interests, and this is quite clear in these exceptional offenses that require a motive for liability. What makes these offenses exceptional, however, is not the concern about interests that they prompt, for as we shall see, there are numbers of other offenses that prompt that concern. It is the fact that the interest being pursued is *explicitly* made a liability determining consideration in the legislative prescription of the offense.

CRITICISM OF THE ORTHODOX CONCEPTION

To appreciate why motives are normally excluded in determinations of liability, it is necessary to understand what motives are. Once again, accepted learning tends to mislead us by resorting to mysterious mental processes. Motives, like intentions, are taken to be mental states, or sets of mental states. Motives are responsible for designing and executing an act, and consist of ideas and of feelings associated with the ideas, to provide a pushing or pulling force. An idea may be produced by recollection or by imagination, and to that there is added an affective element consisting of a desire for what has then been brought to mind. The naked mind's eye engaged in introspective observation can perceive a motive only faintly if at all; and, even when seen faintly, motives tend to vanish mysteriously whenever one attempts to fix one's gaze on them. Still, there is abiding faith that they are there to be perceived even if only partially and indirectly, through techniques in introspective psychology that are akin to astronomical observation.

Motives conceived in this way are of two types—the backward-looking and the forward-looking. Backward-looking motives make reference to what has already come to pass, and produce a kind of pushing power, as when one acts out of revenge, or pity, or indebtedness. Forward-looking motives make reference to what yet might be, and exert a pull, as when one is moved to do something for financial gain, or to hurt someone, or to gain one's freedom.

Motives differ from intentions with respect to both duration and function. Though some motives are more ulterior than others, any motive for doing something relates to the ulterior thing to be achieved or satisfied through that act. It is thus more abiding than an intention, whose life must end with the act that fulfills it. With respect to function, motives differ from intentions in that motives are the source of *power* for the act, while intentions supply the *direction*. "The intention is the aim of the act, of which the motive is the spring," in John Austin's words.

The mentalist account must, however, be rejected. Mental states are not in fact usually offered even as evidence of what the motive for an act is. More than that, accounts of motives are not accounts of mental occurrences or states at all, nor in fact are they accounts of any sort of personal occurrence or state. These points need some explanation.

Evidence of the actor's state of mind is not normally what is sought when the motive for his act is in dispute. This is clear if only we consider what we actually count as evidence when motives are in question. Suppose it is maintained on one side that Napoleon and Hitler had the same motives in invading Russia and, on the other, that they acted from quite different motives. After there has been sufficient specification of the supposed motives to insure a case of genuine disagreement, evidence is sought to back up each claim. But what sort of historical evidence is then relevant? Is it the letters, diaries, and reports of intimate conversations in which are revealed the personal fantasies and desires of each at the time? Or is it rather materials that disclose the personal, military, political, and ideological *interests* that each was pursuing at the time, and what the expected effect of the invasion would be in that regard?

Anyone posing the question why each invaded Russia (as a motive-seeking question) can read works of history to get the answer, in which case he will soon find that it is material of the second sort that historians look to. And while the abundance of historical evidence that is available to determine motives makes the procedure more visible (as well as more complex) when motives are sought in history, the procedure is no different when motives are sought on a smaller scale for everyday acts. Whatever the activity, when we seek motives we ask *for the sake of what* was the act done. Only occasionally would mental states be relevant in answering that question—for example, if the act were done solely to make oneself feel more at ease, or to produce some hallucinatory experience. In such cases the interest prompting the act is psychological; and hence mental states are relevant in the same way that political or military affairs would be relevant when the acts have political or military significance.

The other objection to mentalist theory stresses the fact that accounts of motives are not accounts of personal occurrences or states, mental or otherwise. Motives, we have said, designate those things for the sake of which the act is done. Hence it is perfectly coherent to suggest that two of Napoleon's motives in invading Russia were to test his army's capabilities in a hard winter campaign and to seduce a lady at the Russian Court. It is not coherent, however, to suggest that his motives included a powerful urge to fight in the snow and a keen erotic desire. Nothing else he experienced or had happen to him, nor anything else about him at the time, will serve any better as a motive. The reason is that an account of motives does not tell us what caused an act to be done, but tells us rather *in what cause* it was done. An account of the motives for an act is not an explanation telling why the act occurred, but rather an explanation of the role of the act in a larger story of the actor's pursuits. A point worth noting incidentally follows from this. Since the causes in which persons act are often not in the interest of the actor at all, but are rather in some other interest, acts often have motives that are not at all selfish.

WHAT A MOTIVE IS

Motives are reasons for conduct, but they are reasons of a specific sort. Four conditions must be satisfied if something is to qualify as a motive for a particular act, and whatever meets these four conditions qualifies.

In the first place an act must have the purported motive as its purpose. There are purposeless acts, and these can have no motive. When I stop to make a deposit at my bank I may absentmindedly leave behind the bomb I have been carrying, and it will then make no sense to seek a motive for my act of reckless endangerment.

But even if I have a purpose, my act will be motiveless if it is not what might be called "an interested act." If I leave the bomb just to blow up the bank, I have a purpose that will explain why I left the bomb, but unless there is more to the story the act is wanton and no motive exists to explain why I did it. In such cases of purposeful but motiveless activity the act was done "in order to . . ." but not "for the sake of. . . ."

Even when purposeful acts are done for the sake of something else, *the actor* may not be doing it for the sake of that thing. Thus, I may leave the bomb just to blow up the bank, although others who are terrorists with political motives and know the pleasure I get from blowing things up have provided me with the bomb. The act might then in some sense be said to be for the sake of the revolution, but still it is an act without a motive, since the reasons that might provide a motive for doing it are not my reasons for doing it.

Finally, acts that are perfectly straightforward, normal, and not the least bit fishy do not have motives. If I am apprehended and brought to justice, the question of my motive is certainly in order, for it is not usual for people to leave bombs in banks. But ordinarily it makes no sense to ask what my lawyer's motive is in defending me or what the judge's motive is in presiding over my trial. My lawyer may defend me for the sake of the fee he will get, and the judge may preside for the sake of seeing that justice is done; still, it would be odd to speak of either of them as having a motive. Motives attach only to conduct that is in some way a deviation and that *calls for* an explanation—most often in terms of some other pursuit of the actor that it is designed to serve.

A motive, then, is a reason for doing the kind of purposeful act that calls for an explanation and that is done by the actor for the sake of something else. Motives are reasons that explain such acts in terms of the things for whose sake the act is done. Motives should be distinguished from intentions in two ways. When "intention" refers to the complex anticipatory mental state that a person may have, a motive can be distinguished from an intention by the fact that the intention but not the motive has a beginning and an end, like all other mental states. When "intention" refers to the intention in acting that can be part of the description of an act—which the criminal law calls "specific intent," a motive can be distinguished from an intention as an explanation of an act and not a description of it.

One philosopher has pointed up the distinction between motive and intention in this way. If a rich man has an ugly daughter, he is concerned about her suitor's motives. But a poor man with a beautiful daughter is concerned about her suitor's intentions. Explanation of suspicious conduct is what is wanted in the first case. In the second, it is either a fuller (and, hopefully, reassuring) description of what is going on, or else a satisfactory report of what the young man has in mind in view of conduct that so far is all too plain.

IMPLICIT MOTIVE CONSIDERATIONS IN THE LAW

Turning again to the question of why motives are not usually included in the legislative definition of an offense, we see that the harm associated with particular conduct can normally be specified quite adequately without reference to any interests being pursued; and that for the grosser business of setting limits of liability, matters of the actor's control over the harm can be managed by reference to intention only. More often than is usually recognized, however, motive considerations are implicit in the definition of an offense, as well as in legislative provisions that furnish an affirmative defense by way of justification. Culpability of an act in its fourth dimension is affected by these considerations.

If a legislature wishes to treat in a special way acts done from a particular motive, it may incorporate the motive in the definition of the offense by a special use of the term *intent*. If murder for money or for vengeance is to be singled out, the proscribed act may be "causing the death of a person with intent to profit financially thereby" or "with intent to avenge the death of another." Here the phrase "with intent to" signals the pursuit of an interest as the purpose of the act. It designates a *motive* rather than a *harm* as a required element of the crime, and so the phrase is used in a different way than when specific intent is designated. The two different uses of *intent* both appear in, for example, the New York Penal Law definition of kidnapping in the first degree. That offense is constituted by abducting another person when (among other things) the abductor's intent is to compel payment of a ransom by a third person; or when the abductor's intent is to inflict physical injury on, or sexually abuse, the victim. It seems clear that the first of these alternative *intent* requirements is not a specification of harm but of motive. The illegitimacy of the interest pursued is what is stressed, not the seriousness of the harm, which would in fact be no less were ransom not the motive.

The second *intent* requirement, however, is the specification of a greater harm than is constituted simply by the abduction. This requirement might, by a strained reading, be taken to be a specification of motive, but that would be an odd reading indeed, since it would mean that the illegitimacy of the abductor's interest in injuring or abusing, rather than the greater harm he then threatens, is the aggravating element. It is not always easy to tell whether an "intent" requirement goes to motive or to harm, and indeed in some cases it goes to both. Yet a third provision of the same kidnapping law prescribes liability in the higher degree when the abduction is "with intent to accomplish or advance the commission of a felony." Is there higher liability because the harm is then greater, or is it because the purpose for which there has been an abduction is especially illegitimate, or is it because of both?

Matters of motive may also have an opposite thrust tending to exonerate from liability. Doing harm may be justifiable, and certain justifications of harmful conduct are valid ones simply because of the interest that was being pursued. This is so when one does harm for the sake of avoiding greater harm, or for the sake of protecting against harm wrongfully threatened by others; when a reasonable assertion of one's interests in response to provocation causes harm; or when the harm consists in an exercise of reasonable force that is justifiable because it is for a legitimate purpose in the discharge of one's duty. In all these cases the motive of the actor is crucial to his exoneration.

Besides general principles such as these there are many special affirmative defenses of justification that look to motive—as when, for example, in a prosecution for unlawful imprisonment in New York the defendant asserts that the person restrained was under sixteen, the defendant was a relative, and his sole purpose was to assume control of the child.

CHAPTER FOUR

Conceiving Criminal Conduct: Harm and Attempts

Crimes without harm or without conduct would hardly be recognizable to us. It is true that such crimes are not inconceivable. The state might punish persons simply for having green eyes, and then, without any insult to intelligence, we might speak of having green eyes as a crime. But more than a certain form of liability under the law is needed to make a duly enacted crime morally acceptable. Criminal liability without conduct and without some harm associated with it, at least in the offing, would be unjust. Without conduct, liability would be for what a person could not help; and without harm or the threat of it there would be liability for no good reason. Because of this, some harm and some act is required of any crime validly on the books in our legal system.

In this chapter we investigate the concept of criminal harm and the concept of a criminal attempt. Harms are as fundamental to crime as conduct itself, and in fact impart to conduct its criminal character. In general, it is harms that make conduct criminal, because the conduct produces or threatens the harm, or even in some cases constitutes the harm. Moreover, a particular criminal act is the kind of criminal act it is because of the kind of harm associated with it. An understanding of criminal harm is therefore essential to an understanding of criminal conduct.

In another perspective, the conceptual questions dealt with here appear only as a preface to normative questions. But such questions fall outside the bounds of this book and call for other work of equal scope combining legal, political, and moral philosophy with prudential discussions of public policy. They are the questions of which activities the criminal law ought to make its business, and which it ought to regard as none of its business. The questions pursued here do not depend upon the answers to those further questions, though what we shall discuss here does help to clarify certain ideas that play an important part in answering those other questions.

Attempts are criminal acts on occasions when the harm does not occur, and are therefore criminal conduct in the raw. Since conduct provides the basis and sets the lower limit of criminal liability, a close look at attempts helps us to understand this minimum condition of criminal liability.

I. HARM

THE NOTION OF HARM

The notion of *harm* has played a large role in our discussion already, and will play an even greater part as new topics are pursued. It is thus important to be clear about what harm is, and especially to understand, for purposes of criminal law theory, how harm and conduct are related.

As we speak of it here, harm is an untoward occurrence consisting in a violation of some interest of a person. All natural persons have interests, but so do those social creations of persons that are collective bearers of personal interests: humanity, the State, the community, the family, corporations, and many other varieties of human associations. Persons and their surrogates may be in being; or they may no longer exist; or it may be that they are yet to be born or created. When they are not in being, their interests may anticipate them or survive them. Ancestors and descendants may, for example, both have interests—the one in giving something, the other in receiving it—even though one is already dead and the other not yet born. If someone living appropriates that thing, the interest of each is violated, and the interest of each may then be asserted by someone else on behalf of those not in being. In the context of criminal liability, interests of persons not in being may also be protected by laws that prohibit trespass upon those interests.

An account of harm in terms of interests calls in turn for some account of interests. It is enough, for present purposes, to bring that otherwise mysterious entity out of the shadows and to introduce it as a notion already familiar to everyone, though not to be confused (as it often is) with other familiar notions brought to mind by the same word.

A has an interest in X if two conditions are satisfied, but only if they are. For one thing, X must be of value to A. And for another, X must be of sufficient value to A that the assertion of a claim by or on behalf of A based on the loss or significant impairment of X is not unreasonable. It is most important to note that while X must be of value to A, A need not value it in order to have an interest in it. A may not want X and may make it clear that he doesn't, but his interest in it exists just the same. Since there are no psychological conditions required for A to have an interest in X, A may not be in existence and may still have an interest in X. Since A need not value X in order to have an interest in it, A may be the sort of entity that is not capable of valuing anything, and still A might have an interest in X so long as X is of value to A. Accordingly, Alfred might regard his inheritance of Xanadu as an unmitigated disaster requiring him to sign papers and make decisions about its upkeep when he wants only to write poetry and engage in metaphysical contemplation. But his interest in Xanadu is undiminished even though (to put it mildly) he does not value it at all. Further, if Alfred should suffer a massive brain hemorrhage that leaves him incapable of valuing anything, his interest in Xanadu will not be impaired as a result of his misfortune. Since, under Alfred's father's will, Alfred's firstborn son stands to inherit Xanadu, and since this inheritance is a thing of value to the one receiving it, there is an interest in Xanadu which is Alfred II's even though no such person now exists and perhaps never will.

There is of course the still more fundamental notion of what it is for something to be *of value*. Though there is much to be said about that, we need not say it here. Unlike the case with interests, our unexamined understanding of value can be relied upon to guide us for the limited purpose at hand, and we may safely turn back to the topic of harm itself.

Animals *may be harmed;* and harm *may be done* to a work of art, to the environment, and to the economy. To the extent that they may be harmed (and not simply have harm done to them), animals are possessors of interests and so, to that extent, are endowed as persons even though they do not become persons when so endowed. Like persons not in being or persons lacking the capacity to protect their interests, animals must rely upon others to act on their behalf to assert claims and otherwise protect their interests.

With inanimate things such as works of art, and with nonpersonal abstractions such as the environment or the economy, it is a different matter. These things have not been recognized as possessors of interests, and when harm *is done* to them it is the interests of those who *have an interest in them* that is violated. Harm done to Michelangelo's *Pietà* is not a violation of *its* interests but of its owner's and of mankind's.

Thus, harming something does not always mean violating *its* interests, but it does always mean violating an interest *in it*. This applies to persons, all of whom do have interests, as well as to things that do not have interests. Members of a family may be harmed by loss of support when the head of the family is killed, in which case the relevant interests violated by harm to the breadwinner are possessed by the members of his family and not by him. Regarding harm to the unfortunate father, two things might be said: he *was harmed* by being deprived of his life; and his family *was harmed* by loss of support when that *harm was done* to him.

Harms are not all equally serious. The difference in seriousness among them depends upon the importance of the interest that is violated by the conduct in question. And since the consideration affecting culpability in its second dimension is seriousness of harm, this aspect of culpability turns out to be largely a matter of the importance of the interest that is thus violated.

Harm may be attributable to some personal agency, but it need not be. Harm suffered in a natural disaster is harm no less than the same harm inflicted by human actions. But only when harm is attributable to some person does it interest the criminal law, for only then is conduct brought into question.

Not all harms are offensive. Only harms attributable to conduct may be offensive, and then only if the conduct is culpable. There are two ways in which conduct may be harmful and yet not be culpable. One person may harm another under circumstances that make the harmful conduct justifiable, as in cases of self-defense or avoidance of a greater harm. In such a case, though the harm has been done, the harmful act did not have fourth-dimension culpability. Because of that it was not culpable, and so the harm was not offensive. Similarly, harmful conduct is not culpable when it fails to meet the prescribed standard of first-dimension culpability. Carelessly taking and keeping another person's property is not culpable conduct according to the standard of culpability set by the law of larceny, even though it does work the same harm as a larceny. And again, because the conduct is not culpable the harm is not offensive.

It is only offensive harms that concern the criminal law. Harm not attributable to culpable conduct is no more a proper part of the concerns of criminal justice than harm attributable to a natural disaster.

VARIETIES OF CRIMINAL HARM

Harms that concern the criminal law are distinguishable according to the kind of interest violated, the one having the interest, and the effect of its violation. Four broad groups of harms are discernible.

The first group of harms consists of *violations of interest in retaining or maintaining what one is entitled to have.* Interests regarding life, liberty, property, physical well-being, and security are the most general and the most important classes. Violation of these interests is the harm of many crimes, common and uncommon. Murder, rape, theft, arson, incitement to riot, reckless driving, kidnapping, and forgery are samples from a very large stock. The gravamen of the harm is a *loss*—temporary or permanent—and loss of a kind that deprives or diminishes the victim either in his person or in his circumstances. After the harm has occurred a victim is, or has, less than before. It is harm of this variety that is the paradigm when we speak of an untoward occurrence as "harm."

Offenses to sensibility comprise a second group of harms. An interest in avoiding unpleasant experiences is shared by all who depend upon a common environment, and that interest is transgressed by those who are responsible for unpleasant experiences. Harms consisting in annoyance, inconvenience, alarm, fear, embarrassment, or disgust do not usually leave those who have been harmed any different than they were before. The experience itself, however, is objectionably unpleasant, and under certain circumstances it is serious enough to become a matter of public concern. Such concern is reflected in penal provisions that deal with publishing pornography, publicly uttering an obscenity, loitering to beg in a public place, simple common-law assault, open and notorious cohabitation outside of marriage, necrophilia, prostitution, exhibitionism, and the like. The harm is to those who may reasonably be offended in places or situations where such offense to sensibility is expectable.

A third group of harms comprises those that are neither a loss nor an offense to sensibility but consist in *some impairment of collective welfare.* Social life, particularly in the complex form of civilized societies, creates many dependencies among members of a community. The welfare of each member depends upon the exercise of restraint and precaution by others in the pursuit of their legitimate activities, as well as upon cooperation toward certain common objectives. These matters of collective welfare involve many kinds of interests that may be said to be possessed by the community. Protecting or promoting health, safety, security from foreign enemies, and a sound economy, are examples of these interests. Violations of these interests occur in such crimes as mislabeling of food products and violations of building codes, as well as in counterfeiting and espionage.

There is, finally, a group of harms that consists in *violations of some governmental interest.* These interests are possessed only by the State, and are generated in the very activity of governing. When policies and programs of government are frustrated, there is violation of interests in effective government, quite apart from the violation of interests of other sorts that may also take place. In a society in which political power is not abused, there are interests of government only for the sake of the governed, while in other societies interests of government are sometimes only for the sake of the government. Regardless of how just a society is in this regard, protection of governmental interests is sure to be a prominent feature of its legal system. Hence we have such crimes as filing a fraudulent tax return; failing to register as an alien, or for military service; evading Customs inspection; escaping from prison; selling unregistered securities; bribing a government official; taking photographs of court proceedings.

Any penal provision in a modern legal system is directed to some harm classified in one of these four groups. Not infrequently, however, there is more than one reason for making something a crime, and in that case there is more than one harm that concerns the law. The penal provision then bears multiple credentials, which may be of unequal strength depending on how good each reason is. Not only may concern center on more than one harm, but the harms may be of different sorts. As we shall see, correct interpretation of a law, and sound discretion in enforcing it, depend in large measure on rightly perceiving the reasons for having such a law.

Not all crimes seem rooted in harm, and only those of the first group appear to involve full-blooded harms. It is somewhat odd to speak of the government's suffering harm when a taxpayer's income is not fully reported, of the community's being harmed when an unlicensed driver is at the wheel, or of those offended by obscene displays being victims of some harm. Indeed, much current criticism of "victimless crimes" exploits a narrower and more proper usage. In stipulating a broader usage in this book, so that "harm" refers in a weaker sense to all the varieties of interest violation, nothing that is peculiar to its paradigm use is meant to be imported into the other contexts. The term "harm" has been adopted here as the master term for untoward occurrences only because other expressions seem even more likely to mislead. Historically its chief rival has been the term "evil," but to modern ears that word inevitably carries a suggestion of moral judgment. Its overtones would tend to make a statement like "Deprivation of maidenhood is the evil dealt with in statutory rape" into something more than a description of legislative concern, and in consequence would tend to confuse an attempt to explain a law with an attempt to justify it.

It is well to repeat once more a caution against misconstruing what is said here about the "harm" that is dealt with in criminal legislation. In our discussion we are concerned with conceptual rather than normative matters. It is another labor, no less arduous or important than the present one, to develop a theory of criminal harms. Rather than simply pointing out that something in fact concerns the law as untoward, the burden of that theory would be the formulation of principles that rightly determine what harms the criminal law ought to concern itself with. It would address fundamental questions of personal liberty and the proper limits of public authority. It would seek the facts about supposed untoward effects of conduct, make prudential assessments of the social costs of making particular activities criminal, and consider alternatives that are preferable to penal legislation when public concern is warranted. Its job, in short, would be to answer the question "What deserves to be recognized as a criminal harm?" Important as that answer is, it is not important for any investigation undertaken in this book.

CRIMES MALA IN SE AND MALA PROHIBITA

There is in criminal law theory a much confused distinction between crimes that are *mala in se* and those that are *mala prohibita*. What this distinction means to get at is best understood as a difference regarding harm. When a crime is *malum in se* the interest whose violation constitutes the harm has an existence that is independent of any legal recognition of it. Before a law creating such a crime, or after its repeal, the same interest that is the law's concern while the law is in effect would still exist, and violation of that interest would be the same harm regardless of legal recognition. The law merely defines the wrong conduct which violates the interest and for which it creates criminal liability.

At times, of course, repeal of such a law might create doubt about what conduct is wrong. Quite clearly on contemporary views, embezzlement would be considered *malum in se:* regardless of what the law is, the possessory interest of the bank in its depository funds continues even after they are entrusted to an employee. When he goes off to Rio with the bank's money, the bank has suffered a loss regardless of the state of the law. But if embezzlement were struck from the books, we would be unsure about precisely what conduct violates the bank's possessory interest and is therefore wrong. We would be unsure, for example, whether a bank employee who regularly comingles the bank's money 'with his own, quite aware of what he is doing yet without any purpose to enrich himself, is nevertheless engaging in the same harmful conduct as the straightforward embezzler.

By contrast, crimes of the *mala prohibita* variety depend upon the law for their harm. Once again the law tells us what interest-violating conduct is required for legal liability; but the law now does more than that, for the very interest violated by what is designated as legally wrong conduct is itself a creature of the law. In the absence of legal prohibition, bringing heroin and bringing talcum powder into the country are equally harmless acts. Only when a governmental interest in drug traffic control is created through law is there opportunity for harm through mere acts of introduction. But it would be incorrect to conclude from this that the multitude of penal provisions creating offenses *mala prohibita* are arbitrary legislative exercises, or at any rate fiat without any antecedent interest whose protection is the reason for the law.

Governmental or collective social interests are normally created and protected by these laws. But these interests exist, as do the laws that create them, because there are other underlying interests to be protected—and these the law does not create. The government, it is true, has an interest in regulating the availability of heroin only because the law creates such an interest. The harm done by violating this regulatory law would not occur if the law did not exist. The law exists, however, because the use of heroin is deemed harmful, and restriction of its availability is deemed a suitable way to prevent the harm. Any penal law enacted without regard ultimately to preventing some harm that exists independent of the law would indeed be arbitrary. Because normally there is that kind of further regard, and because protection of some interest whose existence is independent of the law is usually the reason for such an enactment, crimes on the books that are only *mala prohibita* nevertheless are normally more than mere legislative will and whim.

CONDUCT AS HARM

The relation between conduct and harm is more complicated than might appear from our discussion so far. Until now, harm has been viewed as violation of interest, and conduct as something to which that may be attributed. But conduct itself may be the harm, or may be tantamount to harm. In this regard, three varieties of crimes might be distinguished.

The first consists of crimes in which the occurrence of the act is itself sufficient for the occurrence of the harm, even though the act does not constitute the harm. If there has been an act of rape, there has then been a violation of the interest that the law is concerned to protect in rape legislation.

The second variety consists of crimes in which there is liability for the completed crime when conduct results in harm, but in which there is attempt liability for the conduct itself when harm does not result. Doing an act that causes the death of another is homicide, but if such an act does not result in death there may still be liability for attempted homicide. When there is only attempt liability, the conduct itself may usefully be regarded as a second order harm: in itself it is the sort of conduct that normally presents a threat of harm; and that, by itself, is a violation of an interest that concerns the law. The interest is one in *security* from harm, and merely presenting a threat of harm violates that security interest. Still, it is only a second-order harm. If what it now threatens were no harm it would itself be no harm, for then it would no longer pose a threat of harm and so no longer be a violation of an interest in security from harm. Other inchoate crimes, such as conspiracy, or solicitation to commit a crime, or facilitation of a crime, are also second-order harms. They also are crimes in which further harms are threatened by the prohibited conduct, and are therefore also crimes whose harm consists in the violation of a security interest that would not be violated if no further harm were being threatened.

The third variety is closely related to the second. It too consists of crimes whose harm is simply violation of a security interest that makes reference to some further harm. This time, however, the conduct itself *is* the completed crime. For these crimes, the conduct itself is the harm; the harm is one of endangering security; and that harm is of primary and independent concern. A clear example is the crime of reckless endangerment, in which dangerous conduct in willful disregard of life, limb, or property is made a crime. There are, in addition, crimes such as common-law assault requiring only a threat of further harm, and though this crime might have been cast simply as an attempt to commit some other crime, it is prescribed as a completed crime because the threat itself is recognized as an independent harm. Crimes in which conduct consists in doing something "with intent to" do something further, or to have something happen as a result, are of this sort. Crimes thought of as inchoate are also of this variety whenever the conspiracy or solicitation to commit a crime, or the facilitation or even the attempt of it, are conceived to be themselves items of conduct that are social harms independent of the harm of the prospective crime. This is particularly clear in those crimes where the very attempt seems offensive in its own right, as in attempting to fondle the genitals of a child under the age of fourteen, or attempting to negotiate unlawfully a negotiable instrument.

Conduct, then, may be a sufficient condition for harm; or may itself be a dependent harm; or quite independently may itself constitute the harm. In fact, in all crimes except those of a rather small group, the conduct itself constitutes a harm either of the first or the second order. That small group of exceptions consists of crimes for which there is not even attempt liability for the conduct alone. There are both trivial and serious offenses in this group.

If someone tosses a piece of paper out of the car window as he speeds along the highway, no littering offense is committed if the paper blows right back in. Nor would there normally be attempt liability in such a case. The reason is that the threat posed by the conduct itself is too trifling, since the prospective harm is trivial. The serious offenses in this group of exceptions are all crimes of negligence or of recklessness; crimes, that is, in which the harmful result is unintended. Vehicular homicide, for example, requires that someone be killed. If there is no fatality there is no liability for attempted vehicular homicide even when it is perfectly clear that the driver's conduct was just the sort that commonly results in death. Merely creating a great risk of serious harm is not itself enough for attempt liability here. The point merits a more detailed discussion, and this we shall undertake in the next section, where creating a risk is distinguished from simply posing a threat.

Conduct, then, is itself a harm whenever there is liability for conduct alone, and this is so whether liability is of the attempt or of the completed crime variety. But when conduct by itself is not enough for liability, conduct itself is not a harm.

II. ATTEMPTS

WHAT CONSTITUTES AN ATTEMPT

Since a criminal attempt is pure conduct, an investigation of criminal attempts is bound to be especially profitable for the study of criminal conduct. Attempts have already been mentioned in Chapter Two in connection with the distinction between an act and its consequences or its circumstances. In this section the essentials of the very notion of a criminal attempt are looked into briefly, while in Chapter Six and again in Chapter Ten there is extended discussion of the more substantial problems concerning attempts.

When there is only an attempt, conduct threatens the harm of the completed crime, but does not bring it about. There are three forms that this failure may take.

Some offenses require that a certain consequence follow from the conduct of the accused. Death must be caused by the conduct in question for a homicide to occur. If the bullet misses—whether because of mistake, accident, or chance—there can be only an attempted homicide, even though everything normally necessary for the harm to occur has been done.

Some offenses require a circumstantial element to be present, and without it there is not the required harm in what is done. If the articles bought by the accused turn out not to have been stolen, he has not committed the offense of receiving stolen goods—though, again, if it is only because of mistake, accident, or chance that things turn out differently in this regard than he intended, there might still be attempt liability.

In either case something necessary for the occurrence of the harm is lacking, but still there is conduct sufficient to pose a threat of it, and even sufficient normally to bring it about. Sometimes, however, less is done than is necessary to bring about harm on a normal occasion, although there has been enough done to pose a threat of the harm. Someone may have been lying in wait for his victim, or may have been tracking him, or luring him, or been busy setting a deadly device to kill him. If what is done indicates unambiguously that the accused was already thoroughly involved in the job of committing the crime, there may still be attempt liability for it. Here, however, it is no longer mistake, accident, or chance that accounts for nonoccurrence of harm. In these cases a deficiency of conduct distinguishes the attempt from the completed crime. The attempt may be of the deficient conduct variety when the completed crime requires a particular consequence or when it requires particular circumstances, and also when the completed crime requires only particular conduct. For this last species of offense, attempt liability is always of the deficient-conduct variety.

ATTEMPTED ATTEMPTS; AND ATTEMPTED NEGLIGENCE

We noted in the last section that trivial offenses normally are without attempt liability because the conduct is too trifling as a threat of harm. Two other types of crimes that are without attempt liability shed further light on the rationale of attempt liability itself. First, there is no liability for *attempting an attempt*. Second, *crimes of negligence or recklessness* admit of no attempt liability.

The idea of an attempted attempt is commonly regarded as incoherent. The argument may be stated in the following way. An attempt is simply conduct, and so the only species of attempt that might be an attempt at attempting would be some partial conduct as it related to the anticipated whole. Unsuccessful squeezing of the trigger of a loaded gun aimed at another person might be said to be an attempt to attempt to cause his death, if successfully pulling it would in itself constitute an attempted homicide. But, it is argued, that claim would be incoherent: the unsuccessful squeezing either is itself an attempted homicide; or else it is merely preparation for homicide, which is something other than an attempt. What is called an attempted attempt, then, is either nothing else than an attempt *simpliciter;* or it is not an attempt at all.

This concern about logical constraints is needless. It is true that ordinary usage does not encourage speaking of attempting to attempt. What is attempted can always alternatively be spoken of simply as an act, and this preserves the special force of the *attempt* at it to indicate those efforts that may meet with success or with failure. But on the other hand mere exertions to act are commonly counted as attempts, and the act may itself be a further attempt. A drowning man attempts to shout, and the shouting in turn is his attempt to save himself. Squeezing the trigger is an attempt to shoot, and the shooting is an attempt to kill. So in a perfectly straightforward way we do have coherent attempts to attempt.

The reason that the criminal law does not have liability for attempted attempts is not because there is no such thing, and certainly not because such a thing is inconceivable. It is because conduct either poses a threat of harm, in which case it is sufficient for liability as an attempt; or because it does not pose a threat, in which case it is not sufficient for liability as an attempt. In the latter case there is no good reason for criminal liability at all, since there is not even the threat of the harm that has been recognized by the criminal law, but at most only some danger of such a threat. Such "third-order harms"—as they might be called—are simply too speculative to warrant intrusion upon our lives by the forces of law and order.

On the other hand, when conduct is thought to merit criminal prohibition either as a first- or as a second-order harm, appropriate provisions are enacted. Some of these might indeed, in ordinary usage, be spoken of as an attempt to attempt. In its traditional form, burglary requires a breaking and entering with intent to commit a felony. Breaking and entering itself might therefore be thought of as an attempt. If a would-be thief is caught while trying to break in, attempted burglary would be a proper charge, and this well-recognized offense in the law is in ordinary (though not legal) terms an attempted attempt.

Simple assault is another example of what might be called an attempted attempt. This offense is sometimes defined as an attempt to commit a battery. Because, on this definition, attempted assault would be an attempted attempt, liability for attempted assault has not been recognized in a number of jurisdictions. But in deciding whether it ought to be, the crucial question is whether a sufficiently definite second-order harm is constituted by what has been done. When certain menacing conduct is sufficient for the completed crime, earlier stages in the same course of conduct might warrant attempt liability. Someone apprehended still miles away from the one he intends to menace might well be made to answer attempt charges if he is already armed with his club and on his way.

Crimes of negligence do not ordinarily admit of attempt liability, and this is true also of most crimes of recklessness. It is usually said that the very notion of attempted negligence (or recklessness) is incoherent, since whatever is attempted must be intended. Once again it turns out that though there is infelicity calling for a happier expression, there is no incoherence. We noted in the last section that there are two varieties of these offenses, one requiring a particular *outcome* of conduct, the other requiring only a particular *kind* of conduct. An illustration of attempting each should dispel logical misgivings.

Negligent homicide requires that a death be caused by negligent conduct. But precisely the same negligent conduct that has time and again been found sufficient for liability when death resulted from it might also (by good fortune) be engaged in without death's resulting. It would then satisfy the *conceptual* requirement for an attempt in the criminal law. Similarly, reckless driving—an offense that requires no special outcome—might quite plausibly be said to have been attempted when an extremely intoxicated person started his car and was about to pull onto the road. In neither case, however, would there normally be attempt liability. The reason is that in such cases the law has chosen to make *culpability* of the conduct depend upon its outcome, or upon the character of its actual performance.

Presumably it has been decided that without reference to those things culpability cannot be determined with sufficient certainty. Without culpable conduct, no threat of harm is presented in the eyes of the law, and it is for this reason that crimes of attempted negligence and attempted recklessness are not to be found. It might be said that in both these cases there is nevertheless a risk of harm that is created or at the very least ignored by the driver, and that there should be liability for that. And indeed, if the legislature deems it to be punishable conduct, the legislature may then provide liability for it, either by broadening the terms of the existing offense to cover such conduct or by creating another less serious offense.

THE DIFFERING CONCEPTION IN ORTHODOX THEORY

Much of Chapter Six is devoted to questions of when it is that conduct poses a threat of harm. The law of attempts must answer this question in order to distinguish attempts from mere preparation, and also to decide when (if at all) the impossibility of committing a crime means that there ought not to be even attempt liability for things done that point in the direction of some crime. In dealing with these problems, much of modern criminal law theory has in general (and most notably in the Model Penal Code) proceeded on premises sharply at odds with those that have emerged in this section. It is thought that the law of attempts is designed to catch criminally dangerous persons before they do harm. The conduct in question then serves only as evidence of the dangerousness of the actor. As a basis of liability the conduct then need not be truly dangerous so long as it would be if things actually were as the actor believed them to be. On this view a person is subject to criminal liability not for what he has done, but for being (so it is thought) a person of a certain sort.

Curiously, and without explanation, there is here a radical change from conduct-regarding principles of liability to person-regarding principles when attempts rather than completed crimes are the basis of liability. This is one of several instances in which two different questions tend to be muddled by some theorists of criminal liability. The first question is what reasons there are for imposing liability in a particular class of cases. The other question is what reasons there are for having a system of criminal liability in the first place. Insinuated into this confusion is another that has been noted already in Chapter One. The idea that a dangerous person is a person who has a disposition to do harm is scrambled with the idea that anyone who does something dangerous is a dangerous person.

III. CRIMINAL CONDUCT RECONCEIVED

In these three chapters our effort to develop a sound conception of criminal conduct has moved us away from mere bodily movements and mental states toward an open sea of events and states of affairs which may be attributed to persons who are answerable for things that take place in the world. Criminal acts are items of criminal conduct which give rise to accusations. They are fit subjects of criticism because they threaten harm that is deemed socially intolerable. Extended courses of action and complex activities by individuals and by collective entities—waging war no less than taking aim and pulling a trigger—are comprehended as criminal acts. Some acts can only be engaged in, some can only be performed, some only are done, and there are even some that can only take place; and this suggests the richness and variety of those bits of the world that we may choose to regard as acts.

The act itself, or rather the very idea of an act, still remains veiled in mystery. We become better acquainted by first asking ourselves why we want to understand the concept of an act. Three good reasons suggest themselves. First, we want to distinguish acts from mere intentions to act, since it is only acts that we regard as a proper basis for criminal liability. Second, we want to distinguish *being* something from *doing* something, since *doing* but not *being* is regarded as a proper foundation for criminal liability. Finally, we do not want to make a person liable simply because something untoward happens, but only when he is involved as an agent in its occurrence.

It is important to distinguish acts from mere intentions to act because, although acts may break my bones and harm me in countless other ways, mere intentions to act can do me no harm. What I *am* must be distinguished from what I *do* because I cannot (merely) avoid being anything, but can only avoid doing something. It is true that I may be responsible for what I am. But it is only because of what I have done and so only because of what I could (presumably) have avoided doing, that I may be responsible for what I am. Finally, what just simply happened and wasn't done couldn't have been prevented simply by choosing otherwise. When an act is defined in this way and contrasted with mere *intending, being,* an*d happening,* it serves as a coherent basis for criminal accusation. The fundamental principles of culpability and responsibility, which we shall elucidate further in Chapter Five, make use of an act conceived to meet these conditions, and for that reason this conception of an act has much to recommend it for criminal law theory.

Two cautionary observations about acts may be offered as a closing word here.

The critical judgments for which criminal acts serve as a basis are not an invention of the law. True enough, the law places limits on these judgments and devises proceedings that must be followed in making them for legal purposes. But we can understand what is going on in the criminal law because it is similar to what goes on elsewhere in life when conduct is criticized. This suggests quite rightly that a sound conception of crimiɪal conduct is not simply of parochial use to lawyers, but is also of wider interest wherever there is concern about matters of responsibility and culpability. But we must remember, too, that acts are also of theoretical concern when other matters are at issue, and the conception of a criminal act presented here may then be largely, or even entirely, useless. One can easily imagine accounts of behavior which, for example, are formulated not to judge acts but to explain them, and which make good use of a notion of an act that can be wholly understood in terms of abstractions from psychological and physiological descriptions.

The moral here is simple, though often not heeded. "Act" is a term used to designate bits of the world which we wish to give some account of. There are different kinds of accounts which serve different purposes, and the account we wish to give will determine which bits are of significance. What is usefully counted as an act in one kind of account might not be usefully counted as an act in a different kind of account. Much argument at cross-purposes about what an act is can be avoided simply by making explicit the kind of account in which an act is to play its part.

A second caution concerns acts and their descriptions. There are difficulties well-known to philosophers in telling whether "John caused Bill's death" and "John aimed the loaded gun at Bill and fired at his heart" are statements describing in two different ways the same act, or are statements describing two different acts. A criterion of individuation of acts is hardly less important than a criterion of identity. While the identity criterion is necessary to ensure that there is a basis for an accusation, the criterion of individuation is necessary to ensure that there are not more accusations than there are acts. We should not want to have two different charges made when there is only a single criminal act described in two different ways.

The criterion of individuation, like that of identity, derives from a concern about responsibility and may be formulated in this way. If what is described in two descriptions might be the basis of a coherent accusation, and not simply the basis of a pseudo-accusation that seems nonsensical in its fundamental disregard of responsibility, what is described in each is an act. If according to standards for responsible acts (which we discuss at length in succeeding chapters) it is the case that what is described in one of these statements might not be a responsible act when what is described in the other statement is a responsible act, the two descriptions are descriptions of two different acts. Otherwise, they are two descriptions of the same act.

CHAPTER FIVE

Exculpatory Claims

There are many ways that those confronted by criminal accusations may avoid criminal liability. Many defenses (and especially those of recent origin) spring from a need to protect citizens from abuse of their liberties by the guardians of the law, and to keep enforcement of the law humane, accurate, and fair. These defenses, however, do not concern us here. Other defenses that do concern us are intimately related to matters that have so far been under discussion. In one way or another all of them deny that the actor may be blamed for what is alleged to be a basis of liability, and so deny that he can properly be held liable.

In this chapter a survey of these exculpatory claims is presented. It is preceded by a statement of two master principles upon which all such defenses rest. These principles may be viewed as a general statement of what is more particularly stated in negative form by the various exculpatory claims taken together. Only by examining these claims can the importance of the principles be appreciated, for only then do the consequences of ignoring them become clear.

I. RESPONSIBILITY AND CULPABILITY

THE RESPONSIBILITY PRINCIPLE

There are two principles under which all exculpatory claims of the criminal law are to be found. Some of these claims rest on one of these principles only, but some rest on both. The first principle may be called the principle of *responsibility*. It announces that *criminal liability is unjust if the one who is liable was not able to choose effectively to act in a way that would avoid criminal liability, and because of that he violated the law.*

Major difficulties suggest themselves at once. Persons are sometimes unable to act as they might wish because they lack opportunity to do so, while at other times they are unable because they do not have the personal capacity. It is unclear how the line between lack of opportunity and lack of capacity is to be drawn, and whether the principle of responsibility equally credits the claim "I couldn't help it" regardless of whether one or the other deficiency is offered as the reason. A mountain climber may dangle in mid-air, while his companion tied to the same rope is dangling beneath him. Does he lack the capacity or does he lack the opportunity to survive together with his companion? And does that matter when he is later charged with homicide after cutting the rope and letting the other man fall?

A second problem is this. It is often exceedingly difficult to know when the capacity to act in the required way is lacking. Can we truly distinguish those cases in which, because of some deficiency in personal resources, it is rather more difficult to act in a particular way from those cases in which the deficiency leaves the actor unable to do so? Can we tell when a kleptomaniac simply feels an urge to steal that others do not, and when he finds it impossible to control himself? Can we distinguish these two kinds of cases with sufficient rigor to make with any confidence those awesome judgments about criminal liability that turn on the distinction?

This suggests yet another difficulty. When we say that a person was not able to act in the required way, that it really was not possible for him to do so, we often do not mean that it was truly impossible. We consider some weaker claim of inability good enough to deny responsibility. What often we want to say is that the accused could not *reasonably* have done otherwise, or that he had no *fair* opportunity to do so, thereby admitting by implication that he could have done so had he chosen to ignore the risks or the consequences (whatever they might be), or if he exhibited extraordinary powers under the circumstances. Since we believe that the qualified inability counts in his favor just as much as a claim that it was utterly impossible for him to do otherwise, it is exceedingly important that we know when the actor could not *reasonably* do otherwise or did not have *fair* opportunity to do so. Until we know that, we do not know where to draw the line in order to exclude certain claims of inability as being too weak.

There is one further difficulty to be noticed at the outset. With reference to influences that shape one's choices and one's dispositions to act, much is made in the philosophical literature of the ability to determine freely what one does. Responsibility is measured by this freedom, and only a person who is truly free is thought to be truly responsible. The question then arises whether there ought to be criminal liability at all for a person who is not truly free and so not truly responsible.

Resolution of these difficulties is part of the business of those who pass on exculpatory claims, and the conclusions to which their efforts ought to lead them will be discussed in the second section of this chapter, in the next two chapters, and in the first section of Chapter Eight.

THE CULPABILITY PRINCIPLE

The other principle upon which exculpatory claims may rest, either in whole or in part, may be called the principle of *culpability*. Since culpability is itself a more complex notion than responsibility, this principle of criminal justice has more provisos that furnish platforms for exculpatory claims of different kinds. This principle, which reflects the four dimensions of culpability that were distinguished in Chapter Three, can be expressed summarily in this way. *Criminal liability is just only when it is for an intentional act that illegitimately poses a threat of the harm with which the law has concerned itself.*

Like the principle of responsibility, in its very statement the principle of culpability presents us with difficulties. In Chapter Three we discussed at length the problems of an intentional act, but other difficulties remain to be considered. In the first place it is important to know in what way, if any, the posing of a threat of harm by an act differs from its simply being dangerous. Presumably, conduct is to be regarded in a different way from other occurrences in the world which equally endanger us, and so conduct is to be judged dangerous or not in a different way. Further difficulties surround the notion of a threat. When is a threat of harm real and of sufficient stature to warrant the intervention of the law through criminal liability? We do, after all, imagine dangers in many things that are done, even though our fears turn out to be groundless or very much exaggerated. Even when they are not, and we are justified in our concern, the risk of harm may not be substantial enough to justify criminal liability for creating the risk. The magnitude of the threat, moreover, may not be simply a matter of risk. If the prospective harm is very serious, is the activity that might bring it about a substantial threat, even though the harm is still remote?

Another problem here concerns the likelihood of harm. In some way, the likelihood of harm's occurring is an important consideration in judging the seriousness of the threat of harm which particular conduct represents. But a probability calculation cannot be relied upon to determine how serious a threat was posed by an act. Often it will be apparent later that a highly dangerous act had no chance at all of causing the harm that at the time was quite reasonably thought to be imminent; or that an act that was deemed quite sensibly at the time to be perfectly innocent was in fact certain to cause serious harm.

There are also questions of just what harm it is that in fact concerns the law. It is not enough for liability that some harm which might concern the law was threatened. Though the threat of harm was a very substantial one, the harm threatened might not have been the one that the law which is invoked actually had as its concern—in which case liability would be unjust. This, as we shall see in Chapter Six, is an important question for attempt liability, since sometimes the occurrence of what is required for the completed crime is impossible under the circumstances, and it is not clear then whether the right sort of harm has been threatened.

Finally, there is the matter of posing a threat of the harm illegitimately. Truly dangerous conduct of the sort the law has in mind to prevent may take place under circumstances —or for a purpose—that confer a legitimacy upon it. Criminal liability is then inappropriate, since what is criminally wrong in the abstract is not criminally wrong in this case. Sometimes it is difficult to distinguish justifiable from unjustifiable acts, especially when innocent people are threatened by conduct that is necessary to protect the interests of others who are no less innocent.

Only by examining with care the vital parts of different

exculpatory claims can we solve these problems—and then not in any wholesale way, but through an indefinite number of detailed elaborations of the principle.

THE RELATION BETWEEN RESPONSIBILITY AND CULPABILITY; AND SOME PRELIMINARY CLARIFICATIONS

Separately or together, these two principles of exculpation support a variety of exculpatory claims. In fact, all exculpatory claims known to the criminal law rest on one or the other principle, and some in different aspects rest on both. There are excuses and justifications, and there are other exculpatory claims that are neither. The membership and characteristics of each group of claims are closely examined—though in a summary way—in the next two sections. But before embarking on that survey, a few preliminary points are in order.

When the principle of responsibility is invoked for purposes of exculpation, there is a denial that the accused is *eligible* for blame. When the principle of culpability is invoked, there is a denial that the conduct was blameworthy— either not blameworthy at all or not so blameworthy as it must be to make the accusation stick. The connection between responsibility and culpability is an important one. Being responsible is much like having a bank account, and being culpable is much like having it debited. When a person is not responsible, he is not eligible for blame, just as a person without an account is ineligible for debiting. And just as a person who does have an account may still claim that a debit ought not to be made, so a person who is responsible may still claim he ought not to be blamed. The point of exculpation, as the word itself suggests, is to escape blame, and there are two ways to do this. The direct method is to deny culpability. The indirect method is to deny responsibility. Whichever way is chosen, the point is to establish that what was done does not deserve blame according to legal standards of culpability, for only culpable conduct merits the law's condemnation, and only culpable conduct can properly serve as a basis of criminal liability. It is no wonder, then, that ways of escaping blame make up a large and important part of the entire body of criminal defenses.

In all this talk about conduct, we must not lose sight of the actor. It is he, after all, who is to be blamed for what he has done. When an exculpatory claim denies responsibility, there is a direct denial that *he* is blamable, and the same thing is denied indirectly by exculpatory claims that deny culpability. Still, when he is blamed, it is according to the blameworthiness of what he has done, and only that. In this respect, judgments of criminal liability and moral judgments differ, for in moral judgments it is not uncommon for things about a person to serve as the basis of condemnation. It may well be that those traits and habits which support moral judgments about a person and are spoken of as his character turn out to be nothing more than his conduct viewed in a general way through time. In that case the distinction between judgments of criminal liability and moral judgments can be drawn even more sharply. It is, then, the distinction between judgment of a particular act which is his conduct on a particular occasion, and judgment of patterns of conduct disclosed through many acts, and expressed in terms of the actor.

A further preliminary point of importance concerns the term *responsibility*. "He is responsible" is commonly used as a paraphrase of "He is liable." Since being criminally liable normally requires culpable conduct, it then appears that "He is responsible" implies that his conduct is culpable. To avoid this mistaken implication, we must be alert to the quite different senses of "responsibility" when used (as here) to refer to eligibility for blame, and when used (as it never is here) to refer simply to eligibility for punishment.

But there is yet another trick that "responsibility" will play on us if we are not alert. We speak of a person who is eligible for blame as *responsible,* sometimes meaning that he had the ability to do otherwise, and sometimes meaning that he caused what happened. There are exculpatory claims that counter each of these two different kinds of assertion, but they rest on different foundations. When we say that the accused was responsible and mean that he had the ability to do otherwise, we are relying on the responsibility principle. But, as we shall see later in the present chapter and again in the next chapter, when we say that the accused was responsible and mean that his conduct can be treated as a cause of what happened we are relying largely on the culpability principle.

Describing the practice of exculpation and examining the various forms it takes leaves open the question of why culpability, or even responsibility, is necessary for criminal liability. Though much of the time it seems self-evident that we ought to punish only for blameworthy conduct, there are those who view this requirement as an impediment to the achievement of the aims of the criminal law, and advocate its abandonment. It is also contended that the requirement is even now not universal in the criminal law and therefore that, in the interest of more effective crime prevention without any radical reform of our criminal jurisprudence, we might extend the areas in which we dispense with the requirement. In Chapter Eight and Chapter Ten we shall look into these important matters—with, one might hope, a better appreciation of the claims whose abandonment is proposed.

II. A SURVEY OF EXCULPATORY CLAIMS DENYING RESPONSIBILITY

In this section and in the next, all the important exculpatory claims to be found in the criminal law are noted. Claims that do not receive special treatment in the next two chapters are

Exculpatory Claims

1. Exculpatory Claims That Deny Responsibility		2. Exculpatory Claims That Deny Culpability Directly		
1.1. Conduct-regarding	1.2. Actor-regarding	2.1. Conduct-regarding	2.2. Actor-regarding	2.3. Interest-regarding
1.1.1. There was no act.	1.2.1. Mental abnormality	2.1.1. There was no act (3rd dim.).	2.2.1. There was no act (1st dim.).	2.3.1. There was no act (4th dim.).
1.1.2. The act was involuntary.	1.2.2. Infancy	2.1.2. Mens rea requirement not met (3rd dim.).	2.2.2. Mens rea requirement not met (1st dim.).	2.3.2. Compulsion (4th dim.).
1.1.3. Harm is not attributable even *prima facie* to the accused.	1.2.3. Compulsion	2.1.3. Invalidity, inapplicability, or nonexistence of the (alleged) law (2nd dim.; 3rd dim.).		2.3.3. Military orders (4th dim.).
1.1.4. Harm was caused by someone or something else.	1.2.4. Military orders	2.1.4. Insufficient conduct (3rd dim.).		2.3.4. Justifiable ignorance of the law (4th dim.).
	1.2.5. Justifiable ignorance of the law	2.1.5. Harm, which did not occur, was no expectable (3rd dim.).		2.3.5. Entrapment (4th dim.).
	1.2.6. Mens rea requirement not met	2.1.6. Harm, which did occur, was not expectable (3rd dim.).		2.3.6. Provocation (4th dim.).
	1.2.7. Entrapment	2.1.7. Renunciation (3rd dim.).		2.3.7. Justifications for: use of force; acts of public duty; violation of property rights (4th dim.).
	1.2.8. Provocation			2.3.8. Consent (2nd dim.).
	1.2.9. Impossibility of compliance			2.3.9. Lack of offensiveness (1st–2nd dim.).

considered at greater length here, though all discussion here is confined (and sometimes quite uncomfortably) to making clear the force of each claim and the place it occupies in the general scheme of exculpation. The survey is meant to be thorough, but not utterly exhaustive. No doubt a thorough refinement process will turn up many bits of exculpation elsewhere in the criminal law among claims that are not mainly exculpatory; in fact the defense of entrapment is one such claim that has been included here, even though its grounds are only partly exculpatory.

Another point is this. The scheme presented here is not thought to be uniquely correct. Other useful ways of arranging these claims are possible, and some no doubt would make more explicit certain exculpatory moves that are mentioned here only by way of example or that are not mentioned at all, since they turn out to be only more specific instances of a more general claim that is discussed here. It is important also to keep in mind that many claims as they appear in the law have more than one string to their bow and are therefore distributed here under two, three, or even four headings.

CONDUCT-REGARDING CLAIMS

Exculpatory claims that deny responsibility deny that the accused is even eligible for blame, much less to be blamed. These claims are of two kinds, the first of which may be called conduct-regarding since it is something about what was done that gives the claim its force, or (even more important here) something about what was not done. Four different claims of this sort emerge.

1.1.1. There was no act. Being something rather than *doing* something, is not unknown in the law as a purported ground of criminal liability. "Status crimes," as they are sometimes called, purport to make a person liable to punishment for what he is. In the law, a person's being something objectionable is usually expressed in terms of his being in a certain condition, place, or relation. Being addicted to the use of narcotics, for example, was made punishable in California as a crime, though ultimately the highest court in the land decided that it could not be made a crime. The reason that being an addict cannot be a crime is that it is not an act, which means in part that nothing amenable to a judgment of responsibility has occurred. There is, in other words, not even a *prima facie* case to be made that a narcotic addict was able to do what was necessary to avoid criminal liability under the law. This notable non-act stands in contrast to being found intoxicated in a public place. In Texas that was made a crime, and the Supreme Court of the United States decided that this could indeed be made punishable. A *prima facie* case could be made out that a person found intoxicated in a public place did have the ability to avoid that, and so there was not the preliminary bar to liability presented in the case of narcotic addiction.

Further objections of this preliminary sort sometimes emerge when there is an attempt to impose liability on one person for the criminal acts of others simply by virtue of some relation between them. The very first question to be asked is whether an act of dissociation could reasonably have been undertaken which would have destroyed the relation or, even earlier, would have prevented its formation. If not, the mere existence of the relation cannot be the basis of criminal liability. Such instances of presumed vicarious liability are presented in situations where one person is said to be an accessory or a co-conspirator; or where a person for whom services are rendered is said to be liable for what is done by the one rendering them. In all such cases the first question to be asked is whether avoidance or termination of the relation was reasonably within the power of the person who is accused vicariously.

1.1.2. The act was involuntary. A second conduct-regarding claim denies responsibility by asserting that though the alleged act appeared at first to be an act, it turns out really not to be one. These we call involuntary acts, having already exposed their pretensions in Chapter Two. When we learn the truth about what happened, we conclude that there is not even a *prima facie* case for the accused person's being responsible—though that much, at least, seemed possible at the start. The usual case is one in which initially the cause of physical movements that result in harm is obscure, and this allows us to assume that there has been an act. When the truth is known, we see that there were *mere* movements that could not be helped, perhaps because of epilepsy, perhaps because one stumbled, or was stung by a bee. In any case it was, as a non-act, not the sort of thing one could help doing, for indeed one didn't really do it. It was just something that happened to one, with unfortunate consequences for others. The gist of exculpation here is simply that one really cannot help doing what one really has not done.

1.1.3. Harm is not attributable even prima facie *to the accused.* The most obvious and most commonly asserted of all exculpatory claims is not usually thought of as a plea by way of exculpation at all. In actual proceedings as well as in fiction, the defense most often made is that not the accused but someone else (or even something else), known or unknown, is the culprit. In essence it is a claim that there is no material connection between anything the accused did and the harm prompting the accusation. But what is disputed is not *the materiality* of the connection between what happened and what is alleged to have caused it. Rather, *the occurrence* of those events (or states of affairs) that are alleged as the act of the accused is denied. *Whodunits* have as their vital substance these issues of exculpation. *Whatdunits* are another variety in which the mystery is resolved by establishing that it just happened, and blame is similarly avoided then: "It was just an accident—the loaded gun had been lying on the shelf for years, and that day the heat just caused it to discharge." In either case, the alleged act upon which the accusation rests is in a most straightforward way denied, and so, therefore, is responsibility. For surely no one could have avoided doing what he has not done.

1.1.4. Harm was caused by someone or something else. There is a claim of exculpation no less fundamental which denies that the accused *caused* the harm that occurred. The more interesting parts of this claim rest on the culpability principle, but here we must note two parts that are denials of responsibility. The first is a claim that harm happened by accident. Untoward events may occur in the course of our activities, and at first it appears that the mishap was our doing. The appearance, however, may be quite false, and although we are willing to concede that without the activity the harm would not have occurred (if he hadn't picked up the gun it wouldn't have gone off, killing poor Smith), still, what he did was not the cause of what happened (it was just one of those unaccountable mishaps that occur every now and again). But rather than simply pointing away from the accused by declaring that it happened by accident, one can claim that it was not an act of the accused that caused the harm by pointing to someone or something else. It is important, once again, that the accused not be involved in any material way in the events (not Smith, but a faulty repair job or a worn safety catch caused the gun to fire).

Under either version of this exculpatory claim, the accused is involved in the events in some way, but not in a *material* way. But without a criterion of materiality, we will have added here to the obscurity we seek to dispel. The responsibility principle in a further unfolding not surprisingly furnishes that criterion. If the accused in doing what he did had no reason to expect the harm, then he could not avoid it, and so when it occurs he is not even eligible for blame. In the next chapter we discuss at length what it means for the actor to have reason to expect the harm, for that notion plays a prominent part in our analysis of attempt liability and of causation. Here we observe only that what is not an expectable result of what one does is not something that one can reasonably be expected to keep from happening, and so liability based on its occurrence would be unjust according to the responsibility principle.

ACTOR-REGARDING CLAIMS

We come now to the second class of claims that deny responsibility. Those of the first group were all conduct-regarding. These are all actor-regarding, for in all of them the force of the claim is not found in what was or was not done, but rather in something about the actor, who, for one reason or another, was unable to do otherwise.

1.2.1. Mental abnormality. Mental abnormality is the most prominent and the most intriguing of these exulpatory claims. Because of some abnormal condition from which he suffered, the accused may have been incapable of effectively choosing to pursue a course of action that would avoid violating the law, and this furnishes him with a defense. The personal abnormality may have meant defective powers of self-restraint, inability to appreciate the dangerousness or unlawfulness of what he was doing, incorrigibly unrealistic notions about the world, inability to avoid harmful consequences as he acted. Whatever form the abnormality takes, it is relevant if (but only if) it means that the accused was incapable of choosing effectively a course of conduct that did not violate the law.

Since it is incapacity *to choose* effectively that matters, physical abnormalities that debilitate do not furnish the basis of an excuse of this sort. When he causes harm, a person who is deaf, blind, paralyzed, or lacking some of his limbs might be said because of his physical incapacity also to be unable to conform his conduct to the requirements of the law. But because his incapacity does not impair *choice,* he could have avoided doing harm, and so when he does harm under such circumstances we do not accept his physical abnormality as an excuse of personal abnormality but hold him to account as a responsible person. If the physical abnormality is of a kind that does not allow for effective choice in acting (uncontrollable movements, say, that one had no reason to expect or guard against) the abnormality may rightly be invoked by way of exculpation. Mental abnormality may be chronic or it may be only episodic, and in either case it may furnish grounds for exculpation. When the abnormality is only an episode, it may be the abnormal state of consciousness of a perfectly normal person; or it may be a reaction (typically anger or fear) that puts him in an emotional state so extreme that his responsibility (as we say) is diminished and he cannot be held fully responsible.

1.2.2. Infancy. Criminal liability has always been affected by the fact that the offender was young, although legal policies at different times and places reflect different views about how young he must be and about what legal effect his youth ought to have. In part (but only in part) the defense of infancy has nothing to do with exculpation but is simply a matter of humane treatment. It is cruel to subject the young to criminal punishment, and for much the same reason that punishment of sick persons is inhumane. In either case there is cruel neglect in depriving such a person of things necessary for well-being that every person is entitled to simply because he is human. Humane considerations tend even more readily to exempt the young than the sick. The needs of the sick we may satisfy by medical treatment after subjecting them to criminal liability, but the young are harmed in their development by the stigma and traumatic interference with natural psychological dependencies that in some degree any regime of public correction must cause, no matter how benign it might be.

There is also, however, an exculpatory aspect to the defense of infancy. It derives from the limited ability that children have both to appreciate the risks of doing certain things and to appreciate the significance of the resulting harm. Knowing what the risks are, and having regard for the interests of others, requires a social intelligence that the young are only in a process of developing; and because of their more meager capacities it would be wrong to treat the young as fully responsible. Some of our assumptions in this regard have recently been brought into question by the prevalence of criminal behavior among young people who show full appreciation of what they are doing and who exhibit adult capacities of understanding and planning in deliberately choosing to commit crimes. As a result there is a conflict between humane considerations which incline us toward exempting the young from normal criminal liability, and our revised judgments of responsibility which incline us toward holding young offenders to higher standards of liability than those that now prevail.

1.2.3. Compulsion. Another person, or mere circumstances, may impose constraints on what one can do. One may be forced to act in violation of the law because of threats or because of prospects of harm inherent in the situation in which one finds oneself. Force itself may directly constrain unlawful conduct, and the force may be exerted by another person or by some nonpersonal agency. In any of these cases a person may well say, "I couldn't help myself, I had to do it," and this will be given serious consideration as a claim by way of exculpation when it rings true. We consider this kind of exculpation at length in Chapter Seven, distinguishing duress from necessity, and justification from excuse. Here we need note only that any of these claims is in part a denial of responsibility, and that there are two slightly different versions of each.

"I had no other choice," the accused may say as he begins to explain his alleged inability to help himself. He may mean by this that no opportunity was presented for another course of conduct. He had, he says, no (reasonable) alternative; it was a situation in which his circumstances dictated his conduct. On the other hand, "I couldn't help myself" might be given backing by showing that there was no opportunity to choose to act differently—no opportunity to *choose* what to do at all, really—though, admittedly, the circumstances in which the accused found himself allowed for alternative courses of action. In the first case, either I alone survive or both my climbing companion and I fall to our deaths; and after careful assessment of the situation I do the only thing I reasonably can and cut the rope that ties him to me. In the second case, I suddenly find myself dangling perilously in space, and though in a cooler hour it would have been apparent that I probably could save both my companion and myself by gradually swinging in and grabbing outcropping branches, I act like the desperate man I am and quickly cut the rope that ties us, to prevent my being pulled down by his weight. The lack of choice and the failure to choose are equally grounds for denial of responsibility.

1.2.4. Military orders. Military orders may command acts that are crimes, and those ordered to perform them may later be charged with these crimes if they followed the orders. Both civilian law and military law have long recognized a defense of superior orders under these circumstances, though with qualifications that are never entirely clear and that vary considerably from one country to another and from one time to another. As a doctrine of international law, superior orders has an important place among the principles comprising the laws of war, and has been much appealed to in war crimes trials. As an item of domestic law, the Model Penal Code version affords a defense of military orders to one who "does no more than execute an order of his superior in the armed services which he does not know to be unlawful."

Under most views, this is unduly generous, for if the defense is not allowed when what was ordered was known to be unlawful, it would seem that it should not be allowed either when it would simply be unreasonable to believe that what was ordered was lawful. It is not clear, furthermore, whether the same rule governs when orders are given in a wartime situation (and especially under the exigencies of combat), and when orders are given in a more relaxed setting in which questioning is not an immediate threat to military efficiency. Leaving aside these finer points, it is clear that the defense of superior military orders is in part an exculpatory claim that denies responsibility because the actor is (in a meaningful sense) unable to do otherwise.

For one thing, military discipline allows no room for disobedience to orders, and a well-disciplined military force obeys orders unquestioningly. As a practical matter this means depriving a soldier under orders of any opportunity to deviate from them, and a denial of responsibility for what is done in carrying out orders makes sense under such circumstances. There is a second point that is closely related to this. Military penalties for disobedience are typically swift, sure, and drastic. Opportunity to litigate the propriety of what was ordered may not be available; even if it is, the forum is normally predisposed by the perceived requirements of the military enterprise to favor those who give orders over those who refuse to obey them. Under these circumstances, every military order carries with it an implied threat that gives it great coercive force, and those who receive orders may therefore rightly claim that they were coerced and unable to refuse.

There is, finally, a third reason for giving some credit to this denial of responsibility. Persons who act under military orders must assume that the orders are proper. On the exceptional occasion when what is ordered appears unlawful, the one who receives the order and wishes to question it must overcome the presumption of lawfulness. In all but the most obvious cases, overcoming that presumption requires a knowledge of the law, for, under conditions of war in which killing and destruction are commonplace, most activities that would normally be taken to be unlawful are countenanced and encouraged. Acquiring a knowledge of the law so that one may judge the lawfulness of what is ordered is often not possible under these circumstances, and this furnishes further grounds for claiming that it would have been unreasonable to refuse to obey.

Although formerly a wife might claim a defense of coercion when ordered by her husband to commit a crime, in the modern world only military orders provide the basis of a defense of superior orders. A wife is no longer subject to her husband's authority as she was at an earlier time, but others in the modern world are subject to superior orders given by those who are in positions of authority over them in institutions other than marriage. In business organizations, professional firms, government agencies, religious orders, and police forces, orders are regularly given and carried out, and with penalties for disobedience that are sometimes more drastic in their consequences than those imposed for military disobedience. The reason that superior orders of a nonmilitary variety do not serve as a defense to a criminal charge is that the requirements of discipline, the administration of penalties for disobedience, and the opportunities for inquiring into lawfulness are all different, and a person ordered to engage in unlawful acts in any of these other settings is not deprived of his ability to question and to refuse to comply.

1.2.5. Justifiable ignorance of the law. Although ignorance of the law has exculpatory force only under very special circumstances, it does serve to avoid blame when ignorance or incorrect belief about the law misled the accused or kept him in the dark and made him unable to act as the law required. If reliable authoritative pronouncements assert that something *must* be done, and later it is determined that resulting acts are unlawful, one who so acted because he believed the law required it may claim that he had to do it, for he was truly (though mistakenly) coerced by the authority of the law.

There is a second way in which ignorance of the law may deprive a person of meaningful ability to do·otherwise. If a law is not promulgated sufficiently and a privilege to act contrary to its provisions exists prior to its enactment, those affected by the law might rightly claim that their privilege continues, since no public notice of its termination was given and there was no reason to inquire whether the privilege was still in existence. In effect such persons lacked the opportunity to conform their conduct to the law, inasmuch as they lacked the opportunity to acquaint themselves with it. And as we know, lack of opportunity is one way of being unable.

1.2.6. Mens rea *requirement is not met.* It is often claimed by way of exculpation that *mens rea* requirements have not been met. When this means what it should, it means that what was done intentionally by the accused does not measure up to the standard of first-dimension culpability which the law has set for the crime charged. In part this is a claim weakly denying responsibility. Suppose, by way of illustration, that under the law there is criminal liability for knowingly appropriating another's property. I see something that I assume (wrongly) to be abandoned and take it, though under the circumstances any prudent person would first make inquiry. When charged with theft, I admit that I took the article negligently, perhaps even recklessly, but certainly not knowingly. In part (and it is the weaker part) my claim is that my assumption made me unable to appreciate the harm I was doing, hence unable to choose because of an appreciation of the harm not to do it. Such a claim would by itself rightly be regarded as much too feeble to enable me to escape blame, for surely the debilitating assumption I made could have been questioned by me, and should have been. Another and stronger part of this claim rests on the culpability principle and would (as we shall see) avoid blame altogether. Weak though it is, however, the denial of responsibility will moderate blame and leave an accused person better off than he would have been had he assumed that the item he found was someone else's property, and so had been able to appreciate the harm in what he did.

1.2.7.   Entrapment.   Entrapment is a defense well recognized in the United States, and is available when a law enforcement officer or his agent instigates the commission of a crime in order to obtain evidence for a prosecution, even though the perpetrator was not independently disposed to commit the crime. The main reason for allowing such a defense is to discourage undesirable law enforcement practices, and so, just as with exclusionary rules that prevent introduction of evidence obtained illicitly by the police, exculpatory considerations are not the main reasons for recognizing the defense. There are, however, certain exculpatory aspects to the defense. Usually entrapment is accomplished by undercover police officers or by those cooperating with them, and the true identity or affiliation of the entrapping party is not known to the one who is entrapped. Sometimes, however, this is not the case, and it is by virtue of the very authority of the law that the entrapment is brought about.

A police officer might direct that a criminal act be done, and unwilling or at least unenthusiastic compliance might be forthcoming because the authority of the law stands behind the order. As part of a crackdown on police bribery, people in businesses in which bribes are customarily given to the police might be solicited by policemen and arrested when they comply. There is then a form of coercion in which the authority of the law with its implied threats is used as an instrument of extortion. In such a case the defense of entrapment available to the hapless businessman when he is prosecuted for bribery rests in part on his seriously impaired ability to refuse the solicitation and remain law-abiding. Seen in this light, the defense is a denial of responsibility of the same sort that appears more generally in exculpatory claims based on coercion.

1.2.8. Provocation. Provocation is a defense available to a person charged with murder who can show that he lost his self-control as a result of some provocation that normally might cause loss of self-control. If the defense is successful, he is liable for manslaughter rather than for murder. The mental state of such a person is unusual but not abnormal. Although there is disagreement about the admission of idiosyncracies as part of the circumstances, it is a point much stressed in the law that the extreme emotional reaction of the accused and his loss of self-possession must be normal under the circumstances. His behavior must be of a kind that is occasionally part of the reaction repertory of most people, even though for most of us it does not often take a homicidal form.

Incidents such as being assaulted or witnessing an act of marital infidelity by one's own spouse are well-established provocation sufficient for the defense, but many other situations also are now widely recognized, so long as the loss of self-control might reasonably be expected as a consequence of the provocation. There is here an extremely strong exculpatory claim, one based in part on the inability of the actor to moderate his reaction because of a temporary failure of his inhibitory resources. In this aspect of the defense, it does not matter whether the provocation was an act of the victim or whether it was something else.

1.2.9. Impossibility of compliance. A person cannot help failing to do the impossible. If by law roads must be kept in repair by property owners, but the roads are under flood waters, that fact will furnish grounds of exculpation. If the presence in the country of an unregistered enemy alien is against the law, but the alien has been forcibly brought into the country by the authorities and kept unregistered in their custody, that fact again will provide the substance of an exculpatory claim that points to the impossibility of doing what the law requires. The claim is simply that there was no opportunity to comply with the law—which is one way of being unable to. It is an extremely strong denial of responsibility, since the claim of inability in this form needs little, if any, qualification.

III. A SURVEY OF EXCULPATORY CLAIMS THAT DENY CULPABILITY DIRECTLY

So far all the exculpatory claims that we have looked at cut the ground from under an accusation by denying that there is even eligibility for blame, much less conduct that merits blame. Now we come to those exculpatory claims that deny culpability directly by pointing to some deficiency in one or more of the four dimensions of culpability which we distinguished in Chapter Three. The claim now is that the act, be-

cause of this deficiency, does not meet the minimum standard
of culpability for the crime which the law has set. Since liability depends upon that standard's being met, there is no liability
if this denial of culpability is successful.

CONDUCT-REGARDING CLAIMS

While denials of responsibility have two main branches, direct denials of culpability have three. The first is, once again,
conduct-regarding, for all claims along this branch call attention to something about the conduct alleged that diminishes
or eliminates its culpability.

    2.1.1.   There was no act.   As we have already seen, it is
an affront to the responsibility principle to have criminal liability simply for *being,* without *doing.* But the claim that
there was no act appeals to the culpability principle as well,
for, in denying that there was any act at all, it denies that
there was dangerous conduct.

    One form that this claim may take is the simple assertion
that, although there was an untoward occurrence, it was a
mere happening and not an act. The sheet of glass in the wall
of the skyscraper was under stress in high winds and just
popped out—no one pushed it, or installed it defectively, or
in any other way *did* anything to bring about the mishap.

    Another form of such claim is an assertion that, although
there may have been an intention, there was no act. The accused may simply have intended to do something criminal,
and may have furnished evidence of his intention by communicating to others what he had resolved to do and by other
activities which indicate that he had such an intention. But
if activities serving as evidence of an intention do not serve
to fulfill it, the activities are not criminal simply by virtue of
the intention they evidence, for it is no crime simply to intend, no matter what is intended.

    Lawyers and judges often say that this is because no one

can be sure what is in the mind of the accused—"The thought of man is not triable, the devil alone knoweth the thought of man"—and that, in any case, a person has a right to privacy that includes the right to be free from intrusion by others for matters exclusively mental. The general concern for certainty and for privacy which underlies these explanations is admirable, but the reasons given are not the right ones. Since matters of intention are often made abundantly clear through words and deeds, the concern for privacy in such cases is otiose. Furthermore, a crime such as compassing the death of the king bears witness to the possibility of prosecutions for intention that are based on evidence no less reliable than that which is commonly introduced when ordinary crimes are prosecuted. Although it is true that often no clear evidence of intention is available, quite often there is also no clear evidence available to establish liability for common crimes, and in either case the prosecution fails for want of evidence.

There are two closely connected reasons why mere intention is not enough for criminal liability, and both relate to the third dimension of culpability. A person who merely intends but has not yet acted to fulfill his intention may still change his mind and abandon his private criminal purpose. (Abandonment is considered more fully in the discussion of renunciation at the end of this group of claims.) But it is the fact that intentions by themselves are not truly dangerous in the first place that allows the possibility of a changed mind to have its exculpatory significance. Sticks and stones may break bones, and acts that direct them at people are therefore dangerous; but mere intentions to use them against others do not threaten harm.

The objection to punishing for intentions is not solely of academic interest, for throughout history conspiracy laws have been in disfavor when they represent punishment for criminal intentions. A common intention formed and harbored in concert by two people or by a hundred may still be an intention and nothing more, just as it would be if it were a private intention formed and nurtured by a single person alone. The shared criminal intention is the essence of the criminal conspiracy, and although there are dangers presented by shared intentions which are not inherent in private intentions, the danger represented by the conspiratorial intention is not sufficient by itself for criminal liability. Reflecting this, the law of conspiracy requires for liability an act in furtherance of the purpose of the conspiracy and not simply an act in furtherance of the formation and development of the conspiracy.

2.1.2. Mens rea *requirement not met.* Another exculpatory claim that has already been mentioned shows a second face here (and soon will show a third). When looking at conduct rather than at the actor, we may again say that *mens rea* requirements have not been met, and for that reason a crime has not been committed. Now we point to a deficiency in the conduct rather than in the actor, for the conduct is not sufficiently dangerous to meet the culpability requirement set by the law for the crime charged. There is, then, a deficiency in the third dimension of culpability, and this will in turn cause a failure in the first dimension. An art dealer, we might suppose, notices certain things indicating that the painting he wishes to sell is a copy, but he proceeds to sell it as an original just the same. The law makes it a criminal offense knowingly to sell a work of art as an original when it is a copy, and the dealer is indicted. He claims that the signs of a copy were not unambiguous and that he may have acted negligently, even recklessly, but not knowingly in selling the copy as an original. In essence his claim then is that his conduct was less dangerous than the law requires it to be for liability.

2.1.3. *Invalidity, inapplicability, or nonexistence of the (alleged) law.* Sometimes a law on the books that is said to create liability for what was done turns out not to be a valid law. Sometimes the law, although valid, turns out not to cover this case. And sometimes (though not often) it turns out that there is no such law on the books. In all these cases, from a legal point of view there is nothing criminally wrong in what the accused has done. In all of them it turns out that the criminal law has not effectively recognized the thing that was done as a crime, and so did not create liability for the conduct alleged in the accusation.

Denying criminal liability in this way comes down in part to a denial that conduct is culpable as a threat or an instance of some harm that the law has effectively recognized. In this aspect it is the second dimension of culpable conduct that is brought into question. But the claim is also in part a denial that from a legal point of view the conduct can be regarded as in any measure dangerous, since without applicable law effectively on the books there can be no threat of what the law sees as harm constituted by what the accused does. Looked at this way, the exculpatory claim points to the third dimension of culpability.

Although these claims are all ultimately exculpatory in either of the two ways just indicated, much of the time it would be misleading to represent them as primarily exculpatory.

In the United States, for example, it is true that a constitutional argument attacking the validity of a law sometimes points to a harm that the legislation purports to deal with, and maintains that such harm is not a fit subject for legislation; or, alternatively, that the act prohibited by the law does not threaten a harm that the law admittedly may deal with. More often, however, constitutional arguments for invalidity are based on the purported violation by the law of specific rights guaranteed by the Constitution, such as free speech or free press or free religious practice. And sometimes the law is said to be invalid because it is too vague. The claim is then not primarily exculpatory, though ultimately it has that effect by nullifying the law's definition of harm and of dangerous conduct. Furthermore, when arguments for invalidity rest simply on claims of legislative irregularity, they do not at all question the government's right to prohibit what the law purports to prohibit; and so again in spite of their exculpatory effect they cannot be regarded as essentially exculpatory.

When the law is attacked as inapplicable, once again the claim may be exculpatory in intent or it may be exculpatory only in effect. Arguments interpreting the provisions of the law so as to exclude from its coverage the conduct of the accused may be to the effect that such conduct does not fall within the bounds of what was intended to be prohibited by the law. The issue, then, must inevitably be, What exactly was the legislative conception of the harm and of threats of it? But the argument might not raise the issue of legislative intention at all, only the question of what meaning may reasonably be given to the terms of the statute so that only conduct that is clearly prohibited by its language is punished. In that case, once again the argument has an exculpatory effect even though it does not touch on anything that directly affects culpability. A claim that a law does not prohibit certain conduct with sufficient clarity to bring that conduct within the law's coverage is not itself a claim that the conduct lacks culpability; yet it furnishes the foundation for a further claim that this is the case, since as a result the law does not prohibit such conduct.

A claim that no such law exists always has an exculpatory effect, though it is an odd claim rarely heard in the context of ordinary legal proceedings, since officials usually know whether or not a law is in fact on the books. But sometimes the jurisdictional powers of a court or of a legislature are put in question because there is uncertainty about the boundaries of the sovereign power of the political entity from which the legislature or court derives its authority. In such a case the very existence of a law within the legislature or adjudicatory jurisdiction of the government that now seeks to prosecute under it may be brought into question, with direct exculpatory consequences if the challenge is successful.

2.1.4. Insufficient conduct. Sometimes not enough has been done to pose a clear and present threat of the harm that concerns the law. When that is the case, there is in the eyes of the law not even an attempt to commit the crime, and so no criminal liability. The exculpatory claim is, in essence, that the conduct was not sufficiently dangerous for liability to be imposed for it. It is therefore a clear case of conduct that is deficient in the third dimension of culpability. This form of exculpation is often presented in criminal law texts under the rubric of "mere preparation," and an examination of the claim will occupy us at the beginning of the next chapter. It is not only charges of attempt that provide opportunity for exculpation of this sort, however. Accusation of any other "anticipatory" or "inchoate" crime, such as conspiracy or solicitation to commit a crime, or of being an accessory to a crime, also invites the defense that not enough was done by the person accused; or more exactly, that what he did was by itself not sufficiently dangerous to warrant liability.

2.1.5. Harm, which did not occur, was not expectable. When not only does harm not occur, but the conduct in question is not even of the sort to pose a threat of it, it might be said that the harm is simply not expectable, and hence there ought not to be liability for an attempt. Such an exculpatory claim again points to a deficiency in the third dimension of culpable conduct, and we shall consider this claim in detail in the second section of Chapter Six where defenses of impossibility to charges of attempt are investigated.

2.1.6. Harm, which did occur, was not expectable. When harm *does* occur, there is opportunity for the same sort of defensive strategy, but this time by claiming that the conduct of the accused was not the right sort to cause the harm; or put another way, that with regard to the conduct, the harm was not expectable. Again it is the dangerousness of the conduct that is put in issue, and so once again culpability in the third dimension is in question. Our discussion of causation in the third section of the next chapter takes up these matters.

2.1.7. Renunciation. Though the law on this point is not well settled, there is much in principle as well as in authority to support the claim that a previous renunciation of criminal purpose by the accused may under certain circumstances serve him later as a defense. Even though what he did presents a *prima facie* case of liability for attempt or for solicitation of a crime, or for conspiracy to commit it or facilitation of it, the accused may escape liability if he had voluntarily and effectively abandoned his criminal activity before doing any harm. He cannot simply postpone the criminal project or divert himself from one crime to another; nor can he make use of the defense if his abandonment was motivated by events that created a fear of apprehension, or by some obstacle to success which he encountered and which discouraged him. To enjoy the defense he may even be required to have taken strong measures to prevent the perpetration of the crime by others, particularly when he has solicited someone else to commit a crime, in which case timely countermanding in the strongest terms would be the very least that the law ought to require of him if he is to enjoy this defense.

The defense is primarily (though not exclusively) an exculpatory claim whose point is that the full course of conduct that includes an effective renunciation is not a criminal act sufficiently dangerous to warrant liability. It is a claim akin to the claim of insufficient conduct noted above, for though in the case of renunciation there is conduct that is sufficiently dangerous when it is abstracted from the whole and viewed in isolation as a part, still the entire course of conduct taken as a whole is not sufficiently dangerous. It is not the case that, having passed the point of dangerousness at which liability may attach, there is no longer the possibility of return. Dangerousness of conduct may be diminished or increased so long as it is not yet fixed by the occurrence of harm.

In part, the defense of renunciation does not rest upon an exculpatory claim at all, but rather upon a policy of the law that aims at providing an incentive for the abandonment of criminal projects by those who pursue them before they do harm. It is thus the carrot of immunity whose complementary stick is punishment. But providing this inducement cannot be the whole or even the main reason for recognizing a defense of renunciation. If it were, there would be no need to require a voluntary abandonment which is self-originating and not the result of risks or difficulties that present themselves in the course of the criminal endeavor. Indeed, if immunity were also available to those who hesitated for these reasons, it would serve a valuable purpose in many borderline cases, for in conjunction with the risks or difficulties that stand in the way, the welcome prospect of immunity from prosecution would be just the additional weight needed to tip the balance in favor of abandonment before harm is done.

It has been suggested in the comment of the Model Penal Code that the dangerousness of the person is shown to be less by his renunciation; and it is this, rather than the lesser danger of conduct, that is offered there as a reason for recognizing the defense. In one sense of "dangerous person," of course, anyone who engages in dangerous conduct is a dangerous person, and he is exactly as dangerous as his conduct is. But that sense is trivial, since it amounts only to an elliptical way of talking about dangerous conduct; and the statement asserting that everyone who engages in dangerous conduct is himself dangerous turns out to be nothing more than a license for this elliptical usage, and likewise trivial. What is important is a way of telling which persons among those who engage in dangerous conduct have a continuing disposition to engage in it, and nothing about that can be inferred simply from the fact of renunciation on some particular occasion. Many who are not normally disposed to commit crimes may abandon their extraordinary criminal adventure and enjoy the benefits of renunciation, but so may many persons who in general are disposed to commit crimes but on this occasion find that their resolve has for some reason weakened.

ACTOR-REGARDING CLAIMS

Exculpatory claims that deny culpability directly have a short second branch that is *actor-regarding*. Both claims on this branch deny culpability in its first dimension.

2.2.1. There was no act. The first of these actor-regarding claims is yet another aspect of the claim—already noticed twice—that there was no act. If the accused merely *was* something, or merely *intended* something, nothing was done, and so nothing was done *intentionally*. Since culpability requires something to be done intentionally, under such circumstances culpability is impossible, even though there may have been a dangerous occurrence with which persons can be associated simply by their intentions or by what they are.

2.2.2. Mens rea *requirement was not met.* There are several ways in which the *mens rea* requirement is not met, because things are done *unintentionally*.

Sometimes *what the actor did,* though dangerous enough, was not done intentionally, which is the case when *a mistake is made*. This act of his then diverged from the course of activities upon which he had embarked ("The art dealer, failing to notice the marks of a copy, sold an imitation to his customer by mistake"). Sometimes *what happened,* though dangerous enough, was not intentional, in which case there was *a mistake in what happened*. Not his act itself then, but the result of it, diverged from the enterprise ("The art dealer, because of his confusion about his customers' identities, swindeled Alfred Smith by mistake, for he meant Arthur Smith to get the fake and Alfred Smith the genuine work").

In addition to mistakes there are accidents, and they, too, are ways in which things are done unintentionally. Exculpating accidents come in two varieties, and the claims based on such accidents parallel claims based on mistake. "The art dealer sold the imitation by accident" is an instance of the general claim *he did it by accident*. If what brought about his selling of *that* picture was simply not within his control, even though it resulted from what he did, we have such a case. The art dealer might, for example, sell it by accident if a switch that he knows nothing about had been made in the warehouse sometime before, and he now orders the picture stored there to be shipped to his customer. In contrast to *he did it by accident* we have the claim *it happened by accident*. "The customer was swindled by accident," we might say, in which case the suggestion would be that even though the art dealer may appear to have caused his customer to be swindled, such an appearance is wrong: the art dealer actually did not order *that* picture shipped, but rather the genuine one, though his instructions were misunderstood.

For a mistake, then, it is necessary only that *control not be exercised;* whereas for an accident the act or the result *must not be within the actor's control*. In all these cases of something's being done or of something's happening, whether by mistake or by accident, what is done or what appears to be done is unintentional. When what is done or when what appears to be done is sufficiently dangerous but is nevertheless unintentional, the *mens rea* requirement set by the law is not met. While resort to "by mistake" or "by accident" does cover a multitude of unintentional things, it does not cover all. "They did not kill anyone intentionally. They planted

the bomb to blow up the government offices as an act of protest, and as a result killed several employees." By mistake?
By accident? Neither captures properly the available claim.
But what does hold true whenever *mens rea* is absent is that
what was done (or what happened) was unintentional.

INTEREST-REGARDING CLAIMS

The third branch of exculpatory claims that deny culpability
directly are *interest-regarding*. All such claims urge the legitimacy of what was done in spite of its harmful character, so
that what at first might appear to be wrong turns out upon
fuller consideration to be an act that does not deserve condemnation.

In judging harmful acts the interests of the victim always
have first claim on our attention, but often other interests are
also served by these acts, and these interests deserve consideration as well. Thus, I may have very good reasons for killing a man, and sometimes these reasons are so good that my
homicidal conduct ought not to be regarded as criminal at
all. My own legitimate interests or the interests of others may
require that injury be done, or at least allowed as an option.
Usually the circumstances make it clear that certain interests
must yield to others, and that interests whose protection is
beyond dispute can be protected only if other interests are
sacrificed. Sometimes, though more rarely, the harm is justified when it is not grievous, when the benefit to be gained
through it is a matter of social necessity, and when no other
method of obtaining the benefit is feasible.

It is the distinguishing feature of this range of exculpatory
claims, then, that a larger field of interests is admitted into
deliberation, so that not only the interests whose violation is
said to be a criminal harm is considered but also the interests
that are served by doing that harm. This way of escaping
blame is commonly called a justification, and in all its varieties it denies culpability by reference to what we have called

the "fourth dimension," in which countervailing interests are weighed in the balance. Many (though not all) justifications are governed by a principle of necessity holding that useless or needless acts in support of worthy interests are not justifiable if the actor is bound to appreciate that they were not necessary. This principle receives more extended consideration in Chapter Nine, when justification of punishment is investigated.

In addition to justifications for harming another person, there are in the interest-regarding group two exculpatory claims that are found in some cases in which there are injuries, but some doubt about whether there is harm. Not the fourth dimension of culpability, but the second, is appealed to by these claims of consent and of inoffensive conduct, for the gist of the claim is that there is at most *injury* but not *harm*.

2.3.1.   There was no act.   The assertion that there was no act appears here with yet a fourth face. Regardless of what he is or what he intends, everyone has an interest in being left alone so long as he does not engage in what is designated as criminal conduct; and this interest takes precedence over interests in security that may be marginally encroached upon by the existence of undesirable people in the community or by the presence of people who have some intention to do harm. One is therefore justified in being what one wishes to be or in harboring whatever intentions one has. Laws purporting to disregard this are subject to challenge on these grounds in ways that were indicated earlier.

2.3.2.   Compulsion.   Either circumstances or other persons may in some way compel acts that on their face are criminal. We have already noticed that *actor-regarding* denials of responsibility are available when this happens, but there are also important *interest-regarding* aspects to these exculpatory claims. All these features of the claim will be examined in the second section of Chapter Seven, and we need take only brief preliminary notice of the interest-regarding aspects here.

In general, only unlawful force, and not any coercive force or threat of it, will serve as grounds of exculpation, for if the coercive force is lawful it does not threaten legitimate interests of the person who is being coerced. A second point concerns the nature of the coercion, for in general it must be one's person or the person of another that is being made subject to coercion. Threats to a person's property or other kinds of threats that foreshadow harm only to those things which a person enjoys are not generally regarded as sufficient, nor are threats relating to interests possessed not by persons but by entities other than persons, such as pets, or governments. In some legal systems the rule is even more restrictive, so that only when the person threatened is closely related to the one being coerced is the exculpatory claim recognized—presumably on the theory that only then does the one coerced have an interest substantial enough to justify his compliance.

A third *interest-regarding* feature is a weighing in the balance of interests to be protected and interests to be sacrificed, requiring for justification that the harm to be avoided in situations of danger be greater than the harm that is done or that is threatened in order to avoid such harm. In some bodies of criminal jurisprudence there is the further qualification that only the avoidance of especially serious harms will justify harm done in order to avoid harm.

Finally, principles of criminal jurisprudence not uncommonly diminish the exculpatory force of compulsion when it was the culpable conduct of the accused that brought about the need to do harm in order to avoid harm. A man may recklessly place himself in a situation of danger and then be forced to take reckless measures that are criminal in order to escape harm. In denying his claim of compulsion, the law in effect gives less weight to his interests because by placing them in peril he has himself already disparaged them.

Claims of compulsion are of two main kinds, the first pointing to coercion by some other person, while claims of the second kind point to some regrettable necessity imposed by circumstances. In legal theory, constraint by another person is usually regarded as grounds for excuse rather than justification, while constraint by dint of circumstances is regarded as the basis of justification. We learn more about excuses in Chapter Eight, but in the meantime might observe here that only justifications and not excuses are interest-regarding. A good reason why only necessity imposed by circumstances is usually taken by lawyers to be a justification is that necessity normally presents a choice between two sets of interests—one to be respected and one to be protected—which both the actor and those who later judge him must weigh in the balance. Coercion, on the other hand, is a claim that places emphasis on the typically nondeliberative state of mind of the actor who is subject to the threat of force or to force itself.

2.3.3. Military orders.   In our first glimpse, military orders were viewed as an *actor-regarding* denial of responsibility, for the constraints of habitual discipline, the threat of punishment for disobedience, and the difficulties of challenging the lawfulness of the order all conspire to make a person who is subject to military orders unable to refuse to obey. But there is an *interest-regarding* aspect as well. There is a social interest in having military orders obeyed unquestioningly to enhance the efficiency of the military machine, and that interest counts heavily in favor of anyone who (in the absence of manifest unlawfulness) does what he is ordered to do without question. There is not an exorbitant cost incurred in protecting this important social interest, which the obedient soldier invokes when he is accused of criminal conduct, for the law imposes criminal liability at a higher level. Those ordering the criminal acts are themselves subject to criminal prosecution for what their subordinates have done in carrying out their orders. Indeed, under a principle of command responsibility recognized in the laws of war, they may even be held liable for crimes committed by those in their command though nothing in their orders required or countenanced such crimes.

2.3.4. Justifiable ignorance of the law. Ignorance of the law has already appeared in two forms as an *actor-regarding* denial of responsibility. In addition to the claim of authoritative requirement of unlawful acts and the claim of unpromulgated legal curtailment of what one is previously privileged to do, there is an *interest-regarding* claim. The best authoritative opinion at the time may have held that one may lawfully act in a certain way, and later a contrary view— again on the best authority—supplants that opinion. By appeal to the earlier view, an accusation based on the later view may be defended against. The theory of the defense is that there is a strong social interest in being able at any time to ascertain and then rely on responsible authoritative opinions of the state of the law, free of any risk of criminal prosecution should another view be deemed better at a later time.

2.3.5. Entrapment. Entrapment has already been identified as a marginal exculpatory claim when as an *actor-regarding* denial of responsibility it was viewed as a kind of coercion to crime under some threat that bore the color of legal authority. Under color of legal authority, there is also an *interest-regarding* aspect of entrapment.

Normally, a police officer who directs that some act be done is entitled to a citizen's cooperation, since he is presumed to be enforcing the law or performing some other duty in the public interest. Because public safety and public order much depend upon it, there is an important social interest in having citizens generally disposed to comply with police instructions. When a person not independently disposed to commit a crime does so as a result of instigation by a police officer acting under color of his authority, that social interest may (within limits) be invoked by way of exculpation. The Model Penal Code, for example, allows the defense of entrapment under such circumstances when (knowingly) false representations are made to induce a belief that the proposed act is not prohibited. But though the social interest in compliant citizens is in some ways similar to the social interest in obedient soldiers, police instructions are not given the exculpatory weight of military orders, since the need for uncritical compliance is not nearly so great. The defense of entrapment in such circumstances is therefore more qualified than the corresponding defense of military orders.

2.3.6. Provocation. There is yet another exculpatory claim that is an *actor-regarding* denial of responsibility in one aspect and a direct *interest-regarding* denial of culpability in another. Provocation will sometimes reduce murder to manslaughter when the actor has lost control of himself because of the emotional state produced by the provocation. But what the law admits as sufficient provocation it admits very charily, and it does not infer merely from a loss of self-control brought about by some act of the victim that the act constituted legally sufficient provocation. A court may agree that the accused had lost all control as a result of provocation by the victim and was acting in precisely the emotional state required by the law for a defense of provocation—and yet reject the defense because the provocation was not of a kind that the law recognizes. It was not reasonable (as some judges put it) to react in that way to such provocation; or (as some judges say) the "reasonable" or "ordinary" or "average" man would not react in that way to such provocation.

This limitation of the defense is really a restriction to cases in which the accused had an interest that he was entitled to vindicate. There is only a limited measure of exculpation in pointing to the provocative assault or scene of infidelity to which one responded homicidally, and so provocation is not a complete defense. But a great many interests are so important that extreme reaction to what offends against them is not unreasonable; and the defense, though only partial, might plausibly be invoked even when the provocation is only a barrage of particularly offensive insults. Changing moral values elevate in importance some interests while reducing others, and this is reflected in the changing standards of acceptable provocation that are exhibited in jury verdicts, so that racial slurs of an extreme kind might in some circles now be regarded as a more substantial provocation than the sight of marital infidelity.

2.3.7. Justification for use of force; acts of public duty; violation of property rights. Justifications for the use of force under a variety of circumstances can be found in any penal code. Each justification has as its gravamen some interest or set of interests which the accused is privileged or is obligated to serve, and which furnish exculpation when in the service of these interests there is a use of force that would normally be criminal. Because justifications for the use of force are more purely interest-regarding than are other exculpatory claims, several general points about interest-regarding exculpation shine through them with special clarity.

Interests are by their nature opposed to one another. At a very high level of generality we might say that interests in security are often in opposition to interests in liberty. This means, among other things, that an interest in apprehending those suspected of criminal acts is opposed by an interest in not being interfered with when the authorities have only strong suspicions but no proof.

Again at a high level of generality, there are interests in security that are in opposition to interests in justice. This means, for example, that there is an interest in protecting oneself from a burglar who might conceivably use deadly force to escape if he is not disabled first by deadly force, and that this interest is in opposition to another interest of social importance: that every man is entitled to his day in court if that is at all possible. Deciding claims of justification when one person's interests are violated in the course of protecting or vindicating the interests of others requires some sorting and weighing of the interests that are opposed to one another. Several different considerations enter into this.

Some things that are of value are legitimate, others are not. It is no surprise, then, that some interests are legitimate and others are not. But only legitimate interests are to be taken into account in deciding whether what was done is justifiable. Burglars have an interest in escaping, and all criminals have an interest in remaining at large. The question of what a householder may do when he surprises a prowler at night or what the police may do when they have reason to take a suspect into custody cannot be affected by those illegitimate interests.

Since things of value may be of a greater or a lesser value, interests may be more or less weighty, and this introduces a second consideration. Human life is of greater value than property, and so a greater weight attaches to an interest in life than attaches to an interest in property. For this reason, shooting a mere trespasser cannot on the face of the matter be justified.

The weightiness of an interest reflects value to anyone in general. But there are special considerations which make certain of our interests stronger and improve our standing to act when these interests are threatened. When regarded simply as human life, everyone's life is of equal value, and an interest in any human life is of equal weight with an interest in any other human life. But I have a stronger interest in my own life and in the lives of those near and dear to me than I have in the life of a stranger. As with interests in general, value is determined by objective standards. What matters in gauging the strength of my interest is the value to me of those lives according to standards that generally prevail, and not simply how much I happen to value them. How much I may like the stranger or hate my wife is not a consideration that bears on the strength of my interest, and so it does not enter into decisions about whether I was justified in using force to protect one or the other.

Interests are often countervailing; and when countervailing interests are all legitimate, some legitimate interests are in effect sacrificed by the law in order to protect and to vindicate others. Not infrequently, deciding what to sacrifice seems to involve an assessment of the relative weight and strength of legitimate interests that are in competition with one another so that those of greater and more immediate value will prevail. The balancing model is commonly adopted as the model of resolution, but it is the right one only if it is used to evaluate the interests of the accused in the particular situation in which he found himself. What is being decided is not whether the victim deserved the harm he suffered, but only whether the interests of the accused were sufficient to relieve him from blame for what he did. What is called for is not an equitable weighing of interests to see on which side the balance lies, but a consideration of whether the interests of the accused were substantial enough under the circumstances to warrant impunity. Since the value of our legitimate interests must inevitably be affected by the legitimate interests of others when ours and theirs come into conflict, balancing of a sort is always appropriate.

Except for a special group of paternalistic justifications to be discussed later, plainly avoidable harming is never justifiable even though an assessment of interests discloses a clear preponderance in favor of the harm-doer; and so it is always appropriate to ask whether the harmful act was necessary. If a reasonable alternative was plainly available to the actor so that harm could be avoided, he cannot then claim that the course he chose was not wrong. His worthier cause does not confer upon him a right to do as he wishes, but only the more limited license to act as he must, even though harm is done by it. It is often no easy matter to decide when an alternative is reasonable, and the law must sometimes draw lines that seem morally mislocated in order not to call either for risk or for sacrifice that is unreasonable. There is also the problem of mistakes. An actor may not see his situation as it plainly is and may wrongly believe that there is a need to do harm. Again the law must draw lines, so that the accused is judged with proper allowance for ordinary human failings, yet with not so great an allowance that he may be judged only according to his own beliefs no matter how unreasonable they are or how rash his acting on them might have been.

Standard justifications for the use of force as they are formulated in the Model Penal Code reveal the significance of these general points. Self-protection heads the list, and scrutiny of the terms used to define and qualify the defense, though a somewhat tedious affair, will disclose much about the fine points of justification.

2.3.7.1. Self-protection. To be justifiable, the use of force for self-protection must be *believed* to be necessary by the actor (which allows for his mistakes), and must be believed by him to be *immediately* necessary (which would not be the case if he believed that alternatives were available to him). Protection against the use of *unlawful force by such other person on the present occasion* must be the purpose. This purpose speaks first to the illegitimacy of the aggressor's interests under the circumstances, and then to the dearth of alternatives, which depends on the threat against which action is taken being here and now.

There are further important qualifications on the justifiable use of force for self-protection.

Resisting an arrest which the actor knows is being made *by a peace officer, even if unlawful,* is not a justifiable use of force (which points to an important countervailing social interest, and announces that it is still a legitimate one even in circumstances that taint it). There is also a qualification when force is used to resist force by an occupier or possessor of property, or *by another person on his behalf* when such a person uses force to protect the property *under a claim of right* (which points to the importance of a countervailing interest, acknowledges its strength even when the one acting in that interest does so only in a representative capacity, and sets requirements that must be met in order for the interest to be regarded as legitimate). In that case the use of force is justifiable only under special circumstances. It is justifiable if the actor is a *public officer performing his duty* or *a person lawfully assisting him* (which points to a social interest that weighs against property rights but is of paramount importance only when there is lawful action under public authority; it also indicates the breadth of that interest).

The use of force is also justifiable if the actor has been *unlawfully* dispossessed and is making *re-entry,* or if he believes that the force is necessary to protect himself against death or serious bodily harm (which again indicates the importance of certain interests, requires that the act truly serve the interest, and in the case of the first qualification requires that the countervailing interest not be a legitimate one).

The use of deadly force must meet special conditions if it is to be justified. Death, serious bodily harm, kidnapping, or sexual violation must be what the actor believes he is threatened by when he resorts to such extreme measures to protect himself (which points to the importance that the actor's interests must possess if he is to have the right to violate the interests of the one who acts against him). And one who provokes force against himself in the same encounter for the purpose of causing death or serious bodily harm is not then justified in his use of deadly force (which brands his interest illegitimate under those circumstances).

Subject to certain exceptions, the use of deadly force is also not justifiable when one can safely avoid it by retreating, or by surrendering possession to one who asserts a claim of right, or by complying with a demand that he abstain from doing anything that he has no duty to do (which says in effect that when there are *reasonable* alternatives to the use of deadly force, the principle of necessity bars the use of deadly force as needless). There are, however, exceptions that make the use of deadly force justifiable even under these circumstances. Retreat from a dwelling or place of work is not required unless the actor was the initial aggressor or is assailed in his place of work by another person whose place of work the actor knew it to be (which stipulates that there is no *reasonable* alternative to the use of deadly force under the specified circumstances, and suggests how the interests on balance are affected by matters affecting their legitimacy).

Another exception applies to a peace officer justified in using force in performing his duties or a person justified in using force to assist him or to make an arrest or prevent an escape. Such persons are not obliged to desist from their efforts because of resistance or threat of resistance by or on behalf of the person against whom the effort is directed (which points to social interests of paramount importance, to the range of activities that serve these interests, and, by implication at least, suggests that there is no reasonable alternative).

There is a provision allowing any person who uses self-protective force to estimate the necessity for such force in the circumstances as he believes them to be at the time (which provides maximum latitude for mistakes without affecting justifiability). Furthermore (perhaps bringing Plato's *Euthyphro* to mind), when the protective force consists of confinement other than arrest on a charge of crime, it is justifiable only if the actor takes all reasonable measures to terminate it as soon as he knows that he safely can (which is a straightforward assertion of the rule of necessity). Finally, in a blanket provision of the Code (which covers other justifications for the use of force as well), the use of force for self-protection is not justifiable when the actor is in error about the lawfulness of an arrest he endeavors to make by force, or about the unlawfulness of force used against him (which is a provision that sharply alters the balance of interests in situations of error by setting broader limits of legitimacy on one side and narrower ones on the other).

In the same section the Code also makes a defense of justification unavailable when the crime charged is one of negligent or reckless use of force, and the actor's determination of the necessity of using force was negligent or reckless; it makes the defense unavailable also in prosecutions for these crimes when innocent persons are the victims of the negligent or reckless use of force (which bars the defense for situations in which no argument based on interests can be devised, and gives full effect to the interests of innocent third parties, which on balance are even more important).

2.3.7.2. *Protection of others.* Protection of other persons is a second way in which the use of force may be justified. There is no limitation placed upon the relationship between the actor and another person whom he may justifiably protect (which as a kind of universal altruism makes equal in weight the interest each of us has in protecting anyone else or ourselves from harm). Throughout, the defense is shaped to conform with self-protection. Retreats, relinquishments, and compliances are not required unless the safety of the one being protected is ensured. The actor's belief is similarly qualified to allow for error. And location in the dwelling or place of work of either person would call for the same rule that applies when force is used for self-protection.

2.3.7.3. Protection of property. Use of force for the protection of property can take place under many different circumstances, and these differences make the difference between justifiable and unjustifiable use of force. The significance of all these different features can be understood by reference to the same general considerations that bear on protection of persons by the use of force. In cases of protection of property, the legitimacy of interests is affected by established rights of property, or by claims of property rights, or by possession under such claims.

The different weight of interests in property, and of countervailing interests in life and in physical safety, is pointed up by numerous qualifications. When force is used to protect property by a person who acts under the authority of another person, there are questions of strength of interest that are answered by limitations on the defense. No defense of justification puts more stress on matters bearing on the necessity of what was done. What one may do is hedged about by requirements of requests to be made and notices to be given prior to taking action, regard for the efficacy of less drastic measures, and a general preference for legal remedies over self-help whenever that is feasible.

2.3.7.4. Law enforcement. The use of force in law enforcement has its complications as well. Force may be used to make an arrest, to prevent escape from custody, to prevent commission of a crime, or to prevent someone from harming himself. The actor may be a law enforcement official, a private person assisting him, or a private person acting on his own. The force used may be deadly or something less, and the situation in which the use of force seems necessary may be one of greater or lesser urgency with regard to the dangers of the situation or to other matters prompting the use of force. The authority under which the actor purports to act may or may not be lawful. As with all other situations in which force seems necessary, what the actor believes about relevant legalities or about matters of fact may or may not be correct. All these circumstances bear on interests that are in a conflict, and the provision for justifiable use of force seeks to meet the legitimate needs of law enforcement at a cost in harm that does not make of it violence under law.

2.3.7.5. Special responsibilities. Many persons have a special responsibility for the care, discipline, or safety of others, and under certain circumstances the use of force may be required to discharge those responsibilities. Parents, guardians, teachers, nurses, doctors, wardens, flight attendants, and ship captains all might find themselves in a situation requiring the use of force. Safeguarding and promoting personal welfare, prevention or punishment of misconduct, maintenance of discipline, treatment of illness or injury, enforcement of prison rules, the safety of a group or of an individual, and even decorum might all at times require that force be used. Children, incompetents, patients, prisoners, passengers, and crew members might be the victims of such force. Death, bodily injury, disfigurement, pain, mental distress, and humiliation are harms that may occur because of the forcible measures taken.

With respect to the underlying interests that bear on justification, situations in which force of this kind may be employed are typically quite different from the other situations we have been considering. For one thing, force is often used for what is supposed to be the victim's own good, as when a child is disciplined, a patient subjected to medical treatment, or an unruly passenger made to stay in a safe place. Since these paternalistic measures are taken in the victim's own interest, the question of their justifiability involves consideration of two sets of the victim's interests that are now in conflict. One set of such interests is violated when the harm is done; another set of his interests is served by what was done, and is said therefore to justify it.

A second unusual feature in cases of force used against those who are in the care or custody of others is that often no harm is threatened by the victim to prompt the actor's paternalistic use of force, and so the situation does not call for an assessment of competing harms in deciding justifiability. Finally, justification in these situations does not turn so much on whether the use of force was really necessary as it does on whether it was warranted by the responsibilities borne by the actor in his special role, and whether it was the sort of measure that generally is deemed proper in discharging those responsibilities.

2.3.7.6. *Public duties.* The use of force is sometimes required for the execution of a public duty. Lawful military activity is a striking example, but there are others. Besides the use of force, execution of a public duty may require other acts that normally would be unlawful, and those too then need to be justified. This is generally a simple matter, for if the law authorizes or requires an act, it is justifiable just because of that. An interest in being able to act in conformity with the law must within a legal system pre-empt any countervailing interests. The social interest in being free to follow the law is of such importance that, according to the Model Penal Code, even when there is lack of jurisdiction in a court, or defects in legal process, or official acts that exceed legal authority, those who act in good faith—relying on the court order, the legal process, or the supposed authority of the official—are nevertheless justified in their use of force or in doing any other kind of act normally in contravention of the law.

2.3.7.7. Violation of property rights. Finally, certain acts may constitute property crimes and are sometimes justifiable. Destruction, appropriation, damage, intrusion, and interference all suggest acts of this sort. The Model Penal Code contains a simple blanket justificatory provision. Unless expressly or by clear implication the relevant criminal provisions preclude the justification, any circumstances that would establish a defense of privilege in a civil action based on the same acts furnish grounds of justification in a criminal prosecution. In effect this incorporates in the criminal law the assessment of conflicting interests that has gone on in the law of torts and, to a lesser extent, in the law of property.

2.3.8. Consent. Consent to inflict what the law regards as a harm, or to engage in conduct that threatens it, is sometimes a defense if the consent was given freely by the victim. In such case there is really no harm at all, but at most an injury. By his consent the victim has rendered inoffensive what the actor did, which means in effect that for the occasion he has renounced the interest whose violation would otherwise represent a harm done to him.

Though voluntary consent may sometimes be effective in this way, often it is not. There are two major restrictions. If in the eyes of the law a person is not competent to judge and to protect his interests, his consent is for that reason of no consequence. Those who are below the age of discretion and those who are mentally incompetent cannot be relied upon to know where their interests truly lie, and they may make victims of themselves when mature and normal persons would not. Under such circumstances the victim's consent cannot be allowed to convert harm to innocent injury.

The other restriction relates to the nature of the harm. If the harm in question is serious, and if the risk-laden conduct producing it is not privileged by social acceptance, consent is

ineffective to relieve from criminal liability. While it is true
that the injury we suffer might be only our business, the conduct producing it is a social concern. In spite of the consent
of the victim, such conduct may exceed the bounds of decency; and when it does, that is reason for it to be condemned
as a crime. In this, criminal liability and civil liability are
not alike. Civil liability must attach greater weight to consent in such cases since by his consent the victim normally
assumes responsibility for the injury that civil liability seeks
to redress.

In some cases of serious and unprivileged harm-doing,
there is another reason for disallowing consent as a defense
to criminal charges. Sometimes the harm done extends beyond the victim to those who depend on him and to those
upon whom he must depend. A man who agrees to be
harmed in ways that disable him may not be able to serve his
country or support his family. He may also become a burden
on those who must care for him—either as a public charge or
through family ties. In such cases the harm done appears to
be undiminished in spite of the victim's consent, for others
who have not consented are made to feel its effect; and because of this the culpability of the conduct through which the
harm was inflicted is no less by virtue of the consent. But in
cases that do not have such consequential features there is
reason to see the harm as somewhat less serious, and the conduct as therefore somewhat less culpable. In such cases the
victim's consent somewhat reduces in importance the interest
being violated, even though what is left after his renunciation is important enough to warrant some criminal liability
for its actual or threatened violation.

2.3.9. Lack of offensiveness.   When there is consent that
is effective to exculpate, it is because the consent renders inoffensive any conduct that causes an injury; hence there is no
harm. But inoffensiveness may be available as an exculpatory

claim under other circumstances as well. Three varieties suggest themselves, and the first two at least are what might be called *de minimis* defenses. Sometimes there is no harm because the act is too trivial as an encroachment upon the interest in question. For that reason a slight deliberate shove as one makes one's way to the back of a crowded bus cannot be an assault. But even when the encroachment is more substantial it may fail to be offensive because the give-and-take of social intercourse requires toleration of certain encroachments—at least if no refusal to tolerate them has been communicated to those who may otherwise rely on conventions of toleration. Thus, e.g., a hearty slap on the back, even though thoroughly disagreeable to the recipient, may nevertheless be inoffensive from a criminal point of view, since it is within the ordinary bounds of social intercourse, and no narrower bounds have been previously set by the victim.

Sometimes there simply is no encroachment upon an interest of the one who receives a blow, and this is a third case of inoffensiveness. If the blow is just accidental there is no harm, though the same blow delivered deliberately would certainly be an assault. In either case the blow may be far below what normally causes any kind of bodily injury, but when the blow is deliberate it is an offense to sensibility, since it normally humiliates the victim and puts him in fear of violence. The accidental blow, however, does not touch the dignity or security of the person who is struck, and for that reason there is no harm in it.

SPECIAL INTEREST-REGARDING CONSIDERATIONS

Most of the interest-regarding exculpations so far considered have been claims appropriate in special circumstances when alleged acts appear *prima facie* to be wrong under the criminal law. But justifications are not the only important form in which interest-regarding exculpation shows itself.

Certain classes of activities are deemed not *prima facie*

wrong but legitimate and beyond the purview of the criminal law, even though they often cause serious harm and are a
matter of continuing public concern. Automobile driving
and tunnel construction, for example, have strong credentials
as thoroughly dangerous activities posing very real threats
of death and bodily injury even when carried on in a safe
way, for there are hazards always present in these activities
which defy attempts to insure against all harm. But these
activities are regarded as legitimate and allowed because the
interests served through engaging in them are deemed more
important than countervailing interests in avoiding harm.

It is not, of course, that a tunnel is deemed more important than so many human lives, and thus on balance good
value at the statistically estimated cost. If it were necessary
at some stage in tunnel building to seal up one man who cannot be brought out after performing his work, and hence to
make the tunnel his tomb, we should certainly on those terms
prohibit tunnel building because it required deliberate human sacrifice. We should then have to weigh human lives
against tunnels, and choose the lives as more important. But
the assessment we are actually called upon to make is quite
different. *Risk* to human life is what we weigh in the balance.
A social interest in preventing loss of life competes with a
social interest in having tunnels, and on balance the interest
in preventing loss of life is found wanting. There is, after all,
a price to be paid for anything of value, and not infrequently
it must be paid in diminished protection of human life.
When we allow driving or tunnel building, we tolerate a statistical risk that can be translated into lives that actually are
lost and that would not have been lost had we not tolerated
the activity. But this is in no way inconsistent with our refusal
to tolerate the deliberate sacrifice of a single life.

Taking a life stands in sharp contrast to *not affording that
life maximum protection* by prohibiting activities that involve considerable risk of loss of life; and this contrast with

taking a life becomes especially clear when we think of the elaborate precautions that are taken to protect the life of each person on the job—precautions that make it far more likely than not that each person will survive. Even so, if the expected loss of life were far greater than it now is, we might well decide to prohibit tunneling, or at least allow it only when circumstances make it exceptionally important; for, if a great loss of life were in prospect, there would be a more serious compromise of our social interest in preventing loss of life whenever a tunnel was built, and as a consequence more weighty countervailing interests would be needed to avoid prohibition.

When activities are not regarded as legitimate and are deemed criminal according to prevailing views in society, there is another form that interest-regarding exculpation may take. This time the point of view is extralegal and the aim is to justify what was done in spite of its being unlawful and plainly not justifiable under the law. Within any society, save the simplest and most homogeneous, there are always different opinions about the legitimacy of certain types of activities. This is a reflection of different values that are at odds within the community, though often there is a strong consensus which has been given the force of law and holds that a particular activity is illegitimate. Others with dissenting views will then claim that the law is unjust because interests more important than those upheld by the law—libertarian interests—are transgressed by making such activities criminal.

Even broader criticism of this sort can be found outside of one society when those in one country criticize another country's prosecutions, which they say are political, even though they admit that valid criminal laws in the other country may have been broken by those found criminally liable there. The gist of their objection is that other and higher interests than those upheld by the criminal law are at stake. Freedom, equality, social justice, or some other high ideal to which all mankind must own allegiance is seen to have been served by the criminal act, and so, on this view, the more important interest in whose service the crime was committed justifies the crime.

Even more striking contrasts in viewpoint take place through the passage of time, which makes events appear altogether different in historical perspective. A man who was hanged, drawn, and quartered for high treason in England three hundred years ago is in our time made a saint, spoken of as a martyr, and is generally regarded outside his Church as well as in it as a moral hero. Finally, we must notice those figures like Socrates and Jesus who were condemned as criminals under law which, judged by the standards of the day, still seems sound enough, though in the perspective of history that fact seems curiously irrelevant to us now.

CHAPTER SIX
Conduct-Regarding Exculpation

Claims that we have classified as interest-regarding can lead us into vast regions of philosophical discussion and social controversy, for these claims raise questions about what really is harmful, and about what harmful acts ought to be tolerated or condoned by the law. Our inquiry into criminal justice merely skirts these questions because they are not important to the foundations of its theory, though in their own right they are most important and call for a separate investigation that is no less painstaking. In this chapter and the next an examination of the most prominent conduct-regarding and actor-regarding claims is undertaken, for it is claims of these two types that raise the crucial jurisprudential questions in developing a theory of criminal justice.

The claims discussed in the present chapter are found in the law of attempt liability and in cases in which liability turns on questions of causation. In the criminal law the defenses forming around these claims are to some extent complicated by subsidiary claims of other sorts, and to preserve these defenses in a form familiar to lawyers we shall take notice of these subsidiary features while concentrating attention on parts that are relevant to present theoretical concerns.

I. INSUFFICIENCY

In the criminal law it is sometimes necessary to distinguish
between attempts for which there may be liability and conduct which is less than an attempt and for which there is no
liability. It is usual to speak of this lesser activity as "mere
preparation." Efforts to discern the distinguishing marks have
not met with notable success. It is usual to rely on a model
of activity in which there is a sequence of events in three
stages—preparation, attempt, and consummation. It is assumed that attempt liability arises when there has been sufficient progress toward the final event in the sequence representing consummation, even though that event has not taken
place. It is as though a film that recorded a crime were to be
viewed in order to determine exactly which set of frames in
the reel comprise each of the three stages. Depending on the
precise point at which each division is made, there will be
liability for the completed crime, liability only for an attempt, or no liability at all.

When it comes to drawing the line between an attempt
and a completed crime there is hardly ever controversy. Since
the occurrence or non-occurrence of the harm prescribed for
the completed crime settles the matter, it is simply a matter
of seeing whether the harm has occurred. Only on those rare
occasions when the law has not made itself clear, and the exact character of the harm is uncertain, does dispute arise. In
principle, the difference between an attempt and mere preparation is no less clear. But there is no correspondingly easy
test to distinguish the two, and so there are often controversies as to whether conduct is one or the other.

There are good reasons for abandoning this model, for in
two respects it is seriously misleading. In the first place it mistakenly represents all criminal activity for which there may

be attempt liability as the sort of activity that has discrete stages—as though these criminal transactions were all like building a house, or performing surgery, or launching a rocket. Certain criminal activities do of course suit the model, and the planned crime comes immediately to mind. Weapons, tools, and a getaway car are first procured; the building is surveyed, then broken into; its rooms, and then the vault are penetrated; and finally the diamonds are taken. But many other criminal ventures that may call for drawing the line between preparation and attempt do not unfold so conveniently. A sales clerk realizes that a customer has just accidentally been short-changed and puts the difference aside, resolving to take the money himself, but the customer, having in the meantime discovered the mistake, returns to the counter and receives his change. A museum visitor sees a picture that deeply offends him and, thinking himself unobserved, he strikes a match intending to burn the painting; but when a nearby guard cautions him that smoking is not allowed, he blows out the match. A merchant deliberately misrepresents his merchandise in an advertisement, but unknown to him a better item conforming to the description in the ad has been erroneously delivered to the store by the manufacturer and has been put on sale as the advertised product. In all these cases we wish to give serious consideration to the possibility that the conduct in question was mere preparation; yet the conduct has not taken place at a preliminary stage occupied with preparation, for the purported criminal activity has no such preliminary stage in cases such as these.

The second problem with the usual model is converse to the first. Some activities do have stages of preparation, but acts that are part of the preparation may constitute an attempt. For example, preparations for an illegal abortion are sufficient to constitute an attempt to perform it, so that sterilizing the instruments, arranging the equipment, and preparing the patient on the operating table are no less the substance of an attempt than the medical procedures that aim at aborting the fetus.

The reason the model of sequences must be rejected is that what matters ultimately is not how far things have progressed toward the objective, but rather what the relation is between what has been done and the harm thought to be in prospect. If one claims that conduct constitutes mere preparation and is not sufficient for attempt liability, one must show that a true threat of harm was not created by what was done. There are three ways to do this.

The *first* way is to show that the conduct in question is itself innocent, and would raise a prospect of harm only when considered in combination with other conduct and in the light of special circumstances that would make it unambiguously dangerous. If a man planning arson buys matches, that conduct itself is innocent, even though his state of mind is not. What he did remains innocent unless there is other conduct or special circumstances that make the acquisition of the matches especially significant. That would be the case if the matches were acquired in prison where they were difficult to obtain, by a prisoner who had no need of them for any other purpose, and after he had arranged materials in a way that had no apparent purpose other than that of starting a fire. The act is then no longer ambiguous, and unless the obvious inference from what was done to the harm intended is rebutted, the act will serve as a basis of attempt liability. But if the act remains ambiguous, with nothing more than the actor's intention to connect what he did to the harm in prospect, it is an innocent act to be classified as preparation but not attempt.

The *second* way of denying attempt liability because of insufficiency is by pointing to lack (though not total absence) of commitment to the criminal enterprise in which the accused was involved. Normal inhibitory restraints that prevail most often do not disappear altogether in a moment of criminal resolution. Even after a person has done things that clearly are aimed at a criminal objective, inhibition may stand between what he has done and what he yet must do to bring about the harm. For this reason the criminal law includes a doctrine of abandonment by virtue of which timely voluntary renunciation of criminal purpose frees one from liability. The doctrine both encourages change of mind and gives due moral effect to it. It is altogether reasonable, then, that the law should also want to insulate from liability one who may not yet have fully made up his mind. The tinder may already have been carefully arranged, and even in isolation that can hardly be considered an innocent act like buying matches. Yet by itself it is insufficient commitment to a course of harm-producing conduct to be considered harm-threatening.

A *third* claim of insufficiency points to inability. A person may construct an elaborate incendiary device at home under circumstances making it perfectly clear that it is to be used to set fire to a building some miles away. There is no question then of its conceivably being an innocent act, nor can there be much doubt about commitment to a harm-producing course of conduct. Still, under the circumstances so much remains to be done before there is any chance of harm that we judge him not yet able to accomplish his purpose. His conduct cannot then be said to pose a real threat of harm, and so he cannot be said to have done enough to warrant attempt liability.

It is not inadequacy of means under the circumstances that matters here, for, as we shall see in the next section, simple impossibility is not a defense. What does matter is that *not enough has yet been done* to gain ability. That, it should be noted, is crucially different from having done the wrong thing in view of the circumstances, and as a result finding oneself without the ability. In such a case, conduct generally deemed harm-threatening may well have been engaged in;

but never is that possible when, regardless of particular circumstances, not enough has yet been done to acquire the ability.

Three questions, then, are to be asked initially when it is alleged that certain conduct constitutes an attempt. First, were the acts, when taken in context, unambiguous as of a kind that pose a true threat of harm? Second, on the basis of what had been done, is it reasonable to say that the actor's commitment was not in doubt? Third, did he do enough to put himself in a position to inflict harm? A negative answer to any of these questions bars the conclusion that a true threat of harm was posed and an attempt committed.

II. IMPOSSIBILITY

THE VARIETY OF CLAIMS; CLAIMS BASED ON
MISTAKEN BELIEF ABOUT THE LAW, AND
ABOUT LEGALLY SIGNIFICANT CIRCUMSTANCES

In the criminal law as elsewhere, it is commonplace to accuse a person of wrongdoing when he has attempted without success to do something harmful. "Success" and "failure," like their companion term "attempt," suggest a striving by the actor. In a discussion of criminal attempts, this is somewhat misleading. An attempt consists of conduct that poses a threat of harm. "Success," then, consists in the occurrence of the harm contemplated by *the offense,* and "failure" consists in the failure of that harm to occur. When the harm occurs, there is a completed crime; when it does not, there is only an attempt. But in either case the harm need not be the object of the actor's striving.

When the actor is (in this sense) unsuccessful, he may sometimes say that success was impossible. At times such an assertion seems natural enough. Though one realizes only afterward that what one did could not under the circumstances have had the untoward outcome that normally might be expected, still the fact that harm simply was not possible seems to restore to the act a measure of innocence that it otherwise lacks. In seeking to take account of this, the law of criminal attempts has so far not been provided with a firm footing in principles of criminal jurisprudence, and theorists in their attempts to provide such footing have had greater success in uncovering difficulties than in disposing of them. Confusions have been compounded, moreover, by extending the rubric of impossibility to cover the claim that what was done would not be legally wrong even if it were successful. Conventional theory refers to this as *legal impossibility* and contrasts it with *factual impossibility*.

In its simplest form the orthodox rule is that if what the accused intended to do was no crime, there is legal impossibility and hence no criminal liability. But if what he intended to accomplish was a crime, though in fact its accomplishment was impossible, there is only factual impossibility, and that does not avoid liability. In both instances it is the mistaken belief of the accused that receives attention. In the case of legal impossibility, it is held to make no difference that the accused (incorrectly) believed what he was doing to be a crime, and so he cannot be liable by virtue of his belief. In the case of factual impossibility, it is thought to make no difference that things would have had to be as the accused (incorrectly) believed them in order for him to have succeeded in his endeavors, and thus he cannot escape liability because of the certainty of failure.

But matters are not that simple. What might be included under the headings *legal impossibility* and *factual impossibility* turn out to be not two claims but six, each with distinct grounds that are best preserved by avoiding these two headings altogether. Three of the claims rest on the proposition that, even if successful, what was done cannot be judged wrong; the other three attach significance to the fact that success was not possible. The first three claims are these:

1. There was a mistaken belief about what acts are prohibited by law, or about who may be liable for doing them. *Legal impossibility* is usually used to designate cases of this kind, and is usually limited to cases in which the actor believed what he did to be prohibited.

2. There was a mistaken belief about legally significant circumstances under which something prohibited is done. This presents the case of *legally justifiable acts*—that is, of acts which only because of some special circumstance are not unlawful, but whose justifiability the accused fails to appreciate because of his mistaken notion about the circumstances.

3. There was a mistaken belief about some matter of fact upon which criminal liability depends, so that there could be liability only if things were as the accused mistakenly believed them to be.

It is conceded universally that an incorrect belief by the accused regarding his criminal liability cannot cause him to be liable. Illustrations in the literature usually depict some mistake by the accused in thinking that there is a law that makes what he does a crime. But these mistakes are not the only kind. Anything upon which liability may depend under our system of criminal jurisprudence will do. Accordingly, there is no inculpatory force in the accused's (mistaken) belief that under the law he had capacity or lacked immunity or was not justified, for example.

Claims in our second and third groups have generally been thought by commentators to present cases of *factual* rather than *legal* impossibility, and thus they have generally been rejected. It is especially curious that there should be attempt liability in cases of the second group, since they are indistinguishable from completed crimes with respect to the occurrence of harm that universally distinguishes the completed crime from the attempt. First, then, these cases of mistake regarding justifying facts.

Professor Glanville Williams discusses two hypothetical cases which in his view present instances of attempted murder, though not of murder. In one case a sheriff executes a prisoner according to the authority conferred by a warrant for the execution, but the sheriff does not know of the warrant and has acted in pursuit of some unlawful purpose of his own. In another, a soldier in combat kills an enemy soldier, having formed a belief that it is his own drill sergeant whom he is killing. In each case the homicide is apparently *justified,* in the first by the existence of specific legal authorization for it, in the second by its setting; but in each case the mistaken belief of the accused raises a doubt about his innocence, and Professor Williams concludes that both are cases of attempted murder.

But circumstances that provide a justification in answer to an accusation of murder must surely have the same force when the charge is attempted murder. The very point of justification is that by virtue of the circumstances the otherwise wrong act is not wrong. If something is not wrong under the circumstances, how can an attempt to do it under those same circumstances be wrong? Of course it might be argued that what the accused believed is a material part of the circumstances, and that in cases such as these the belief of the accused deprives him of the benefits of the defense of justification, since his act is not justified if done with such a belief. Thus, in the sheriff's case it might be crucial that he believed himself without authority to execute, and in the soldier's case that he believed he was not killing an enemy. Professor Williams, however, has decided the question of justification without regard to the actor's belief when in each case he exonerates from murder. The justification on these terms is then equally available whether the charge is murder or attempted murder. In either case it is the same conduct that is being judged, and under the circumstances the conduct must be found not to be criminal.

The point may be put this way. If the belief of the accused is a material part of the circumstances and is held to make his act unjustifiable, this leaves the killings without justification, and the completed crime is constituted under the facts in each case. If the belief of the accused is not a material part of the circumstances with regard to justification, then the circumstances in these cases provide the grounds of justification without it, and the conduct in each case provides no basis for criminal liability of either sort.

CLAIMS THAT SOMETHING NECESSARY FOR THE CRIME WAS LACKING

The *third* class of cases has proved the most troublesome. In essence the defense again is that conduct said to be wrong is in fact not legally wrong, and so not a proper basis for legal accusation. But now it is not claimed that what was attempted is nowhere to be found among the prohibitions on the books; nor that even if it is prohibited, it is still justified in this case. Rather, the claim now is that something necessary for the existence of a crime—completed *or* attempted—is lacking.

In the New York case of *People v. Jaffe* the defendant purchased certain cloth which he believed to be stolen but which in fact at that time was not stolen goods, since it had been restored to its rightful owner and then with the owner's consent delivered to Jaffe in order to get evidence against him. He was convicted of attempting to receive stolen goods, but the conviction was ultimately upset by the appellate court on the curiously inapposite grounds that "[i]f all which an accused person intends to do would if done constitute no crime, it cannot be a crime to do with the same purpose a part of the thing intended." It is, however, tolerably clear that the court meant to rest its decision on its reading of the statute

as providing for a crime of receiving goods which *are in fact
stolen,* and to decide as it did because this requirement for
liability had not been met. The decision has been widely criticized in the literature, and its authority nullified by the section now governing attempts in the New York Penal Law. Its
rejection in the Model Penal Code is perhaps the most igno-
minious disapproval of all.

We are not concerned here to determine whether *Jaffe* was
correctly decided. It is important for present purposes, however, to show why it may have been. It might well have been
a case of innocent belief of the third variety. If that is so,
there should indeed have been no liability.

To see this possibility more clearly, we might imagine another Jaffe who is a respectable citizen and a man who is fond
of good music. This Jaffe is approached on the street one day
by a shabbily dressed fellow who holds in his hand a dirty paper bag. He stops Jaffe and offers him the dozen stereo tapes
the bag contains for five dollars. Jaffe knows that tapes are
often stolen from cars—he has recently been a victim himself—and he believes without a shadow of doubt that these
cassettes were stolen. The selections and the price are very
appealing (and he thinks *If I don't buy them someone else
will*); so he completes the transaction. Actually the seller is
an itinerant car washer, and the tapes are a gift made to him
by a customer who had traded-in his car and disposed of its
contents a few days earlier. It seems appalling to suggest on
these facts that good citizen Jaffe should be liable for an attempt to receive stolen property because he believed the
tapes to be stolen. Yet a similar suggestion by critics of *Jaffe*
is not alarming and at best only controversial.

Two assumptions account for this: that the defendant in
Jaffe was a fence rather than a casual buyer; and that the law
punishing receipt of stolen goods should be construed in a
way that makes it applicable only when dealing with the
practices of receivers. The first assumption is correct in point

of fact; the second remains in doubt, for the issue of construction was not raised in the case. If it had been, arguably the goods need not be stolen for harm to be threatened but only for harm to occur. If the business practices of receivers of stolen goods were deemed in themselves a threat of harm to be dealt with criminally, then whether or not goods received were in fact stolen would not matter for attempt liability, so long as the goods were being *received as stolen goods*. The belief of a receiver would then be of significance, not because the belief itself imparts some element of wrongfulness for which liability is imposed, but because a receiver's belief that goods are stolen is part of what, for the law's purposes, identifies him as a receiver engaged in receiving. When read as written, however, the statute under which Jaffe was prosecuted lends little support to such an interpretation, with the result that goods would in fact have to be stolen for there to be any liability under the statute.

We are left, then, with a class of cases represented by *Jaffe* in which there is no attempt liability—and for the same general reason as in cases of the first two classes. In the criminal law we do not have criminal liability for conduct simply because the actor believed it to be unlawful, or believed something which if the case would make it so. If we did, we would in effect confer legal status upon foolish, unjust, and inexpedient rules that people believe to be the law because of their ignorance, their private feelings of guilt, their idiosyncratic moral views, or their mistaken notions of public policy; and we should also have to regard a rule as broken whenever an actor's belief—even though incorrect—about what he is doing makes it reasonable for him to believe that he is violating the rule.

Two distinctions are important to note at this point: the first, between being mistaken about what one is doing, on the one hand, and doing something by mistake, on the other; the second, between two different cases of doing by mistake something that poses a threat of harm. In the first such case, if what was done by mistake had been done as intended, the conduct would not pose a threat of harm; in the second, that would make no difference, so that, whether done by mistake or as intended, the conduct still would pose a threat of harm.

It is one thing to entertain false beliefs and thus be mistaken about what one is really doing. It is quite another to do something by mistake. When one is mistaken about what one is doing, one always has a false belief; and being mistaken about what one is doing is one reason why one does something by mistake. But there are many other reasons, and in any case, in its significance for criminal liability, doing something by mistake is unlike being mistaken about what one is doing.

. The distinction is particularly important for the problem of attempt liability that we are examining. Suppose, for example, that Jaffe not only believed that he was receiving stolen goods, but had actually bargained for and arranged delivery of goods that were in fact stolen. Because of a mistake in the instructions given to the person who picked up and delivered the goods, what Jaffe received was not the stolen goods he bargained for, though he believed it was. He then has received the goods by mistake in addition to being mistaken about what he has received. In that case there would be good reason to find attempt liability even when reading the statute in the way that bars liability under the facts of *Jaffe*. What Jaffe now has done poses a threat of the harm that the law contemplates, for he was engaged as a receiver in a transaction for goods that were in fact stolen. Certainly that conclusion is not warranted under the quite different facts of *Jaffe,* assuming of course that one still adheres to the suggested reading of the statute as requiring more for liability than an act of receiving by a professional receiver acting in that role. In *Jaffe* only his belief about the character of the goods was mistaken, and so he was mistaken about what he was doing. But that does not change what he was doing and, regardless of his belief, his conduct did not threaten the harm contemplated by the statute. In this new case, however, the actor is doing something by mistake, and what he is doing threatens the harm contemplated by the statute. Furthermore, had he not done it by mistake, his conduct would still threaten that harm, and so there is no reason to count the mistake in his favor as grounds of exculpation.

The crucial distinctions emerge with consummate subtlety and refinement in a notable invention of the literature known as the two umbrella cases.

> *Case 1.* D finds an umbrella left in his house after a party. He hides it, intending to steal it. It has been left by P, and there is a note inside it saying that it is a present to D. D is not guilty of an attempt.

> *Case 2.* D sees P, a celebrity, put his umbrella in a stand at D's club. D resolves to steal it. When no one is looking, he goes to the stand and takes the umbrella in the place where P's was. But someone has moved the umbrella, and D has taken his own. He is guilty of an attempt.

The stated results seem correct. In the first case D's mistake was about *whose* umbrella he was taking. There is no question that he took the umbrella he intended to take, but *he was mistaken* about its ownership. In order for the harm of larceny to occur, however, there must be a loss, and for attempt liability that harm must be threatened. But no loss is threatened by activities aimed at taking one's own property, for the simple reason that even if such activities are successful there would be no loss. In the second case the matter is quite different. D has again made a mistake about *whose* umbrella is being taken, and again that is in itself innocuous, since it is only a matter of mistaken belief. But D in this case *took the umbrella by mistake,* because someone had moved the umbrella he intended to take. He was engaged in conduct that threatened the harm of larceny, for, had he been successful, a loss would have occurred. Though he took by mistake the umbrella that belonged to him, the mistake does not relieve him from blame, since his conduct is the same whether or not the mistake is made.

In essence the rejected arguments are these. The argument for liability in Case 1 is based on giving inculpatory effect to *D*'s belief. But since criminal liability is for acts and not for beliefs, that argument fails. The argument against liability in Case 2 is based on giving exculpatory effect as an excuse to *D*'s mistake in doing what he did. But since his conduct was of the same harm-threatening sort in spite of that, and since the act that threatened the harm was still intentional, that argument too must fail.

There are, to be sure, alternative ways of interpreting the facts and attaching significance to them. In Case 1, for example, instead of appropriating a particular umbrella that had been left behind, *D* might take an umbrella *at random* from among the many left by his guests when they went off to dinner after the weather had cleared. *D*'s purpose is to appropriate to himself the umbrella of someone else; and he has been told previously by a guest of his that one of the umbrellas, with a note inside, is a birthday gift to him. In that case, the fact that the umbrella *D* happened to take was the subject of the gift, and so already his, would not avoid liability—no more, that is, than would his ownership in Case 2. Now, as in that case, there is something more to pin liability on than *D*'s mistaken belief about whose umbrella he was taking. Since in acting as he did he intended to take one of the umbrellas that actually did not already belong to him, he was engaged in conduct that posed a threat of the harm of larceny. In Case 1 as originally presented, although *D* has an *intention* of stealing the umbrella he takes, his *act,* by contrast, is not of the sort that threatens the property of others; for in fact only his own umbrella is in the zone of danger in which anyone else's umbrella would have been imperiled by what he did.

Elaboration may similarly affect liability in the second case. *D*'s friends, for example, may in that case have played a trick on him by telling him that Neville Chamberlain is visiting the club and that the umbrella in the stand, although the same model as *D*'s, is the famous umbrella carried by the Prime Minister. In fact Chamberlain is miles away at the time, and the umbrella in the stand is *D*'s own, put there by his friends. In this case there is no other umbrella in the field of choice when *D* acts, and hence what he does in taking his own umbrella can hardly be construed as conduct threatening a loss of property. There is only his naked belief that the umbrella belongs to someone else, and that does not change the character of his conduct from innocent to dangerous.

Whether conduct will be thought to threaten harm depends on general expectations about harmful outcomes under particular circumstances. These expectations may vary, and so then must judgments regarding attempt liability. The expectations may be heightened, and conduct now deemed unthreatening may then be thought dangerous. Conversely, expectations may be diminished to a point at which no harm is believed to be threatened by an act now regarded as very dangerous indeed. Harm and what threatens it both may be seen in a different light at a different time or place. Two elaborations of the umbrella cases illustrate this.

Suppose in Case 1 that the scene of the party were a distant desert island, and that the company were survivors of a shipwreck. Ownership of what little has been salvaged is the subject of considerable dispute, and there is general concern that each person should at least be secure in his possession of what he already has. Accordingly, the group adopts a rudimentary penal code that contains a straightforward common law larceny provision making punishable the taking of another's property with intent to appropriate it as one's own, with a preamble indicating the purpose of the provision and expressing the special communal concern that prompted it. What *D* did in Case 1 could then be reasonably construed as an attempt. Threats of loss would be posed under such social circumstances merely by acquisitions that were indifferent to the question of the ownership of some item that was lying about, and so *a fortiori* loss would be threatened by someone's taking with the belief that what he takes belongs to another person.

In Case 2, expectations and so liability may likewise change with changes in the social setting. This time, however, we have a case in which the expectation of harm is sufficiently slight to make what *D* did no threat of harm. We might imagine a society in which attitudes toward property are different from our own. People there are more possessive, and regularly keep what they own in their immediate possession, or lock it up, or place it in the close custody of someone they can trust. Their law of larceny is the same as ours, and persons who wrongfully take the property of others may expect to be punished. If *D*'s club were an institution in that society, and *D* took an umbrella left unattended where anyone might carry it off, his act might well be judged not to be a threat of harm. In such a society, property left open and unattended would normally be abandoned property, and so no longer subject to loss. *D*'s conduct then, according to general expectations, would present no threat of the harm of larceny.

CLAIMS THAT SOMETHING NECESSARY FOR THE HARM WAS LACKING

In all the cases considered so far, the accused had a false belief that might (it was thought) have some inculpatory force, but this suggestion has been rejected. Furthermore, all except the second umbrella case have turned out to be cases in which there is no attempt liability for the reason that there was no harm-threatening conduct. But another problem arises, and this puts even the second umbrella case in doubt once

again. The occurrence of the harm in Case 2 was no more possible than in any of the others. If harm could not possibly have
occurred, then why should there be liability?

The three claims comprising a second group under the rubric of impossibility share a common defensive posture: that
the endeavor was utterly without prospect of success, and so
there ought to be no liability for it. These claims, all of
which are regarded under conventional theory as claims of
factual impossibility, may once again be distinguished by the
mistaken belief that the actor entertains about relevant matters. All such claims would, under conventional theory, be rejected out of hand as defenses because they merely assert that
the facts made the completed crime impossible, and there is
no good reason (it is thought) to count that in the defendant's favor when he is charged with the attempt. Whether
any or all of these three defensive claims deserve to be recognized is something we shall now consider. The claims are the
following: 1. A circumstantial element that is necessary for
the harm—and hence for the completed crime—was missing,
though the actor believed otherwise. This is the second umbrella case. 2. The act itself was defective or deficient in a
way that made it impossible for the harm to occur, though
the actor believed at the time that he was acting in a different way, and in fact, if he were acting as he thought, the
harm would have been possible. 3. Although his act was what
the actor believed it to be, it is impossible for the harm to result from such an act, though the actor believed otherwise.

As for the first of these propositions, perhaps the clearest
case of such a defense would be a pickpocket who claimed
that since his victim's pocket turned out to be empty, he
could hardly be said to have attempted a larceny. "After all,"
he might say, "how could I have attempted to take the property of another when there simply wasn't any?" Theorists
were in fact blessed with some early English cases holding

that there indeed was no attempted larceny under such circumstances.

The error in such a conclusion has already been exposed in our discussion of the umbrella cases. While it is true that the pickpocket's belief cannot serve as a reason to blame him criminally, there is something else that can. Though he made a mistake in picking an *empty* pocket, he picked a pocket intentionally; and no matter whether a pocket is empty or full, the picking of it to steal is an act that threatens larceny. Since in spite of his mistake he did not do unintentionally the act that threatens harm, and since his act is dangerous even in view of his mistake, his mistake does not afford him an excuse.

Another notable invention of the literature deserves attention at this point. We are told that, on her return to England from the Continent, Lady Eldon was discovered to have secreted in her coach some lace purchased abroad which she believed to be French lace and thus dutiable, but which was in fact non-dutiable English lace. On the orthodox view she faced liability for an attempt to smuggle, since her mistake was a mistake of fact. That case is contrasted with a variation in which the lace is indeed French. Believing correctly this time that it is French, Lady Eldon again has hidden it. But French lace has in fact just been removed from the duty list, though Lady Eldon does not know this. On orthodox principles there presumably would be no liability for attempt here, since this time her mistake was about the law. Even commentators who reject the orthodox distinction among impossibilities have acquiesced in finding liability in the first case but not in the second, though they do not deny that this seems paradoxical.

There indeed is cause for displeasure with such a result, for in fact either the harm has been threatened in both cases or else in both cases Lady Eldon's conduct does not pose a threat of harm; and on either alternative each case should have the same result. Which result is the correct one depends on a more ample understanding of the penal law under which Lady Eldon is to be charged. It is not possible here to argue for one or another interpretation of that smuggling provision, since no text of the law is provided by the inventors of the cases, nor is there any indication of the exact purpose the law was to serve. The possible alternative interpretations can be made clear, however—and for our purpose that is enough. These cases, then, can be analyzed in the following way.

If Lady Eldon's mistaken beliefs had significance at all, her beliefs had the same significance in both cases. In the first case, believing wrongly that the lace was French, she hid it; in the second case she wrongly believed the lace to be on the duty list, and, once again, because of her belief she hid it. True, in both cases she believed that she was hiding a dutiable item, but her belief about what she was doing does not in itself have any inculpatory significance in the eyes of the law. In both cases also, Lady Eldon's belief that the lace was dutiable prompted her to hide it. This act of secreting the lace was done intentionally; and if, but only if, this act posed a threat of the harm that concerned the law, it was culpable in the eyes of the law. The question of whether harm was indeed threatened by the act depends on specifically what harm it was that the law had concerned itself with.

It might be decided that undeclared introduction of a dutiable item is the harm, and that dutiability of the article is necessary only for commission of the completed crime. A threat of the harm (and so a criminal attempt) is then constituted by mere secreting in order to introduce free of customs something *believed* to be dutiable, whether it is so or not. This seems a plausible view of the harm intended to be dealt with in an ordinary smuggling provision, and it would be supported by argument that the government policy to be served by this law is discouragement of evasive practices. On this assumption about the law, both Lady Eldon cases would sort with the picking of an empty pocket as instances of an attempt, since her conduct, like the pickpocket's, is dangerous with respect to the harm that the law seeks to prevent, even though under the circumstances the harm could not occur.

A second possibility is that, under the law, dutiability of the article is necessary for the attempt as well as for the completed crime. Under this view the completed crime would be undisclosed introduction of an article in fact dutiable, and the attempt would be conduct tending but failing to accomplish that. This conception of the harm being dealt with in an anti-smuggling law is plausible in a country where customs control is efficient and schemes of evasion are rare. In such a country there might still be concern that, if no law prohibiting evasion were on the books, evasive practices to avoid payment of duty would grow, and for that reason there is a law punishing the undisclosed introduction of dutiable items. Because evasion is rare, however, there is no need to punish mere secreting of items that are not dutiable but only *believed* to be, and a construction reflecting this fact can fairly be placed on the law as enacted. The harm, in other words, is non-payment of duties, and that harm is not threatened unless the item is dutiable. If the law were to be viewed in this way, there would not be attempt liability in either Lady Eldon case, and both cases would then sort with *Jaffe*.

Beliefs, though themselves without inculpatory force, may still affect culpability, and it is important to avoid confusion on this point. Lady Eldon's belief might be quite different in a way that would be most helpful to her in avoiding criminal liability. Suppose, for example, that she had hidden some very expensive lace bought in France, even though she believed it to be exempt from duty, for it had always been exempt, and only very recently (unknown to her) had it been made dutiable. She had hidden the lace to keep knowledge of its purchase from her husband, since he often criticized her extravagance and she feared that he might make a scene when she produced it for Customs inspection. If charged, Lady Eldon might well protest that although she failed to disclose the item as the law required, she honestly believed that the lace was not dutiable and that she was therefore not required to disclose it. Under either of the two versions of the law just suggested, this might well avoid liability. But under a third version, which made undisclosed introduction of dutiable items an offense, and hence acts of concealment at Customs for whatever reason an attempt, her claim would not avoid liability. Whether it is accepted or rejected, however, Lady Eldon's claim is a plausible one that bears good credentials as a recognized mode of exculpation.

At this point an error having grave consequences for criminal law theory is commonly made. It is assumed that when Lady Eldon's belief counts in her favor it is because the belief shows that her mind was innocent; and that a belief counting against her similarly has the significance it does because it shows her to be of a wicked or a dangerous mind. But the belief itself is in no measure a reason for blaming or exempting from blame in the criminal law. Earlier discussions have already indicated that certain denials of responsibility and of culpability rest on belief in an altogether different way, and further discussion in the next chapter should make that even clearer.

If Lady Eldon truly believes that the lace is not dutiable, in at least a limited measure she is unable to conform her conduct to the law, since she does not know that she is violating it. In addition, what she does intentionally is then in some measure less dangerous, for her activity is not guided by an evasive design. It is for these reasons alone that her belief furnishes grounds of exculpation. Lingering doubts on this point might be dispelled by imagining that a law reform commission is considering a change in the law so that no longer will it matter for conviction that someone in Lady Eldon's position believed that the dutiable item she hid was not dutiable. Considerations of fairness to persons not engaged in acts of smuggling will likely be weighed against the government's interest in more efficient and economical Customs control. The less ample freedom from regulation that will result from casting a broader net will be considered in the light of the benefits to accrue from a law more easily enforced. But it is virtually inconceivable that one item on the commission's agenda would be the assessment of the wrongness or dangerousness of certain beliefs and of the importance of punishing persons who entertained such beliefs when they acted in accordance with them. That, however, would properly be an item of the highest priority for any law reform commission doing its job in a society that took seriously the explanations of attempt liability to be found in many standard texts.

CLAIMS BASED ON MISTAKEN BELIEF ABOUT
WHAT WAS BEING DONE

The next kind of exculpatory claim is appropriate when a person is mistaken about what he was doing. He may at the time believe himself to be doing what normally produces the result he intends, but in fact is not doing that at all; and what he intends cannot possibly result from what he actually does. A stock example is the man with homicidal intentions who shoots at a tree stump thinking it to be his enemy. As one English judge said, the man was simply not "on the job"; and almost certainly the man will say something to that effect if accused of criminally attempting what he intended. The question, once again, is whether the impossibility is a good defense. The answer is that it depends on the situation in which the accused acted, more particularly on those elements in it that are significant regarding attempt liability generally.

We might imagine two different settings, one almost certainly disposing us to see a criminal attempt, the other equally certain to incline us toward the opposite conclusion. In the first a man with gun in hand is closely pursuing his intended victim through the woods. At a turn in the path he loses sight of his quarry for a moment, and then with a clear view fires in the failing light at a tree stump that he thinks is his man. At the time the intended victim is hiding behind a rock some distance from the stump.

Contrast this with the case of a man who while sitting in his study late at night is drawn deeply into paranoid fantasies in which he imagines that his partner has been plotting to kill him. He is convinced that at that very moment his partner is in fact lurking outside. He jumps up and, rushing to the window pistol in hand, fires at a stump which he takes to be his partner. But his partner is in fact asleep at home miles away at the time, as indeed there was every reason to believe he would be.

Between these two extreme cases there are intermediate ones that seem less certainly an attempt than the first, yet more so than the second. Suppose instead of close pursuit through the woods there is only a search of the area where the intended victim was seen some time before. Is the shot at the stump then an attempted homicide? Suppose in the second case that the intended victim often took walks in the vicinity at that hour, and that the man who shot from his window at the stump had that in mind? Perceiving the ebb and flow in the conclusions to which we are inclined, we want a principle by which to give a good account of these changes.

At first the temptation is to say that one is disposed more or less to see an act as an attempt according to how likely it is that harm will occur. In the two original stump-shooting cases, however, there is *ex hypothesi* no possibility of harm in either, hence in both the harm is equally improbable; and yet one seems a very strong case for attempt liability, while

the other seems a very weak case indeed. A clear case of at
tempt liability when there is zero probability of harm makes
the same point. When a person out to kill someone sends a
fusillade of bullets into the intended victim's bed in the middle of the night, there is the clearest *prima facie* case of attempt liability even though, unknown to the assassin, his
intended victim is halfway around the world at the time.

Wisdom in these matters begins when we gauge the dangerousness of what was done and turn attention to the *expectability of harm* rather than to the *probability* of its occurrence in the particular case. When the actor is "on the
job," what he does qualifies as genuinely dangerous with respect to the harm he intends; when he is not "on the job," he
misconceives what he is doing with respect to the harm he
intends, and so what he does is not genuinely dangerous.
Cases in which the actor is "on the job" can be separated
from those in which he is not by reference to the expectability of harm, so that only when what he does makes harm expectable is he "on the job." This places a great deal of weight
on the still obscure notion of expectability, which must now
be made clearer.

If the actor had reason to believe that what he was doing
would bring about the harm he intended, then, and only
then, was the harm expectable. Cases like that of the man
firing at the tree stump in hot pursuit of his enemy are, arguably, of the "on the job" variety; and unquestionably the
assassin firing into the bed is on the job. In these cases the actor had reason to believe that what he was doing would bring
about the harm he intended. But the man who fires at the
stump from his window while in the grip of his delusion is
not "on the job," for he does not have reason to believe that
what he does will bring about what he intends, though indeed he firmly believes that it will.

The actor "on the job" always has reason to believe that
what he does will bring about what he intends. Those who

do not have reasonable expectation based on what they are actually doing are not "on the job," and so not properly subject to liability. The reason for this is simple enough. Liability is for culpable conduct only, and when what is done is not dangerous it is not culpable. The actor *supposes* that he is engaged in dangerous conduct, but that does not make it so. The innocence of his conduct (if not of his heart and mind) endures in the face of his delusions and radical misconceptions.

Outcomes, then, may not be expectable, even though expected by the actor. The other feature of the expectability principle is also tinged with paradox, for according to the principle some impossible outcomes are expectable nonetheless. Attempt liability is preserved in the face of impossibility by requiring only that *the actor* have reason to believe as he does. Beyond that, there is no requirement that there be a general reason for so believing. So, for example, since the person who usually sleeps in the bed that was the assassin's target was thousands of miles away, there was no reason to believe that he would be killed; yet the assassin, who knew nothing of the victim's absence, had reason to believe that his murderous act would be successful, and so the expectability requirement is satisfied.

Since everything here turns on what the actor *believed* to be the case, it might seem after all that it is not the dangerousness of what he did that matters, but rather what he believed. The argument then would be that the relevant conduct consists of shooting into the bed; that, whether or not the actor believed the bed to be occupied, his conduct was the same; and that only something about his belief in each case could account for attempt liability in the one but not the other. But the error lies in supposing that conduct is the same in both cases. The man who shoots into the bed believing (not unreasonably) that it is occupied is intentionally doing something that may be described as shooting into someone's bed; and what is then done *intentionally* cannot be described as shooting into someone's *empty* bed. What is done intentionally (rightly) alarms us even if we happen to know that harm is impossible, for it is a very dangerous thing to do. But a man who shoots into a bed that he knows to be empty is intentionally doing something else, and this may be described as shooting into someone's empty bed. That may perplex and even vex us as we take notice of a perfectly good mattress wantonly wasted, but we are not alarmed by such an act of pointless destruction since it is not dangerous.

Two objections have to be faced here, the first of which deplores what is taken to be a confusion of acts and their descriptions. Thus it is objected that what we really have is one and the same act under two different descriptions, and not two different acts. A reply to this calls for a criterion for the individuation of acts to supplement the one presented at the end of Chapter Four. It was suggested there that two descriptions of an act are descriptions of different acts if—and only if—according to principles of responsibility the act described under one description might be a responsible act while the act described under the other is not. A further criterion of individuation—admittedly weak but still adequate for the limited purposes at hand—relies instead on principles of culpability. When the act described in one description is culpable and the act described in a different description is not, or when the culpability of the two acts is different, the two descriptions are of two different acts. If this were not so, and the culpability of an act could be altered by changing its description, we should make a mockery of moral and other critical judgment of conduct, for then it could rightly be said that acts are more or less blameworthy according to how they are described.

The second objection takes an altogether different line. It concedes that the man who shoots believing the bed to be occupied engages in conduct different from that of the man who shoots believing the bed empty. According to this view, however, it is a wicked or a dangerous state of mind that makes the difference, for in both cases the bed is empty and the shooting itself therefore no more dangerous in the one case than in the other. Since it is something internal and private to the person that makes the difference (so runs this objection), it is the wickedness or the dangerousness of the person, as displayed on this occasion, that warrants attempt liability in the one case but not in the other.

A good deal has been said already about criminal liability imposed not for conduct but because of what a person is, and more is to be said in later chapters. Such liability is opposed by the principles of criminal jurisprudence that we have, and proposals to abandon those principles and adopt instead a system that seeks out socially dangerous persons have yet to meet even the most obvious objections. Postponing these matters until later, it is sufficient here to reply simply that conduct is plainly more dangerous in the one case than in the other, regardless of how dangerous the one engaging in it turns out to be, and that, under the criminal jurisprudence we have, this furnishes grounds for finding attempt liability in the one case but not in the other.

CLAIMS BASED ON A MISTAKEN BELIEF ABOUT
WHAT COULD BE DONE

The sixth and final version of the impossibility defense is appropriate when the actor's mistake is not about what he is doing, but about what may result from it. These result-regarding claims differ mainly in emphasis from act-regarding claims. In the previous group, stress was put upon the actor's mistake regarding what he was doing. This might be a mistake about his own efforts, or more likely, about one of the situation's features that made of his efforts an act different from the one he believed it to be. By contrast, it is the absurdity of the expectation entertained by the actor that is now stressed in this final group. Since the expectation was an absurd one, the defense now is that the act presented no threat of the completed crime and therefore does not qualify for attempt liability. In phrases familiar to the literature, what the actor did was "utterly without prospect of success," or "a grossly inadequate means" to bring about the harm of the completed crime, although admittedly in acting as he did he believed otherwise.

A single aspirin is put in a cup of tea by someone who wishes to kill the person to whom it is served, and the cup is presented in the quite unreasonable belief that one aspirin will do the job. Water is charged with a satanistic incantation and is then added to whiskey and served for the same purpose by someone believing in the efficacy of the magic words. Is either a case of attempted murder?

We might first notice our inclination to treat such a suggestion just a bit more seriously in the aspirin case. We see at least the shadow of a threat of harm in a single aspirin because aspirin is a toxic substance, as suicidal adults and curious children sometimes remind us. By contrast, a swallow of drinking water (with words or without) seems to present no danger at all. Our intuition serves us well here, for if there were to be a difference in the two cases it would rest on a difference in the dangerousness of what was done. But although aspirin may be more dangerous than water, the difference is not great enough to make a difference for the question of liability. Expectability of harm once again is what matters, and in neither case is the harm expectable.

Barring special knowledge of some abnormal circumstances, the man who puts an aspirin in tea has no reason to believe that it will kill as he intends it to; nor, clearly, does the man who puts water in whiskey. Once again, it is neither impossibility nor improbability that matters. It is not impossible in either case that death may result from what was done. There might be a severe hyperallergic reaction to the aspirin, resulting in death. The man who drank the diluted whiskey might have acute gastritis that would cause him to regurgitate the undiluted drink, but because of the water with which it is taken the alcohol is tolerated, and it then combines in effect with barbiturates already in his system to put him into a fatal coma.

Harm, though not impossible, is admittedly most unlikely; but it is not the improbability that matters either. Instead of the single aspirin, a small amount of strychnine no more toxic than an aspirin might be put in the tea by someone who once again is quite naïve in the means he has adopted to commit murder. The probability of causing death is then no greater; yet this time there may well be attempt liability. Because strychnine is a dangerous poison, a person who administers strychnine to kill is doing something dangerous. He does have some reason (though not very good reason) to believe that his expectations will be fulfilled, and this is so in spite of the fact that failure is virtually certain.

Magic as it is known and practiced in societies to which it is indigenous raises an interesting question under this analysis. Glanville Williams suggests that "an attempt to kill by conjuration or sympathetic magic in a backward territory might well be held criminal, for when such beliefs are common, the magic may work through the mechanism of the victim's mind," and he notes South African legislation making these practices an offense. This phenomenon is found elsewhere in the world, and among the Australian aborigines the ritual "pointing of the bone" causes serious deterioration and ultimately the death of the victim by just such a process. There is indeed no problem of supporting an accusation of attempt, at the very least, where the practice in question may in fact harm the victim in the way suggested. With such a possibility there is not even room for a claim of *impossibility*, for in such societies the dangers are manifest and part of the commonsense world. But what if the magic were in fact no more effective in such a society than it would be in a more sophisticated community? Is the mere fact that such magical practices are generally, albeit unreasonably, regarded as dangerous in that society enough to warrant treating them as dangerous when in fact they can do no harm?

Whenever acts are of the sort about which members of the community are apprehensive, that alone is reason enough for taking seriously the suggestion that they qualify as offenses. Many well established laws aim to protect sensibilities and to prevent acts that make people *feel* unsafe, whether reasonably or not. If it is only members of a special group in the community that are likely to be put in fear—Haitian emigrés, gypsies, or satanists in New York, for example—it would be more appropriate to make criminal only specified conduct that actually causes or threatens apprehensiveness on particular occasions. The law will then provide in effect that only when there is a susceptible victim will there be a crime. If, on the other hand, conduct is generally regarded as harmful in the community, fear of it on particular occasions should not be required for criminal liability. In either case, however, if harm is not expectable, liability ought not to be of the attempt variety.

What is proper is criminal liability for a crime of causing or threatening apprehensiveness (which in turn may admit of attempt liability for partial conduct when causing or threatening is itself threatened but does not occur). Since the harm intended by the practitioner of magic is not expectable, conduct purporting to be a threat of harm is not an *attempt* with reference to that harm. Generally mistaken belief that is widespread in the community (and so *a fortiori* mistaken belief widespread in a subcommunity) is no different than the idiosyncratic mistaken belief of an individual. In both instances the truth of the matter is that the harm intended has not been threatened, and hence whatever culpability the conduct has does not derive from that harm. What is warranted is legislative assessment of the harm done by acts that frighten, in order to prescribe liability for inducing the (admittedly irrational) fear.

The point has general importance for attempt theory that should not be lost sight of in the panoply of exotic illustrations. We constantly change our ideas about what harm may befall us, and learn that some activities that seemed to threaten us are in fact quite harmless. It is part of our progress as civilized persons to move from irrational apprehensiveness to rational expectations as we discover more about the true causes of our evils and the true effects of our acts. It is often the case that informed opinion in these matters is well in advance of popular notions, and that conduct still regarded as socially dangerous under prevailing views may be regarded as harmless in more enlightened circles.

If genuine and substantial fearfulness is a result generally to be expected from certain activities in the community, then those activities may be prohibited even though in truth there is little or nothing to fear from them. The reason is that the fear itself is properly a matter of public concern, and though enlightened government must foster understanding to dispel irrational fears, measures to protect against what is feared irrationally may in the meantime remain among the penal laws of the community. At the same time, however, it is proper for the law to be responsive only to enlightened views in deciding questions of attempt liability and to reject ill-founded beliefs, even when they are widely held. Only if enlightened views will sustain his expectations does an actor have reason to believe that what he does will bring about harm, and so only then is he properly subject to liability for an attempt.

The permissible and the impermissible creation of criminal liability can be illustrated in this way. Imbecility, sexual maladjustment, and the destruction of healthy family life are thought to be threatened by incestuous sexual relations, and so the law prohibits incest. Under enlightened views, the prohibitions on the books in many jurisdictions are unnecessarily restrictive since the interdiction of certain relations in order to prevent these harms is without rational support. Powerful sentiment against such relations nevertheless exists, with underlying fears made stronger by psychological predispositions that are inhospitable to the facts. Until fears and other strong emotions are moderated, incestuous relations of the questionable sort might still be prohibited for the offense to feeling that typically they cause, particularly to feelings of other members of the family. But though a man has quite unreasonably convinced himself that the stranger he is marrying is his long lost sister and advertises this to all his neighbors, his open cohabitation with her cannot properly subject him to liability for attempted incest, despite the greatest consternation and alarm among members of his family and in the neighborhood where his story is believed.

FURTHER EXPLANATION OF EXPECTABILITY AND DANGEROUSNESS

Six kinds of claims have been looked at. Any of them might be used to defend against charges of criminal attempt and, in conventional theory, all of them are deemed to be claims of impossibility. The first three assert in effect that even on the face of things there is nothing criminally wrong in what was done. If established, any of these three should indeed serve to avoid liability. The other three claims assert that harm is not expectable. The first of these three turns out to be unsound in principle, but the other two are sound and can serve to exculpate. All but the first two of the six claims fix attention on the expectability of harm, by questioning whether conduct threatens harm. Till now we have thought of this as a question about the dangerousness of conduct, and thus a question about the culpability of conduct in what we have been calling the *third dimension of culpability*. Some remarks about *expectability* and *dangerousness* are therefore in order.

Conduct threatens harm, and hence is dangerous, only when the actor has reason to expect the harm. Much of the discussion of problems of exculpation in this section rests on this idea of dangerous conduct, even though the notion is burdened by certain difficulties. Four problems have to be confronted, the first of them concerning the use of the term *dangerous.*

It seems wrong to say that conduct is dangerous *only* when the actor has reason to believe that harm will occur. For one thing, there is a weak sense in which conduct might be said to be dangerous even when there was no reason to believe that harm would result from it. In all innocence and under circumstances which give not the slightest hint of danger to anyone, I open a letter and a bomb goes off. In this weak sense what I did may be spoken of as dangerous, especially when spoken about after the catastrophic event. But it would be odd to assert that what I did *threatened* harm, since there was no reason to believe that harm would occur, and in that stronger sense the conduct was not dangerous.

Suppose next that there *is* reason to believe that harm might occur, even though the actor had no reason to believe that it would. Letter bombs are a known danger at the embassy, but the clerk is newly arrived from his own country and not yet briefed when he opens the letter on his first day on the job. In a stronger sense of "dangerous," he does something dangerous when he opens the letter. Anyone normally informed about the situation would describe it that way before as well as after the fact. But if we wish to speak of what he did as dangerous conduct *qua* conduct, still more is necessary. The clerk must have reason to expect what those who are not in the dark have reason to expect, for when we are interested in dangerousness of conduct *qua* conduct we are interested in what threatens harm when the agency of harm is capable of choice. A responsible agent who does not have reason to expect harm is not in a position to avoid it by choosing to alter his normal course of activity. Although what he does may be dangerous, it is not dangerous as conduct.

As a precaution against misinterpretation, it is well to take note of a still stronger sense in which conduct threatens harm. If we state that an actor threatens harm, we may sometimes be taken to imply that he threatens it *intentionally*. But such a sense of *threatening harm* is too strong for present purposes, for when an actor has reason to expect harm he still need not *intentionally* threaten harm in order for harm to be expectable. The dangerousness of his act is the same whether done intentionally or unintentionally, even though indeed its culpability will be affected by this consideration (in what we have called the *first dimension of culpability*). Obviously, a man who threatens harm *unintentionally* by accidentally discharging the gun he has just loaded in a crowded room has done something that makes harm expectable, and it is therefore dangerous conduct; the same can be said of the man who shoots *intentionally* in the same circumstances, though no doubt the culpability of the two acts will often be judged differently.

A second problem is the obscurity of the notion of having a reason to believe. What is it exactly, to have—or not to have—reason to believe that harm will occur as a result of what one does? It is important that we know the answer so that arguments as to who has reason and who does not are kept on the track. Present purposes call only for a narrow rule that allows us to tell when the actor does not have reason to believe. Such a rule stated simply might at first be thought disappointingly obvious. Only if there is reason to believe that something is the case can the actor have reason to believe that it is. But even then, if, in spite of there being reason to believe it, there is no reason for *the actor* to believe it, then he has no reason to believe it.

The first part of the rule sets as a necessary condition that there be reason to believe; this would exclude cases such as that of the man who shoots out the window at a figment of his imagination, and of the man who believes that ordinary drinking water has been given lethal powers by his magic. The second part of the rule sets special conditions applying to the actor, and covers cases like that of the embassy clerk who acts quite reasonably when opening the mail in a state of complete innocence. In all these cases harm is not expectable, since the actor does not have reason to believe that harm will occur.

The rule is easily put to work, but more subtle points have to be observed if it is to work properly.

There is reason to believe that something is the case whenever the belief is, under the circumstances, a rational one. But false beliefs as well as true ones may qualify. Many beliefs not altogether unreasonable turn out to be palpably false, and their falsity is so manifest that we think it unreasonable that the belief should be entertained in the first place. Nevertheless, even though there is no *good* reason to believe, so long as the belief does no violence to common sense and is supportable within the rational communion prevailing locally, there still may be reason to believe even when there is very little reason.

Another point is this. The actor need have no belief whatever in order to have reason to believe. It is commonly the case that those who act negligently (and even recklessly) do not appreciate what they are doing and do not believe that harm will follow as a consequence of what they do. Yet they have every reason to believe it, as any reasonable person would. The point can be made more general: Whether a person has or has not reason to believe something is independent of what he actually believes, or whether he has any belief at all.

There is a further point that draws attention to the actor's having *his* reasons. He may indeed "have his reasons" for believing as he does, but that does not mean that he has *reason* to believe as he does. "It stands to reason" is what the irrational actor may say, though there is no reason to believe as he does; and, according to his own queer logic, he may make inferences from premises that are no less odd. Having taken all that in, however, we are still in a position to reject the claim that he had reason to believe as he did.

And still a further point along this line. Why a person believed as he did might always be explained. With such an explanation in hand, we can say that there was a reason *why* the actor believed as he did, and we can tell what the reason was. But this does not entitle us to assert that the actor had reason to believe as he did, only that there was a reason for his believing as he did.

Does *expectability* admit of degrees? Two actors who do the same thing may each have reason to believe that what he does will bring about harm, though one of them has better reason than the other. Is the harm, then, more expectable in the one case than in the other? This poses a third problem about dangerousness and expectability, and it is an important one. If expectability can be measured in this way, we then have a yardstick to take the measure of dangerousness, and so can tell how culpable an act is in its third dimension by reference to how good a reason the actor had for his expectation. Anything affecting culpability affects liability (as we shall see), and therein lies the ultimate importance of this question.

Happily, expectability does furnish just such a measure. Once an actor has reason to expect that what he does will result in harm, we may view what he does as dangerous, and then we may satisfy ourselves about *how* dangerous it is by asking just how good a reason he has. He may have some scant reason to believe that he will be successful, though under the circumstances it is quite unlikely, and his expectations can fairly be called wishful thinking. Or, on the other hand, he may have every reason to believe that he will be

successful, for only the intervention of something quite un-
forseeable could prevent the anticipated outcome. In both
cases the actor had (some) reason to believe that the harm
would occur, though in the first case he had hardly any reason to believe it and, in the second, hardly any reason to
doubt it. Many cases fall between these extremes, and one
can determine where they fall in different cases by viewing
and comparing prospects of success as the actor might reasonably see them.

There is, finally, the problem of *probability*. It seems at
first glance that dangerousness of conduct comes down simply to what the probability is that harm will result from the
conduct. If this were true, it would embarrass an analysis of
dangerousness in terms of expectability. But it will not do to
say that the actor's having better reason to expect harm
means nothing more than that harm is more probable. As we
saw earlier, harm may be a virtual certainty even though the
actor has no reason to expect it; and, conversely, it may be
utterly impossible for the harm to occur, and yet the actor
has every reason to expect it. Expectability of harm and dangerousness of conduct are measured not by the probability of
harm's occurring but by how good a reason the actor has for
expecting harm to occur. The further question, then, is
whether judgments of dangerousness and expectability ought
to take probability into account at all. Not surprisingly, the
answer is that probability has significance only as it may affect the question of how good is the actor's reason for expecting harm.

Imagine an assassin who is determined to kill a certain
prime minister by planting a land mine along the route the
prime minister will be traveling in his car. The assassin, who
has only one mine, knows that the prime minister will be
traveling along one of several possible routes that are already
closed to all other vehicles. The assassin is completely in the
dark about the specific route to be taken, and finally decides

by lot where to plant the mine. If when he plants it the prime minister has already decided on his route, the probability of his killing the prime minister will be different than it will be if the prime minister has not yet made his decision. But nothing affecting the assassin's reason for expecting the prime minister's death has changed, and the dangerousness of his conduct is therefore the same. True, the situation he has created will be more dangerous—or less dangerous—depending upon whether a decision has been made by the prime minister; moreover, we sometimes speak of acts that create more dangerous situations as more dangerous acts. But since we have no warrant to infer dangerousness of acts simply from dangerousness of situations, we should regard this as loose usage to be avoided here.

A third possibility will make clear the relation between probability and dangerousness. Suppose that the prime minister's driver has been instructed simply to take the most scenic route, and the assassin, learning of this, plants his mine along the route he thinks the driver will choose. What the assassin now does is more dangerous because he has better reason to expect the harm he intends. He has better reason because, based on what he knows, no longer do all routes appear equally likely, and he has acted accordingly. In this way greater probability can affect the dangerousness of what was done, for, when the actor knows the greater probability and is guided by this knowledge, he has better reason to expect the harm he intends.

REJECTION OF LIABILITY WITHOUT EXPECTABILITY

Making an actor's reasonable expectations a touchstone of his liability does not sit well with everyone. One argument in particular can be relied on to rally formidable opposition. Its foundations have already been found faulty, but it deserves more thorough examination.

It is perfectly possible for the seemingly impossible to happen. Against all odds, whiskey and water meant to kill can turn out to be lethal, even though the undiluted drink would not be. Again—though it seems barely credible—the person imagined to be outside the window might have decided to take an unprecedented nocturnal stroll, and after miles of aimless walking, he might happen to be in the path of the bullet just as the shot is fired. In such a case, the actor has engaged in conduct in order to bring about the harm, and the harm occurred just as he intended it to and as a result of what he did. Why, then (it is asked), should there not be liability in such a case—for the completed crime when harm occurs, and for an attempt when it does not?

Those proposing liability in these cases are usually ready, even eager, to concede that there are good reasons for not holding liable a person who causes harm unintentionally. If it were otherwise, punishment would befall us as bad luck over which we had no control, just as the harm we had caused others in such cases would have befallen our victims as misfortunes over which neither we nor they had control. Such a world would be congenial only to people who are blindly vengeful or to misanthropic souls whose satisfaction lies in a balance of misfortune. But those who argue for liability in the cases at hand remind us that no objection of this sort can be made in these cases. What happened was intended, and in the strongest sense, for it was precisely what the actor had in mind that he brought about. More than that, the actor embarked on a course of activity designed (as he saw it) to produce precisely the result that it did produce. He chose to act in pursuit of that harmful objective; and had he not acted as he did, his victim would not have been in any danger. In the face of so powerful an indictment, the matter of reasonable or unreasonable expectations seems paltry and irrelevant to advocates of liability. There is enough here in the conduct of the actor (so they say) to constitute an attempt if harm does not occur, and a completed crime if it does.

True, a very important reason for exempting from liability those who cause harm only by chance or by accident does not apply in these cases, even though we should certainly say that the harm occurred only by chance or by accident. But there are other good reasons for rejecting liability in these cases. One is that liability could not be for what the actor *did,* since only by chance or by accident could it result in harm. If there were liability on the theory advanced, even though the conduct were deemed necessary for liability, there would be liability for what was *intended,* not for what was done. Punishment for what is intended is more objectionable in the absence of any conduct, since it is an even more profound transgression of the culpability principle. But punishment for what is intended is objectionable in any case; and this is no less true when what is *done* is prompted by the clearest desire to bring about what was *intended.*

There is a second reason for refusing to find liability in these cases. If we treat as dangerous whatever the actor regards as dangerous, we accept and in effect regard as reasonable those groundless notions that flourish in the mind of the actor. On this principle, it would be proper to regard as not dangerous anything that he regarded as not dangerous, and to accept as a defense against criminal charges his notion that what he did was safe, no matter how preposterous and insulting to common sense that idea might be. Acts of the grossest negligence and sheerest recklessness would have to be excused simply because the actor was convinced that there was no need for concern.

There are still further consequences of this principle. It is implied that we are justified in accepting as dangerous whatever the actor regards as dangerous because, even though his notions might be stark delusions or misconceptions of a radically irrational sort, still for him they are the basis of an expectation of the same harm that all of us recognize as harm. Suppose, however, that not only are his notions of what may produce harm absurd, but that his appreciation of harm itself is equally absurd. If he is convinced that, instead of doing harm when he kills another person, he benefits that person through an act of purest charity by freeing the dead man's spirit for a far happier existence, what reason is there for not crediting this notion of his as well? If such a benign intention can be shown in the cases we are considering, ought that not then to result in a refusal to find liability—a refusal which those who previously argued for liability would be bound to concur in by the very premise upon which their argument rests?

The principle has general consequences that are more alarming still. If the actor's notions about what is harmful and what is innocent are to be adopted in judging him in these cases, there appears to be no reason why they should not be adopted in all cases. If when I shoot you I believe that I do no harm, and do it only to transport you to a far better place, why should I not then be free from liability according to this new principle that liability is for intentions that are acted on?

III. CAUSATION

WHAT CAUSATION ISSUES ARE ABOUT

Reasonable expectations have a role to play in judgments of liability when harm occurs as well as when it does not. We have seen this already in those extraordinary cases in which the intended harm occurred even when the actor had no reason to believe that it would. Even more interesting and certainly more important are cases in which the harm occurring is neither intended nor brought about by chance. There are many such cases in which an association of the harm with someone's act suggests itself; yet the link is uncertain. Imagine that a gunman enters a store, points a weapon at the proprietor, and demands his money. A frightened customer standing nearby clutches his chest, gasps, and collapses. The gunman flees, a doctor is called, and the customer is pronounced dead, apparently of a heart attack brought on by the fright he experienced. It does no violence to language or to common sense to say that what the gunman did caused the customer's death. Yet it is far from clear that the gunman caused the death in any way or in any sense that would warrant charging him with homicide. It would still not be clear if the gunman had threatened the customer as well as the proprietor—though in that case there appears to be a firmer link between what he did and what happened. It is not easy to account for this appearance: in both cases the gunman's conduct played precisely the same role in the unfolding of events. This point about cause and effect we are bound to acknowledge, and yet upon reflection it seems curiously irrelevant and out of place. A quite different sort of point appears to be more helpful. In the second case the gunman would have somewhat better reason to expect what happened.

We might well ask what having reason to expect what happened has to do with causing it. This turns out to be a profitable question the pursuit of which is rewarded by answers to the three main problems of causation in criminal law theory. First, what exactly do we mean when we ask whether an act caused harm? Second, how can we tell whether a particular act caused a particular harm? Finally, a question that seems to present no problem at all until an answer is required. In cases presenting causation issues, why is it of any importance that the accused have caused the harm? To answer these questions it is necessary first to understand the notion of a cause that concerns the criminal law. A good beginning can be made by looking into the characteristic contexts of its use.

One person may cause, or attempt to cause, another person to engage in some crime (or to do something harmful even though not criminal)—and that itself can be a crime. Criminal conduct itself is a harm quite apart from what it produces, and hence activities designed to bring about criminal conduct can themselves be criminal. Criminal solicitation and criminal conspiracy are two broad categories of crime in which one person acts so as to cause another to commit a crime. There are, in addition, specific crimes on the books in which such words as *solicit, request, propose, advise, command, coerce, importune,* and *induce,* as well as simply *cause,* are used to mark conduct designed to bring about the unlawful conduct of another person.

The ways in which one person may persuade another to commit a crime are as various as the ways in which he might persuade him to undertake a lawful activity. But only when the acts of the person who is said (with whatever words) to cause a criminal act are performed in a role that makes those acts dangerous is there properly criminal liability for the actor. By requiring that one man's act truly cause (or tend to cause) another's, we want to protect against liability that rests upon a palpably unjust principle of *post hoc ergo propter hoc.* We may talk frivolously about committing crimes and may even in an angry hour speak in dead earnest about violence that we say we are willing to have done, but we do not in these cases embark upon a criminal venture. If our idea acts as a seed in someone else's mind and flowers in criminal activity, or if we are taken seriously by someone prone to seize and act upon mere suggestions of crime, we do not want to be treated as criminals because of that. Certainly, in one clear sense what we said was the cause of what was done subsequently. But in that sense our causing is not something that matters in determining our liability. Even though at the time we may have meant what we said and were taken to mean it, still, under the circumstances we had no reason to believe that it would be taken seriously as a criminal project that we meant to have carried out. The effect upon others of what we say and do is one thing. What we *cause* others to do through words and deeds is something different.

In the second context for causation in the criminal law, causing harm appears in a more straightforward way. One may cause harm to another person simply by one's own devices without any other person's participation. Linking up as a cause what a *person did* with *what happened* is important in difficult cases if we would preclude liability for what someone (or something) else and not the accused brought about. But this is easier said than done—and certainly easier done than understood.

Simple commonsense tests prove to be miserably inadequate. It would be little enough to be able to say that one man's act is not the cause of another's death whenever the act is not necessary for death to occur; but even that exceedingly modest proposition is insupportable. Thus, if I deliver a fatal blow to a dying man, I cannot avail myself of his already certain death when I am subsequently charged with having caused his death. Nor will a hardly less modest claim be of any use, for it cannot be said either that whatever is necessary is a cause. An act enjoying perfect innocence will not lose that innocence even though, under the circumstances, had it not been done the harm would not have occurred; and so it is no cause. If I had not given my car keys to my friend he could not have had the accident; yet giving him the keys was not a cause of the accident. The more onerous demand of common sense is no help, for it is not the case, either, that conduct must be sufficient to produce the harm if it is to be the cause of it. Almost never could what was done have resulted in the harm without other things, yet without doubt simply in doing what he did the actor often causes the harm.

A third context to be examined for clues stresses the distinction between *doing harm* and *causing harm*. There are times when we want to say that the accused did not *do* harm, even though he may have *caused* it. We require this distinction because there may be less liability for causing harm than for doing harm, or even no liability at all. It may be that under the law a person is guilty of unlawful imprisonment when he unlawfully restricts another person's freedom to move about, but not when all he does is cause such restriction. If *A* makes a reckless accusation against *B,* and *C* (to whom *A* has made the accusation) springs into action and locks up *B, C* may be guilty of the offense, but not *A,* for *C* has done the harm, but *A* has only caused it. Though in a trivial sense *doing harm* always implies *causing harm,* the reverse is not the case, and we wish to preserve the distinction between the two so that merely dangerous conduct that is not deemed serious enough to punish may be distinguished from harmful conduct that is.

In drawing the distinction between *doing harm* and *causing harm,* it becomes clearer that the job at hand is not to explain how harm came about, but to decide whether expectation of harm was reasonable. There is a further point of great importance which this distinction lays bare. When one causes harm, unlike simply doing harm, one creates a perilous situation or condition that eventuates in the harm. In *causing* harm, one does something that sets the scene for what then happens, as the actor had reason to expect it would. When one simply *does* harm, there is no intervening situation of danger between the act and the harm. Some criminal acts are by their nature not capable of *causing* harm, since the very *doing* of them amounts to the harm's occurring. Criminal attempts are themselves harms, and in a crime such as rape the act is itself a sufficient condition for the harm. No room is left in such crimes for a situation threatening a harm that is yet to occur, and so in these crimes the harm is never, strictly speaking, *caused.*

In order for an act to be conceived as *causing* the harm, the situation of peril that the act brings about need be of only a moment's duration; still, such a situation must exist.

Once a situational construction of the events is made and the matter is conceived as one of a person causing harm by what he does, the door is open for rebuttal. The issue then is not the conceptual one of whether the actor did harm or caused harm. Rather, the question to be answered is whether or not the actor caused the harm. That answer is the one that may defeat liability, for if the admittedly dangerous situation was not really created by what the actor did, or if the harm occurring did not really result from that situation, or if the actor didn't really have reason to expect that the harm would occur as a result of what he did, he cannot be said to have caused the harm. If that is the case, he cannot be held liable.

What warrants the situational construction of events, and how the rebuttal of causal imputation can be accomplished, we shall consider shortly. But first we must consider a competing view of acts as causes of harms. It is an altogether different view, and one that manages to confuse the issues.

A DIFFERENT KIND OF THEORY, AND ITS ROLE

Common sense, science, and philosophy are all concerned about cause and effect. Explanations of how things came to be as they are, and predictions of what may yet come to pass, are surely as important as any task to which human intelligence is applied; nor is it any wonder that there is a quest for general principles to account for the connections among causes and effects. Theories of causation or causality not only seek warrants for saying that the existence of one thing may be attributed to that of another; in addition they seek ways of insuring that such warrants are valid. This enterprise of attribution we may call explanatory accounting, and the theory guiding and sustaining it we may call an explanatory theory of causation.

In contrast to this huge enterprise, there is a far more modest—though not unimportant—endeavor seeking answers to questions of whether conduct has caused harm. This we may call the enterprise of liability accounting, and its theory—our subject in this section—we may call a liability theory of causation. In furnishing an account of conduct and harm for purposes of determining liability, the precise history of events and conditions that brought the harm to pass is of scant interest. In weighing liability, it matters little precisely what role the act of the accused person played in relation to the roles of other things going on in the world and making their presence felt. It matters little—but the little that it does matter is important, for explanatory accounts do have something of importance to contribute to liability accounts. If a man is found dead in his garage with his skull crushed, it will be most important in dealing with a suggestion of homicide to know just what it was that caused his death. Was it carbon monoxide poisoning, which seems plausible in view of his suicide note and the car engine's fumes? Or was it the blow to the head allegedly dealt by the defendant while the dead man was still alive?

The coroner's examination is intended to enlighten us as to the cause of death, and if it supports an account unfavorable to the defendant we may expect it to be questioned critically and even challenged with countervailing expert testimony in court. Such a defensive posture rests on a conduct-regarding exculpatory claim that denies repsonsibility. Its gist is that the harm was caused by someone or something other than the act of the accused. The reason recognition is accorded to such an exculpatory claim is simple, though seldom appreciated. When in this straightforward way someone or something other than the conduct of the accused caused the harm, the accused could not, as we say, help it. Indeed, when not his act but someone else's, or something else, is the cause, he is most obviously not able to help what happened. As a consequence, making a man liable for harm he simply did not cause would be as stark a violation of the responsibility principle as may be imagined.

In a liability account, then, we first satisfy ourselves,

through a preliminary explanatory account, that it is not the case that no act of the accused was the cause (in an explanatory sense) of the harm. Having done that, we go on to those considerations that are peculiar to determinations of liability, and in altogether different ways decide whether the act caused the harm. Notice a nuance of language that helps to identify what kind of account is being provided. When X is an act and Y is a harm, the statement "X was the cause of Y" is always part of an explanatory account; but the statement "X caused Y" may either be part of an explanatory account or part of a liability account, ambiguity being resolved by deciding what sort of evidence or argument is appropriate to establish or impeach the claim. "Smith's blow was the cause of Jones's death" can be offered only as an explanation of the death. But "Smith's blow caused Jones's death" might be an explanation, or it might be part of an account concerned more immediately with liability and not at all with explanation. In that case we shall want to know about the creation, risks, and outcome of a situation connected with Smith's act and Jones's death, rather than whether it is someone or something else that accounts for Jones's death.

THE SITUATIONAL CONSTRUCTION OF EVENTS AND
THE EXCULPATORY CHALLENGES

Causation questions in the criminal law are about acts causing harm, and yet the question fixes attention on a situation for which an act is said to be responsible. The situation is said by those who make the accusation to be dangerous and to have eventuated in the harm it threatened. It is said also that the act of the accused brought about or materially enhanced the dangers in the situation, and because of that the act itself is deemed to have been dangerous. Yet, as we know, dangerous acts may themselves threaten harm and so may themselves be enough for liability, in which case no causation issue arises. One may well ask, then, why there is a causation issue in the one case but not in the other. Situations, after all, are always there to be perceived if only we choose to see them; and we must account for our choosing to see a situation in one case but not in another.

The answer lies in our appreciation of the facts. If we see nothing else bearing on the threat of harm lying between what was done and the harm that we suppose occurred because of it, we say simply that harm was done. But often after our acts take place, events take on a life of their own beyond our efforts and control. The acts of others, as well as other forces in the world that are foreign to our acts, influence the outcome of what we have done. Situations develop in which the danger lying simply in what we have done is overshadowed by conditions and events that are alien to our acts, and the danger is made to depend upon things over which we have no control. If our acts are dangerous, we expose ourselves to whatever liability the law may have established for such acts. As for the harm that grew out of a dangerous situation, we do not expose ourselves to liability unless reasonable expectations concerning the consequences of what we have done in creating that situation give our acts an ominous aspect with regard to the harm. Whether our acts are dangerous in that way is the question posed by a causation issue.

Five challenges must be faced by any claim that an act has caused a harm. The first—the preliminary one already discussed—borrows from an explanatory account of the events to claim that someone else or something else caused the harm. The other four all look to the situational construction of events, and the first of these four asserts that, even though the act of the accused may have been dangerous in some way, it was not the act of the accused that brought about or contributed in any material way to the dangerous situation from which the harm issued. Auto races and Russian Roulette furnish cases in point.

A number of drivers organize a race to see whose car is the

best. Details are arranged to minimize the chances of mishap, and the rules are followed by all the drivers save one. He disregards every precaution and drives recklessly until finally at a curve he veers off the track and kills a spectator. Without doubt he has caused the death of the person he hit. There is, however, a much weaker case (and perhaps no case at all), to be made against the other participants for causing the death of the spectator. Because of the precautions and their care in observing them, it is difficult, though not altogether impossible, to see the dangerous situation as being a thing of their creation.

Another illustrative case is a game of Russian Roulette being played by the three men who have organized it. The revolver is passed from one player to the other, each risking his life on a spin of the cartridge chambers. After the game has been in progress for some time, they are joined by a fourth man who takes his turn, passes the gun, and watches in horror as the man to whom he has passed it brings the game to an explosive conclusion. However the question may ultimately be decided, a weaker case on a charge of causing the unlucky player's death can be made against the fourth man than against the two surviving originators of the game. The reason is simply that it is more doubtful whether the situation whose dangers were realized was created by what the fourth man did.

A third way of challenging the accusation that an act caused a particular harm is to argue that, even though the actor may have created a dangerous situation by what he did, its dangers did not include the harm that occurred. As we already noted, when a robbery precipitates a fatal heart attack, there is an odd look to the proposal that the gunman's menacing act caused death. The reason is that heart attacks are not generally thought to be among the clear and present dangers created by a robbery. A case may be made (though not a strong one) if the victim is the person threatened, a weaker case if it is a bystander who might reasonably feel himself in some danger, and no case at all if it is merely an onlooker who is not in any danger but is frightened by what he sees. In each case the danger of what occurred is successively less, although in each the dangerous situation created by the gunman is the same.

Even if the conduct of the accused created the dangerous situation, and even if the situation threatened the harm that occurred, the harm may have occurred for other reasons. When this is so, it is, once again, wrong to say that the actor caused the harm—and this is the fourth of our challenges. An unusually subtle invention in the literature is instructive here. Three men in the desert have had a falling out, and two of them wish to kill the third. Each of the two devises his own plan unknown to the other. In the middle of the night the first man puts a fatal dose of poison in his companion's supply of drinking water. The second man knows nothing of this, but, a few hours later, knowing that the third man will be setting out on a trip alone at dawn, he proceeds to punch holes in the third man's canteen. The ill-fated companion sets out as planned and subsequently dies of thirst.

Both the first and the second man can properly be charged with attempted murder, for what each did quite clearly threatened the harm. The first man, however, cannot properly be charged with murder. True, he deliberately created a life threatening situation by putting poison in the water, but the death that subsequently occurred was not among the dangers of the dangerous situation that *he* created. When we look closely at this exculpatory claim, it turns out to be, once again, the preliminary challenge, though this time in a new form. The act of the *second* man was the cause of the death in the desert, and it would therefore be a stark violation of the responsibility principle to hold the first man liable, since nothing that he did, if left undone, would have spared the third man's life.

The man who drained the canteen does not have any of the challenges available to him as a defense, and so he continues to face homicide liability. Since the victim died of thirst in the desert, nothing could be plainer than that the act of depriving him of his only source of water created a dangerous situation whose dangers were indeed realized. Nevertheless, it has been argued that in effect the preliminary challenge provides a way out. Thus, the victim would have been finished off by the poisoned water had it not been made to dribble away by the man now charged with murder; and even though removing the victim from harm's way at one point will not excuse placing him in harm's way at another, the previous peril does provide a defense by another route. In order (it is said) for the act of one man to cause the death of another, it must be the case that without the act the death would not have occurred. In our case, however, it would have, and so the condition *sine qua non* for a cause has not been met.

The answer to this objection has already been given in general form. *Sine qua non* plays a major role in explanatory accounts, and any event that cannot prove itself to be *sine qua non* can hardly be taken seriously as a cause. But the matter is different in liability accounts. If according to a correct explanatory account of the death, the act of someone else was its cause, respect for the responsibility principle does indeed require that we not hold the accused liable, for if we did we should be making him liable for harm that is beyond his ability to prevent or avoid. But neither the responsibility principle nor anything else bearing on liability requires that we not hold the accused liable when what someone else did would have caused the death in any case (though it didn't). We determine liability not according to what fate had in store for the victim, but according to the conduct of the accused and the harm that it produced.

Two of these situation-regarding challenges to the proposition that an act caused a harm are denials of expectability, while the third one rests on the responsibility principle. In each of the two that deny expectability, it is said in effect that the accused had no reason to perceive among the dangers in what he was doing the harm that actually befell the victim, and hence no reason to expect that what he did would bring about what happened. A final challenge of this sort does not altogether *deny* expectability, but makes the expectation of harm seem tenuous indeed. Although the actor may have had reason to expect that what he did *might* bring about the ensuing harm, we are unwilling to say that he had reason to expect that it would, and so are unwilling to say that he caused the harm. In these cases the dangers of the situation are too uncertain, the outcome too speculative.

Consider the avaricious son who wishes to inherit as soon as possible from his wealthy mother. She has a delicate cardiac condition, and her doctor has told him that any upsetting news is very bad for her. To worsen her condition he tells her that he is himself dying of an incurable disease—an invention that he is certain will cause her great distress. Immediately, to his considerable surprise (and satisfaction), his mother suffers a heart attack and quickly succumbs. It is difficult to take seriously, for purposes of homicide liability, the suggestion that the son's story caused his mother's death. In an explanatory account it would not be an implausible conclusion, and certainly in condemning the son as a kind of moral monster we would connect in that way what he did with what happened. But for purposes of criminal liability the situation is much too uncertain. The beating of a chronically ailing heart depends upon conditions so complex that the effect of any item of bad news is speculative in the extreme. Though the doctor's warning is sensible enough—what, after all, is to be said against it?—it would be foolish to interpret it as a prediction of likely consequences should his admonition be disregarded.

The uncertainty of danger is made clearer by supposing that the son meant to kill his mother by telling her the news and that his mother was unaffected medically by what he told her, but that the authorities, having heard about what he did from shocked relatives, charge him with attempted homicide. It is the uncertainty of danger that makes such an accusation at the least profoundly disquieting. Conversely, one may imagine that the son chose to bring about his mother's death by means that create a situation the dangers of which are clearer. After being cautioned by the doctor not to alarm her in any way, he steals silently behind her chair and emits a piercing scream. Fatal consequences then seem much less problematic, since the effect of what was done upon the mother's cardiovascular system is quite certain and quite dangerous.

CAUSATION CLAIMS AND THEIR RESOLUTION

Situations, unlike most acts, are broad affairs that embrace the doings of many persons and the workings of many things. When harm occurs, it is sometimes tempting to look for *the* cause and to dispute the claim that a particular act was the cause—and this by arguing for another act or another feature of the situation which is said to be in some way or other more advantageously situated to fill that office. In explanatory accounts this makes sense, for we want to know what would have made a difference and, in order to make clear how the harm came about, we will choose as the cause the element that best instructs us as to how that harm might have been avoided. The office of cause will often be shared by a number of causal factors, each playing a partial role and together providing a full account. When a liability account is wanted, however, it is not a matter of *the* cause at all. It is a question of whether some particular act will qualify as *a* cause.

In any situation there may be many different acts that qualify, and thus for a single crime it is possible without inconsistency or duplication to have many different accusations based on these different acts. Unlike the case with explanatory accounts, there is no single office of *cause* to be filled (whether by one or more elements in the situation), for in liability accounting there are places open for any dangerous act that qualifies to become *a* cause of the harm. With this in mind, we turn now to the ways in which acts are sought to be disqualified in the criminal law as causes.

There are situations in which two or more acts appear as possible causes, and it might be suggested that a later act ought to be disqualified because of an earlier one. A person might be fatally wounded and then wounded again by a second attack. Death would have occurred anyway, says the second assailant, and so he claims that his assault ought not to be accounted a cause, even though it was a deadly assault.

The claim of a previous wound sufficient to kill does not disqualify the second fatal wounding as a cause. That second act is conduct of a kind to threaten death and to produce a situation fraught with the perils of death. It therefore merits treatment as conduct that caused death when death occurs in the normal course of events. The previous act, of course, created the same sort of situation. But that only makes that act a cause and hence a basis of further liability, without changing the status of the subsequent act. Again, as with the case of the men in the desert, one must be careful not to introduce surreptitiously a proviso that if the second act was unnecessary for the harm to occur, then that act is not to be regarded as a cause.

Alternatively, the second assailant might claim that the wound he inflicted was in itself not serious enough to have caused death, and for that reason ought not to be considered a cause. There are here the ingredients of a good defense. There might still be attempt liability for the homicide if the conduct itself were a deadly assault, for although the wound was trivial the conduct was of the sort that threatened death. But the *situation* created by the attack when a trivial wound was inflicted was not one of danger to life, and thus the act creating that situation is not a cause of death. We should take special note of this case, for in it we have both an *act* that *threatens* the harm, and the *occurrence* of the harm, yet with no liability for the completed crime, since the act did not cause the harm.

A slightly but crucially different case is, however, presented when there is a slight but crucial change in circumstances. A person may be seriously, but not fatally, wounded by a homicidal assault: barring unforeseen complications, he could reasonably be expected to survive if he receives prompt and competent attention. While lying seriously wounded, however, the victim is the object of a second homicidal attack—one in which a wound is inflicted that would normally be regarded as trivial but proves fatal in these delicate circumstances. In this case the person inflicting the second wound is properly said to have caused the death. It was his conduct that created a situation fraught with the dangers of death, though admittedly the abnormal circumstances in which he acted were not of his creation. His homicidal attack was conduct that threatened the harm that occurred; it created a situation that was dangerous with respect to that harm; and the dangers were realized. Since death is not normally the result of a trivial wound, the assailant might claim that the harm was not expectable. Such a contention is without merit, however, for harm must be expectable *only* with reference to his conduct, not with reference to its result. Given his homicidal attack, death of the victim was expectable, even though, given the trivial wound, it was not.

Further problems about causation emerge under the rubrics of *intervention* and *arrest*. After the act in question some other causal factor may intervene, or else the harmful consequences of the conduct may be arrested for a time. In either case the earlier act may seem to be nullified. Thus, a fire started by Smith to collect insurance may be swallowed up in a raging blaze of quite different origin. Or the fire he started may have gone out before doing any damage, but the tinder is later set ablaze quite by chance because of faulty electric wiring. Both cases present the question of whether Smith's conduct is properly accountable as a cause of the fire and hence possibly as an act of arson.

A true intervention (and not simply a merger) occurs when the second fire has its destructive effect before there is damage from the first. In that case a dangerous situation has been created by Smith's activity, and it is dangerous with respect to the harm that occurred; yet the harm does not occur because of that dangerous situation. If an act is to qualify as a cause of harm, the harm must occur because of a situation created by the act; in this case, however, that condition is unsatisfied. Even though the harm must occur because of the situation, it is not necessary that all, or even a substantial part, of the harm occurring be attributable to the dangerous situation in order for the act creating it to be regarded as a cause. If only some small part of the loss is definitely attributable to Smith's fire, that is enough for his act to be a cause. Extent of damage is not a consideration that enters a judgment concerning liability for arson, and so it is immaterial that Smith's very small fire resulted in only a very small part of the total loss.

It has been suggested in the leading work on legal causation, Hart and Honoré's *Causation in the Law,* that certain cases of intervening acts are to be regarded differently. On this view, when a subsequent act intervenes and assumes a role of cause in relation to subsequent events, by its intervention the subsequent act in effect pre-empts the role of cause and discharges the prior act as a cause whenever the subsequent intervening act is *voluntary*. From the examples provided of a "voluntary" act it is fairly clear that any act which the actor freely chooses to do would qualify.

But such broad special treatment for all cases of "voluntary" intervening acts seems unwarranted. Sometimes, of course, one person may deliberately take advantage of an opportunity for harm provided by another person, and the harm that he brings about by seizing on the opportunity is attributable to him and not to the person providing the opportunity. Thus, if I dig a hole in the street and cover it with a newspaper, I have reason to expect that someone will step into it and injure himself. But if a young man who saw what I did then amuses himself by bringing around a blind man and leading him onto the spot, his ("voluntary") act, and not mine, would be the cause of the injury that results. The reason is that in such case the dangers of the situation created by me were not realized, even though harm of the sort that made it a dangerous situation did occur. Had I eliminated all danger by appropriate measures of precaution I would still leave the hapless blind man as prey for the malicious youth. Building upon what I have done, the wicked youth creates another situation supplanting mine and eventuating in harm.

On the other hand, there may be intervening acts no less "voluntary" that do not place a limit on the consequences of my act and do not discharge it as a cause. If malicious mischief that extends even to victimizing the handicapped is the order of the day in my neighborhood, and I notice a smiling youth standing and eagerly watching as I dig my hole, I might well be said later to have caused the blind man's fractures, even though he would have suffered nothing without the malicious intervening act. Though in both cases the "voluntary" intervening act is the same, the manifest hazards of the situation that I have created are different with the young man plainly in the picture, and so therefore is what I have reason to expect and what I might then rightly be said to have caused.

True arrest (and not simply temporary interruption) yields to much the same analysis as intervention. If Smith's fire went out before doing any damage, and the tinder is later ignited by faulty wiring, there is then a question of whether he caused the destruction that followed. The crucial question is this. Did the dangerous situation created by Smith no longer exist once his fire stopped burning? If the fire no longer existed, the loss occurring later is attributable only to the dangers of a new situation produced by other events, in which case Smith's act could not be the cause. The answer to the question will depend on our appreciation of the hazards that comprise the situation created by his act. One or another mode of occurrence (we might say)—under such circumstances, it's all the same once tinder has been set, for the hazard of a fire existed so long as the tinder was there. Or, adopting the opposite view, we might argue that even though the tinder was necessary it was far from enough, and standing alone did not present any danger.

An act is sometimes said to be too remote to constitute a cause. This objection is the one raised most often, and yet its grounds are not well understood. Although physical remoteness may play some part, the touchstone is not the remove between act and harm in time or space. As a cause of death, dispatching a gift of poisoned sugarplums from the other side of the world is an act no more remote than placing the package in the victim's mailbox. A lingering illness from wounding to which the victim succumbs after six months need present no problem; whereas, an attack only six minutes before death from the wounds inflicted might be held too remote to be a cause when the victim is subjected to grossly improper treatment in the interval.

Lack of *proximate* cause (as the legal jargon would have it) is determined, not surprisingly, by reference to the dangerous situation prevailing. If the harm occurring is comprehended by the dangers of the situation created by the act—and not otherwise—the act has met the requirement of proximity and may be regarded as a cause. If a mugger knocks down his victim and leaves him lying unconscious in the road in imminent danger of being run over, there is little difficulty in viewing the attack as a cause of death when the expectable mishap occurs. If, however, while lying in the road the unfortunate man is, with the same fatal result, bitten by a poisonous snake escaped from the zoo, we should be very much inclined to reject the mugger's attack as a cause of death. Move the events to a primitive road through a snake-infested jungle, and the altered dangers of that situation militate in favor of an opposite result in each case. We can discern a simple but sure sign of remoteness for all cases. When we consider the actual risks in the dangerous situation created by the accused, we conclude that these risks did not comprehend the harm that occurred.

CAUSATION AND THE FIRST DIMENSION OF CULPABILITY

Two curious features of causation remain to be accounted for. The first is a rather mysterious connection between causation and what we have been calling the first dimension of culpability. It appears, for example, that when harm is done purposely we are less in doubt about an act's being its cause than we are when harm is done recklessly, and that this holds true generally for all degrees of culpability in the first dimension. Illustrative cases summon supporting intuitions.

Imagine in each of four different cases that a shot is fired by one person, and because of that another person dies of fright. In the first case the victim is shot at in an unsuccessful murder attempt; and although the bullet misses its mark, the fright it produces causes the victim to suffer a fatal heart attack. In the second case an enraged customer leaves a store and fires a gun blindly through the plate-glass window, fatally frightening another customer who is inside. In a third case a man who amuses himself by startling others shoots into the air in a crowded store, whereupon a fainthearted customer is fatally stricken. Finally, in a fourth case a round carelessly left in a gun is accidentally discharged while the weapon is being cleaned, and someone sitting nearby in the same room is frightened to death. In each case of successively diminished culpability there is also an apparent weakening of the causal tie between firing the gun and death from fright; and that weakening is significant in a liability (though not in an explanatory) accounting. This needs to be explained.

The analysis of culpability in Chapter Three pointed out that what was done *recklessly* was more dangerous than what was done *negligently;* that what was done *knowingly* was more dangerous still; and that what was done purposely was even more dangerous than that. It was pointed out also that when a more dangerous act is *intentional* it is (other things being equal) more culpable. Earlier in the present chapter we noted that when conduct was more dangerous there was better reason to expect the harm, and in this section we noted that when the actor had better reason to expect the harm there was better reason to regard his act as a cause of it. One further link, and the mysterious connection between culpability and causation is explained. The actor has better reason to expect that harm will occur if he intentionally does the sort of thing that provides one with a better reason for expecting harm to occur.

Since a more dangerous act done intentionally is more culpable, and since a more dangerous act done intentionally is also more reasonably to be regarded as a cause, it becomes plain that the more culpable act in these cases is quite rightly regarded as more certainly a cause. Notice that if the actor did not have good reason to expect what occurred, the greater culpability of his act will not strengthen it as a cause. If, for example, the store was in fact deserted but the bullet that was fired struck a hidden gas pipe and produced an explosion that killed someone in a nearby building, it would not matter whether the gun was fired to frighten persons thought to be in the store, or whether it was fired by accident. If the harm was not expectable, without any reference to culpability the act will rightly be judged not to have caused the harm in either case.

Not surprisingly, the correlation of causal standing and culpability obtains only when there is a causation issue in the first place. Suppose the victim in each of our four cases is struck by a bullet that causes his death. Death may be instantaneous or it may come only after weeks in a hospital bed. The coroner's report may state as the cause of death one or another fatal consequence of being shot. No causation issue is presented unless there is controversy regarding the creation, risks, or outcome of a dangerous situation said to have been created by the accused. Consequently, although the act is different in its first dimension of culpability in each case, there may well be no question of its being less a cause in one case than in another. It is then simply a matter of the act's being the cause of death according to an explanatory account tailored to meet the preliminary needs of a liability account, with questions of expectability never being raised. If they were—in each case, say, the medical treatment received was questionable, and the person firing the shots claims therefore that not his act but the treatment received by the victim was responsible for his death—then, once again, we should see culpability in this way matched with causal imputation. The murderer's act will then be more readily judged a cause than will the act of a careless, a reckless, or even a malicious person who fires the shots without intending to kill the victim.

Similarly, if the subsequent treatment deserves more blame than mere negligence would warrant—say, the doctors decide to experiment on the victim, with disastrous results—the status of that subsequent activity as a cause of death would be enhanced. There are greater dangers in affirmative departures from proper medical practice by doctors who experiment than there are in lapses from proper practice by those who are merely negligent. Because the dangers are greater, there is better reason to believe that harm will occur; and this strengthens the argument for improper treatment as a cause. When the dangers in improper treatment are great enough to overshadow the original dangers created by the shooting, not only will the treatment be accounted a cause of death; but the shooting will *not* be, for no longer can it then be said that *its* dangers have been realized in the death of the victim.

CHAPTER SEVEN
Actor-Regarding Exculpation

Exploration of the major areas of exculpation that were mapped in Chapter Five continues in this chapter. Attention is turned here to claims based on the predicament of the actor rather than claims based on the character of his conduct. In a reversal of roles, the responsibility principle now assumes the lead in giving these claims their force; though the culpability principle does show itself quite regularly to make important supplementary contributions when an essentially actor-regarding claim turns out to have in addition some conduct-regarding or some interest-regarding feature, and when an actor-regarding claim denies culpability directly by reference to the intentionality of conduct. A term familiar to everyone in its general use is introduced here and given harder edges as a term of art. Actor-regarding exculpatory claims are all *excuses,* standing in contrast to justifications on the one hand, and to a miscellany of conduct-regarding exculpations, on the other.

I. IGNORANCE AND MISTAKE

DISTINGUISHING IGNORANCE AND MISTAKE

One way to meet an accusation is to say, "I didn't mean to . . . ," completing the sentence with a statement of the act of which one has been accused. It avoids blame—or at least purports to—by claiming that the act was unintentional. If the accusation has been a gentle one—perhaps no more than implied—the suggestion that the whole thing was unintentional will itself usually serve to excuse. When the charges are serious and the accusation is more determined, one who offers an excuse will usually be asked to explain it. To make sure that the excuse is a credible one, an account of how the thing came to be done unintentionally is called for. Was it absentmindedness, inattention, insufficient skill, clumsiness, or sheer forgetfulness? Or perhaps it was a matter of not knowing, or realizing, or appreciating something—in which case it would be an excuse of a very special sort, one especially personal, if no more idiosyncratic or private than the others. The excuse would then rest on matters that are, strictly speaking, mental. When that is the case, and when the excuse is designed to meet a criminal accusation, such excuse is likely to be classified as one of ignorance or of mistake.

Ignorance and mistake are not the same, and exculpatory claims based on each are different. Intuition can be relied on to certify that they are different, but the difference between them cannot be learned simply by an appeal to intuition. *Being mistaken* and *being ignorant* appear at first to be contrasting mental states whose difference lies in the presence of some (wrong) belief when one is mistaken, and in the absence of any belief when one is ignorant. Here, however, ignorance is being offered to explain away something that was done; and people who offer their ignorance for that purpose, no less than people who offer their mistake, had better have a wrong belief to back up their claim.

Since ultimately the claim of ignorance rests also on a wrong belief, a person who properly claims that he was ignorant *was mistaken* as well. I glance in my wallet, fish out a twenty-dollar bill, and put it on the counter to pay for my purchase. The cashier inspecting the money notes unmistakable signs of a counterfeit. Suspicions are aroused, and I feel a need to defend myself by assuring everyone that I was not intentionally passing counterfeit money. "I certainly didn't know it was counterfeit," I protest. "I had no idea I had anything like that in my possession. The question never entered my mind!" Ignorance is what I claim; yet if I were asked whether I believed that the money was good, I should rightly reply that I most certainly did.

In the same circumstances, however, I might offer an excuse of mistake rather than ignorance. I had earlier noticed a suspicious-looking bill, had placed it (I thought) at the back of the wad in my wallet intending to show it to the authorities, but quite unwittingly I have just fished it out and placed it in front of the cashier. This time when I protest that I didn't intentionally pass a counterfeit bill I cannot rightly claim *ignorance* of its counterfeit character. It is true that I no more believed in this case than I did in the previous case that I was putting counterfeit money on the counter. But my knowledge that I well might have a counterfeit bill in my wallet puts out of bounds a claim that I was *ignorant* of the counterfeit character of the bill I produced. What I may rightly claim is that I believed I was offering a perfectly sound piece of currency and hence presented the counterfeit bill by mistake.

In both cases I performed unintentionally an act for which the law provides criminal liability when it is done intentionally. In the first case I presented counterfeit money *in ignorance,* since I hadn't a suspicion that it was no good;

whereas, in the second case I presented it *by mistake,* since I mistakenly believed it to be one of the good bills and not the suspicious one in my wallet. An exculpatory claim that is rooted in ignorance has greater strength than one rooted in mistake. Since I am better able to prevent the counterfeit from being passed when I know of its existence in my wallet, I can then mount only a rather feeble claim that I couldn't help presenting it. If, on the other hand, I simply do not know that I have counterfeit money on me, my ability is greatly diminished, and so my excuse is a much stronger one.

For cases of ignorance as well as of mistake, however, the culpability-regarding side of exculpation will prove more important than this responsibility-regarding aspect. Quite apart from the question of my ability to avoid the unlawful conduct, how dangerous is the act that I have done *intentionally?* In the case of ignorance, that act is less dangerous because harm is less expectable. A person who believes it likely that he is carrying a counterfeit bill has better reason to believe that he might offer counterfeit currency than someone who does not know that he carries a suspicious item in his pocket. The harm is more expectable and the act more dangerous. Since what is done intentionally is more dangerous in the case of the mistaken person than in the case of the ignorant person, it is more culpable. And this can have consequences that are crucial in the determination of liability.

The law might be designed to make liable only those who purposely or knowingly pass counterfeit money. The harm that is done or threatened by negligent or by reckless acts might be viewed as a tolerable burden that need not concern the law in its policy of protecting the currency; in which case those acts, though culpable, would not be deemed sufficiently culpable for liability. Either ignorance or mistake will serve to excuse if the law has this shape. But a different policy to protect the currency might be adopted by the law, and it may well be that only ignorance and not mistake will then do the job. In view of the greatly increased supply of bad money now in circulation, it might be deemed desirable to create liability for reckless acts or even for acts that are merely careless. If one of my bills has aroused my suspicions—or should have—my failure to make sure that I do not offer it by mistake would then be enough for liability, should I offer it by mistake. But if I offer it in genuine ignorance I would still have an excuse.

It is *mens rea* (to use the familiar jargon) that is denied when either mistake or ignorance is offered as an excuse. In either case it is being claimed that what for liability must be done intentionally has in fact been done only unintentionally. But just what it is that must be done intentionally is not always made clear. In legislation terms like "negligently," "purposely," "believing it to be," and the rest serve as qualifiers of culpability; and sometimes it is not clear what scope they are intended to have. It can be unclear, then, whether a mistake about the character of the bill tendered is required to exculpate, or whether a mistake about which bill it was that was being tendered is enough. When there is ambiquity of this sort in what is expressed, or when legislation simply fails to include the terms of culpability even though some excuses were clearly meant to be recognized, courts manage as best they can to resolve the uncertainty that then exists, by determining precisely what harm the legislation was meant to deal with and precisely what conduct merits liability as a threat of that harm.

THE MISTAKES THAT MATTER

The law provides that certain things have to be done if a person accused of doing them is to be made criminally liable. But not all these things are elements of the dangerous conduct that concerns the law; and if something not an element of such dangerous conduct is done unintentionally, that fact offered as an excuse will not serve to defeat liability.

At first it seems unjust to ignore such an excuse when it is offered, for it appears that punishment is then imposed in spite of the fact that the accused did not mean to do what is prohibited by the law. Upon reflection, however, it becomes clear that this is not so. If what was done unintentionally is not part of the dangerous conduct, it is not part of the conduct prohibited, for the law is concerned to prohibit only dangerous conduct. Sometimes, of course, part of the conduct required for liability is not of that sort; but then that part has no significance for culpability, and the fact that it was not done intentionally has no exculpatory force. Illustration helps make all this clear.

Suppose the federal government wishes to regulate traffic in dangerous drugs by requiring that shippers be licensed. It also wishes to impose licensing requirements upon those trafficking in whiskey, but for an altogether different purpose. Licenses for shipment of certain drugs are to be required in order to prevent their distribution outside of pharmaceutical channels; whereas, licensing of whiskey shipments is a measure designed to produce revenues for the federal government. Both laws provide criminal penalties if there is unlicensed transportation across a state line, for it is supposed that only when there is interstate shipment is there a clear jurisdictional basis for a federal drug-control law or for collection of federal whiskey revenues. But, it may be asked, should these laws further provide that the crossing of a state line must be done knowingly, so that one engaged in transportation without a license would not be liable if he goes into another state by mistake?

Such qualification seems appropriate in the case of whiskey, but not in the case of dangerous drugs. The governmental interest in revenues from interstate commerce in whiskey is not violated when what is intended as intrastate shipment includes by mistake an interstate detour. The reason is that the shipment is not part of interstate commerce, from which the federal government has an interest in deriving revenue; hence the inadvertent interstate detour is not a violation of that interest. There is, then, no harm and thus no conduct that is culpable with reference to such harm. When the same mistake is made in the unlicensed shipment of dangerous drugs, the matter is crucially different. While, once again, there is liability only when a state line is crossed, there is culpability without that. The harm—or threat of harm—is in the illicit drug trafficking, and that occurs regardless of whether a state line is crossed. What was done unintentionally—the crossing—was necessary only to furnish a jurisdictional basis for invoking the federal law. Culpability does not in any way depend upon crossing a state line, and so in no measure should culpability be affected by the fact that the accused didn't mean to do that. Since claims of mistake serve to avoid liability only if they have exculpatory significance, the mistake in this case should not provide a defense.

Not all harms are equally serious, and an actor may believe himself to be doing something that threatens a less serious harm when in fact what he does threatens a more serious one. Breaking into a home is a more serious form of burglary than breaking into a place of business, since security of persons in their homes is a more important interest. A burglar may break into a home that is located in a converted commercial building, and the burglar may believe that he is entering business premises of the sort usually found in that neighborhood. When charged with the higher degree of burglary, he pleads his mistake as to the character of the premises as an excuse. Should his mistake affect his liability? The answer depends, once again, on whether the mistake affects culpability. In this case the burglar had reason to believe, as he did, that the premises were business premises. The act done intentionally thus threatened the harm occurring when premises of that sort are broken into, even though the occurrence of that harm was not possible in this case. The bur-

glar is therefore entitled to have his mistake recognized in exculpation, and is properly charged with attempted burglary
of business premises.

This conclusion does not sit comfortably with everyone,
for, although theory may dictate otherwise, intuition makes
it appear that something more serious has occurred when a
home is broken into. But a fuller account should pacify
intuition, since once the intruder discovers his mistake, he is
no longer mistaken and is therefore unshielded by the excuse
against criminal liability for anything after that. The result
and the argument to support it are in principle no different
when business premises are invaded under similar circumstances by a burglar who thinks that he is entering a home.
His liability then would be only for attempted burglary of
the home; though again his excuse will not shield him for
what he does after he has discovered his mistake.

REASONABLE, UNREASONABLE, AND HONEST MISTAKES

It might have been unreasonable for the intruder to make
such a mistake or to persist in it when he became aware of
certain things. This presents the general problem of whether
a mistake that is unreasonable is nevertheless serviceable as
an excuse.

When a mistake is said to be unreasonable, it is not always
clear just what is meant. Four possibilities must be distinguished, for each presents the issue in a different light.

On the first interpretation the excuse is challenged since,
even if it is credited, the person offering it is still to blame. "He
made the mistake by not acting reasonably," is the way the
challenge might be put, implying clearly that not acting reasonably is the very fault that the accusation rests on in the
first place. When negligence or recklessness is charged, the
accused is held to account for doing what one reasonably
should not do, or not doing what one reasonably should. "I
didn't mean to do (or neglect) that," the accused may say by

way of excuse. "It was just a mistake." The reply "But it was an unreasonable one" reaffirms that the prescribed requirement for culpability has been met, that the mistake was not of the sort that might happen in spite of reasonable precautions. When this is what is meant, establishing that the mistake was indeed unreasonable defeats the excuse, for then the excuse fails to meet the force of the accusation.

A second possible challenge to the excuse is that to say that there was a mistake is not reasonable. Although a mistake has been claimed, there may be little reason to believe that one was made; indeed, the evidence at hand may even point in the other direction. And although the mistake is said to be unreasonable, it is really *the claim* of mistake that is then being called unreasonable. This challenges the proponent of the excuse to furnish sufficient backing for his claim so that it will not appear unreasonable: evidence, that is, to support his claim that his act was not intentional—and for the reasons that he claims. If not adequately backed, the excuse offered must give way, as any assertion must, to a denial that is stronger.

A third possibility has to do with reasonableness of belief. Looked at closely, this turns out to be a challenge of the same kind as the previous one, albeit an especially important challenge of that kind. If the accused insists that he thought the home he broke into was a place of business, it might be objected that *holding* such a belief was unreasonable. "There it is, plain as day," says the prosecutor, pointing to a picture of the vine-covered cottage, "a dwelling and not a place of business." The accused must then show that he had reason to believe as he did (e.g., someone familiar with the neighborhood told him it was really an antique shop). Otherwise his claim of making a mistake based on his being mistaken must be rejected, since there would then be stronger backing for its rejection than for its acceptance.

There is a fourth and final interpretation with which the

third is easily and often confused. It is sometimes suggested that a belief that is unreasonable results in an excuse that is invalid. The thought is that only when a wrong belief is reasonable will *acting by mistake* because of the belief be a valid excuse, for otherwise there will be no limit to the foolishness and imprudence that a person may successfully employ as the grounds of an excuse.

A belief may, of course, be unreasonable to the point of absurdity, and then a claim that it was actually entertained by the accused will usually be exceedingly difficult to establish. At times it will be virtually impossible to convince others, but at other times new insight into the mind of the accused at the time of the crime, or a fresh appreciation of some unusual features of the situation, may lead us to see that what first seemed an insult to common sense is in fact an eminently plausible claim. Once we conclude that the accused did have such a belief, we cannot refuse to recognize the excuse based on that belief simply because the belief is unreasonable. Service in providing an excuse is all that we ask of the belief; no matter how bizarre the belief may be, it may render that service if it truly was held by the accused, for even at the fringe of madness such belief still explains that the accused did not do intentionally what must be done intentionally if there is to be liability.

Though mistaken beliefs that are unreasonable will always serve in this way to excuse, they will usually be rejected when the defense seeks to justify, rather than excuse, what was done. In such cases the mistaken belief involves some matter of fact that would allow for a defense by way of justification if it were as the defendant believed it to be. The question then is whether the defendant's honest belief is enough to provide him with a defense no matter how little reason there may have been for him to believe as he did. When that question is answered in the negative—as it usually is—a further question can arise, for even a reasonable and honest belief that is mistaken may not be sufficient. An illustrative case makes clear the importance of these questions.

Suppose that a man convinces several companions that his wife wishes to have sexual intercourse with them, even though the story is without any basis in fact and has been contrived by the husband for reasons of his own. He also tells the men (all strangers to his wife) that her unusual sexual proclivities include a wish to be taken by force, and that they may therefore expect her to enhance her own excitement by resisting their advances. They all arrive at the man's house, awaken his wife, and, overcoming the predicted resistance, proceed to have forcible intercourse with her. When the men are later charged with rape, they claim that they honestly believed that the woman wished to have forcible intercourse with them. The question then is whether this is a good defense even if the belief was not a reasonable one.

The defense seeks to justify an act of forcible intercourse, which on its face is an act of rape. Consent by the person who appears to be the victim will sometimes justify what appears to be a criminal act. While the law will not allow the defense of consent in cases of more serious crimes, it will certainly allow it in the case of forcible intercourse, since the consent of the woman makes impossible a violation of her sexual autonomy—so that the harm of rape cannot occur. In our case, however, the woman has not consented, even though the men presumably believed she had.

Those violating rules of conduct sometimes have a right to do so, and for that reason ought not to be punished. Sometimes they have good reason to believe that they have such a right; and again it would be wrong in many of these cases to punish them, since their having good reason to believe that something is the case is often enough a good reason for allowing them to act in accordance with the belief, even though certainty is lacking. Otherwise we should be severely inhibited in the enjoyment of our rights—a right to have sex according to our tastes no less than a right to protect ourselves from those who threaten us. But unreasonable beliefs are another matter. Requiring people to make sure that they act on only reasonable beliefs inhibits only reckless acts, not acts that one is entitled to believe he has a right to do. Those who break the rules without having good reason to believe that they have a right to do so ought not to be accorded impunity, for, unlike those who have a reasonable belief, the reckless person could have avoided the criminally dangerous act simply by acting in a normally prudent fashion. Unlike punishment in spite of reasonable mistake, punishment in spite of unreasonable mistake encourages circumspection and restraint in situations in which circumspection and restraint are needed to avoid harm.

It is, however, not inconceivable that even some reasonable mistakes will not be acceptable as part of a defense of justification. There are situations in which *certainty* and not simply reasonable belief is what a person ought to have before he acts. If a woman who has for some time sought and enjoyed forcible intercourse now decides suddenly that it no longer interests her, and now refuses calmly, firmly, and in earnest her lover's violent advances, it seems not entirely implausible to argue that, even though the mistake that led him to persist was a reasonable one, it ought to be disregarded and his defense of consent rejected. If his own interests are not urgent or weighty, and the situation is so fraught with danger or the prospective harm is so serious that a person ought to ascertain the facts and not simply act on reasonable surmise, he cannot then claim that he had a right to act, even though he did not know how things actually stood.

As we have already observed, in a case that is fit for excuse rather than for justification the reasonableness of the mistake does not matter. Imagine that before he left the house the husband had coerced his wife's subsequent submission by threatening her with violence if she did not give herself to the companions he proposed to bring home later, and that his companions in their ignorance of the true situation had what in the eyes of the law is forcible intercourse when the frightened wife to whom they were introduced docilely submitted to their advances. They would then have had forcible intercourse *unintentionally* and would therefore not have done *intentionally* the act required by the law to be done intentionally in such a situation if there is to be liability for rape.

Even if the atmosphere of intimidation and other circumstances lead to the conclusion that the belief in the wife's willingness was unreasonable, the excuse offered by the men is still a good one, for they still would not have engaged in forcible intercourse intentionally. In spite of their excuse, they will then appear to have acted recklessly, and it might be urged that there ought to be criminal liability for what they did. Having such liability under the law might indeed be a good idea, even though it would be liability not for rape as we know it but for conduct less culpable—conduct engaged in by those who are heedless of the danger inherent in a suspicious situation but are not aware that what they do is the act of forcible intercourse prohibited by the law of rape.

We have noted in passing that beliefs must be honest if they are to be accepted. Whether the exculpatory claim is by way of justification or of excuse, and whether the belief is reasonable or unreasonable, it must be honest if it is to carry any weight. Although this requirement of honesty is regularly recited in judicial opinions, scant attention is given to what an honest belief is. It appears at first that only a *claim* that a belief was held can be honest, just as only a *claim* that a pain was felt or that a ship was seen can be honest: the thing claimed is itself neither honest nor dishonest. But the statement of such a requirement of honesty in this elliptical form would be utterly superfluous, for it goes without saying that every claim, not only claims of belief, must be honest if they are to be credited for exculpation. In fact it is the beliefs themselves that may be honest or not honest—just as the claim suggests; and there is good reason why only honest beliefs deserve to be taken seriously.

As we make our way through life we develop passions and acquire prejudices that make us want to see things in a way that suits us. Our beliefs are not always the outcome of disinterested exposure to those facts that are available to us, but sometimes result from our refusal to acknowledge certain facts that we find disagreeable or inconvenient; and we end up believing things to be as we wish them to be. There is, in short, a process of self-deception by which we seize upon and maintain beliefs that suit us, even though we ought to know better. Whether such beliefs are instances of willful intellectual dishonesty or are merely convenient misconceptions that we allow ourselves to slide into, *we* are responsible for holding such beliefs, for we have chosen not to look at the truth that is there for us to see if we only are willing to see it. If in the cases we have been discussing, the men refused to see what was plainly to be seen and instead persuaded themselves that things were as they wished them to be, there would then be no reason to allow their belief to weigh in their favor. After all, their belief matters—when it does—since, believing as they did, it would be unfair to require them to do other than what they did. But when the mistaken belief is held only because the accused chose to believe what suited him instead of what quite plainly was the case, how can it be unfair to require him to conform his conduct to the law instead of deluding himself and then violating it?

MISTAKES OF LAW

So far our discussion of mistakes and of ignorance has had reference only to what the actor did or to what he thought he was doing. No reference has been made to his ignorance of the law or to mistaken notions about it which he may have entertained when he acted. This second department of exculpation under ignorance and mistake bears the tag *of law* in conventional legal theory, where it is contrasted with what is called (without further discrimination) ignorance and mistake *of fact*. *Law* is far less busy than *fact* as a forum for exculpation. Its governing maxim has traditionally been *ignorantia juris neminem excusat,* which suggests that whatever claims are presented are summarily refused. This is misleading, however, for under certain unusual circumstances relief is sometimes available.

Claims of ignorance and of mistake are on an altogether different footing here. The accused can seldom find comfort in the fact that he was uninformed about the law, for true ignorance matters in one class of cases only. Sometimes, though only rarely, the law makes knowledge that the prohibited conduct is wrong a condition of criminal wrongdoing. Some few statutory provisions defining crimes do include a phrase like "knowing it to be unlawful"; and ignorance of the law is then a defense. One specimen of this unusual sort of legislation is a provision creating criminal liability for a public official who uses the powers of his office in deliberate disregard of the law, even though he might also violate the law quite innocently in the course of his duties and incur no criminal liability. Apart from these exceptional cases, being ignorant that it is wrong, in the law as elsewhere, does not itself excuse what is done.

Mistakes of law, on the other hand, do serve to exculpate under special circumstances. Only recently has this received explicit recognition in the law, and even then such recognition as has been accorded, though eminent, is not widespread. There are three forms that these exculpatory claims may take, one interest-regarding, the other two actor-regarding. Since mistakes of law do not come ready titled, however, it is necessary before discussing these claims to distinguish them as a group from mistakes of fact. Lawyers have not spared themselves in their effort to draw this distinction, but results have often been disappointing.

In the context of criminal accusation, when something legally impermissible has been done there may be either a mistake of law or a mistake of fact. When there is a mistake of law, what has been done is based on a mistake, but it is not done by mistake. When there is a mistake of fact, even though what is done is also based on a mistake and occurs because of it, what is done is done by mistake. Doing the impermissible *by mistake* in the one case but not in the other serves as a distinguishing feature.

The actor's mistake about the law may be either a mistaken belief that it is not legally wrong to do as he does, or that it would be legally wrong not to do as he does. But not any mistake about the law will do. The mistake must be about some provision of the law that bears on culpability. The reason is simple enough. Accusations are based only on culpable conduct. What makes conduct culpable is those provisions of the law that bear on culpability. Since excuses must meet accusations, only mistakes about legal provisions bearing on culpability are relevant for purposes of excusing. A mistake about some provision of the law bearing on liability but not on culpability, like a mistake in doing something that bears on liability but not on culpability, would lack exculpatory force because it would fail to meet the accusation.

We can turn again for illustration to the two federal licensing laws governing interstate shipments—one enacted to control dangerous drug traffic, the other to derive revenues from commerce in whiskey. For the unlicensed shipper of dangerous drugs whose wares were transported across state lines, a mistaken belief that the law did not require for liability the crossing of a state line would have no exculpatory force, since his activity is culpable without that; and his mistake would therefore not qualify as a mistake of law that might be useful in meeting an accusation. But under the revenue measure requiring a license for interstate shipment of whiskey, the same mistaken belief about what the law required would have exculpatory force against a charge of unlicensed interstate shipment and would be regarded as a mistake of law, for the shipper's mistake was about a matter that bears on culpability.

Only under special circumstances will mistakes of law have sufficient exculpatory force to avoid liability. There are then three different claims that might be made.

The first claim, an interest-regarding rather than an actor-regarding one, is in essence that a person is justified in relying on an authoritative opinion of what the law is, since otherwise a very important social interest would be compromised. There is a social interest in preserving citizens' confidence in those persons whom the legal system has designated as its spokesmen, for otherwise official statements of the law will no longer serve as a guide in deciding what to do. When there is doubt about what the law is, it is usual to consult official pronouncements and to obtain professional opinions. But legislation is often not plain on its face, and judicial interpretations as well as administrative elaborations may still leave the matter unclear. Eminently qualified lawyers may, and often do, disagree about what the law is at any given time. And, to compound uncertainty, even the clearest shape imparted to a law by judicial decisions may be changed by later decisions. In view of this, it is no wonder that a person acting on the best available authority concerning the state of the law may subsequently find himself accused on at least equally good authority because a different view now prevails.

One might argue that the earlier view was the better view, and if successful that argument will provide a good defense. But in fact the earlier view may not have been the better view. The burden of the argument then must be that under the circumstances the accused was justified in acting as he did, even though his view of the law was mistaken. The argument points to what was from the citizen's viewpoint an eminently reasonable reliance on statements of the law. If a later view of the law can result in liability, there could never be reliance on the law at any time, and speculations as to what the law might be in the future would then supplant the present state of the law as a guide to conduct. The law would lose its authority, and the law-abiding attitude of the good citizen would weaken as the notion of settled law upon which his attitude depends is eroded.

But not any reliance on a mistaken notion of the law will do to avoid liability. Such reliance must be reasonable—which means that the opinion being relied upon must have very strong credentials. If a merely plausible opinion were enough, the law would be exposed to subversion on another front. Such a rule would mean that, when there was doubt about the law, each person could resolve it as he chose; and so long as his view of the law had some merit he would avoid liability. Uncertainty about the law would then be an invitation to circumvention, for nothing more than a competent exercise of the lawyer's craft in construing the law to favor his client would be needed to gain exoneration. There is a social interest in being able to rely on good professional advice about the law from one's lawyer, but the interest is not important enough to allow for the exploitation and the compounding of uncertainty in the law. Even though his lawyer's view of the law—which the accused acted on in good faith—may well serve to reduce the extent of his liability, it will not exonerate from liability. For that the law requires an opinion that is authoritative and official.

The other two versions of the claim of mistake of law are both actor-regarding denials of responsibility.

A person may act because he thinks the law requires him to. The law, as we know, may be uncertain and even changeable. Later it turns out that one need not have acted and—

even worse—that what one did is against the law. It is not reasonable reliance on the law that one now argues, but rather that one felt compelled to act as one did and that it was quite reasonable to feel that way. A person believes that, had he not acted in accordance with what were authoritatively presented as requirements of the law, he would be subject to penalties that he had good reason to believe would be imposed. It is the case of a person compelled by the law as he quite reasonably understands it.

The threats of the law are certainly to be taken seriously, and one who acts in response to threats that he reasonably understands the law to make is entitled to assert an exculpatory claim of compulsion (to be considered more generally in the next section of this chapter). He, like the person acting at gunpoint, has a greatly diminished ability to choose to do otherwise. Even if the threat should turn out not to be real, it was reasonable for the actor to believe it was real, and these are plausible grounds for exculpation. But if the opinion on which he acted was merely the unofficial opinion of someone in a position of authority, it was not reasonable for him to feel threatened, for rather than acting as he did he might reasonably have looked into the matter and discovered that the law had not been promulgated or interpreted officially in the way he thought it was.

There is, finally, the other actor-regarding denial of responsibility that presents itself as a mistake of law. Certain mistakes about the law tend to exculpate on a theory of privilege arguing that an act may be done free of liability when its prohibition is not sufficiently well-known. Some of the things the law prohibits—the best-known crimes in any penal code—have antecedents in social prohibitions that are independent of the law. In such cases members of society cannot claim to be at liberty to do as they wish without restriction under social norms apart from the law. But any legal system that is at all sophisticated also places restrictions on what one is free to do apart from the law, rather than simply endorsing (or granting dispensations from) those restrictions that exist independent of the law. In order for a legal restriction to curtail a prior privilege to act by making the act a legal wrong, those affected by the new law must have opportunity to conform their conduct to it. This is a practical constraint upon the law, for without such opportunity the law cannot succeed in its purpose.

Even more important for present concerns is the fact that lack of opportunity to conform one's conduct to the law is grounds for invoking the responsibility principle. In general, anyone who is not able to abide by the law, and who breaks it because of that, has his inability available as the basis of an excuse. When there is no normal opportunity for the law to be known, it is as a practical matter unknowable, and those who are supposed to be bound by its requirements are then unable to comply. In order for the law to be knowable, there must be publication adequate to enable those affected by it to inform themselves by those methods conventionally relied upon by law-abiding citizens. Though that is the essence of the matter, it is not quite as simple as at first it might seem.

On the model of prior privilege there must be reason for the citizen to seek to inform himself about the law. It is not usual under any legal system for each person affected by a new law to be notified of that; but neither is it usual for a citizen to ascertain the lawfulness of each activity he wishes to engage in. A legal system does not rely upon either a general obligation of the state to inform its citizens or upon a general civic obligation on the part of citizens to inquire. There is a presumption that a person either is informed about the law because the matter is sufficiently well-known, or that he is prompted to inform himself when the activity at hand is notoriously of the sort that falls within the general concerns of the law.

There are two broad and overlapping categories of such activity. One consists of conduct that under current views in the community is considered wrong, offensive, harmful, immoral, dangerous, or in some other way untoward, and would normally be regarded as a matter of public concern for that reason, even though a person may be at liberty legally to engage in it. The other category consists of conduct which, according to generally known interests of government, might be the subject of legal regulation for reasons other than the character of the conduct. Typically such conduct is the subject of laws establishing regulatory offenses, and these laws prohibit certain activities or require certain others only to implement some policy. Since, however, not all conduct falling within these two categories is made the subject of legal restriction, one who does not know of such restriction may rightly claim that he should be excused for having violated the law when it has not been adequately published. Further, if a law restricts conduct not falling within either of these categories, a person violating such a law without knowledge of it may rightly claim to be blameless even when there has been publication that would otherwise be adequate. Notification of those who may be affected is required in order for these somewhat eccentric legislative specimens to have the force of law in curtailing the prior privilege of those affected, since nothing about the activity restricted in such a case would prompt inquiry. When such laws are drafted, it is usual to include a provision for prior notification of anyone affected as a condition that must be satisfied if the law is to be enforced against him. The theory of exculpation is the same whether it is insufficient promulgation or lack of notice that furnishes the grounds of exculpation. The accused in such a situation has been deprived of fair opportunity to conform his conduct to law. Lacking opportunity to do otherwise, he could not help what he did.

II. COMPULSION

Sometimes people are forced to do what they do. When what they are forced to do is wrong it seems that the compulsion ought to count in their favor. After all, we say, such a person wasn't free to do otherwise—he couldn't help himself, not really. No claim to avoid blame appeals more urgently to our moral intuitions, yet none presents more problems of detail. There are times, after all, when we ought to stand firm and run the risk of harm to ourselves instead of taking a way out that means harm for others. In such a situation we must expect to pay the price if we cause harm when we prefer ourselves, for then the harm is our fault even though we did not mean it and deeply regret it. But how shall the line be drawn to separate cases in which the constraint is sufficiently powerful to make blame inappropriate from cases in which constraint is simply a challenge to avoid harm to oneself as best one can while doing no harm to others? A line too far in either direction means injustice, for it is not right to allow with impunity harming that should have been avoided, nor is it right to punish for harm whose avoidance cannot reasonably be expected.

To begin with, the very notion of compulsion that concerns us here must be clarified. "Being forced to do something" will serve as a rough paraphrase for ordinary purposes, but it cannot be used for more demanding work. It is doubly undiscriminating as a phrase used to deny responsibility, for it admits too much and then fails to make important distinctions among what is properly admitted. Often I rightly say that I was forced to do something, though I do not for a moment doubt that I am responsible for what I did, since after a careful assessment I chose the path of prudent self-interest rather than another path that was fraught with unpleasant consequences. But even when I am forced to do something in a way that makes holding me responsible for it seem wrong, I may be relieved from blame by claims other than that of compulsion. This is so when, for example, I did what I did because of dark and unmanageable urges within me, or when I was compelled to do it by nothing more mysterious than the force of gravity.

The phrase "I couldn't help it" is more promising. Though it, too, admits certain cases in which culpability is denied for reasons other than compulsion, it will not let in cases of thoroughly responsible action. There are four different ways to interpret "I couldn't help it," though only the third and the fourth express a claim of compulsion of the sort that interests us at this point.

"I couldn't help what happened" is what we might say when something happened by accident. It is appropriate when we were involved merely as an instrument of harm and nothing more, or when we were merely in the vicinity, and a false appearance of involvement was created. In such a case we were subject to forces with which we could not cope—either because they were beyond our power to control or because there was no opportunity for us to intervene. These exculpatory claims are conduct-regarding denials of responsibility, not claims of compulsion, for, instead of asserting that we were compelled to act, they argue that we did not act at all. We were acted on, or had something happen to us, or (even more starkly) there we were when it just happened and we could do nothing, even though the outcome harmed others.

"I couldn't help what I did" is a second rendering of "I couldn't help it," but with very different implications. A person may have an urge so strong that he finds himself unable to resist, or he may be overcome or even overwhelmed by emotion and may lose control of himself. He then may declare, "I couldn't help what I did" to register his inability to restrain himself from doing as he did. Such a person is not really claiming that he had to do anything, even though ordinary descriptions make it seem that he is. What he claims is that he *felt* that he had to and—even more important—that he was precluded from *making a choice not to do it* because of something that was wrong with him. Such personal incapacity may be episodic or chronic; in either case it furnishes grounds for excuse that are stronger even than compulsion. Such a person often is left truly unable to do otherwise by his urges or his emotions, while this is only rarely the case with a person who was forced to do what he did under compulsion. In the law these excuses are spoken of as irresistible impulse and diminished responsibility. Along with kindred claims of mental abnormality, they are investigated in the next section.

We come now to the two interpretations that represent the claims of compulsion of interest to us here. The first might be expressed by saying "I couldn't help doing it," and the claim so expressed would be classified as an actor-regarding denial of responsibility. This is a claim of inability to do otherwise because of lack of opportunity, and the lack of opportunity may be brought about either by a dangerous situation leaving the actor without choice, or by menacing conduct precluding a choice that would avoid harm both to himself and to others.

There are two forms that his inability may take: he may have no opportunity to choose, or he may lack any other opportunity, and so have no choice. The difference was illustrated in Chapter Five by the perilous situation of two mountain climbers dangling in mid-air, one above the other, on a single rope that will break unless one cuts the rope and lets the other fall. Menacing conduct, and not simply the dangers of the situation, will also illustrate this difference.

Suppose that a third man already firmly anchored above these two had deliberately tugged on the rope to cause them to become suspended this way, and had then threatened to cut the rope and kill them both unless one cuts the rope and finishes off the other. The man ordered to cut the rope might then be compelled to do so. In his terrified state he might not be able to make a choice that would save both himself and his companion; he would be unable, that is, to avail himself of some opportunity for safety that he would normally have perceived if he had his wits about him. Or again, it may become clear as the situation is calmly surveyed that the threat leaves no alternative to compliance. But the excuse appropriate in either case has as its ground lack of available opportunity, not lack of personal capacity.

When the excuse takes the form of inability to choose, it often appears that the person was unable to choose because his state of mind precluded choice, and that because he was frightened he acted impulsively instead of choosing what to do. Many times this is indeed the case; still, however, it is *lack of opportunity to choose* and not his state of mind that furnishes grounds for an excuse of this form. For one thing, people who are frightened and act impulsively sometimes do have opportunity to choose, and when they do we dispute the claim that they could not have done otherwise. Choices in great profusion are commonly made by persons "running scared" as they seek to escape harm, and such choices stand as clear examples of ability to choose even in a state of abject terror. For another thing, a person may be in a perfectly normal state of mind and fully in possession of himself, yet without opportunity to choose—in which case precisely the same excuse is available to him. Thus, the rope is frayed and unraveling, and upon reflection it seems to the man above that both he and his companion will plunge to their deaths unless he cuts the rope at once and eliminates the weight below him. If he then proceeds without delay to cut the rope, his lack of alternative will serve him as an excuse, even though his personal capacities were in no way impaired.

There is, finally, a fourth way of interpreting "I couldn't

help it" to express a different claim of compulsion that is interest-regarding. As he dangles in mid-air, the experienced climber, coolly surveying the situation, may consider gradually swinging with his injured companion toward the side of the cliff until he himself is close enough to grab hold of an outcropping branch. The risk in this is great, however, for the attachment of the rope to the ledge of rock above is precarious and the swinging motion might pull it free. He decides finally that to prevent both of them from losing their lives the only reasonable course is to cut the rope and eliminate the weight of his companion, so that he can pull himself to safety. When accused of causing his companion's death he well might say "I couldn't help myself." This is a claim of regrettable necessity, declaring that what was done was justifiable because, all things considered, it was necessary to save his own life. To be sure, he had an alternative course and an opportunity to choose it. He therefore was able to do otherwise and is not entitled to an excuse. But since he had good reason (so it seems) for rejecting the alternative, what he did under the circumstances is (so it seems) justifiable.

LIMITATIONS UPON EXCULPATION

Two different interpretations of "I couldn't help it" have yielded two different claims of compulsion. The first denies responsibility because there was a lack of other available opportunity. "I couldn't help doing it" is the declaration that makes this more clear. The other, "I couldn't help myself," seeks to avoid blame more directly by justifying what was done.

Both the excuse and the justification present serious problems. If a person feels himself threatened and genuinely believes that he must act in a certain way to avoid harm, does that always provide the foundation of a good excuse? In spite of honest convictions, some notions about dangers and about measures of protection are unreasonable. Will honest but unreasonable belief provide a good foundation for the excuse "I couldn't help doing it"?

The difficulty with justification also is one of qualification, and it is more complex. The actor is surely not entitled, no matter what the cost, quite simply to prefer his own interests over others and to do anything necessary to protect them when they are wrongfully threatened. Life in society depends upon suitable regard for others as well as for oneself; and when the man who stands accused replies "I couldn't help myself," we have a right to require of him more than a bare showing that self-interest prompted what he did.

Turning to the problems of excuse, we have mistakes to deal with as the first order of business.

The accused may be quite wrong in claiming that he "couldn't help doing it"; yet his mistake may have been a reasonable one. A mountain climber dangling in mid-air cannot be expected to appreciate certain possibilities that would save both himself and his companion, even though such possibilities are obvious enough to me as later I sit watching films of the misadventure. He was altogether wrong about what he should do or could do. But his mistake was not unreasonable, since the situation in which he found himself deprived him of insights that as a mere observer he should certainly have had. Nothing more than the responsibility principle is needed to excuse him, for, given the limitations that the situation imposed upon him, he could not do otherwise.

Unreasonable mistakes make more interesting as well as more perplexing cases, and they reveal an important point about lack of opportunity. Like reasonable mistakes, unreasonable mistakes can be made in several different ways. A person may believe that he is being threatened when he is not, and his mistake is so obvious that we have no hesitation in asking how he could ever have seriously believed that he was in danger. Unlike the case of reasonable mistake, the actor then has no reason to believe as he does. Sometimes the

threat is actually far less serious than he thinks it is as he
tries to escape it, and his actions in protecting himself then
seem much too drastic. If he had no reason to exaggerate
the threat as he did, once again his mistake is unreasonable. Another problem is presented when a person in danger fails to see an obvious course of action that would avoid
harm to the other person as well as to himself. When such
a course is normally as obvious to a man in his position as
it is to anyone else, his mistake, again, is unreasonable. In
any of these cases, when what is done to protect against harm
is unreasonable, the actor may claim that even though it was
mistaken and unreasonable it was honest and thus ought to
furnish grounds of excuse. Those who accuse him will argue
that what he did was not only needless but inexcusable as
well, for, unlike the situation in a case of reasonable mistake,
the actor in this case had no reason to do as he did.

Refusal to credit unreasonable mistakes can be endorsed
as sound policy so long as they are carefully distinguished
from reasonable mistakes. When the actor's mistake was unreasonable the opportunity to avoid harm was available to
him, and yet for *reasons of his own* that are not good reasons
he did not avail himself of it. When the actor's mistake is
reasonable, the opportunity to avoid harm also was available
to him, but it was not simply for reasons of his own that he
did not avail himself of it. Rather, he had good reasons for
not acting as he might have, even though the facts of the matter provide better reasons for a contrary conclusion about
how he should have acted. Since he was not in possession of
those facts, nor had he reason to seek them out, they cannot
be counted as part of what he knew or ought to have known
in determining whether he had good reason for acting as he
did; hence in spite of them his mistake remains reasonable.

It is different with unreasonable mistakes. True, the man
who made unreasonable mistakes was likewise not in possession of the facts, and likewise that will not count against him.

But unlike the perpetrator of a reasonable mistake, he who makes an unreasonable mistake makes his mistake in spite of what he knew or had reason to look into. A person making a reasonable mistake is disabled by what he does not know and has no reason to find out, and it would therefore be a transgression of the responsibility principle not to give effect to his mistake. This, however, is not the case when the mistake is unreasonable, for the actor then is not unable to appreciate and seize the opportunity, even though for reasons of his own he does not do so.

Though the reason for rejecting unreasonable mistakes is clear enough, one still feels that perhaps, after all, these mistakes do deserve credit in an excuse *if they are honest*. All honest mistakes, it seems, stand on the same footing, for in all cases the actor who was a victim of an honest mistake truly believed without self-deception that what he did was necessary, no matter how foolish or obtuse such a belief may have been. But we are misled by this feeling—quite likely because we confuse the excuse here with the excuse of mistake discussed in the previous section. There we noted that unreasonable mistakes, no less than reasonable, resulted in the accused doing *unintentionally* the act that the law required to be done *intentionally* if there is to be liability for it. But with the excuse of compulsion the argument is altogether different, and rests upon the principle of responsibility instead of the principle of culpability. While it makes perfect sense to say that an act is done unintentionally whether the mistaken (though honest) belief prompting it is reasonable or unreasonable, it makes no sense to argue that because of his admittedly unreasonable (though honest) mistake the actor was unable to do otherwise.

The defense of compulsion has its aspect of justification—and this too, like exculpation by way of excuse, presents problems of limitation. When the defense admits that the actor had a choice and so concedes that he is without excuse, it may still claim that he had to break the rules to protect himself or others. But it would be unconscionable to allow harming with impunity simply because the harmdoer could escape or prevent harm in no other way. Such a broad principle would permit great harm done to avoid slight harm, and would countenance harm that was immediate and certain when done to avoid harm that was remote and speculative. It would allow a person in peril who is to blame for his own predicament the same right to harm others as it would allow a person who is merely a victim of circumstances beyond his control. Hedging is necessary to prevent unsuitably wide exculpation, and seven different considerations bear on the determination of proper boundaries. Easy cases of justifiable harming can be analyzed with reference to these considerations, and even though such cases provide no ready formulas by which hard cases can be made easy, there are arguments by analogy with respect to these considerations that guide the decision of new and difficult cases.

The first point to be considered is the *seriousness of the harm* to be avoided. Loss of life is more serious than loss of property; and because of that, certain harmful measures are justifiable to protect life but not property. A subsidiary consideration attaches importance to *who is being protected.* Harm to me or to those whom duty or affection constrain me to protect is for me more serious than harm to someone who is a stranger. Using force to protect one stranger from another may therefore not be justifiable, though the same act might well be justifiable if done to protect a person who is naturally an object of protection.

The *harm inflicted to prevent harm* may be more or less serious—and this must weigh as a second consideration in deciding what is justified. A thief seeking only to escape with one's money may justifiably be stopped by forceful measures that injure him, although acts calculated to stop him by killing him are not justified.

A third and a fourth consideration are likewise counterparts. Harm to the person threatened may have been imminent or it may have been remote, and the risk of harm in what he did to avert the danger he faced may likewise have been either great or small. Some principle of *proportion between threat and response* must be observed, so that manifestly empty threats do not serve as well as truly ominous ones to justify a drastic response.

The next two considerations also are counterparts addressed to the accused and his victim. Having engaged in harmful or dangerous conduct, the accused now claims that he was compelled to do what he did in order to protect himself. If he exposed himself to harm, however, we should look into the full context of his activity, for otherwise people might be allowed to run risks of harm to themselves without good reason and then ask others to pay the price of their imprudence. Having disparaged their own interests by the risks they so cavalierly took, they cannot then claim that their interests ought to prevail and justify doing harm to others. The victim of harm must have his conduct scrutinized in the same way. Did he in some way provoke the harm that he suffered, or was he an innocent victim who had done nothing to diminish the respect to which his interests were entitled?

Prudence and *necessity* combine as a final consideration. If what the accused did was, strictly speaking, necessary to escape harm, he has the ingredients of an excuse and needs no justification. In that case he had no opportunity to do otherwise so as to avoid harm and so, having been unable to do otherwise, he was not responsible for what he did. But necessity is not always that strict, and more permissive though no less correct imputations of it are often made in order to justify what was done. It is then claimed that the course of conduct pursued by the accused was necessary to escape harm, even though admittedly he had opportunity to do otherwise and could have adopted another course. What is meant is that it would have been imprudent to have chosen some available alternative, since interests meriting protection would then have been compromised. Thus, for example, additional lives might have been saved by allowing everyone in the water to climb aboard the lifeboat; but preventing some from doing this was necessary, it is said, for otherwise the survival of everyone in the overloaded boat would be seriously jeopardized. One may be justified in rejecting available alternatives that involve risks or concessions in excess of what prudence would dictate, and one may then rightly claim that the course one adopted was (so to speak) necessary.

These considerations are not all openly embraced in the law by the principles of justification to be found in a penal code, and some of them are generally neglected altogether. The provisions of the Model Penal Code, for example, set forth a defense of justification by necessity, and present only a "choice of evils" test. This test makes justifiability depend simply upon whether the harm produced by the conduct is less than the harm it avoids. Only the seriousness of the harm done and of the harm avoided need then be considered. But surely this will prove too meager when, for example, the harmful act is done in anticipation of some possible harm that is still distant and uncertain, or when the person who does harm does it to avoid harm that he has invited upon himself.

CRITIQUE OF THE CONVENTIONAL DEFENSES

Two different defenses based on different principles have been distinguished. Claims of both kinds are rightly called claims of compulsion, though one is a defense by way of excuse and the other by way of justification. But the law's grasp of fundamental principles in this region of exculpatory claims is particularly unsure, with evidence and arguments that are really beside the point admitted and even encouraged through unsatisfactory statutory provisions. The Model Penal Code, which has served as a prototype for much enlightened law reform in the United States, serves here also as a source of instructive mistakes.

The Code contains a general defense of justification-by-necessity that we have just noted. Under this provision, conduct believed by the actor to be necessary in order to avoid harm to himself or to another is justifiable if the harm that he seeks to avoid is greater than the harm that the law seeks to prevent in creating the offense with which he is charged. There is no suggestion either in the text of the Code or in the accompanying comments that prudential considerations may enter the actor's deliberations and that he is free to reject unreasonable courses and to adopt as a matter of necessity the course he takes then. Rather, the actor is held to a test of strict necessity in which alternatives, as a practical matter, are simply impossible. This would leave the actor unable to do otherwise, and so furnishes grounds for an excuse rather than for the justification that the Code purports to provide here. But the Model Penal Code also provides a defense of *duress*. According to its terms, it is an affirmative defense that may be invoked when the accused engaged in criminal conduct because of unlawful use of force upon his own person or upon the person of someone else, or because of a threat of such use of force. A proviso is added, however, that the force—or threat of it—must be such that a person of reasonable firmness in the situation would have been unable to resist.

It is clear that the defense of duress was intended as an excuse. The reporter in his comments speaks unmistakably in the language of excuse, describing the typical case as one in which "the actor makes a choice but claims in his defense that he was so intimidated that he was unable to choose otherwise than as he did." This inability, spoken of as "psychical incapacity," is made the focal point of whatever exculpatory force duress is to have. But insofar as the suggestion is of an abnormal mental state it misconceives the excuse. There is a

defense of "diminished responsibility" that is based on para-
lyzing or overwhelming fear, and, though not universally recognized, it is not unknown to the criminal law, and is examined, along with other claims of mental abnormality, in the
next section of this chapter. Such a defense relies naturally
enough on evidence of the accused's psychological condition
at the time. A claim of duress, however, neither calls for nor
admits of such evidence. As an excuse it calls attention to the
dearth of opportunity to do otherwise, either because any
other course was blocked by its dire consequences, or because
the threat created a situation in which making a choice was
impossible. In either case there is no "psychical incapacity"
to which appeal need be made, for the actor may have been
in full possession of his undiminished "psychical capacities"
and still unable to do otherwise.

What kind of excuse *duress* might be is one question, but
there is then a further question of whether duress is really an
excuse at all, since its formulation in the Model Penal Code
makes it appear more like a justification than an excuse. Under the Code provision the actor's inability entitling him to
his excuse must be produced by force, or threats of force,
against the person. But imagine a man living without opportunity in abject and hopeless poverty, and depending for
his very survival upon the meager employment provided by
another man who now threatens to cut that off and leave him
destitute if he does not do as he is ordered. Or imagine a
famous man who is widely admired but will certainly become
an object of contempt and ridicule if a threatened disclosure
about him is made. The Code provision makes no allowance
for such coercion, even though in principle the threat in
these cases provides as good a basis of excuse as a threat of
force against the person. This limitation to the use or threat
of force against the person makes sense in the design of a
justification, though not of an excuse, for interests in remaining free of physical harm may be deemed sufficiently impor-

tant to justify acts undertaken for their protection, though interests in income or reputation may be thought not to be important enough.

A second feature marking duress in the Code as a justification rather than an excuse is this. The use of force or the threat of its use does not exculpate according to the Code provision unless the use or threat of use is unlawful. That is reasonable enough when blame is to be avoided by way of justification, for wrongful conduct engaged in to protect against force or threat of force remains *prima facie* criminally wrong in spite of what prompted it if the force or threat was lawful in the first place. If that were not so, law enforcement and legitimate self-help would be unprotected against whatever resistance might be made. Viewed as an excuse, however, the matter is quite different. Force or its threatened use, whether lawful or unlawful, will equally deprive the actor of his ability to do otherwise, for opportunities are equally foreclosed regardless of the legitimacy of the acts foreclosing them.

Although duress as it is formulated in the Code is more plausibly regarded as a *justification* than as the excuse it purports to be, there is still a case of sorts to be made for it as an *excuse* by accommodating within the shape of an excuse both the form the coercion must take and its unlawfulness. When coercion deprives the one coerced of fair opportunity to do otherwise he has an excuse for what he does. When coercion is lawful, compliance is a reasonable course open to the one coerced. A course of resistance is then not the only one he could reasonably have taken, and it is therefore not excusable. Similarly, when only his livelihood or his reputation is at stake the actor still has opportunity to resist coercion, since there are available to him (in theory, at least) satisfactory remedies that he may later pursue to repair the harm that is done. This, however, is not the case when there is injury to his person, for then even the best remedies that can be devised are inadequate, and for this reason his resistance is excusable. But conceived in this way as an excuse, the defense of duress seems forced and unnatural, while as a justification its special requirements come naturally into play.

Desperate acts done by a person in danger are treated differently by the Model Penal Code depending upon whether the danger is presented by some other person or by some nonhuman agency of harm. Though the general defense of justification because of necessity is available in both cases, duress is a defense available only when compulsion is by another person. The justification defense, however, requires that the harm prevented be greater than the harm in what was done, and it is therefore less readily available than the defense of duress. The upshot of all this is that in dangerous situations that merely *happen* there is less latitude for measures that can be taken with impunity to escape the danger.

It is never made clear in the Code and its commentaries why the defenses are qualified in this way, but one good reason for recognizing such a difference suggests itself. A threat presented by another person is livelier than the dangers presented by impersonal agencies of harm. Even if harm is no more imminent, the presence of human intelligence on the job and of a will to bring about harm makes escape more difficult. When the source of prospective harm is as canny and determined as we are, there is less room for us to be circumspect and it is harder for us to devise less harmful means of escape. But it is wrong to leave the matter there, as the Code does.

Sometimes harm is presented by nonhuman agencies on an urgent basis that likewise leaves no room for plans and choices to minimize harm. There is only one gas mask, one life preserver, one dose of antitoxin, one tank of oxygen, and in a matter of moments all is over without it. One of us can survive, but the other must then die. In the face of criminal accusation, the person who saves himself and thereby fatally deprives the other is entitled to the same excuse as would be available if the threat were presented not by circumstances but by another person. In either case he is no moral hero, and perhaps he is even morally deficient. But in neither case does he deserve blame as a wrongdoer in the eyes of the criminal law.

MORAL WRONGS AND EXCULPATION UNDER THE LAW

People who are compelled to act as they do sometimes harm others who are innocent. Three of us are castaways, adrift, starving, and at the outer limits of hopelessness. You hold a gun to my head and in dead earnest order me to take my knife and provide us with food by cutting the throat of our companion who lies asleep at the bottom of the boat. A person of reasonable firmness would have been unable to resist, and so under the Model Penal Code I am shielded by the defense of duress if I play the butcher. If I take it into my head myself to provide us with the food that we need now for our very survival and proceed to hack off the leg of our unconscious companion, under the Model Penal Code the law will again shield me, this time because I believed it to be necessary to keep alive.

Not everyone will be happy with these results. Philosophers will ask if it is morally right to kill an innocent person to save one's own life, and some will question whether even to save one's own life it is morally right to inflict upon an innocent person serious harm that cannot be adequately redressed. Clearly, a strong case can be made in a moral forum against the moral propriety of taking an innocent life to save one's own, and a plausible, if weaker, case against the moral propriety of savaging an innocent person even for one's own survival. Since killing an innocent person to insure one's own survival is surely morally reprehensible in some degree, the law in allowing it would seem to endorse an act that on its face appears to be criminal and that in addition turns out even under the circumstances to be morally unacceptable. The answer to this objection has already been given in Chapter One, where moralistic conceptions of precisely this type were criticized. In considering this especially strong case for legal rules that are moralistic, we do well to remind ourselves again that the law must be designed to allow with impunity what ordinary men must ordinarily do in the circumstances, even when the extraordinary character of their circumstances require them in desperation to do what is morally reprehensible.

III. MENTAL ABNORMALITY

THE VARIETIES OF RELEVANT ABNORMALITY

At the time a person engages in criminal conduct he may not be able to conform his conduct to law because of his mental condition. He has the opportunity but not the capacity to do otherwise, and so may claim that he was not a responsible person at the time. This is the most personal of all excuses, since it is something about the actor himself and not his performance or his circumstances which gives the claim its exculpatory force.

Mental abnormalities are of many different kinds, and clearly not all of them disable a person in a way that matters here. Those abnormalities that do have relevance for purposes of excusing can be sorted in four groups. The first consists of mental illness that formerly in medical literature and still in legal literature would be characterized as a *disease* of the mind because of a sufficiently definite pathology and sufficiently pronounced morbidity. Intoxication, whatever its source, is a second variety. Mental defectiveness is a third sort of relevant abnormality, encompassing cases of serious deficiency, mainly in intelligence, but including deficiency of any mental capacity necessary to control behavior. Finally, there is the variety conveniently referred to as automatism, and this includes behavioral phenomena that are diverse in origin but are all instances of a gross separation of consciousness and action such as exists during hypnosis, somnambulism, and epileptic seizures.

Relevant impairments of mental capacity may have origins that are *extrapsychic* or *intrapsychic,* and both present difficulties in formulating principles of criminal liability.

Drugs, alcohol, hypnotic suggestion, a blow on the head, emotional shock, an extra chromosome, or a brain tumor are all extrapsychic impairments, for they are all ways in which relevant incapacitation may be produced by external intervention upon normal functioning. A person may himself be responsible for some of these interventions, either by his own acts or by acts of others that he allows. He may incapacitate himself by drinking or by taking drugs, or he may submit to hypnosis under circumstances that portend harm. In such cases the difficult question is whether the incapacitation can still serve as an excuse, and the answer is that it can. No matter what its origin may be, an incapacitation that renders an actor unable to help himself is, according to the responsibility principle, available as ground for an exculpatory claim. There may, however, be liability for the act of self-incapacitation engaged in by the actor, or for his willing submission to incapacitation at the hands of someone else. The reason is that his causing himself to become incapacitated is a dangerous act and culpable because of the harm he may do when incapacitated; and so long as he had the ability to avoid incapacitation there is no offense to the responsibility principle in holding him liable for his culpable conduct. Liability may be created for acts of incapacitation, or liability may be designed to attach only when there is dangerous conduct while in such a state. But not any act contributing to incapacitation can be regarded as itself dangerous and a basis of liability.

For example, a person may cause himself ultimately to suffer sieges of delirium tremens by the gradual effects of his own alcoholic indulgence. The long course of drinking does not, however, consist of separate acts that individually or together threaten harm in a way that is definite enough to satisfy jurisprudential requirements for dangerous conduct, and for this reason there cannot properly be liability for those acts.

When acts of self-incapacitation are sufficiently dangerous to allow for liability, the culpability of such acts is properly measured by the danger of lost self-control and not by the harm in what is done when control is lost. Thus, one person may kill another deliberately, under delusions produced by drugs taken deliberately; yet culpability is not for deliberate killing, since the accused is not responsible at all for his homicidal conduct but only for the dangerous act of taking such drugs. Not without some awkwardness in principle, the lesser culpability is usually reflected in the criminal law by liability for homicide of a lesser degree.

When mental impairment is intrapsychic in origin, the excuse based on it is received more charily. The same debilitation that would easily pass muster for an excuse if externally induced is regarded with skepticism when its origin is palpably not outside the mind of the actor. Initial suspicion is indeed warranted because of increased opportunity for deception. But even after the genuineness of the psychopathology is established, often there is lingering skepticism regarding its significance for judgments of responsibility. This skepticism is justified to the extent that it reflects sound opinion that the actor was perfectly capable of doing otherwise despite his illness. It is not justified when it is based on the belief that, since the origins of his illness are within him, it is somehow of his creation and under his control, and hence a defect for which he is ultimately responsible. In general, holding a person responsible for his mental illness is even more unjust than holding him responsible for physical illness. Such medical knowledge as we have bearing on the etiology of serious mental illness makes it clear that in most cases a sick person could neither prevent the onset of his illness nor by caring for himself bring it to an end, while often in the case of physical illness effective measures of precaution and care are easily taken.

VERSIONS OF THE INSANITY DEFENSE

Not every mental abnormality excuses. Even when the abnormality is of a kind relevant to responsibility, certain conditions of incapacitation must be met if there is to be an excuse. In the criminal law these conditions have been formulated as rules governing the insanity defense. Although these rules look mainly to mental illness and defectiveness, the conditions for excusing under them have a rationale extending to mental abnormality of whatever variety.

Four different versions of the insanity defense have developed in the criminal law, though the conditions that must be met under each version are not so dissimilar as the formulations of each version at first suggest. Considered in the light of general principles of exculpation, the first version, which dominates among Anglo-American jurisdictions, turns out to be too meager. The second version (which in some form is now the law in about a third of the American jurisdictions and under the Model Penal Code) represents the most satisfactory statement. The third and fourth versions, though possibly lending themselves to suitably restrictive interpretation, offer too great opportunity for unwarranted excuses as they stand without such qualification. We need first to acquaint ourselves with each version and can then go on to a critical examination to distinguish among them those that are good excuses from those that are bad. Our concern here is only with the reason a person is not responsible. Very difficult medical questions about which states of abnormality leave a person not in a responsible condition will remain unexplored. The basic question of what it means not to be responsible because of mental abnormality is all that concerns us. But without an answer to that question one does not know what exculpatory significance, if any, to attach ultimately to the medical facts.

The first version of the insanity defense is represented by the M'Naghten rules. In their original statement these rules provide that a person has a defense of insanity if he did not know the nature and quality of the act he was doing, or did not know that it was wrong, because laboring under a defect of reason from disease of the mind. Included among the original M'Naghten rules was a further proviso that, even if not so afflicted, a person would have a defense if at the time of his act he was suffering from an insane delusion such that if—but only if—things were in fact as he thought, it would furnish a defense. This part of the M'Naghten rules has been generally disregarded because of the limitation it places on delusions that may excuse—though, as we shall see, rarely is the right reason given for ignoring this part. The need has always been recognized to have the defense cover all cases in which the accused had insane delusions about the circumstances under which he acted, and this has resulted in strained applications of the remainder of the M'Naghten doctrine to cover all of those cases.

Despite variations in language and differences in fine points of interpretation, the substance of the M'Naghten formula has remained unchanged in the many jurisdictions that have adopted it since its introduction in England well over a century ago. Serious incapacitation may make it impossible for the actor to be sufficiently aware of what he is doing so that he could choose to do otherwise. It may deprive him of his ability to appreciate the dangerous character of his conduct, or to appreciate the very fact of the harm in what he does, so that a normal disposition to avoid harmful conduct is not possible. His incapacitation may deprive him of the ability to comprehend the circumstances in which he acts and thus makes it impossible for him to choose not to do what under the circumstances is not justifiable, though he thinks otherwise. It may make him incapable of knowing that the law prohibits what he does, when only the fact of legal prohibition is a reason for not doing it. In any of these cases, because of a deficiency or a defectiveness in his personal resources he cannot help what he does.

The second version of the insanity defense consists of some form of M'Naghten to which is added an excuse based on grossly deficient inhibitory capacity. This addition is usually referred to as the irresistible-impulse rule—though any suggestion that the act need be impulsive to qualify would be seriously misleading. Under this provision, if the accused was incapable of restraining himself from doing what he knew he was doing and knew that he ought not to be doing, he may invoke as an excuse his inability to exercise self-control.

The gravamen of this excuse is, again, the actor's helplessness in being unable to avoid doing the proscribed acts. This excuse is even stronger than the claim of compulsion asserted when one had been forced to do something criminal. Instead of succumbing to pressures that one is nevertheless able to resist if only one chooses to act unreasonably, the person without significant capacity for inhibition is simply unable to resist. The excuse is sometimes misconceived, however, so that the untoward urge rather than the inhibitory failure receives primary attention. This distorts the rationale of the excuse. We do not excuse because the actor wanted desperately to do what he did. Of itself powerful determination to do harm is not grounds for exemption from judgments of culpability. On the contrary, such strong determination furnishes supplementary grounds for a judgment of greater culpability. But failed inhibition that results in an inability to do otherwise supplies the necessary excuse.

The third version of the insanity defense makes mental disease or defect, *when it produces criminal conduct,* the basis of an excuse for that conduct. This version, known best as the Durham rule, has been adopted in four American jurisdictions (though discarded subsequently in the one that gave it its name). It relies heavily in practice on the same rationale of excuse as the previous version but offers certain opportunities for troublesome departures that will be discussed shortly.

There is, finally, a version of the insanity defense in which mental derangement or deficiency at the time of the criminal act constitutes the basis of an excuse without further qualification. The actor need only be seriously defective or not in possession of his faculties in order for his conduct in such a state to be excusable. Unlike the previous version, the relation between the abnormality and the criminal conduct is not of concern so long as the two are contemporaneous. In somewhat primitive forms this version preceded M'Naghten in the common law, and in modern times it is to be found in the criminal law of some civil law jurisdictions. It enjoys strong support among those of the medical profession interested in these forensic matters, and its popularity in those circles is probably even greater than that of the Durham rule. As with Durham, there is in practice heavy reliance on the same rationale of excuse that support M'Naghten and irresistible impulse; but again, as with Durham, opportunities for excusing on other grounds are made possible by this rule, and those other grounds must be carefully investigated.

CRITICISM OF RATIONALES THAT IGNORE RESPONSIBILITY

The preceding discussion has indicated the several different ways that the law has gone about recognizing an excuse of mental abnormality when the excuse is presented in its most dramatic form as the insanity defense. Many of those who favor the third or fourth version of the insanity defense think it a good defense simply that a person was mentally ill at the time of his criminal act, or that his criminal conduct was a result of the mental illness he suffered at the time. There are important arguments here, one rooted in moral considerations regarding avoidance of cruelty, and two others rooted in exculpatory considerations thought to apply to sick persons.

The first contention is that it is wrong to punish a person *when he is sick*. It is generally regarded as inhumane to neglect the suffering of those in a debilitated condition, and even more inhumane to inflict further suffering on them. It would therefore be barbarous if the criminal law not only withheld comfort and cure from the sick who are subject to its processes but imposed upon them the rigors of a penal regime. Directed to present concerns, this principle of humane treatment clearly requires that a person mentally abnormal at the time of his crime not be subjected to punitive treatment while he continues to be in such a state, but that instead he receive medical treatment.

The principle of humane treatment must certainly be respected and given full effect at all times. But it does not confer a cloak of immunity on a person who is sick when committing a crime. Conduct may be culpable even though the actor had chicken pox, pneumonia, multiple sclerosis, or terminal cancer. It may be culpable when the disorder is mental rather than physical. When a sick person's conduct is culpable and forms the basis of criminal liability, he is to be cared for and treated for his illness so long as it continues by those in whose hands he is placed because of his criminal liability. But liability for culpable conduct is not avoided by illness. In his *Commentaries on the Laws of England* Blackstone suggested that "lunatics" (and, analogously, "idiots" as well) are "excused from guilt" by the rule *furiosus furore solum punitur*. Viewing madness in this way—as itself a madman's punishment—makes of his madness a reason for the law not to inflict punishment on him even if he recovers, for a single crime deserves but a single punishment. This is not a good reason for exemption from punishment, however, since there is nothing in the insane person's suffering that warrants exemption from punishment when those who have suffered no less through other afflictions are not granted exemption by the law. As we shall see in the final chapter, humane considerations are included among the many reasons for moderation and dispensation in sentencing, and surely the ills a man has suffered cannot be ignored. But it is the extent and form of liability that is then being determined, and not the propriety of imposing liability in the first place.

A second argument derives from general requirements imposed by the responsibility principle. It is pointed out that it is wrong to punish someone *for being sick*. The reason is that in being sick a person has not done anything that he could have helped doing. Since merely falling ill cannot be regarded as culpable conduct, it may not be punished. (A person might of course be rightly blamed for making himself sick, or allowing himself to become or to be made sick, and we might decide that such conduct indeed deserves punishment when, for example, it was understood that the well-being of others depended upon the fitness of the one who became sick. In such a case the conduct can be judged culpable because the accused could have acted to prevent his illness.)

Insofar as a person is being punished for his conduct and not for his disorder, the responsibility principle is not transgressed. But sometimes it is claimed that when a mentally disordered person is punished for his conduct, he is being punished for his disorder, since the conduct is a symptom of it. Such claims are especially prominent in arguments advocating extension of a mental abnormality defense to persons characterized as psychopaths or sociopaths, persons whose dedication to wrongdoing is especially strong and free of internal conflicts. The claim rests on a misunderstanding of what it means to be punished for something. A person may be punished for a criminal act, and that act may in various other perspectives be viewed quite accurately as a symptom of his illness—or indeed of society's illness, or as an act of dedicated self-sacrifice, or as an act to advance a socially worthwhile cause. Still, in all these cases we are punishing him only for his culpable conduct. We may punish in spite of causes, motives, or intentions, so long as they do not furnish an excuse or other reason for not punishing.

The third argument is that it is wrong to punish someone for what he does *as a result of being mentally ill*. The position here differs from the previous one in emphasis, for it is no longer argued that it is wrong to punish for illness as evidenced by criminal conduct. Rather, in this argument it is wrong to punish someone for his conduct when it is *produced* by the disorder, there being then a tacit admission that the criminal conduct need not be viewed as symptomatic behavior but only as having been in some important way dependent for its occurrence upon the existence of the illness.

The fact that conduct resulted from mental abnormality is by itself not enough to excuse the conduct, for that alone leaves us with no principle on which to rest the excuse. True, exculpation would indeed be warranted by a principle that what is morbidly determined is not wrong; yet there is no reason to accept as a governing principle that condemnation ought to be restricted to healthy determinations to act harmfully. Of course a person's mental abnormality, if it is to excuse his criminal conduct, must be related in some significant way to that conduct as its cause. This may be put even more strongly. We ought to excuse when, but only when, conduct is the "product" of abnormality in the sense that the abnormality is a sufficient condition for the conduct. In that case, but only in that case, the accused was unable to do otherwise because of the abnormality and so is entitled to be excused. But it is not true that we ought to excuse simply because what was done would likely not have been done but for the abnormality. Otherwise we should have to excuse anyone who acted from some untoward tendency attributable to a mental abnormality if he is unlikely to have done the act if he were normal, even though he was quite as capable of acting differently as any normal person would be if subject to the same tendency. This would mean that a bank employee ought to be excused when his embezzlement is morbidly determined by a powerful unconscious wish to be caught, even though he could effectively have chosen not to succumb to that wish; while another employee who embezzles only because tempted by healthy fantasies of a life of leisure ought not to be excused.

There are arguments for not punishing wrongdoers who suffered mental abnormality—but in effect they require for an excuse too much rather than too little. The logic of the first of these arguments requires that only those who cannot be deterred by the threat of punishment are entitled to the defense of insanity. This argument has eminent philosophical credentials in the work of Bentham, and it is to be heard in the best modern legal circles as well, where the policeman-at-the-elbow test is taken to represent a good rough summary of what the law wants to know.

Those who advance this argument point out that prescribing punishment for what the insane do is futile, since the threat of punishment can have no deterrent effect on such persons. Thus anyone who considers the practice of punishment to be justified by its deterrent effect must hold punishment of the insane to be unjustified and, in fact, a purposeless infliction of suffering. It has been argued in reply that punishment of the insane may still have a deterrent effect on sane persons, since it deprives them of hope of escaping punishment by successfully advancing fraudulent claims of having been insane at the time of their offense. That answer is good only to the extent that a crime is committed when the decision to commit it includes deliberation on possible legal tactics to avoid conviction. Since most crimes are committed without a decision of this sort, the deterrent effect of a threat of punishment is in general unaffected by the presence of a defense of insanity in the law.

There are, however, other answers to the "no deterrence" objection that do not require belief in fictitious deliberations by would-be criminals.

If it is being suggested that the non-deterribility of the insane has been the rationale for the insanity defense in the law as it has developed, we may ask why the law does not also refuse for the same reason to punish those who were genuinely and blamelessly ignorant of the law they broke. Such persons were in a position indistinguishable from the insane with respect to the futility of prospective punishment, and so to punish them is equally a purposeless infliction of suffering. Yet, as we know, in the law as it stands such innocent ignorance does not generally excuse—and this inconsistency must raise doubts about the rationale proposed to account for the insanity defense.

There is an even more cogent objection than one based on inconsistency. It is not the case that all, or even most, insane persons are incapable of being deterred by threat of punishment. Under the most common Anglo-American version of the insanity defense—that represented by the M'Naghten rules—there is an excuse if the accused by virtue of a defect of reason from disease of the mind did not know he was doing what was wrong. The Model Penal Code similarly establishes as a defense a person's lack of substantial capacity to appreciate the criminality of his conduct (which means more than mere knowledge that it is criminally prohibited) as a result of mental disease or defect. Many persons fit these specifications in being unable to appreciate that what they do is wrong and in fact at the time think it justified for some reason; yet they are as much aware and in awe of the threat of punishment as normal persons. In some notable cases of the insanity defense, the defendant committed murder under the delusion that he was carrying out a divine command, or was giving his due to a man he believed to be very wicked, or was killing someone who was bent on harming him. Less dramatic but far more frequent are the family and sex-intrigue homicides in which the killing was done in a suitably extreme abnormal mental state—often spoken of as temporary insanity—in which the accused was likewise at the time convinced that he was justified.

In general there is no reason to believe that in these insanity cases their abnormality rendered the accused incapable of being deterred by the threat of punishment—though of course, like many normal defendants, they were not in fact deterred by it. There is, further, every reason to believe that certain abnormal persons who would be entitled to exoneration on grounds of insanity were in fact deterred, just as normal persons would be, because the law has made punishable the conduct they contemplated. If these things were not so, the insanity defense could consist simply in establishing the one point that by reason of mental abnormality the accused could not at the time of his crime be deterred by the threat of punishment. What in fact distinguishes the sane from the insane under criminal law standards is the inability of the insane to appreciate the *culpability,* not the punishability, of their conduct. Because of their abnormality, the insane cannot at the time apprehend what justifies condemnation of their conduct. Even though amenable to threats of punishment, they lack a resource of appreciation that is necessary if one is to have a reason apart from avoidance of punishment for not doing what the law prohibits. One who cannot appreciate that what he is doing is wrong is unable to avoid doing what is wrong when—as is usually the case—he depends for guidance upon that appreciation. Punishment of those who cannot help doing what they do is indeed a useless infliction of suffering; and as a failure to recognize legitimate excuses it is most undesirable in ways that we shall discuss in the next chapter.

There is a general argument against mental abnormality defenses. Again it is an argument that, by implication at least, requires too much rather than too little for excuse. Many mentally ill persons who have committed crimes are dangerous; yet the very abnormality that is evidence of his being dangerous serves to shield the accused from liability. Those who see confinement of dangerous persons as a principal purpose of the criminal law are particularly distressed by this, for in effect just those persons who are thought to be most properly the concern of the criminal law are allowed to escape its restraints. On this view, only those few persons who have committed crimes while suffering from disabling mental abnormality of the proper sort but who are no longer dangerous would be entitled to the defense.

The answer to this is that not all restraint by the state need be based on criminal liability. If a person is dangerous because of mental abnormality, he may be prevented from doing harm by noncriminal commitment, regardless of whether his conduct provides a basis for criminal liability. It is true that persons are not usually found to be a menace for purposes of commitment unless they have done something that would provide the substance of a criminal charge. But it is still the dangerousness of the person and not the criminality of his conduct that warrants deprivation of liberty. Since determinations of dangerousness and determinations of criminal liability are independent matters, a successful defense of insanity to a criminal charge does not weigh against the accused's subsequent liability to commitment on the ground that he is dangerous. Conversely, postponement of the question of mental abnormality when determining liability would result in branding as criminals persons who (whether dangerous or not) are not to blame for what they did, with the additional stigma of insanity attached later as their only consolation.

The rationale of excusing for mental abnormality may be summarized in this way. Certain forms of mental incapacity deprive a person of his ability to act other than the way he does because resources for an effective choice are lacking. He is in this condition when he lacks the capacity to tell what he is doing, or what is likely to happen; or when he lacks capacity to appreciate its significance as something wrong, or lacks the ability to restrain himself. A person incapacitated in any of these ways is unable, as a matter of choice, to do otherwise. For this reason an excuse of mental abnormality renders inappropriate an excuse that goes directly to culpability. There is no point in being concerned about whether something was done intentionally when the actor was not even a responsible agent. When there is a full complement of the personal resources necessary for responsible conduct, there is, conversely, a duty to draw upon such resources to avoid harmful conduct. Consequently, when a normal person claims that he did not at the time appreciate the significance of sticking a knife into another person—his mind was elsewhere—he offers a different kind of excuse from that of the mentally abnormal man who makes the same claim. The normal man, by showing less culpability, can only expect to blunt an accusation of conduct of a higher degree of culpability—he didn't harm the victim knowingly, but only negligently through absentmindedness in failing to pay attention to the dangers of what he was doing. But the man who establishes that his failure of appreciation was due to lack of necessary mental resources exempts himself altogether from any judgment of culpability.

The distinction and connections between lack of responsibility and mere lack of culpability are important with regard to several difficulties surrounding the insanity defense.

The usually discarded third part of the original M'Naghten rule provided that even if the accused person who suffered a defect of reason from disease of the mind could know the nature and quality of his act, and even if he could know that what he was doing was wrong, he still might have a defense if at the time of his act he suffered from a delusion such that, had it been a correct belief, it would have afforded a defense. This part of the rule has been dropped—but not in order to exclude insanity defenses based on delusions. In fact, any limitation upon the kinds of delusion that are acceptable has been declared objectionable, since delusion cases have always been recognized as paradigms of criminal insanity, and in all M'Naghten rule jurisdictions the defense of insanity has been broadly allowed in delusion cases by means of strained interpretations of other parts of the rules.

The usual argument is that the limitation in the M'Naghten rules leads to absurd results. For example, in accordance with conventional legal rules precluding criminal jurisdiction over foreign nationals for crimes committed in foreign countries, a homicide defendant in England who, in a delusion at the time of his crime, believed himself to be Bluebeard re-enacting one of his murders in France would have a good defense. Not so, however, for another homicide defendant in England with a similar delusion, who believed himself to be Jack the Ripper. Even when the rule has been confined to delusions that bear on exculpatory claims (typically, provocation and self-defense)—as undoubtedly its original proponents intended it to be—critics have not been silenced, even though often their reasons for rejecting the rule in such situations are not made clear.

It seems, in fact, that the original rule was a sound one based on the factual premises concerning mental abnormality which were accepted by the M'Naghten judges, but that these premises are incorrect. The mistake from which the rule proceeded has been characterized as the doctrine of partial insanity. It holds that a person whose insanity consists merely in delusions is still capable of choosing to act in conformity with the law governing the situation as he perceived it. He is therefore to be held accountable for not acting in conformity with the law as it would apply to the situation he perceived, even though, by virtue of his inability to perceive the situation correctly, he could not be held accountable for breaking the law with respect to the situation as it actually was. According to the better medical knowledge available now, however, the fact of the matter is that such persons in the grip of their delusions are normally so severely incapacitated that they cannot even choose to act otherwise. We therefore cannot regard them as responsible when they act as their delusion dictates, and so must consider them ineligible for blame. Questions raised by the original rule about matters of culpability (usually matters of justification) are for this reason superfluous.

A second problem concerns what is meant by "wrong" under the terms of the M'Naghten rule. If the accused, because of a defect of reason from disease of the mind, did not know that what he was doing was wrong, he has a defense on grounds of insanity. The question that has persistently troubled courts both in England and the United States is whether the required failure of knowledge is of legal wrong or of moral wrong. Does a person have a defense when as a psychotic he knew that murder was a crime but believed he may nevertheless commit it because divinely commanded? What about a mental defective who knows that he is not supposed to hurt other people but does not even know what a criminal law is? The Model Penal Code speaks of the accused's lack of capacity to appreciate the criminality of his conduct, but the difficulty remains, for appreciating the criminality of conduct is not the equivalent of knowing that it has been made a crime. Indeed, the final draft of the Code provision offers "wrongfulness" as an optional substitute for "criminality."

The difficulty is removed by recognizing that what is crucial is *capacity to know*, rather than *knowledge*, and that it is capacity to know something that is *necessary for culpability*. In a just legal system, conduct ought not to be treated as legally culpable unless reasonable opportunity exists to become aware of its legal interdiction. Such opportunity for awareness has significance only if there also is ability to take advantage of it. That in turn depends (as we should suppose after reading the first section of this chapter) on ability to appreciate the untowardness of conduct and to be aware of the range of normal concerns of the law, as well as the ability to become acquainted with the law itself. If a disabling incapacity exists with respect to any of these necessary conditions, the person incapacitated is not responsible, for he then lacks ability to take advantage of the opportunity to become aware of criminal liabilities and so to act in accordance with the law. It turns out, then, that it is misleading to ask whether legal wrong or moral wrong is meant. The question to be answered is whether, because of mental abnormality, the accused was unable to take advantage of the opportunity of becoming aware of the criminal liability that attaches (under the law) to what he did.

Another difficulty concerns the irresistible-impulse defense. There has been great hesitation in legal circles in admitting as an excuse the inability to exercise self-restraint. It challenges commonsense understanding of human behavior to assert that a person who skillfully engaged in a criminal enterprise and was possessed of all the abilities necessary to control what he did, nevertheless did not have the self-control to choose not to do it. The excuse is therefore often construed as analogous to the excuse of external compulsion—he had no choice, he was forced to—rather than as a denial of responsibility by virtue of incapacity. The excuse so construed is then rejected as being too easy a way out for persons who either have not chosen to resist with sufficient determination their own powerful untoward urges or have failed to take precaution against the urge. Such persons are thought therefore to be no less culpable than persons who lose their temper and, while in the grip of their rage, commit crimes.

But this denial of responsibility becomes plausible as understanding of human pathology advances and it becomes increasingly clear that there are serious mental abnormalities consisting of inability either by repression or precaution to inhibit acting on certain urges. The claim of irresistible impulse is then no longer construed simply as one of not having effectively chosen to do otherwise, but rather more—as not having the personal resources necessary to choose effectively. There is a breakdown in the normal system of selection and diversion among our contending inclinations, and so we are dominated by some purpose in the service of which we can make choices with consummate skill but which we cannot choose to abandon.

DIMINISHED RESPONSIBILITY

A stark separation according to mental abnormality of those who are responsible from those who are not seems at times unsatisfactory. Sometimes there is not sheer incapacity with regard to elements of control, and yet there is deviation from normal capacity great enough to make desirable a limitation on accountability. Accordingly, a doctrine of diminished (or partial) responsibility has developed in the law and, though still not widely accepted, it offers a path for receiving into the law new insights about many varieties of limited impairment affecting control of conduct. The most notable development so far has been in England where the Homicide Act of 1957 reduces what otherwise would be murder to culpable homicide when the accused suffered from such abnormality of mind as "substantially impaired his mental responsibility" for his acts.

The rationale for diminished responsibility is simple. If a person who is incapacitated is ineligible for blame, a person who is seriously impaired though not incapacitated is eligible only within limits. While not utterly bereft of resources required for accountability, his resources are diminished to a point where full faulting according to the tenor of the conduct is inappropriate. For reasons previously given, however, it would be a serious mistake to construe the defense of diminished responsibility as a declaration that the *somewhat* sick, simply because they are sick, ought not to be held to a liability as great as that of the healthy person. Indeed, perfectly healthy persons who have perfectly natural reactions that put them in an abnormal emotional state may rightly claim diminished responsibility. Typically, this is the case when a person acts under the influence of extreme anger or fear because provoked or threatened.

Mental abnormality may affect culpability in a more direct way, however, and some confusion about this has arisen in discussions of diminished responsibility. By virtue of his abnormality, a person may be unable to act in a way that is criminally culpable, or at least not in a way that is as culpable as the conduct charged. Or, though capable of such conduct, he may simply not have been acting in the way charged but rather in some other way that was dictated by his abnormal processes. In either case he may lodge an exculpatory claim that his conduct is different than alleged with respect to elements bearing on culpability, and he would rely on the evidence of his mental abnormality to establish this.

Such an exculpatory claim is in essence no different from the sort appropriate when a normal person has not acted culpably, but the kind of evidence and argument supporting the claim is different. Instead of evidence indicating simply that the accused was engaged in a somewhat different enterprise than alleged, the evidence here indicates that, by virtue of his abnormal mental condition at the time, the accused could not or simply did not engage in the activity alleged. Two somewhat different exculpatory claims are made in this way, and both have as their point what in the language of traditional criminal law theory would be called a lack of *mens rea*.

Suppose that a prisoner attacks a guard with a knife and inflicts serious wounds. The prisoner is charged with first-degree assault, one element of which is intent to cause serious physical injury. It is claimed on his behalf that he was at the time suffering severe paranoid anxieties that led him to misinterpret a routine warning and to take it as a sign that he was about to be attacked by the guard. He slashed at the guard only to forestall what he believed to be imminent blows. Evidence of his abnormal state would tend to show that he did not have the specific intent to cause the serious physical injury required for the offense. This would mean that while admittedly he exercised normal control in conducting an assault, he did not exercise normal control in producing serious injury. In a crucial respect the act done was therefore unintentional and therefore less culpable than the act charged. The same would hold true for a person who is accused of burglary (which requires an intent to commit a felony), and who at the time of breaking and entering a home was in such mental condition as to be incapable of having any definite further purpose.

The other challenge to culpability by way of abnormality concerns not the purpose informing the act but rather the planning and the supervision while the activity is in progress. Such operational design and oversight are introduced as requirements in the law by such terms as "malice aforethought," "premeditation," "deliberation," "willfully," and "knowingly"; and they may have been beyond the accused's capacities, or simply absent because of his abnormality. Powerful effects of intoxication or of lingering mental illness may render a person unable or unconcerned to form the plan or to remain in control of its execution, and it must then be concluded that his apparently homicidal attack was not really designed to bring about the death of his victim. The Model Penal Code extends this variety of abnormality defense to all cases in which evidence of mental disease or defect is relevant to the question of whether the accused has a required "state of mind" at the time of the crime, so that even recklessness or negligence may be disproved by evidence of appropriate abnormality.

In both these "criminal intent" challenges based on mental abnormality, it is not responsibility that properly is said to be diminished. Culpability is what is really claimed to be diminished—and diminished to a point where the conduct is less culpable than is required by the law for the offense charged.

THE PURSUIT OF RATIONAL PROCEDURES

The excuse of insanity has presented far greater difficulties than any other for the criminal process. Mainly this is because the point of the proceedings is lost sight of, and as a result confusion arises in deciding who may appropriately answer the very different kinds of questions involved, and also in deciding what the consequences of accepting or rejecting the excuse ought to be.

The controversy in which medical views of the insanity defense appear to be at odds with legal views results principally from a failure to appreciate that the law must ultimately be concerned not with who is sick but with whose conduct is excusable. Deciding that issue requires several subsidiary decisions that fall peculiarly within either medical or legal competence. There must, in the first place, be standards setting forth in general the nature of the incapacities that render a person not responsible. It is these standards that constitute the rules of the insanity defense and the rules of a defense of diminished responsibility. Deciding what these rules shall be is the responsibility of those with legislative and judicial authority who must make the law.

What is called for here is not some general description of relevant clinical abnormalities in language that lawyers are used to. What is required is a statement of the kinds of mental failures (due to mental illness or defectiveness) that entitle us to conclude for purposes of criminal liability that the accused could not help doing what he did. Once there are such standards of mental abnormality, it is possible to judge the alleged abnormalities of a particular defendant. Then the opinion of medical experts must be looked to in order to determine the nature of the defendant's debilitation and the extent to which that debilitation affected his capacity to act in accordance with the law. Such expert opinion may be critically examined by lawyers—as indeed any expert opinion in a legal proceeding may be examined to determine a disputed issue. That is not a means of substituting an inexpert for an expert opinion, but only a way of ensuring that its acceptance is ultimately based on reason rather than on authority. There is, finally, a decision of vast discretion that is usually made by a jury. This is a conclusion about whether, according to the account of the defendant's mental condition that is finally accepted, there is debilitation sufficient to excuse under the legal standards for excuse.

Asking psychiatrists for expert opinions about whether such standards of incapacity are met is asking them to perform a role that is not within their special professional competence. Yet this ultimate determination does require specialized skill in sifting among psychiatric opinions to arrive at a sound appreciation of the defendant's mental condition with reference to those features that are significant for judgments of responsibility. The paramount procedural problem of the insanity defense is to combine this specialist's appreciation with the layman's considered views about when choices to act are no longer meaningful or even possible. For this reason there is a great deal to recommend suggestions, such as H. L. A. Hart's, that we adopt an "apparently coarser grained technique of exempting persons from liability to punishment if they fall into certain recognized categories of mental disorder," on the model of exemption from criminal liability for persons under a specified age. The trouble is that the establishment of a comprehensive scheme of clear categories seems well beyond what medical science can now provide, for persons diagnosed as having similar disorders regularly exhibit vast differences in what they are able to do.

Another sort of misapprehension deflects attention from responsibility to other matters, at the cost of both justice and humaneness in the administration of the criminal law. It is assumed by some that determining the accused to be responsible and so liable to have his conduct judged culpable is a warrant for treating him punitively rather than therapeutically. But since many persons meeting legal standards for responsible conduct are nevertheless quite sick, sending them to prison rather than to a hospital seems uncivilized. Accordingly, it is said that anyone who is mentally ill ought therefore not to be treated as criminally responsible.

The mistake here is in giving priority to existing institutional arrangements and then, under such arrangements, attempting to impose rules of liability that are humane in their effect. A rational and morally concerned society designs its institutions to treat in a humane way those liable according to just principles of liability. When a person liable according to proper standards of responsibility and culpability is also sick, principles of humane treatment (which are in no way inferior moral considerations) require that he be treated as sick. To the extent that inappropriate treatment may at present be expected under existing institutional arrangements and regimes, that is cause not for the reform of the rules of criminal liability but for the reform of existing institutional arrangements and regimes.

CHAPTER EIGHT

Limits of Excuse

Excuses are the subject of controversy carried on within the criminal law by those who shape its rules, and outside by those who are concerned more broadly with its general design. This is not surprising, for those ways of escaping blame that draw attention to the actor still vex us with difficult questions as they have since ancient times. Some of these questions have to do with freedom of choice and with a person's ability to do what he ought to do; others present the dilemmas arising when liberty and justice stand in the way of achieving desirable social objectives.

There are some very general objections to limiting excuses as we do in the criminal law. Certain arguments aim at excusing large numbers of people now held criminally liable, and some even purport to excuse everyone. These arguments are looked into in the first section of this chapter.

There is then the question of why excuses matter at all. Rather than extend the range of excuse, proposals for radical change in the opposite direction seek to eliminate all or most of the excuses now recognized in the criminal law. This suggestion is examined in the second section.

Finally, there is strict liability. Among theorists of the criminal law there is disagreement about which excuses an accused person ought never to be deprived of. Usually, though not always, the excuses in dispute are direct denials of culpability rather than denials of responsibility; and usually, though not always, the cases provoking disagreement are not prosecutions for serious crimes but enforcement of laws that are merely regulatory in nature. In the last section of the chapter strict liability is investigated and its problems sorted out in ways intended to leave less cause for controversy.

I. PERSISTENT THEMES

SOME CONTROVERSIAL CLAIMS

There are a number of familiar arguments of excuse—one might call them exculpatory themes—which have a broad appeal and influence decisions in the world of affairs, and yet carry no weight as a bar to liability in the criminal law. Finding out why this is so is the main item of business in this section. A related matter of the opposite sort should be taken up first, however, for there are two important claims that do not receive the recognition they should. The first relies on an argument that is sound, though often misunderstood and then rejected. The second rests on an argument that wrongly makes it appear to be an excuse and on that mistaken premise the claim is rightly rejected, though it has merit and deserves recognition on different grounds as the claim it actually is.

The first claim brings us back to the problem of mental abnormality. It is suggested from time to time that a particular abnormal condition ought to excuse the sufferer from criticism for his wrongdoing. As our understanding of behavior advances, we have a keener appreciation of its pathological determinants, and we are increasingly indisposed to blame those whose conduct we see as merely pathological.

It is proper, indeed essential, that we take into account new insights in pathology that bear on a person's capacity to conform his conduct to the requirements of the law. In doing this we are not changing the criteria for excuse but only adding new conditions to be tested by those criteria. If it is suggested that certain drug addicts in particularly acute states of craving are without capacity to control themselves in what they do, or that intoxicated persons suffering unusual hyperallergic reactions are similarly debilitated, or that certain persons suffering overwhelming compulsions to indulge erotic desires simply cannot help themselves, we should want to look into the details of the pathology and, if we are convinced that the suggestion is correct, we must allow an excuse.

It is seriously misleading to imagine that statements of legal criteria for excuses are statements of the conditions that excuse—and this is especially true with reference to the criteria for mental abnormality excuses such as the insanity defense. These legal criteria are only touchstones of excuse to test the qualifications of new conditions when they are offered as grounds of excuse. As our understanding of human behavior continues to deepen, our conception of what constitutes relevant incapacity is properly enlarged.

Sometimes a very different type of claim is offered as an excuse. Often those in sympathy with radical causes will attack the law and argue that members of those deprived groups in a community that do not really enjoy the protection of the law ought to be excused from obeying it. A social-contract theory gives some support to this view. When the law is generally enforced in a discriminatory way so that the benefit of the contract cannot be enjoyed by some part of the community, those who are deprived of this benefit might plausibly be

excused (at least in the interest of justice) from their undertaking under the terms of the contract. In a slightly different
version, when laws are enacted or enforced to serve not the
general interest but only more limited interests, a benefit—
in general, the basis of a reciprocal obligation to abide by the
law—is then lacking. It might then be said that violations by
those who are not benefited ought to be excused.

It is common enough to speak of a person's being excused
from some obligation. In contract law we speak of conditions
that excuse performance, by which we mean conditions that
excuse *from* the obligation to perform. A person is also commonly said to be excused *from* liability whenever it would be
improper to impose it. He might not be to blame, for example, when culpability is a requirement for liability, and so
he is excused *from* liability. He might be excused *from* liability because he had a right or a privilege, or because he enjoyed an immunity. If a person has an excuse *for* what he did,
that will also serve as a way to excuse him *from* liability.
There is, in other words, an abundance of ways in which a
person may rightly be excused *from* liability; some of them
are nonexculpatory, and some—like an excuse *for* what he
did—are exculpatory.

When it is said that under certain conditions it is unfair to
require certain members of the community to abide by the
law, the argument is that they have no obligation to obey
and ought to be excused from liability; or that they had a
right to act as they did, and for that reason ought to be excused from liability. Under certain extraordinary conditions
these arguments have merit under civilized standards of political morality, and serve in a just society to avoid liability. It is
not part of our concern here to decide under what conditions
such arguments have merit; our interest now is only to note
that the argument does not purport to excuse an accused person *for* what he has done, but only to excuse him *from* liability for doing it.

The ambiguity in "excuse" may mislead in two ways. It can divert us from the exculpatory considerations upon which excuses properly rest and lead us to excuse *for* what was done when there is no good reason to. It can also confine us unduly and prevent us from turning our attention to matters that entitle an accused person to be excused from liability for reasons other than reasons of excuse, depriving him thereby of a defense to which he is entitled.

Turning now to the excuses rejected by the law, there is first a false excusatory move, and it appears in many forms. It is commonly suggested that certain things caused a person to behave badly, and that since they were not of his making— indeed, their existence was beyond his control—he ought not to be held responsible for their effects. Causes of crime under this view are things but for which the criminal behavior would have been unlikely. Conditioning influences that shape the development of personality are favorite causes; so too are constitutional defects. Childhood experiences, genetic factors, cultural attitudes, and economic privation are among the elements most frequently cited as sources of exculpation. Typically the plea would be, "He's not to blame—look at the conditions he grew up in, the experiences he was forced to endure, the handicap he suffers. Almost certainly, if he were not subjected to such dreadful influences and put at such a disadvantage, he would not have turned to crime."

We take these matters seriously, as indeed we must, in deciding how to treat an offender, for they tell us something about his needs. Even more important for present concerns, these things may help us to appreciate motives. We may come to understand that a person in acting criminally may not have been bent on doing harm, but rather was in the grip of certain unrealistic notions that made what he did seem to him to be something quite different from what it appears to be in the eyes of the law. If we probe deeply and sensitively we may find, for example, that he was really involved in an internal struggle against submission to an authority figure and not in the least interested in doing harm to the victim. In such a case, even though criminally liable, he is entitled to be punished as someone whose conduct is less culpable than it would be if we ignored these background factors.

There is, however, good reason why these considerations do not provide an excuse that avoids liability. Those offering the excuse assume that conduct cannot be blameworthy unless the existence of those conditions necessary for its occurrence was a matter within the actor's control. This, however, is not so. We are all of us all the time subject to such alien influences, but so long as we have control over how these influences affect our conduct we are responsible agents. All that is required for responsibility is that we be able to modify such influences by inhibitory processes. Even though certain background conditions may have been necessary for the behavior that constituted criminal conduct—except for those conditions the conduct almost certainly would not have occurred—we do not excuse the conduct unless the outcome of such conditions is beyond the inhibitory powers of the actor. In short, to be responsible for one's conduct it is not necessary that one be responsible for those things without whose influence one would not have acted as one did. It is necessary only that one be able to frustrate their effect.

One excuse of this sort—probably the most frequently heard of all excuses when crime is discussed by people with generally enlightened views—has its most concise expression when it is said of the accused that "he is not to blame, society is." For the reason just given, this is not a valid excuse and thus does not *shift* blame—though if there is sense in the notion of blaming society and good purpose in engaging in such a practice, the claim may be used to good effect to add society as another object of accusation. Alternatively, it may be interpreted simply as a rhetorical flourish in a call for the elimination of the causes of crime, in which case it is not an excuse at all and has no bearing on the liability of the accused.

There is, however, yet another plausible interpretation to be made. The statement may be understood as a claim that it would be wrong for those exercising public power to punish a crime that likely would not have occurred but for their neglect in dealing with the causes of crime. Under this interpretation there is no claim of excuse *for* doing something but rather a very complicated claim of immunity unaffected by considerations of culpability. It rests on those considerations that determine when there may no longer be an enforceable obligation to obey the law, and thus it is a claim to be excused *from* criminal liability, not an excuse *for* having done something criminal.

DETERMINISM AND EXCULPATION

Underlying all other problems of excuse is the question of whether some metaphysical truth about human conduct provides a general mandate for universal excuse. In the eyes of orthodox determinism, every person is part of nature and is subject quite thoroughly to its influences. No agent, therefore, is as free as he appears to be, for everyone in fact acts as he does because acted upon by forces independent of his control. These forces are largely unknown, but no less efficacious for their obscurity. In its purest formulations the determinist position precludes the possibility of any spontaneous intervention by an agent to determine his own conduct. He is not a cause of his conduct apart from his place in a field of causes that operate upon and through him but are not under his domination. Thus he cannot act to frustrate the influences toward misconduct to which he is subject unless he is fortunate enough to be subject also to contrary influences that are stronger. For this reason, when accused of wrongdoing he may always validly claim that he could not do otherwise than he did.

Orthodox determinism recognizes that we are disposed initially to see self-determination of conduct in ourselves and in others, but maintains that this is an illusion fostered by ignorance of the true causes of conduct. On an extreme determinist view, it is unjust to punish anyone for what he has done, for the very same reason that it is unjust to punish anyone for what he has not done. In either case the untoward occurrence is not properly attributable to the actor, but to something or someone else. Seen in this light, the extreme determinist claim is a kind of conduct-regarding denial of responsibility—"He didn't *do* it"—and hence, strictly speaking, not an excuse at all. On a less extreme view, orthodox determinism would hold that the harm is attributable to the actor, but that he always has available an excuse that the outcome of the combination of causes acting on him was not within his control. The claim is then in essence an actor-regarding denial of culpability, which might be expressed by a declaration that no one's acts are ever truly intentional.

The thesis of universal excuse that might reasonably be attributed to orthodox determinism can be answered without raising objections to its premises. For present purposes we may even accept its conclusion that one is not accountable for acting as one does. If that proposition is then invoked as a defense by those who punish, they in turn must be judged equally without fault for what they do. Those who prescribe and administer punishment are, on these assumptions of determinism, likewise unfree to do otherwise, and so criticism of them for what they do is equally misconceived. Conversely, if determinism, by some concessions in theory, allows for criticism of acts of punishment, it must on the same grounds allow for criticism of the conduct that is being treated as punishable. Though this argument is not deeply satisfying, neither is the argument it seeks to refute, and for present purposes it seems enough simply to establish the fact of *tu quoque*. Confidence is then restored in the commonsense conclusion that a person's conduct is open to criticism and that he may rightly be held accountable for it.

There is, however, an even more telling criticism to be made, since the conclusion suggested by the determinist thesis is itself false. It is not the case that, whenever a person could not do otherwise than he did, he is not responsible for what he did—though this is what the determinist thesis suggests. In order not to be responsible, the actor must have acted as he did *because* he could not do otherwise.

As an illustration, suppose that Smith and Jones both wish to have a counter-espionage report removed from the files and destroyed. Smith is a government employee whose rather serious lapses are detailed in the report, and he is likely to lose his job if the report comes to the attention of his superiors. Jones, a fellow employee, is in fact a foreign spy likely to be apprehended if certain other matters in the report come to the attention of the authorities. Only Smith has access to the report, and Jones knows that Smith intends to destroy it. Jones says nothing to Smith, preferring to avoid the risk of his own involvement if possible, but instead waits to see whether Smith will carry out his intention. If Smith should change his mind, Jones is ready to make him do it— by a dire threat which it is certain Smith cannot resist, or by drugs and hypnotic suggestion that are equally certain to be effective. Smith proceeds on his own to destroy the report, but is found out and now faces criminal charges for the destruction. If Smith learns of Jones's contingent plan to compel the destruction, he may claim quite correctly that he could not have avoided doing what he did. But clearly that would not serve to excuse him. To have his claim taken seriously, Smith would have to show that he did it *because* he could not do otherwise—that, for example, he was undecided what to do but learned of Jones's foolproof plan of coercion and acted under its unuttered but nevertheless real threat.

The claim suggested by orthodox determinism is like the claim available to Smith, and it is invalid for the same reason. Having supposedly discovered that no one could ever have done otherwise, orthodox determinism proposes to excuse universally. But it does not even purport to show that everyone acts as he does *because* he could not do otherwise. Such a claim would place an unbearable burden upon the proponent, for he must argue either that all of us regularly act not on choice but on impulse in accordance with influences that hold sway over us; or else that we are all aware of causal influences constraining us to act in a certain way and either regularly submit to them as a matter of choice in which we willingly accept our fate, or submit against our will as we are overpowered by them. It is plain enough that, far from describing what is universally the human condition, these alternatives describe what can be found only infrequently in some very odd cases and then only in some partial approximation.

Of course, even if the actor does not know that he is doing what he does *because* he cannot do otherwise, he is entitled to be excused if in fact he did it because he could not do otherwise. The man whose behavior is determined ineluctably by the dark psychic forces of the unconscious and who cannot act except in accordance with its dictates is entitled to be excused even though he has not the slightest idea of why he acts as he does. Similarly, if we all are enslaved in a field of causal determinants whose dictates we cannot choose to contravene, even though we do not know this and cherish an illusion of genuine choice, we would be entitled to an excuse because in fact what we then do we do *because* we cannot do otherwise. But determinism only *supposes* that this might be the case. What its arguments purport to *demonstrate* is simply that we cannot do otherwise; but not that we act as we do *because* we cannot do otherwise.

In the absence of such demonstration, our clear intuition

about the possibility of choice remains unimpaired, and is opposed only by a metaphysical supposition of what *might* be the case. True, this supposition may be entertained in good conscience so long as there are no convincing arguments to foreclose the possibility of our being mere pawns whose acts are merely the moves of mysterious powers whose processes remain hidden from us. But a theory of responsibility—and more particularly a theory of criminal justice—need consider only the narrower question of whether it is unjust to criticize conduct and hold people responsible so long as that possibility remains open. It is not a difficult question, for it seems plain enough that the mere theoretical possibility of universal cosmic compulsion need not be banished in order for responsibility to be taken seriously in our dealings with one another.

It is just barely possible, of course, that we may one day find that what determinism now in its extreme moods supposes to be the case is in fact the case. But then we should only be enlightened about choice and responsibility by a great leap forward as we have been enlightened from time to time by much smaller steps through the discoveries of psychopathology or through some new appreciation of a person's behavior in the light of his personal or social circumstances. In the meantime, when we follow our intuitions and assume, in deciding questions of responsibility, that people have the power of choice that they seem to have, we give no offense to those ideals of justice in human society which we are bound to serve.

There is, finally, a theme of universal excuse that is based in part on a less rigorous determinism, and in part on a mistake about what justifies punishment. It invokes the commonsense assumption that everything, including human behavior, has a cause, and attaches great importance to the universal abatement of reproachful attitudes toward conduct once its causes are understood. It proposes to elevate to a standard of civilized social practice the insight expressed by *tout comprendre, c'est tout pardonner*. We tend to pardon behavior when we understand it, and since in principle all behavior is understandable, we ought always to pardon as though we actually had such understanding.

It is true that attitudes of condemnation do tend to diminish as understanding of motivation increases. This psychological fact is perhaps best explained by viewing the condemnatory attitude as a rather primitive protective response to the prospect of further harm once some harm has occurred or has been threatened. Such responses are needed less, and hence are weaker, as understanding of what was done increases. We seek to understand fully, and as civilized creatures we welcome the abatement of condemnatory attitudes. But condemnation of what was done may still take place even when there is complete and sympathetic understanding of its causes; and condemnation then is perfectly compatible with such understanding. In any case, for criminal liability it is the culpable character of conduct that matters, and not the attitude that may be expected in the light of what is or may be understood. Even when we have a deep and sensitive understanding, we are still bound to view what was done as a violation of the law that is more or less culpable according to those standards of culpability upon which our criminal jurisprudence rests; and what was done still deserves condemnation according to its culpability even though we then understand it better.

II. QUESTIONING THE NEED

THE ARGUMENT FOR RECOGNIZING EXCUSES

Excuses to avoid blame seem a natural and sensible part of ordinary life, and normally we should be alarmed by a suggestion that one accused of doing wrong ought to be criticized even though he did not mean to do it or was unable to do otherwise. But even in ordinary life, excuses do not always matter. Criticism sometimes is not aimed at assigning blame, and excuses are then brushed aside as irrelevant. Knowledge is acquired, skills are developed, and bad habits are broken through performance and then criticism of it—and in this program excuses often fall upon deaf ears. Criticism is for the sake of instruction and to encourage keener effort. Excuses are beside the point and a waste of time, or—even worse—a subversive influence. When things go wrong in military campaigns or in business ventures, those in charge are often criticized, and, once again, excuses are either out of place or are only subordinate considerations. Confidence in leaders and managers is all important and, when they fail, often the only question is whether grounds for continued confidence still exist. Usually excuses have only a small part to play in that decision, and often no part at all.

In all these contexts, criticism is not the basis of an accusation, and the exclusion of excuses is therefore not unfair. Since criticism is only to judge ability in the light of performance, the refusal to consider excuses is not surprising; nor is it an offense to justice.

Criminal charges, however, are another matter, for they are the very paradigm of accusation. The criticism of conduct represented by such charges is aimed at assigning blame as a basis of liability. It is for this reason that we are alarmed by suggestions that criminal charges might stick in spite of excuses. Once again, however, special reasons are offered for ignoring excuses in this context. It is said that many socially dangerous persons are allowed to go free in spite of having committed a criminal act—simply because on this occasion they happen to have an excuse. Criminal liability, it is said, is the means by which the law may act to remove and correct socially dangerous people. A socially dangerous person can be identified by his socially dangerous behavior, and once the identification is made, accusation and excuse no longer have a place in the proceedings. At that point the aim is to sequester and to treat, though the diagnosis may take into account whatever grounds of excuse there might be in order to judge more accurately just how dangerous the person really is.

A curious alliance is formed on this issue. Those who cultivate the dilemmas of determinism and believe crimes to be universally excusable would tend generally to favor the abolition of excuses. Usually their arguments are not merely metaphysical but appeal also to what are assumed to be the social and psychological facts of criminal behavior. On their account no criminal is truly responsible, and it is wrong to excuse some but not others. This invidious discrimination based upon specious distinctions can be done away with only if our system of excuse is abolished. Others who advocate the elimination of excuses but start from the premises of therapy and social sanitation simply regard the issues of responsibility and of culpability as irrelevant to the objectives of liability, and so deny that there are times when criminal acts ought to be excused.

In our time, work of exceptional illumination has been provided by two writers on the subject. H. L. A. Hart has presented a variety of arguments in defense of excuses, while on the other side Barbara Wootton has urged their elimination. It is worthwhile to examine their views in detail.

In the essay titled "Changing Conceptions of Responsibility" Professor Hart provides four reasons for preserving excuses in the criminal law. First, official intrusions in our life would be greatly increased without them. Police investigation of apparently accidental or careless harm would be warranted, since under such a system even excusable harm may make the harmdoer liable to treatment of some sort. The strength of this first objection depends, as Hart acknowledges, upon a comparative value judgment balancing the loss of liberty against the safer social environment that presumably would result when this finer net is cast.

Two further arguments advanced by Hart in favor of giving effect to excuses are based on considerations of punishment. One touches its justice, the other its efficacy. He points first to the moral objectionability of a practice that would punish lawbreakers for the sake of deterring them in the future and by their example deterring others as well, even though they could not have avoided doing what they did.

It is surely right, as Hart suggests, to regard as morally objectionable the universal conscription of all lawbreakers in the cause of deterrence without exemption for those having an excuse, since such universal conscription ignores considerations of autonomy. But even our present system of limited conscription, which enlists only those who have no excuse, can be viewed as a morally dubious practice in need of justification, since it inflicts suffering upon certain persons in order to achieve a desirable social objective. The root of the objection is really the sacrifice of individual interests for collective ones. Justification of that sacrifice is the burden of those who regard deterrence as morally right, and it is not clear what part exemption of those with an excuse might play in that.

The other objection posed by Hart is based on doubt about how criminal liability would be regarded under a system that admits no excuses and administers either therapeutic or punitive treatment depending upon which would better serve to prevent further crime. Hart is struck by a dilemma that such a system creates. Either the stigma that now attaches to those convicted of crime will continue to attach—in which case there is a moral objection to stigmatizing those who could not do otherwise. Or, because of the different basis of liability and the different treatment, a person found criminally liable will no longer be stigmatized, in which case an important deterrent resource of the law will have been destroyed.

Professor Hart acknowledges that the supposed dependence of the law upon social attitudes toward lawbreakers is a matter that may appear different in the light of further psychological and sociological research, and that this objection to the new system may then lose some of its force. But even commonsense reflection upon our present system of legal regulation gives strong support to the view that *liability in spite of excuse* does not stigmatize the one who is liable, and that the efficacy of the law is not impaired by this absence of stigma. A person who is a social menace because of his highly contagious illness is not stigmatized when he is deprived by law of his employment in a restaurant kitchen or is subjected to compulsory quarantine. Furthermore, even though he could not avoid having the disease, the law removing him from circulation is effective to prevent other cases of the disease from developing.

Similarly, persons who engage in socially dangerous conduct that they could not help might be made less prone to continue to do so by a regime of corrective treatment that would then prevent further crime. Not unlikely, their excuse will shield such persons from criminal stigmatization, and so the injustice of condemnation for those who could not help themselves would not occur. A system that disregards excuses might therefore be effective without being unjust, and would escape the dilemma that Hart suggests. It would be a system in which no part is played by deterring stigmata—but in such a system there is no need for such deterrence.

The fourth reason advanced here by Professor Hart for retaining excuses shifts attention to *mens rea* in the definition of an offense. Omit all reference to the mental elements in its offenses, says Hart, and a criminal code "could not possibly be satisfactory," though he concedes that there are many important offenses on the books to which this objection does not apply. We shall soon see how important a point this is. As a preliminary observation, it might be said that even the limited concession made by Hart seems unnecessary, for under a rigorous analysis of requirements for liability it turns out that what is properly meant by *mens rea* is in some form required for all offenses. The discussion of strict liability in the next section should make this clear.

In his essay "Punishment and the Elimination of Responsibility," Professor Hart presents yet another set of arguments in favor of excuses. He first argues that in general every man ought to have a fair opportunity to conform his conduct to the law, and that this is the rationale for most of the excuses recognized by the law. This is an important preliminary point, though by itself it serves only to explain why we excuse. More is needed to explain why the law is bound to recognize excuses when they are offered in defense to a criminal accusation. A case must be made out for fairness at some cost in social safety that is stronger than the opposing case for social safety at some cost in fairness.

Professor Hart then reminds us that a world without excuses would severely curtail our ability to plan our lives within the law, since we would be legally accountable for unintended harm resulting from mistakes or accidents. Throughout our lives we would be at the mercy of happenstance, and for this reason we must prize our excuses, for they protect us from such a precarious existence.

This picture of a world without excuses seems reasonable enough, but we must keep in mind that our attitude toward excuses depends upon certain matters of fact. If it could be shown that the cost of accepting excuses was a greatly diminished ability to prevent crime, and that crime made our existence truly precarious, we might seriously consider the huge sacrifice in self-determination that would result from abandonment of excuses, and might conclude finally that, because of our perilous environment, control over our destiny is a luxury we cannot afford. Many misfortunes that befall us in life we have learned to accept with resignation as part of the risks of being alive, and we should then add to those unavoidable misfortunes criminal liability for our acts regardless of our fault.

Professor Hart next suggests that admitting excuses places a premium on self-restraint. The law rewards those who keep the law in what they do by not requiring them to suffer punishment when in spite of adherence to law there is an untoward occurrence born of mistake or accident.

One problem here is that the model of activity suggested by Hart's analysis seems not altogether suitable. To make self-restraint intelligible, there must be a temptation to break the law against which self-restraint can be exercised. But on many occasions when conduct is excusable there has been no such temptation. Certainly there need be none, and Hart's point in support of excusing has force only if temptation was present. But there is a more serious problem. If reward for self-restraint were a reason for recognizing excuses, and on other grounds it was decided that recognition of excuses was undesirable, excuses could still be dispensed with and the inducement to self-restraint preserved by the expedient of punishing more severely conduct that would not in any event qualify to be excused, while still punishing, though less severely, excusable conduct. This would simply amount to an adaptation of the grading scheme found throughout the criminal law—a system in which severity of punishment depends upon the extent of culpability. The nonculpable conduct of one who follows the law would then be rewarded by minimum punishment when it causes harm, and this would preserve the inducement to self-restraint while preserving as well the presumed benefits of not allowing liability to be avoided altogether by excuse.

Finally, Professor Hart points with special emphasis to a basic fact of our social life. We distinguish sharply and with important consequences between a deliberate blow and an accidental blow, treating the one (though not the other) as offensive, and holding accountable the one who acts deliberately while excusing the one whose blow was an accident. "This is how human nature in human society actually is," says Hart, "and as yet we have no power to alter it." The law, he says, must take such basic facts into account, and it fails to do so when it ignores excuses.

Here Professor Hart points to an exceedingly important and special use to which excuses of this sort are put, though in his discussion he does not make explicit the special role played by the excuse. The exculpatory argument consists of two separate exculpatory claims. The first of these is the excuse, which asserts that the blow was unintentional. Unintentional blows, however, are not offensive, for in the case of an unintentional blow there has not been the assault upon sensibilities that the law is concerned to protect when it prohibits offensive touching. Since this assault upon sensibility is precisely the harm contemplated by the law that punishes offensive touching, the second (and ultimate) exculpatory claim is that on this occasion of inoffensive touching there is no harm. This is not an excuse, though it is an exculpatory claim that initially needs the excuse to give it substance. The fact that the blow was unintentional provides a footing for the further claim that the blow was not an offensive touching, and so not an occasion of harm of this sort. Since the blow was unintentional it was not an assault upon one's dignity and one's peace of mind, for there is good reason to be upset or affronted when a blow is meant, but not when it is an accident.

The role of excuse in these cases may be contrasted to the more conventional role played by the same excuse when it is not an offense to sensibility but a more substantial harm of true physical pain or bodily injury that the law takes notice of. If such harm is the law's concern, and purposely causing it is made a crime, the excuse that one caused it only accidentally will itself comprise the whole of the exculpatory argument. There is then not a denial that harm was done, but rather a denial that what was done intentionally was the dangerous conduct for which the law prescribes liability. In terms of our previous analysis of culpability, the mode of exculpation here is a denial of *intentionality* rather than a denial of *harm*. In either the leading or the supporting role, however, the excuse is indispensable if there is to be liability only for the crime that the legislature meant to create.

THE ARGUMENT AGAINST RECOGNIZING EXCUSES

In her book *Crime and the Criminal Law* Barbara Wootton argues that matters of responsibility ought not to be considered when deciding whether to impose liability on a person who has broken the law, and this presents a serious challenge to those who advocate recognition of excuses in the criminal law.

In Lady Wootton's view, the criminal law ought to be forward-looking and, when a crime occurs, the law ought to pursue its objective of preventing crime by taking measures designed to prevent a recurrence. Accordingly, the criminal law ought to facilitate a program of social hygiene that seeks to treat each offender in a way that is likely to cure him of whatever caused him to commit a crime. The job is either to identify and treat pathological conditions or to correct by more frankly penal methods when criminal behavior is not a matter of pathology.

Lady Wootton's scheme of criminal justice has no place for a requirement of *mens rea*. Indeed, such requirement would interfere with the objectives of the program by providing an avenue of escape for the socially dangerous. Though Lady Wootton does not explain exactly what she understands the term *mens rea* to include, it surely includes the state of mind of a person who means by his actions to do harm.

Though her discussion leaves room for some doubt, the term would quite likely include as well the state of mind of one who acts with willful disregard of risks of harm, or with indifference toward the dangers of a dangerous situation. In any event, *mens rea* is for Lady Wootton the criminally wrong state of mind which accompanies physical actions that cause harm, and which she speaks of as "socially damaging actions." Lady Wootton's position is that it is "illogical" to make this state of mind a part of the definition of a crime in view of what it is that we wish (or should wish) to take notice of and treat as criminal. In the first instance only behavior causing harm matters, for then the question is simply whether there should be liability to treatment. When we move on to consider what sort of treatment is appropriate we may then look into the state of mind of the person committing the crime. In principle, at least, that state of mind is relevant in diagnosing the causes of his antisocial behavior, and so it is quite sensible to take it into consideration when deciding on measures to prevent a recurrence of that behavior.

Under Lady Wootton's view it would make no difference whether a denial of *mens rea* took the form "I didn't mean to do that" or the form "I couldn't help doing it." In her discussion, mere absence of a required state of mind and the inability to have it are commingled and rejected as excuses. Her objection is simply that there are many socially dangerous persons—such as the utterly irresponsible, the reckless, the careless, and the accident-prone—who might be rendered innocuous by proper treatment but who are now left dangerous and at large because at the time of their dangerous activity they were not possessed of the morally reprehensible state of mind which the law requires for liability.

One may sympathize with Lady Wootton in her assumption that the law in its concern with *mens rea* seeks to punish for wicked states of mind. That view of the matter receives ample support in the literature of criminal law theory. But since the requirement of *mens rea* really has an altogether different significance, Lady Wootton's position is in reality a much different one than she takes it to be. Rather than certifying the wickedness or dangerousness of a state of mind, the law by having a requirement of *mens rea* seeks to insure that the act for which the defendant stands accused is in fact an act of the harmful sort that concerns the law, and (even more often) to insure that only those who engage *intentionally* in some unlawful act incur liability for what they do. We have just looked into the first of these concerns in our discussion of offensive and inoffensive blows, and have already many times turned our attention to the second when the question of culpability in its first dimension has come under discussion.

These two roles that are played by *mens rea* requirements are both illustrated in the following provision. In New York the crime of custodial interference is committed by a person who "being a relative of a child less than sixteen years old, *intending to hold such child permanently or for a protracted* period, *and knowing that he has no legal right to do so, . . .* takes or entices such child from his lawful custodian." It is thus a defense that the person taking the child did not intend to keep him. It is also a defense that such person believed that he had a legal right to take the child with the intention of keeping him. The first defense would render the taking a harmless temporary deprivation in the eyes of the law, and so would furnish the foundation of the exculpatory claim that what was done did not cause or threaten the harm which is the concern of the law. The second defense is an excuse, for it denies that what the law prohibits was done intentionally.

In seeking to eliminate requirements of *mens rea* from the definition of crimes, Lady Wootton has assumed the burden of showing that these defenses are not needed—either because their purpose may be served in other ways or because their purpose need not be served at all. Nowhere is there an attempt to discharge this burden—hardly remarkable in view of the fact that it is a burden of overwhelming proportions. By eliminating opportunity to argue that what was done was not in fact the harmful conduct the law is concerned to prevent, Lady Wootton would make possible the conviction of those whose conduct is simply not a social danger. Surely she would want to provide against that, and it seems safe to conclude that she would want to see *mens rea* and the claims that deny it preserved for that purpose.

There is a burden of a different sort that would greatly enhance Lady Wootton's proposal if carried successfully. This other burden, though hardly lighter, is perhaps a less uncomfortable one for Lady Wootton in view of her objectives. It may be that unintentional "socially dangerous" acts could be dealt with by a system of criminal law conceived along radically different lines, a system in which penal law would be akin to legislation providing for such things as internment, compulsory education, civil commitment, and quarantine. Conduct then would no longer be the ultimate concern in deciding when to impose criminal liability. Instead, attention would be directed to the condition a person is in, or to the status he occupies. "Socially dangerous" conduct, which would still be the subject matter of criminal prescriptions, would then be of concern simply as an indication that something is wrong with the person who engages in it. It would be the office of those who impose liability simply to arrange for appropriate treatment to prevent further "socially dangerous" activities.

There is bound to be a heavy cost in autonomy when we are made liable in spite of how we choose to act. There are further heavy costs in terms of loss of civil liberty because of increased subjugation to public authority, and we should not want to commit ourselves to pay any of these costs without a very careful accounting beforehand. As a first step, we should want to know a great deal about the Pygmalions to whom we may all be compelled to play Galatea. We should want to know much about their aims, their methods, and their prospects of success. Even without delving too deeply into these larger issues of how men ought to live and how they ought to treat one another, we are beset by two immediate problems that appear to postpone indefinitely the adoption of such a scheme.

The items of "socially dangerous" conduct that are made criminal by the criminal law were not selected in order to identify persons who have something wrong with them, nor do they in any generally reliable way serve that purpose. Legislators when they draft penal legislation are not concerned to devise tests to spot defectives requiring treatment or custodial sequestration. Their interest is simply to give appropriate legal recognition to harmful conduct that is a matter of public concern and to create liability to punishment for those who engage in it. Lady Wootton has not indicated that she believes that a penal prescription ought instead to consist of a specification of behavior symptomatic of a socially dangerous personality. Indeed, she gives no indication that this would even be possible. Nor does she furnish us with warrants for inferring, from an instance of "socially dangerous" conduct as defined in the penal law, the existence of dispositions to engage in such "socially dangerous" conduct. On its face such inference seems no more sound than inferring that a person who breaks a dish probably has a disposition to break dishes, or that a man who divorces his wife probably has a disposition to terminate his marriage. Yet without grounds for a *prima facie* belief that doing harm indicates a disposition to do harm, this conception of the criminal process invites the inhumanity of compulsory treatment for the harmless and the injustice of incarceration for the innocent.

This proposal for the criminal law as it ought to be is undermined at the threshold by yet another consideration. If the benefits of corrective treatment are to justify subjecting to such treatment people who have caused harm even though their conduct is not blameworthy, we should certainly require at a minimum that the treatment have a genuine prospect of success and not be simply a pretext for taking people out of circulation. In order for any compulsory medical measure to be just, it is necessary (though not sufficient) that there be a reasonable expectation of its success. There would be manifest injustice, for example, if the law made innoculation compulsory when immunization followed from it only rarely and unpredictably. Such a law would be unjust as an arbitrary exercise of power, even though the infringement of liberty would be slight.

Injustice is much greater if, when there is compulsory diagnosis and treatment of "socially dangerous" tendencies, uncertainties are legion and the program entails severe deprivation of liberty. Terms such as *treatment* and *pathology* are at present sheer metaphor when relocated from medical to criminal contexts. The idea of a therapeutic model is premature and cannot be given serious consideration as a program for reform without major advances in diagnosis and in techniques of treatment. We are bound until then to accept certain risks in the interest of preserving liberty and insuring justice, just as we accept certain risks when we allow the use of high-speed motor vehicles in the interest of transporting ourselves more quickly and conveniently.

Even so, there is ample consolation for those who may be disappointed when a safer society cannot be promoted through an excuse-free criminal process. In the first place, harmful or dangerous acts under circumstances that indicate some likelihood of mental abnormality warrant measures to determine whether the person is in fact a menace and so properly committed to medical care under principles of civil commitment. But beyond that, persons who are accident-prone, habitually careless, inconsiderate, inattentive, scatterbrained, and in other ways of a kind that cause harm to others are in fact often the object of legal concern that is noncriminal. There are laws requiring tests, permits, licenses, approvals, and innumerable varieties of precautionary measures and examinations, as well as regulatory directives of all sorts, all of which comprise an elaborate system of legal supervision designed in part to prevent harm by dangerous persons, though by measures outside the criminal law. When considerations of justice make penal liability inappropriate, resort is had to these measures, which advance the same ends and are often more effective because administratively more sensitive to the causes of the harm.

This system of regulation dispenses almost entirely with excuses, and yet at the same time it does not offend against principles of responsibility and culpability. A claim that one did something wrong during a driver's test by mistake or by accident gets no recognition in the grading of the performance; those who show themselves to be socially dangerous as unskilled drivers are denied the opportunity to do harm. Still, we do not consider that an injustice is done in excluding excuses, for culpability has no place in these nonpunitive proceedings. It is simply a matter of being able to perform potentially harmful activities in a socially safe way in order to be entitled to perform them at all.

III. STRICT LIABILITY

WHAT STRICT LIABILITY IS

The sweeping revisionist proposals of Lady Wootton and others have taken encouragement from a more modest development within the criminal law. For a large number of offenses falling beyond the bounds of common crime, it appears that excuses either are unavailable altogether or are severely rationed. In the main these are minor offenses, on the books because certain lawful but dangerous activities need governmental regulation through laws that have a penal backing, or because some program of public benefit similarly requires such laws for its implementation. There are also more serious crimes in which violations appear inexcusable, although, unlike regulatory offenses, they are regarded as curiosities and a mysterious departure from normal legislative practice. The excuses to which the law turns a deaf ear when there is strict liability are all claims of mistake or accident. What the law prohibits may be done unintentionally, so it seems; and yet there is liability. Apparently, then, there is liability without culpability.

But there are disappointments in store for those who have been gladdened by strict liability and who see it as the model for a new and enlightened criminal law in which excuses have no place. A more careful examination discloses that in most crimes of strict liability there actually is a requirement of low-grade culpable conduct akin to certain sorts of negligence for which there is civil liability. The remainder of what are thought to be crimes of strict liability are actually crimes of a high degree of culpability. For both classes of offense there are excuses that defeat imputations of culpability. This is the thesis to be defended here; but a preliminary distinction among terms is necessary to avoid misunderstandings. *Strict liability* characterizes offenses that are usually, though incorrectly, said to entail liability without culpability; *absolute liability* is the term used to characterize offenses for which there actually is liability without culpability. Many offenses of strict liability are readily accepted and flourish in the law. Offenses of absolute liability are eccentric and rare. This is hardly surprising, for once their true character is revealed they are rooted out and banished.

VARIETIES OF STRICT LIABILITY

Perhaps the most prominent feature of most strict liability offenses is that conviction does not affect respectability. Neither his conduct nor the punishment he receives for it stigmatizes the offender. These offenses of low culpability are typically of the *regulatory* or *public welfare* variety, and so penal treatment is rightly viewed as simply an expedient way of encouraging or preventing certain consequences that flow from lawful activity, rather than as a public response to wrongdoing. Common examples are traffic offenses and prohibited sales to minors, food and drug adulteration or mislabeling, and those numberless varieties of other petty offenses in which the accused is in a position to prevent some untoward occurrence because of the control he exercises over some activity, situation, or enterprise. When there is strict liability in offenses of this sort, a court will not entertain pleas that the accused did not know, or that he believed otherwise, or that he exercised reasonable care. Not only is there an absence of wrongdoing, then, but the prohibited act might have been excused if only the law allowed the excuse to be heard.

There are, however, other more serious crimes in which the defendant is similarly bereft of opportunity to defend by excuse. In most jurisdictions a man accused of statutory rape cannot present as a defense his reasonable mistake about the girl's age. Similarly irrelevant under traditional views is the mistake of one who reasonably, though wrongly, believed that his former marriage was ended by law or by death and who is accused of bigamy after remarriage. Again, under prevailing views, the claim of accidental death will not help a burglar accused of felony murder when a bullet he had fired into the air ricocheted off the ceiling with fatal results, even though he establishes that he meant only to distract the watchman who surprised him and blocked his escape.

Perhaps the outer limit of severity under strict liability was reached by invoking a principle of command responsibility in the case of General Yamashita. Indeed, it is doubtful that liability was merely strict rather than absolute. The United States Supreme Court reviewed and approved the judgment of the war crimes tribunal by which the Japanese army commander in the Philippines during the last months of the war was sentenced to death because troops of his command engaged in wanton slaughter of war prisoners and civilians and in widespread acts of burning, pillaging, and other barbarous acts. There was no showing that the General in any way condoned, much less ordered, these atrocities, and it was questionable whether he even knew of them. The conviction did not rest on allegations of specific acts of negligence by the commander resulting in these atrocities. Further, it was conceded by the prosecution that normal communications and discipline had broken down as a result of the deteriorating military situation during this time of Japanese retreat, and so apparently Yamashita would have been unable to control his troops by the exercise of his authority as commander even if he knew what was going on. Nevertheless, he was convicted and hanged because he had, in the words of the indictment, "unlawfully disregarded and failed to discharge his duty as commander to control the operations of the members of his command, permitting them to commit brutal atrocities." The legal basis for such criminal liability was said to be the principle of international law that, with regard to protection of civilians and prisoners of war, an armed force in a war zone is commanded by a person responsible for his subordinates.

In view of the apparent injustice of legislation that affords no opportunity for excuse, it is hardly surprising that courts often afford relief by not giving a statute its most literal reading. When words like "willful," "purposely," "negligently," "knowingly," and the like do not appear in the law at all, or appear to have a scope that unduly restricts excuses, courts will often interpret the text in a way that provides opportunity for excuse when simple justice seems unmistakably to require that such opportunities should exist.

OBJECTIONS TO STRICT LIABILITY

Those objecting in principle to offenses of strict liability rely mainly on three propositions: first, that only persons who are to blame for what they do are justly punished for it; second, that it is wrong to punish a person who did not intend any harm to occur; third, regarding serious offenses, that the heavy sentences prescribed are deserved only for conduct that is culpable in a high degree.

The premises upon which the first objection rests have been warmly endorsed throughout our discussions. Penal treatment for those whose conduct is not culpable is indeed unjust, and this principle is generally respected throughout the criminal law. But this does not furnish grounds for objection to strict liability, since the principle is not violated when there is strict liability. On the scale of culpability, offenses of strict liability are very low indeed, but culpable conduct is nevertheless required by the laws that create these offenses.

Three conditions must be met if there is to be liability under these laws: (1) *the risk of the harm for which there is liability must be such that the one to be held liable can appreciate it;* (2) *the one to be held liable must have the ability to prevent the harm;* (3) *the measures required to prevent the harm must not in effect be prohibitive of the activity posing the risk of harm.* In essence these conditions ensure that both the responsibility principle and the culpability principle are respected. When these conditions are met, the occurrence of the prescribed harm because of some activity constitutes negligence *per se* on the part of the one carrying on that activity, and liability is then strict. As with negligence *per se* for which there is civil liability, fault lies only in failing to satisfy legislative requirements; and penalties are prescribed for that.

The second objection is to punishing those who did not mean to do harm and were not even so much as recklessly indifferent to its occurrence. The objection is to punishing acts that are only negligent, and so *a fortiori* to punishing when it is simply a matter of precautions that were unsuccessful. There are two premises on which this objection rests: that only when conduct is generally regarded as wrong can punishment be efficacious; and that only when conduct actually is wrong can punishment be just. Mere negligence, it is said, is not generally regarded as wrong, nor should it be, for it is not actually wrong.

But countless offenses (to which these critics make no objection) sometimes characterized as *mala prohibita,* are, like negligence, not regarded as instances of wrong conduct apart from the law's prohibition. The claim of injustice is answered by pointing out that what is wrong in the violative conduct is a failure to take precaution sufficient to satisfy the law; thus these offenses are no different than other well-accepted offenses of culpable omission. It is indeed less culpable than other conduct, and so deserving of less punishment, but still no less deserving of punishment. It is further objected by some that, when criminal negligence is created, punishment is prescribed for the consequences of a mere mental lapse instead of for the consequences of a state of mind that makes punishment deserved. This argument is no weightier than would be an argument urging no punishment for an intentionally harmful act because it was the consequence of a mental lapse in failing to exercise self-restraint. In either case the actor has breached his duty to avoid doing harm—in one case by pursuing harm and in the other by engaging in risky activity without due precaution.

The third objection condemns strict liability for serious

crimes by appeal to a generally accepted principle of condign punishment which requires that lesser culpability be visited with a lesser penalty. The principle itself is unexceptionable; yet it poses no objection here because, as we shall see, serious crimes for which there is thought to be strict liability are in fact offenses of a high degree of culpability.

It would be a mistake to conclude, because these general objections to strict liability have been rejected, that each offense of strict liability is justifiable. Culpable conduct is necessary for any criminal liability to be sound. But other considerations of justice, as well as considerations of prudence, may stand opposed to a particular prescription of strict penal liability. In general, when there are other ways to accomplish the same end and they do not require coercion and deprivation, it is wrong to resort to penal laws. It is especially wrong when conduct is scarcely culpable and ordinary excuses do not count.

PURPORTED JUSTIFICATIONS OF ABSOLUTE LIABILITY

Absolute liability evokes little enthusiasm, though it is accepted in principle and justified as an unpleasant necessity by many who incorrectly assume that the offenses of strict liability included in the law are really offenses of absolute liability. Four strands of argument appear in defense of absolute liability for petty offenses. Two of them lay stress on what are claimed to be justifying necessities; the other two emphasize that such liability is less undesirable than might be thought. All four turn out to be less formidable than at first they seem, and in the end they provide scant support to those who wish to dispense entirely with a requirement of culpability in the criminal law. It is well to examine these arguments carefully, for, though absolute liability is still rare, its toleration and growth in the law is encouraged if these arguments are accepted.

JUSTIFICATION BASED ON ADMINISTRATIVE CONVENIENCE

The first of the arguments from necessity rests on considerations of administrative convenience. It is conceded that in the interest of justice it would be desirable to allow a defendant charged with a regulatory offense an opportunity to show that he was not to blame. Weighing against this, however, are considerations of effective enforcement. The character of these offenses insures that they will be committed numberless times, and it is said that enforcement on a scale required for effective regulation would be virtually impossible if trial courts were burdened with such issues as whether there really was a mistake, how reasonable it was, whether the precautions taken were all that might reasonably be expected, and the like. The chances of violators' escaping prosecution altogether would be greatly increased because of the time consumed by each case; and opportunities to escape conviction by disingenuous excuse would be far greater than in prosecutions for more serious crimes, since overall considerations of prosecutorial economy would make rebuttal too costly in terms of what is to be achieved by conviction. Because of this a sacrifice of opportunity for excuse is said to be required in the interest of effective regulation of social perils—a compromise of the individual's claim on fairness to promote the common good.

This is a balancing-of-interests argument. Much may be said against the very logic of conceiving fairness as an individual interest to be weighed against some collective social interest. But criticism less subtle is sufficiently telling. When proceedings are unfair, even though fair proceedings would be a heavy burden a morally responsible government is obligated to seek other strategies of regulation. What the law requires may be devised so that almost certainly a failure to comply would be a matter of culpable neglect. In that case the burden upon tribunals would be considerably lessened, since only rarely would the defendant be able to present even a *prima facie* case of excuse. Instead of regretting an administrative need for absolute liability, we must employ legislative ingenuity so that violation of the law by mistake or by accident becomes a rare occurrence. When it does occur, we shall be able to allow that fact to weigh in favor of the defendant, for the overall administrative burden will then be very much lighter.

There are other points that diminish the vitality of administrative convenience as an argument for absolute liability.

Unlike the case with more serious crimes, it is not conviction that matters in keeping these laws effective, but only the threat of prosecution; and the fact that convictions would be fewer if excuses are allowed need not make us uncomfortable. Violators for whom the threat of prosecution has meaning are strongly affected simply by being subjected to prosecution. On the other hand, violators without legal scruples and indifferent to the law as a deterrent coolly write off the penalty they may incur as a cost of their activity to be absorbed by the enterprise or, if possible, to be passed on to others. Whether conviction is more or less difficult will likewise not affect their conduct, but will affect only the economic calculations of the enterprise.

Providing room for excuse need not in any case create the additional prosecutorial burden that is usually supposed. Once facts making out a *prima facie* case of culpable conduct are alleged, the burden may be placed on the defendant to show by a preponderance of evidence that his conduct was not culpable. This departure from normal rules that require proof beyond a reasonable doubt in criminal prosecution is unobjectionable, since those rules have their reason mainly in the devastating consequences of conviction—consequences that are absent when conviction is for a petty offense. For the same reason some curtailment of evidence and of subsidiary issues of culpability is unobjectionable in the interest of more expeditious proceedings. It is already common practice in prosecution for petty offenses to allow evidence having exculpatory force in mitigation of the offense, and it is scarcely more time consuming to consider it in exoneration. It is also a point in favor of requiring culpable conduct that this should in some measure relieve pressure on courts by encouraging, during preliminary stages of enforcement, an administrative screening out of those instances of supposed violation which in fact are faultless.

JUSTIFICATION BASED ON ENCOURAGEMENT OF PRECAUTION

A second argument stresses a presumed need to keep on the *qui vive* those engaged in activities that become dangerous if performed without constant attention to its hazards. If a person engaging in such an activity will have the opportunity to show himself blameless if harm should occur, his striving for foolproof protection against harm will be less zealous—so it is said—and the activity will therefore be less safe than it might be.

One reply to this argument relies on the facts of economic behavior. The assumption that absolute liability will encourage greater precautionary effort seems largely untrue to the facts. A more realistic account would attach great importance to such factors as the profit motive and the need to maintain a favorable competitive position by eliminating the costs imposed on the enterprise by marginal precautions. This reply is not without weight, for surely it is unwise to rely on laws that are often made ineffective by strong economic incentives to disregard them. But ineffective laws, for all their unwisdom, are not therefore unjust. Even though absolute liability may not increase precaution, so long as in principle it reasonably could do so it is not unjust as a measure that violates the principles of responsibility or culpability. Harmful lapses still might be prevented by greater precaution—which is all that those principles require.

Injustice might, however, obtrude itself under such circumstances, though in other forms. When little fault is to be found in the way something is done, and not doing it that way would be exceedingly onerous, it is unfair to hold the actor liable for what he has done. Liability may also be unfair because the prospective harm is easily remedied when it does occur, or because it is remote, or because the burden of protecting against it should in fairness be placed on other shoulders. These, however, are the injustices of strict, and not absolute, liability.

The proposal that we have penal liability without fault to insure precautionary alertness can be dismissed quite simply, and we are spared an anguished balancing of an interest in safety and an interest in justice. If it is possible for reasonable precautions to be taken that can (in principle, at least) be effective, we do not have an instance of absolute liability. But if such precaution is impossible, though there would be absolute liability there is then no longer the reason for having it that has been proposed.

JUSTIFICATION BASED ON SUPPOSED ANALOGY TO TORT LIABILITY

A third line of argument looks to civil liability as a model for penal liability. Considerations that justify absolute liability in civil controversies governed by the law of torts are thought to justify absolute penal liability. Courts sometimes view penal liability as a way of placing a risk and a burden of loss upon the one who endangers by mishandling or mislabeling, rather than allowing the loss to fall on an innocent party. Since on this rationale there are times when a civil remedy is available in the absence of culpable conduct, it is thought that punitive measures may sometimes be imposed under the same conditions. This view of regulatory offenses is reflected in and encouraged by their designation in the literature as "civil offenses" and "public torts."

It is indeed unobjectionable at times to place an economic burden on a party who is not at fault. As between two parties, neither of whom is at fault for a loss that one of them has suffered, it is sometimes right that the other should ultimately bear the burden of that loss. At times considerations of justice other than considerations of fault mandate this.

Sometimes it is said that the loss should fall on the one better able to stand it—which is to say, the one who will on the whole suffer less. This refers not to the crude injustice of a "deep pockets" theory passing itself off as "rough justice," but to decisions on principle. Decisions to grant or refuse an injunction when one party's blameless activity will result in damage to the other party sometimes turn on such an estimate of the very different consequences to the parties by reason of their different economic positions.

Sometimes it is said that the loss should fall on the one in a better position to prevent it, regardless of whether the failure to do so was culpable. An example is the general liability of a building owner for injuries caused by material falling from his building.

There are situations in which the loss is rightly put on one without fault as part of a system of broad risk distribution that renders negligible the impact of the loss. Liability of an employer or of a driver pursuant to workmen's compensation and no-fault automobile insurance plans are illustrations.

Finally, on the principle that risks should follow prospects of gain, it is sometimes held that, regardless of fault, the loss should fall on the one who benefited or stood to benefit from the activity resulting in the loss. Claims for equitable relief are often decided under this principle. In part it is this principle that dictates the rule of liability for those who blamelessly cause injury in the course of hazardous but profitable activity.

Fault turns out, then, to be only one consideration among many that affect the equities between persons who cause and who suffer a loss. These other considerations are the grounds of absolute civil liability. But they are utterly without relevance when the right to impose punishment in the absence of fault is in question. The loss is not shifted from the victim to the defendant by punishing him. Hence, reasons for shifting loss cannot serve as reasons for imposing punishment. Even when there is fault, the rationales of compensation and of penal treatment are altogether different. Compensation is *for* what the victim has suffered and it is due him *because* the blameworthy rather than the innocent suffer more justly. Penal treatment is *for* blameworthy conduct, and is due *because* there is need of a credible threat for purposes of securing conformity to the law (or because of whatever else it is that justifies criminal punishment as a social practice).

The confusion of penal liability and civil liability has several sources. Because the person liable to punishment and the person liable to provide civil remedy are both faced with an undesirable deprivation, it is sometimes assumed carelessly that what justifies absolute liability for one will justify it for the other. Confusion is promoted also by the mistaken assumption that certain forms of civil liability are instances of absolute liability when in fact the liability is rooted in minimum fault and is merely strict—for example, when users of explosives or keepers of dangerous animals are held strictly liable in damages for harm resulting from such activities.

Yet another source of confusion may be the fact that in areas of public welfare there are many instances in which the law creates absolute civil liability and strict penal liability based on the same activity. And finally, confusion might possibly be encouraged by the existence of punitive damages for torts, and of "penal" legislative provisions creating civil liability in multiples of actual loss. The conduct that can sometimes be the basis of civil liability might carelessly be thought to be nonculpable, yet subject to a sort of penal response by such rules. But such an assumption would be mistaken because the conduct informing these "punitive" or "penal" features of civil liability is in fact always highly culpable.

JUSTIFICATION BASED ON MILDNESS OF SANCTION

The fourth line of argument draws attention to the relative mildness of penal sanctions prescribed for petty offenses as compared to the punishment authorized for full-blooded crimes. The difference is not simply in measure, or in kind of deprivation when a fine rather than a prison sentence is imposed. Missing is the reprobative force that stigmatizes as criminal both the conduct and its author, and this missing ingredient is an essential part of true criminal punishment. Because the sanction is of a lower order, it is suggested that for the sake of convenience we may dispense with questions of culpability and determine liability under a simpler set of standards.

The point does indeed provide support for proposals to simplify trial procedures. There is not the awful prospect that one's dignity as a free and equal citizen will be lost, and that one will be subjected to the degradation of life in prison. Some curtailment of extensive procedural protection seems reasonable, simply because the consequences of conviction are less dreadful. But though it is a less harsh injustice, it is still unjust to impose penalties for minor offenses in the absence of culpable conduct, and it is an injustice with an important practical consequence. Violence to a common sense of justice here is likely to be no less pernicious in its long-range effects than in cases of serious crime. Most often it is the normally law-abiding who are convicted of petty offenses, and the injustice they experience then causes a loss of respect for the laws in question by those who abide by the law out of respect for its authority rather than fear of its punishment.

Confusion about the very notion of a penalty undoubtedly reinforces the inclination to make light of mere penalties. Some penalties are in fact not unjust even though they are imposed when there has been no culpable conduct. These penalties are all *nonpunitive*. If one wishes to justify a nonpunitive penalty one does not produce reasons why some wrong conduct ought to be visited with undesirable consequences. Still, these penalties are measures adverse to the interest of the one penalized, and so require some justification, albeit of a different sort. At least three varieties of nonpunitive penalties can be distinguished according to the kind of reason there is for having them.

Some penalties prescribed by the rules of a game are not thought unfair even though nothing in the least blameworthy need be done to incur the penalty. Such a penalty may be warranted by mere chance in the unlucky roll of the dice, or by the involuntary lurch of an offside linesman reacting to a bee sting. The game makes no allowance for such misfortunes, since they are hazards assumed in playing the game. The challenge of chance and the contest between luck and skill is in large part what makes the game worth playing, and both depend upon penalty rules of this sort.

Equally nonpunitive are penalties that are best conceived as a kind of tariff. Costs are sometimes imposed on activities either to discourage them or else to compensate for the loss that they cause others. In either case one remains at liberty to do as one wishes, but one must pay the consequences. Rather than prohibiting the sale of cigarettes whose smoke contains large amounts of tar and nicotine, the government may decide to impose a penalty tax to discourage their purchase. A contract may contain a penalty provision allowing for early termination of the agreement by one party upon payment to the other party of a sum that is calculated to compensate for loss of anticipated profits. In either case there need be no wrongdoing for the penalty to be assessed, and questions of culpability need never arise.

Administrative acts that bring about deprivations are especially apt to promote confusion concerning penalties, since they are employed in the same regulatory arenas in which strict liability is favored. Often the deprivation has harsh consequences, and this strengthens in them the flavor of a sanction. Permits and licenses may be denied or revoked, government benefits and special status withheld or withdrawn. There may be good grounds for this. One good reason is protection against the dangers of substandard performance, so that when the personal qualifications or facilities important for acceptable performance are lacking, opportunity to cause harm may be foreclosed by administrative action. Another ground for deprivation is absence or loss of the very basis of entitlement, and this is common in the many welfare programs that the government provides. In none of these cases, however, need culpability be considered. Deprivation is not for wrong conduct. It takes place because certain conditions that have not been met must be met to give effect to the policy or program.

The feature that distinguishes a *punitive* penalty, then, is that the penalty is for conduct that is culpable. And it is the culpability of that conduct that justifies there being a penalty for it.

TESTING THE PROPOSED CRITERION OF JUSTIFIABLE STRICT LIABILITY

If the law is just, offenses of strict liability which it creates are offenses in which there is minimum culpability. In order for conduct to be minimally culpable, three conditions must be satisfied. In the first place, it must be possible as a practical matter for the risk of harm inherent in what is done to be appreciated by the one who is doing it. A second requirement is that the one to be held liable must have the ability to prevent the harm. Finally, the means by which he is able to prevent the harm must not in effect be prohibitive of the activity in which the risk lies. Liability may then be avoided by the accused if he can establish that he could not have done anything to prevent what happened, that he took all reasonable precaution against its happening, or that it would be unreasonable to require him to have known of the risk.

This formula, like most, is more easily stated than applied. In effect the standards of minimum culpability are an invitation and a guideline for argument. What are the risks that someone in the defendant's position is bound to take account of, and what duties of precaution regarding them are reasonable? The complex issues raised by these questions require for their resolution a sorting and weighing of many further questions when liability is created as well as when it is imposed. But this is the case wherever matters of fault concern the law.

To test our criterion and to make clear its importance, it is useful to consider some leading cases in which strict liability was challenged as unjustified.

Suppose drugs are purchased in bulk from a reliable pharmaceutical manufacturer and repackaged by a seller in retail amounts for mail-order sales, with labeling by the seller according to the manufacturer's specifications. The drugs are then sold. A statute prohibits placing in commerce mislabeled drugs, and these drugs are in fact mislabeled because the manufacturer's specifications were wrong. The seller did not know and had no reason to suspect that the drugs were not as specified by the manufacturer. Is strict liability for mislabeling justified? May the seller be punished even though admittedly he was not careless in any way? The United States Supreme Court thought so, and this seems right for the following reasons.

The activity in which the seller was engaged was one that

could not be carried on safely without attention to the danger of mislabeling, and that danger is what the law is designed to protect against. Further, effective control to ensure that each lot repackaged conforms to specifications is within the power of a party engaged in the designated activity, and such control could be exercised in ways that are not in effect prohibitive. True, the jobber was not *negligent,* in the most emphatic sense of that term, when he relied, without more, on the representation of a reputable manufacturer. But saying that he was not in this sense negligent is saying only that he did not carry on his business in a way that *created* some risk of the harm which occurred. It does not imply that he took whatever affirmative precautionary measures he reasonably might have to make sure that a known hazard inherent in it would be avoided. His failing to do that was conduct of minimum culpability.

A case concerned with drug regulation of a different sort provides a revealing contrast. A woman in England let rooms to persons who smoked marijuana in them. Although she owned the house, she did not herself live in it, and she had no knowledge that marijuana was being smoked there. An Act of Parliament made it an offense to permit premises to be used for such a purpose, and she was duly convicted under the act. The House of Lords ultimately quashed the conviction because of the injustice of liability under such circumstances. Once again, the decision seems right. Although the householder was able to prevent her rooms from being used for the illegal purpose, the risk of marijuana smoking was not manifest as part of her activity in letting premises and collecting rent, and so there was no reason for her to make relevant inquiries about prospective occupants, conduct inspections of their rooms, or take other precautions to prevent the forbidden act. In normal circumstances—and there was nothing abnormal here—there is no reason for one who rents rooms to be on the alert for marijuana smoking or other possible violations of law that might take place in the privacy of the occupied room.

In yet another case, the United States Supreme Court overturned a conviction under a municipal ordinance of Los Angeles which required any person previously convicted of a felony to register with the authorities if staying in the city for more than five days. In this case, the woman convicted under this law had no knowledge of the registration requirement. Liability is objectionable for essentially the same reason as in the preceding case. Being convicted of a felony does not impart notice that one may have to register with the local authorities wherever one may stay later in life. The harm that concerns the law—which in this case is the presence in the community of unregistered former convicts—is not manifest to one whose presence constitutes the harm.

It is instructive to compare this with the case of someone who is unlicensed and engages in an activity for which the law requires a license. Here ignorance of the requirement does not normally excuse, since one engaging in an activity that is specialized enough to be licensed is not unreasonably held to a duty of knowing about the requirement—or at least of inquiring about it. In a society as much regulated by licensing as ours, the legal risk of unlicensed activity is notorious. Still, if a license were required for eating one's lunch in the park, in the absence of a notice to that effect the same defense of unappreciated harm would have much to recommend it—so long, at least, as such licensing remained extraordinary. One expects to be regulated in many activities, but one also expects to be free of regulation in many others.

The risk may be obvious enough and yet conduct may not be culpable, since the actor can reasonably take no greater precaution against the harm's occurrence. This was the situation when in New Zealand an inspection sticker was removed in some unknown manner from the windshield of a parked car during the driver's absence. As a result, the driver was convicted of the traffic offense of permitting a motor vehicle to be on the road without an inspection sticker. His conviction was finally overturned by the Supreme Court of New Zealand, and, once again, that decision seems right. Under the facts there was no failure to take full precaution against being on the road without the sticker, and nothing more could reasonably have been done by the defendant to prevent what the law punishes.

It may be suggested that a person intent on preventing something can—whatever the cost—almost certainly do so. The driver could have left his car in a garage, or hired someone to guard it while it was parked on the street. But requirements of this sort to avoid a taint of culpability are tantamount to prohibiting the activity, since only an activity of a different sort could then be engaged in with safety. The law may indeed decide to go beyond the limits of reasonable precaution and treat an activity in its usual form as culpable when something untoward occurs as a result. If every car on the road without an inspection sticker were a serious menace, like every car without lights, we might expect a legal demand for whatever precaution is necessary to avoid that. We would then in effect be prohibiting conduct that does not include such precaution. But these extreme prohibitions are warranted only when there are serious and immediate dangers. If we do not limit this extraordinarily strict liability to such cases, the result is only inhibition of those who are diffident, but without any encouragement to greater precaution on the part of people who engage in normal activities with reasonable precaution and who risk unjust liability in doing so.

STRICT LIABILITY AND JUSTICE

Even though excuses are few and narrow when liability is strict, such liability need not be unjust. The act for which the law creates strict liability in petty offenses is an act of minimum culpability. That act poses even less threat of harm than ordinary negligent conduct, and for that reason even less room need be provided for excuse.

Consider the pharmaceutical distributor. He sold drugs labeled according to manufacturer's specifications that he regarded as reliable. Since his reliance on the manufacturer's specifications was not unreasonable, what he did was not negligent. But the law makes the sale of a mislabeled drug an offense even though the mislabeling is reasonable under the circumstances. This means that marketing the drug without all reasonable precaution against mislabeling is minimally dangerous conduct in the eyes of the law. If mislabeling were due to circumstances altogether beyond the control of the distributor, he would have that as the grounds of excuse in accordance with the mandates of the responsibility principle. But it seems reasonable that he should not have broader opportunity for excuse. What he is accused of doing intentionally is not harmful, or very dangerous, or even moderately dangerous. Excuses to the effect that a harmful, very dangerous, or moderately dangerous act was unintentional are therefore irrelevant to the accusation. Accordingly, claims that in essence assert "I didn't mean to do it," "I didn't know I was doing it," or "I wasn't careless in doing it" are all ruled out.

Nevertheless, there are two possibilities of injustice. If punishment is immoderate for acts that are only minimally blameworthy, a principle of proportionality between crime and punishment is disregarded, and this does violence to criminal justice—in a way that we shall examine more closely in the final chapter. The other way in which laws creating strict liability may be unjust is by penalizing conduct unfairly even when it is culpable. It is unjust to punish without culpability, but it is also unjust to punish with culpability when the burden of compliance is unfair. There are at least three ways in which that burden might be unfair.

If the burden of compliance is considerable and there are

reasonable alternatives to accomplish the same governmental objectives without creating such a burden, it is a needless and unjust imposition by the law. Instead of requiring in effect that each seller of drugs arrange difficult and expensive testing if it wishes to insure against liability, the law might provide for government inspection to protect the public against dangers of mislabeling. Again, it might be that the law has placed the burden on the wrong party. If the manufacturer is in a better position to prevent mistakes and can more easily absorb the costs of greater precaution, liability probably should in fairness fall upon him rather than upon the distributor, and for that reason the law as it stands would then be unjust. Finally, if the danger against which the law affords protection is a negligible social problem, a law requiring any burdensome precautions may be unjust. Perhaps the law ought not to hold strictly liable those who unintentionally mislabel drugs, unless the items are on a list of especially dangerous drugs calling for especially great precaution.

Though injustice appears in the form of strict liability in each of these cases, it is not strict liability that is the source of injustice, but rather the unfair use made of it in view of more general considerations. These claims of injustice can indeed be made with respect to any instance of criminal liability whenever it is clear that some alternative method of social regulation ought to be employed, or that the brunt of the law ought to fall elsewhere, or that the law need not concern itself about such matters.

STRICT LIABILITY FOR SERIOUS CRIMES

Can strict liability for serious crimes be justified? Earlier we spoke of strict liability for statutory rape, for bigamy, and for homicides committed in the course of committing other crimes. Heavy punishment is prescribed for these crimes and it may fall upon those convicted of them, even though apparently they were not so much as seriously negligent when they broke the law. This must surely disturb us, for these apparent victims of injustice seem to have violated the law only through mistake or accident, and yet seem to be held strictly liable and then punished severely as though they had acted far more culpably. Serious crimes of strict liability appear to be a sharp departure from the principle of proportionality between crime and punishment that prevails generally, and for that reason a grave injustice.

Surprisingly, many who are dubious about strict liability for petty offenses do not think it unjust when it appears to be prescribed for serious offenses, and their efforts are more often directed toward justifying rather than eliminating such laws. Commonly the argument is that the accused has committed a moral wrong regardless of the excuse he may have to meet the legal accusation; and that for this reason the law chooses to ignore his excuse.

A widely discussed English case of the nineteenth century is a fine example. The defendant in *Regina v. Prince* was accused of violating a law that punished the taking of an unmarried girl under the age of sixteen from her father's custody against his will. His defense was that he was told by the girl that she was eighteen, that he believed her, and that his belief was reasonable. Though the jury believed him and shared his view of the matter, he was convicted upon the judges' instructions, and his conviction was upheld mainly on the theory that what he did was morally wrong regardless of the girl's exact age, and so in spite of his excuse.

In the light of preceding discussions, the claim of a moral wrong ought not to detain us here. What Prince did intentionally was to take a young daughter from her father's custody against the father's will. If that is a moral wrong which the law treats as harmful and for which it creates criminal liability, Prince's mistaken belief is of no importance and will not serve to excuse him. The law might be understood differently, however. It might be understood not to regard as a harm the seduction from a father's custody of any young female, but to view as harmful only the taking of a female under age sixteen. In that case Prince has not done intentionally what the law means to prevent, and so his conduct is not culpable. His excuse is his way of arguing that, and he should then be allowed to present it. The point of importance here is that under either version of the law the harm done is a serious matter in the eyes of the law, and the defendant's intentional act that brings it about is understandably met with punishment reflecting its very considerable legal culpability.

The law under which Prince was convicted needs further explanation to remove an uncomfortable wrinkle in the case. It seems odd to claim that intentionally abducting *a young woman* from her guardian's custody is to be regarded as criminal conduct when the law clearly designates her sixteenth birthday as the point at which criminal abduction of this sort can no longer take place.

But suppose the harm does lie simply in the abduction of a young woman still in her guardian's custody. The age requirement then may be taken as a limitation of convenience to make the legislation less vague and to prevent arbitrariness in its administration. Without some definite (though arbitrary) designation of age it would be impossible for a man to know whether a woman was old enough in the eyes of the law to make courtship and elopement against a guardian's will no longer a legally harmful act, and the enforcement of such a hopelessly vague law would result in arbitrary decisions to impose liability in one case but not in another, even though in relevant respects they are indistinguishable. Because the age requirement is merely a matter of convenience for the just administration of the law and is not an element of the crime that affects culpability, a mistake by the accused regarding age does not serve him as an excuse, for what the law prohibits was still done intentionally in spite of his mistake. The difference between mistakes that exculpate and those that do not has already been discussed in general in the preceding chapter, and the knots that are untied by noticing this difference are not peculiar to problems of strict liability.

More commonplace serious crimes of apparent strict liability yield to the same analysis. Statutory rape bears a close resemblance to the crime with which Prince was charged. Once again, the harm that concerns the law seems to rest on notions of community morality, and the person who might at first be thought of as the victim is typically no less interested than the accused in pursuing the activity for which there is criminal liability. It is age, once again, that makes the difference; and, once again, it is a mistake about age that prompts a claim of excuse. If premarital sexual activity by adolescent females is the harm that concerns the law, and if the age requirement is included in the law simply to protect against the injustice made possible by vague legislation, it makes perfect sense to reject the proffered excuse of mistake about age. If the accused intentionally had intercourse with an adolescent female not his wife, he did what the law makes culpable; and if she is under-age he can be held liable for that culpable conduct. If, however, at the last minute a trick is played on him in the dark and an under-age female substitutes herself for the mature woman whom he has seduced, he then has an acceptable excuse, for then he indeed did *unintentionally* the act that the law regards as harmful.

Social attitudes change along with the moral views that underlie them, and when this happens the law is likely to reflect the change. The Model Penal Code, for example, makes reasonable mistake of age a defense to the charge of statutory rape, and as a reason suggests that "Pursuit of females who appear to be over 16 betokens no abnormality but only a defiance of religious and social conventions which appear to be fairly widely disregarded." Here there is recognition of a changed conception of the harm, and so a new view of what is harmful conduct. Sexual relations with a female who is less than sixteen is then the prohibited act, and a suitable mistake about her age is then acceptable as an excuse because the prohibited act is then not intentional and so not culpable.

The earlier conception of the harm is preserved in a companion provision of the Model Penal Code which precludes the excuse of reasonable mistake regarding age when the victim is under ten and the crime charged is therefore the even more serious one of ordinary rape. The reason given for not recognizing the excuse is that "any error that is at all likely to be made would still have the young girl victim far below the age for sexual pursuit by normal males." The harm as the law here conceives it is child intercourse, which is analogous to adolescent intercourse as the harm of statutory rape under the traditional conception of that crime.

Bigamy is a crime in which the law's traditional conception of the harm diverges even more from notions commonly held outside the law. The law founds its prohibition on a belief that the integrity of the family is a matter of the greatest importance upon which the very existence of society depends, and that bigamy destroys a family. For this reason a person who wishes to marry again must make certain that the previous marriage has been terminated. It will not do simply to rely on the assurance of one's first wife that she has obtained a valid divorce even though such reliance is eminently reasonable. If in the eyes of the law the marriage has not ended, there will be liability for bigamy, for the man in remarrying has done intentionally an act that the law regards as a threat of harm, and harm of quite a serious character.

This conception of the harm in bigamy is modified as views of the family change. In a large number of jurisdictions, as well as under the Model Penal Code, reasonable mistake about termination of a previous marriage is now a defense to a charge of bigamy. Taking a second spouse deliberately or through indifference to the question of whether one still is married is prohibited, since there is still humiliation, neglect, and nonsupport of spouse and children as likely consequences. Under this more modern view the law regards as dangerous an act of marriage when careful attention is not paid to the matter of one's marital status at the time. If in spite of responsible precaution one makes a mistake about one's status, the act viewed as dangerous by the law has not been done intentionally, and an excuse of mistake is perfectly appropriate.

Homicide that occurs in the course of some other crime may be punished more severely than it would be otherwise, and indeed may even make the perpetrator subject to homicide liability though otherwise he would be free of it altogether. Homicidal acts of a lower degree of culpability are elevated when they occur in the course of another crime, and blameless acts that cause death become punishable for the same reason. Why the law has fashioned such liability is quite obvious. The criminal conduct of a person engaged in the commission of a crime is regarded as posing a threat of death. He is seen as both desperate and uninhibited, and because of his state of mind he is thought more likely to engage in rash acts that have fatal consequences.

Committing a crime, then, is the act that must be done intentionally, and it is the greater danger that death will occur in the course of doing it that makes that act more culpable. When the death that is threatened does occur, liability for causing it is therefore greater than it would be otherwise. On this view, committing a crime is much like burning a building. If death results, it does not matter that the perpetrator neither meant that to happen nor did anything designed to bring it about. It was part of the risk inherent in what he did and, if death occurred in the course of what he did, it does not matter that it was brought about by mistake or occurred by accident.

Modern conceptions of felony murder are based on a different assessment of the dangerousness of criminal conduct rather than on a different appraisal of the harm, and in this respect the change from older to newer views differs from the change that has taken place in the law of statutory rape and bigamy. In many jurisdictions felony murder may now be committed only in the course of those felonies in which the risk of homicide is thought to be especially great. The Model Penal Code rejects felony murder altogether except when death results from a reckless act manifesting extreme indifference to the value of human life, which would in any case be murder under the Code. Indeed, under the Code version there is not even a suggestion of strict liability, since conduct is sufficiently dangerous for liability only if it is reckless in the prescribed way. Carelessness with a gun, for instance, or even a reckless act that does not put anyone's life in imminent danger is not enough for felony murder. So if a bank robber leaves people in an ordinary storage room from which they cannot escape and in which they eventually suffocate, under the Code he may still avoid liability for felony murder by showing that he did not know that the door would lock automatically when he closed it.

Serious crimes with a legislative origin or a common-law ancestry to which strict liability is alien are sometimes enacted in a new legislative form that is thought to create strict liability. A federal law made it a larceny to "knowingly convert" government property. Bomb casings on an Air Force practice range had been lying there for some time apparently abandoned when a junk dealer proceeded to collect and sell them. He was convicted under this larceny provision without regard to his belief that the metal was abandoned property, and the United States Supreme Court reversed his conviction. The Court's argument was that, although the traditional larceny requirement of an intent to take the property of another did not appear in the legislation, there was no warrant for refusing to read it in and include it by implication, for otherwise a radical change in the law of larceny would result without any indication that Congress intended that.

The radical change that so disturbed the Court can be described as treating what is generally recognized as less dangerous conduct as though it were more dangerous. If the statute were read literally it would mean serious criminal liability for a person who was at worst indifferent to the legal niceties of property interests or who was simply careless in acting on appearances alone. Though intentionally taking articles one believed to be abandoned under such circumstances does have its dangers and might properly be visited with moderate penalties as a regulatory offense, it is not serious enough to be met with the heavy liability of a larceny conviction.

It is true that under very different conditions such deliberate taking of property that happened to belong to another might reasonably be thought to be a serious danger and punishable as larceny now is. This would be the case, for example, in a community of people uprooted from their homes and living in temporary shelter where possessions are commonly in the open and within everyone's easy reach, where abandonment of property hardly ever takes place, and where loss of one's possessions causes especially great hardship. Under such circumstances there are two reasons why culpability would be much greater even though there was no intent to deprive another of his property. One reason is that when ownership is unknown there would be greater risk of doing harm by taking on the mere appearance. The other reason is that the harm to those who lost their possessions would be more serious. But even when the law makes the taking of articles punishable as larceny in this way, it does not create strict liability, for it is the act of taking carelessly that must be done intentionally in order for there to be liability, and that act is under the circumstances an act of a high degree of culpability.

Among cases of strict liability for serious crimes, that of

General Yamashita stands out by itself as a source of shame to a legal system that allowed itself to be caught up in the enthusiasm of victor's justice. All that Yamashita can be said to have done intentionally is to have exercised the authority of the commander of the Japanese forces in the Philippines without having control over the conduct of his soldiers. Short of devoting all of his command resources to maintaining discipline it appears it would have been impossible to prevent the atrocities that were committed, and since he had little if any knowledge of what was actually going on, his ability to restrain his army was in any case a dubious proposition. Assuming and exercising command responsibility as he did can hardly be said under the circumstances to be a very dangerous act, though it is the only thing done intentionally by him for which he was found criminally liable and put to death.

It is true, we come to a different conclusion if we view an army in a war zone as an inherently dangerous force whose normal tendency in the absence of command restraints is to commit atrocities. Though the Japanese army may have been thought of just that way by a people caught up in the emotion of war, it was unconscionable for the Supreme Court of the United States to take such a view when reviewing a prosecution which sought a man's life as punishment for what he did. If the Court took a reasonable view of what he did, its comparatively minor dangers would have warranted at most a comparatively light penalty according to its true culpability.

A SUMMARY

What exactly is strict criminal liability, and what claims of injustice have been lodged against it? A summary in general terms of the answer that has emerged will serve to conclude our discussion.

Strict liability is liability for conduct of minimum culpability. There are two reasons why culpability might be very slight. One is that the harm of concern to the law is not at all serious. The other reason is that in the act for which there is liability there is only a slight risk of whatever harm it is that the law has concerned itself with. Petty offenses in which there is liability for conduct of minimum culpability are rightly regarded as offenses of strict liability. This is because the conduct required by the law to be done intentionally if there is to be liability is not very dangerous conduct. For this reason there is in practice scant opportunity to meet the accusation by the excuse that the prohibited act was done unintentionally, though in theory the same range of excuses is available. It is excuses under the culpability principle that are then scarce, for in the light of the slight harm or the slight risk (or both) it is only very rarely that the person accused may rightly argue that what he did intentionally is not even that dangerous. There still is abundant opportunity, however, for excuse under the responsibility principle. It is sometimes the case that the accused was unable to avoid committing the offense short of restricting his activities in ways which the law neither contemplates nor requires, and this serves as a good excuse. Since opportunities for a good excuse of unintentional conduct are severely restricted, there is strict liability. Since there is no such restriction on excuses of inability, liability is not absolute.

Since strict liability is for blameworthy conduct, it does not violate the culpability principle. It is not a restriction on liberty that is unjust because purposeless, which it would be if the culpability principle were violated. Since there is no liability in spite of the fact that the accused could not do otherwise, strict liability does not offend against the responsibility principle either. It is not unjust as a requirement that something be done which cannot be done.

But further considerations of justice must be taken into

account. A principle of proportionality between crime and punishment must be respected as well and, in prescribing only very moderate penalties for acts of very moderate culpability, this principle is accorded respect in petty offenses. Yet another constraint of justice is a broad principle of fairness that disallows unfair burdens of compliance. When the law places the burden inequitably on the wrong party, or when the facts of the matter make such a burden unnecessary at all, the law and the liability imposed under it are unjust. Though many laws creating offenses of strict liability may be judged unjust according to this principle of fairness, there are many instances of such injustice to be found throughout that portion of the criminal law that lies beyond the bounds of common crime, and it is not a variety of injustice that is in any way peculiar to offenses of strict liability.

Among serious crimes a select few are said to be crimes of strict liability, and yet turn out not to be so. The reason they are regarded as crimes of strict liability is that it seems not to matter that the highly culpable act prohibited by the law was done only unintentionally. The mistake stems from a misconception about what really concerns the law. Sometimes (as with statutory rape or bigamy) the harm that concerns the law is misconceived. Sometimes (as with felony homicide) it is the risk as the law sees it that is misconceived. In either case, there is a resulting misconception as to just what act it is that the law regards as culpable when done intentionally, and it is wrongly concluded that the law is rejecting some excuse of having done only unintentionally the act that the law regards as the basis of liability when it is done intentionally. But when the law's conception of the criminal act is correctly understood, it turns out that unintentionally doing *that* act *is* accepted as a good excuse, and so there is not the violation of the culpability principle that at first there appeared to be.

Neither the culpability principle nor the responsibility

principle is compromised by these serious crimes. Nor is the principle of proportional punishment, since on the law's view of harm and risk the act for which there is heavy punishment is an act of considerable culpability. A substantial argument can be made, however, against the justice of these laws when judged under principles of fairness. In view of changing ideas of how harmful the acts are, and in the light of altered views about what the law may properly concern itself with, the older conception of culpable conduct becomes highly controversial, and the fairness of those laws that are based on that older conception is called into question. New laws and new interpretations of the old ones take heed of this complaint and redefine the culpable act, and this in turn opens up new opportunities for excuse that did not exist before.

CHAPTER NINE

Justification of Criminal Punishment

Much effort so far has been directed to examining questions of criminal liability and to developing a theory of criminal justice that makes sense of the answers provided by criminal law. But criminal liability itself needs examination. As a social institution it is much in evidence throughout history in civilized human society, and never more prominent than at present. By what right do some men hold others criminally liable? This question inevitably leads to others, and we find ourselves puzzling over such matters as reasons for punishing crime, the proper measure of punishment, and whether there are alternative forms of criminal liability that might be preferable to punishment. The issues that form around these questions are the subject of this chapter and the next.

In Chapter One it was suggested that punishment for crime was necessary to preserve the effectiveness of the law and keep society law-abiding. Though punishment may serve a good end, it also cripples people and destroys their lives. Even though we acknowledge that if crimes went unpunished we could not hope for the social life we now have, and see ourselves obsessed in such a world with threats to our survival, still we are bound to admit that criminal punishment produces much misery. It is the truth expressed in Bentham's observation that "All punishment is mischief: all punishment in itself is evil." Like any other necessary evil, criminal punishment needs to be justified, and in this chapter we examine all plausible theories of justification before defending the only one that seems defensible.

I. PRELIMINARY MATTERS

THE NEED FOR JUSTIFICATION

If a practice needs justification, it must be thought to have something wrong with it. Charity is not thought to have anything wrong with it, and so it needs no justification. But imagine a sect in which those who earn money give it away to the needy and in so doing neglect members of their own family who depend on them for support. Such charity needs to be justified, for though it may turn out finally not to be wrong, there is in any case something wrong with it. On the other hand, if a practice is thought to be wrong, and not simply thought to have something wrong with it, it is not in need of justification. Slavery, for example, is now generally taken to be wrong on its face and not thought simply to have something wrong with it. Anyone who would seek to justify it would therefore have to show first that in fact it is not simply wrong, as it is generally believed to be. To justify slavery, one would have to show at the start that there is something right about it which has a redeeming tendency and that might, after due consideration, redeem it. This necessary first step of partial redemption could, for example, be an argument that a carefully selected and willing slave population would be better off living under a humane regime of slavery while at the same time others in the community who benefited from the institution also would be better off than they are now. There would then still be much to be said against slavery, but its advocate would have established a footing for an attempt to justify it by further argument that must take into account what is wrong with slavery.

Criminal punishment is like charity partially impugned and slavery partially redeemed, for it is a social practice that has something wrong with it, yet is amenable to efforts at justification. Its staunchest advocates and its most vociferous critics are almost all agreed in viewing it this way. Those who object strongly to the coddling of criminals do not consider that a coddled criminal has been deprived of something that is simply right, like medical care or wages earned in the prison shop, but say only that he has not received the kind of treatment he should have in spite of its admittedly undesirable aspects. Those who take an opposite view and advocate radical reform of the penal system do no more than urge a radical change in the way those convicted of crime are to be treated—perhaps even the elimination of all treatment having a punitive intent. They are not, however, abolitionists who advocate an end to criminal liability as we know it, which certainly they should if they regarded it as without redeeming features. Opinion at both extremes, as well as in between, holds punishment of those who commit a crime to be a regrettable necessity, though admittedly the regret may be profound or perfunctory and the necessity may seem urgent or simply abiding.

Since punishment, unlike charity, is an evil, it needs justification; and since, unlike slavery, it is not simply evil, it might be justified. Justifications of punishment all perceive some grim necessity which makes it right in spite of the suffering and degradation it produces. Though there are different ideas of what that necessity is, all of the justificatory arguments are arguments from necessity. Any theory that would take punishment of criminals to be a good thing simply in its own right—like care for the sick or charity for the poor—is not a justificatory theory at all, and indeed purports to show, among other things, that justification is not necessary. Certain retributivist theories seem to be of this sort, for they hold that repaying crime with punishment is simply doing justice and is a good in its own right. Other retributivist theories are more disposed to see some evil in punishment and seek to provide justification for it by showing the necessity of giving criminals their just desert.

Most retributivist theories are not purely of one sort or the other; but to the extent that a theory does not deem criminal punishment to be in need of justification because punishment of the guilty is good in its own right, that theory is ignored here. It is ignored not because it is unworthy of serious philosophical attention, but because it cannot hope to be taken seriously as a justificatory theory of criminal punishment in any society of the modern world that professes what might loosely be called liberal democratic ideals. The reason such a theory is unacceptable in such a society has already been discussed in Chapter One, and here we need only briefly remind ourselves of what was said there.

When measures taken by the state in such a society deprive citizens of their liberty and in other ways cause them to suffer, it is not enough simply that in themselves those measures are morally right, for the state itself has no political right to do whatever is in itself morally right when there is not in addition a social need which it is legitimate for the state to satisfy. Because the state has a vast power that is ultimate in society, and because there is always imminent danger of that power's being abused by those who have access to it, there is at the political foundation of a liberal democratic society a principle of parsimony that deprives the state of power to curtail liberties and inflict suffering solely on moral grounds. Such a principle is regularly recognized and boldly advanced when laws on the books only to enforce morality are subjected to a libertarian critique, but unfortunately the principle is rarely invoked when the controversy is about the institution of criminal punishment. This, it may be noted, is especially curious since the purely moralistic presuppositions of pure retributivism are even more pronounced than the moralistic leanings of most arguments in defense of the legal enforcement of morality which regularly point to some supposed social harm that will come about if morality is not enforced. This principle of parsimony, moreover, presents no dilemma to those who wish to see the state do only what is morally right, for though we may require the state in doing its proper job to do only what is morally right we need not and should not allow it to regard as its proper job doing whatever can be shown to be morally right.

OBSTACLES IN THE PATH OF JUSTIFICATION

Since all attempts at justification of punishment appeal to a purported necessity, all are liable to be defeated in the same ways. If punishment does not accomplish what is necessary, it is *useless* in that regard, and so could not be justified by the necessity. If there is an alternative to punishment that will serve well enough to accomplish what is necessary, and is preferable to punishment because its evils are not as great as those that make the justification of punishment necessary in the first place, then punishment is *needless*. Finally, even if punishment is neither useless nor needless, it will still not be justifiable if what it accomplishes is simply not worth the evil it entails. In what follows we shall examine various justifying aims to see whether punishment is useless or needless with respect to them. We shall not pursue the question of whether a purported justifying purpose, if achieved, makes punishment worthwhile in spite of its evils, for any enlightening answer would require an evaluation of supposed consequences too complex even to contemplate.

And, happily, we need not pursue this question, for the

two questions of uselessness and of needlessness present obstacles that only one theory of punishment can surmount. According to that theory, there is a need to uphold the law and to prevent it from becoming so many dead letters by punishing those who violate its rules, and this is what justifies punishment. It may indeed still be argued that upholding the law in this way is not worth the cost in human suffering that punishment represents, and that therefore, even though neither useless or needless, criminal punishment is not justified. But it seems clear that keeping the law alive and effective is a purpose of sufficient worth so long as those laws for whose sake the lawbreaker is punished are on the whole an intelligent and suitably restrained use of public power, and so long as treatment of those who break the law is sufficiently civilized. It seems fair to say, then, that the burden of argument rests squarely on those who believe that upholding the law is not worth the price even if laws are on the whole wise and just and the punishment for breaking them is no more than is required to prevent lawbreaking with impunity.

This suggests a further general objection to be disposed of at the outset. All attempts to justify punishment argue that punishment is necessary for the sake of something else—perhaps correction of criminal tendencies, or the creation of a safer social environment, or preserving the law's deterrent effect. Whether on the whole what is gained is worth the price to be paid in human misery is one question. Whether it is right to *use* the person being punished to attain the objective is another. The criticism implied by this second question is not the traditional objection that utilitarians must meet when they are accused of allowing (at least under unusual circumstances) for punishment of the innocent, for it is punishment of the guilty as a general social practice which is brought into question here. But like punishment of the innocent, punishment of the guilty for the sake of gaining some social benefit is suspect because apparently it too involves the sacrificial use of certain members of society for some social good.

One reply might be that the justice of a social practice depends only upon the justice of what is done according to that practice, and that if each person who is punished is truly guilty then the institution of criminal punishment cannot itself be judged unjust. But the premise upon which this rests is not correct. Imagine that a new system of criminal justice for most common crimes is introduced which is less expensive and less cumbersome than the one we now have. The police conduct diligent and impartial investigations, and when they are completely satisfied that they know who the perpetrator is they prepare a report and certify their conclusion. Without more, the person certified as the perpetrator is then sentenced by a judge for the crime.

If police investigations were always conducted in a thoroughly responsible way, and conclusions were arrived at with the greatest caution, this new system might well be an improvement over what we have at present in protecting the innocent from conviction as well as in preventing the guilty from escaping the clutches of the law. It would in that case result in justice being done even more often than under the system we now have, and yet we would regard such a system as shockingly unjust compared to our present practice, for, unlike the system we know, this new one would not provide a fair opportunity for a person liable to be convicted to show that he is innocent. Similarly, if the system we now have is judged to be unjust because it *uses* the guilty for some general social benefit, though the grounds of injustice are different the system may likewise be judged unjust in spite of the fact that the guilt of each of those punished ensures that there is no injustice based on punishment of the innocent.

A more promising answer argues that not only punishment but indeed the very laws that punishment serves are a *use* of a person for general social benefit. The law represents a re-

striction on what each individual may do, and in prohibiting
certain acts the law deprives each person of a measure of his
liberty in order to promote greater safety and security for all
within the community. The law is therefore itself an affront
to individual autonomy and is open to the same objection as
the practice of punishment when engaged in to achieve
greater safety and security for all.

Such an argument could be expected to provoke a spirited
defense of the law by those who insist that punishment is objectionable when pursued for the sake of social benefit. The
Kantian position would be that the law itself, like punishment, is inherently morally worthy, though this position requires metaphysical presuppositions about the nature of man
and the moral law that are too speculative to serve our purposes here. Besides, it seems plain enough that a great many
penal laws to be found in any modern legal system are enacted as measures of expediency to serve some policy of government evolved through a morally uncertain political process, and these laws could not in any case be taken to be moral
imperatives simply because they are the law. These penal laws
would have to face the objection that they do not conform to
general Kantian notions of the law and that as measures of
social expediency they violate Kantian rights of autonomy.

Three other arguments in support of punishing the guilty
for the sake of social benefit do not present these special
difficulties.

First, the Kantian objection is to *mere use* of a person for
some social (or even personal) benefit so that he is not treated
as an end in himself. But this is not an objection to making
use of persons when the use does not constitute such moral
degradation. Each person being regarded as an end in himself does not require that each of us treat one another as an
island unto himself not to be used for the benefit of others. If
it did, many commonplace and uncontroversial acts of social
intercourse would be forbidden simply because use was made

of a person without his permission. On the Kantian view, when the guilty are punished and they receive their just desert, their moral autonomy is accorded full respect. Indeed, only then is full moral respect shown to the guilty. Having given moral autonomy its due, however, there is no reason why a guilty person may not serve a socially desirable end either as an example or in some other way that contributes to maintaining a less dangerous community than there might otherwise be.

A second argument is this. Since the benefits of laws backed by effective sanctions are in theory conferred on everyone, and since in theory these laws impose on everyone the same restraints, it seems reasonable to view the legal system as the continuing performance of a contract which all members of society enter into and renew by continuing to live under its provisions. Punishment of the guilty is one provision of this social contract, and those who live under and are parties to it are bound by their contractual assent to submit to punishment according to their guilt. Since this obligation is consensual, it is not in derogation of a right of autonomy but on the contrary represents an exercise of that very right.

The third argument places less stress on the give-and-take of mutual agreement, and instead sees greater overall benefit to each individual when certain collective interests are served at the expense of more immediate individual interests. On this view, individual autonomy is to be accorded ample respect. Indeed, it may even be more important than anything else, and for this very reason it is subject to certain curtailments that are necessary for its enjoyment. If collective as well as individual well-being depends upon an effective system of laws, and if an effective legal system requires punishment of those who break the law, then punishment is necessary for both collective and individual well-being. True, punishing a person in order to benefit him individually is a violation of his moral autonomy no less than if the benefit were collective. But part of the individual benefit (and a most important part) is the preservation of those conditions of life that are necessary if personal autonomy is to be worth anything. In a world without law in which human life is lived in a state of nature, the value of free personal choice would be extremely small, since urgent matters of survival in the face of constant peril would dictate the activities that one chose, and to a great extent one's fate would be determined by forces beyond one's control. The possibility of an environment allowing autonomy to be valuable in the first place depends upon effective laws, and they in turn depend upon the punishment of lawbreakers.

These arguments furnish solid grounds for punishment of the guilty with full respect for personal autonomy, even though punishment is for some common good; and since these arguments are in no way inconsistent with one another it is not necessary to choose between them. None of these arguments, furthermore, is consistent with a view much feared by defenders of moral autonomy—namely, the view that a person who is not *responsible* for what he has done may be punished for it nevertheless. If persons who are not responsible were punished, there would in those cases be a use of individuals for the collective good without regard to their powers of choice.

Looking at that possibility under the theory of a social contract, it can hardly be presumed that the general agreement serving as the foundation of social life provides that it does not matter whether a person had the ability to do otherwise when it is almost universally the rule in all areas of social life that ability to do otherwise matters very much. On the other theory, which justifies a limited sacrifice of autonomy to prevent its devaluation, there is likewise no support for punishment without regard to responsibility: in order for the legal system to remain effective and preserve social order, it is not necessary that there be punishment without consideration of whether the one to be punished was responsible when he broke the law.

II. THEORIES OF PUNISHMENT

Attempts to justify the institution of criminal punishment take different routes, and often more than one route is taken in the course of a single attempt. In this section we shall examine five theories of punishment that are commonly adopted in some form by those who seek good reasons for our continuing to punish crimes. What proponents of these theories fail to recognize is that when criminal punishment is viewed as these theories view them, it is a social practice that is needless, or useless, or both, and so not justifiable on any of these theories. Since none of these theories provides even a good reason, we are spared the need to consider which of them alone or in combination might provide a reason that is both good and sufficient. In the next section, however, we shall consider a sixth reason that does appear to be good, and that plainly is by itself sufficient if it is good.

REMOVAL OF SOCIALLY DANGEROUS PERSONS

To most people the most compelling reason for dealing as we do with those who commit crimes is our need to remove dangerous persons from circulation. Our social environment can be counted on to produce a full complement of criminal dangers no matter what we do, but if we do not eliminate dangerous types when they show themselves we should increase the danger considerably, for in abandoning the war against crime we would allow the ranks of the criminal element to swell as veterans remain at large and new recruits constantly join them.

A policy of removal for the sake of social sanitation requires for its success that those who have a *disposition* to commit crimes be identified. But in fact it is impossible to infer a disposition to commit crimes from any occurrence of criminal conduct. In theory, of course, the disposition could be inferred from the behavioral characteristics of a person who commits a crime. But no behavioral characteristics matter in determining criminal liability, and the only ones that may be expected to come even incidentally to the notice of those who make the determination are characteristics associated with the criminal conduct that is the basis of liability. These characteristics cannot in any general way be relied on even to furnish some evidence of *disposition* to crime, for in establishing the basis of criminal liability the law does not concern itself with behavior indicative of a criminal disposition, but only with conduct which it is deemed desirable to prohibit; and in general the behavioral characteristics of those who engage in criminal conduct are as diverse as the behavioral characteristics of those who engage in law-abiding conduct.

Still, it is fair to say that a significant number of those convicted and removed *do* have a disposition to commit crimes, and that their removal therefore represents a gain in social safety. For this reason, criminal liability in the form we have it is not altogether useless as a measure of social safety, but it is nevertheless of relatively little use compared to alternative methods that we might adopt if our criminal proceedings were designed to consider evidence of dangerous dispositions.

Another fact, however, does make it useless—and worse than useless—as a measure of social safety. The places to which those convicted are removed are themselves breeding places of crime. Many of those who were previously without definite dispositions to crime develop firm criminal inclinations, and those already accustomed to living outside the law have their resolve and their sense of community strengthened. Because of this, over a period of time a larger number of persons with criminal dispositions are added to the social environment through release from prison than are removed by incarceration, since permanent isolation is not a feature of criminal liability and since many found liable have no real criminal disposition at the time they are convicted. These further effects of removal and isolation in a community of convicted persons are not adventitious and occasional, depending upon the design and administration of the prison community, but are a feature of penal treatment that is evident everywhere, in the past as well as the present.

But even if the uselessness of criminal punishment were overlooked, an attempt to justify it on grounds of social sanitation must fail because it is a needless practice. Criminal prosecutions are carried on to determine guilt or innocence. Since there is more ample and better evidence of dangerous dispositions than what is allowed in these determinations of criminal liability, a proceeding designed to admit and consider such evidence would be clearly preferable as a means of identifying dangerous persons. There are two reasons why this is so. The greater accuracy in such a proceeding would mean that more dangerous persons would be identified and taken out of circulation; even more important, it would mean that fewer persons who are not dangerous would be deprived of their liberty as dangerous persons. Criminal liability, then, is needless as a means of promoting a safer social environment in view of this preferable alternative, and consequently it is not justifiable as a means of making the community safer by removing its criminal dangers.

REHABILITATION OF SOCIALLY DANGEROUS PERSONS

There are those who wish to make the process seem more human in its dealings with those who have broken the law, and instead of emphasizing the benefits of a purged environment they place stress on the opportunity to straighten the crooked which punishment provides. In their interest as well as ours we may rehabilitate those now considered social dangers when their crime places them in our clutches; and though it is rarely suggested that this opportunity to rehabilitate will alone justify liability to punishment, the purported benefits of a regime of rehabilitation are thought to add weight in favor of having a system of liability for those who commit crimes.

This attempt to justify punishment has some of the same flaws that made the previous attempt unsatisfactory, as well as some defects of its own. It can only be a source of wonder that in imposing penal liability we still avow as one of our objectives the improvement of the person, for almost universally when prison has an effect at all it is of the opposite order, and apparently this is so regardless of what sort of correctional efforts are made. The only benefits in a program of reform or rehabilitation—the way it is styled depends only on how much moral flavor one prefers—are those that undo the harm done by prison itself and that make the prisoner's life more like the life of someone who is not subject to a correctional regime in the first place. When a practice is universally unsuccessful in accomplishing a purpose for which it is said to exist, with reference to that purpose the practice is useless. Rehabilitation is just such a universal failure insofar as it purports to correct those dispositions to crime that do not originate in the correctional experience itself.

There is an even more fundamental objection. Since many of those made subject to a regime of rehabilitation are not possessed of dangerous dispositions that mark them off from the population at large, any rehabilitative effort is for them needless and so not a justification of their being deprived of their freedom. Worse than needless, it is for such persons the compounding of a special humiliation with the general suffering that is normally part of criminal liability. There is no need for these people to be changed since they are not dangerous, and those who in their paternalistic enthusiasm impose corrective treatment that they suppose is necessary subject the innocuous lawbreaker to the special sort of degradation that is suffered when the power of one person over another is exercised wantonly.

Both this theory and the theory stressing social safety have been rejected largely on the facts, and it might be objected that failure—even universal failure—in achieving the avowed aim does not make the endeavor itself unjustifiable when it would be justifiable if in practice it did meet with enough success to be considered useful. It might be argued that even though *engaging in the practice* might well be unjustified because of universal failure, still the aims of the practice do justify it *in principle*. But though this may be so, it is quite beside the point.

A practice is justifiable in principle if it would be justifiable when carried on as intended with intended results. Whether there is success when it is actually engaged in is irrelevant to its justification *in principle,* for justification in principle is a purely hypothetical determination that does not concern itself with the facts. But justification *in principle* of the practice is not what is wanted here. It is justification of the practice *as it is engaged in* that is called for. This is justification *in practice,* in contrast to justification in principle, and *success or failure* of the practice (albeit with reasonable allowance for things that go wrong) is then of crucial importance in deciding whether it is justifiable. When the practice is engaged in without actual prospect of success, which is the case when criminal liability is created and imposed to make the community safer or to make convicted persons less bent on crime, the practice as engaged in is a useless one, and for that reason not justifiable.

PAYING ONE'S DEBT TO SOCIETY

No observation about crime and punishment seems less controversial than that a criminal must pay his debt to society. Not everyone will agree in regarding as a criminal anyone found guilty of committing a crime no matter what the circumstances may be under which he was prosecuted and no matter what the law he has broken requires of him. But almost everyone acknowledges that some things truly are crimes and that those who truly commit them have incurred a debt to society that is paid by criminal punishment. The metaphor of paying a debt is perhaps best understood, once again, by reference to the more elaborate metaphor of a social contract. All of us may be viewed as having entered a compact that binds us together as a society in which each of us has reciprocal rights and duties, including duties to forbear from engaging in harmful conduct. As in many contracts, there are penalty provisions, in this case the items of sanction to be found in a penal code. The public authority created to enforce the contract invokes these when a duty of forbearance is breached. The penalty exacted can be viewed, then, as a contract debt that must be paid to society according to the terms of the social contract.

The metaphor is useful in suggesting where the justice of criminal liability lies. Since each of us might prefer to indulge our own selfish interests and thereby harm others, it seems fair that those unwilling to sacrifice advantage or gratification be put in a relatively worse position when they engage in criminal acts. If retribution has any place in justifying the institution of criminal liability that we know, it is here. The claim by way of retribution would be that something is owed by a person who commits a crime, and that he must pay it just for having committed the crime.

But though a practice may be just, it may still not be justifiable. The existence of a contract will suffice to make a *prima facie* case for the justice of enforcing the obligations it creates, and yet enforcing the obligation may not be justifiable. If the contract is a useless one—when performed it does not gain for those intended to be benefited what it purports to obtain for them—that would be enough to make its enforcement unjustifiable on grounds of uselessness when, as with criminal punishment, there is at the start a presumption against it because of its many undesirable features. And in fact the social contract provision for criminal penalties is useless, since the penalties it provides do nothing to restore either to the victim or to society what has been lost because of the crime committed.

Another version of this metaphorical debt suggests itself. The aim of criminal liability might be to allow one who has incurred the debt to discharge it and thereby restore himself to the ranks of the respectable citizens of the community. Much that is commonly said about paying a debt to society suggests that its purpose is not to benefit a creditor but rather to bring about the benefits which the debtor enjoys when he no longer has the debt as a weight on his conscience and a mark against his good name. But this version of the metaphor is seriously flawed. The position of the criminal who pays his debt to society is analogous to a debtor who goes into bankruptcy and receives a discharge, not a debtor who pays and extinguishes his debt. After having been discharged, there is a continuing stigma and suspicion. A convicted person does not renew his credit and good name by paying his debt to society. On the contrary, he enhances his bad reputation by having been in the company of undesirables. While he may have a clear conscience that the fugitive cannot enjoy, it is not from having had liability imposed, but from no longer having to bear his wrongdoing as a secret. Since, once again, the purported purpose of paying a debt is not achieved, once again criminal liability on this account is useless and therefore not justified.

There is a further reason why the debt payment theory will not serve to justify criminal liability. Quite apart from being useless, criminal liability as we know it is needless. If we wished to provide genuine reparation for those harmed by those who violate the self-restraining undertakings of our social compact, we should enable the criminal to furnish compensation as best he can for the loss he has caused and require him to pay this as a debt. Criminal liability would then be designed in a radically different way to allow the criminal to make his victim whole; and though such liability would no doubt often result in imperfect compensation, it would in that respect be no different than compensation through civil liability. As a means of restoring self-respect to the criminal as well as restoring his respectability in the community, it would certainly represent a great improvement over what we have at present, for it would be an effort to cancel in some measure the very basis of condemnation by adding to the record of one's criminal conduct later efforts to undo the harm. This alternative to punishment, then, is preferable because it is bound to be more effective in achieving the objectives of debt payment, and also because it is a way of achieving them that has less of those objectionable features of degradation and misery that called for justification of punishment in the first place.

Paying one's debt to society can also be understood more directly without resort to the social contract metaphor. Sometimes theories of criminal punishment make much of the fact that at one time responding to crime was a private matter, and that even today the victim and those close to him have a special interest in seeing that the culprit receives his due. In one perspective, it is the victim or his representatives who owe the wrongdoer a measure of suffering for the harm he has inflicted, and it is society that acts as agent in paying it. The same transaction can also be viewed from a different perspective as one in which the wrongdoer has a debt of suffering which is owed to the victim and for which society is the collection agency. It is in any case a matter of vengeance, private or public, in which harm is to be repaid, if not exactly in kind, at least in a way that satisfactorily settles the score.

There is undoubtedly much of value for purposes of explanation to be found in the notions of vengeance and retaliation. When we want to know why a system of criminal liability came into being and why heavy stress on suffering is so often a feature of it, the facts of human psychology exhibited in legal history are the right ingredients of theory. But explaining a practice and justifying it are two different things. We may learn a great deal about the origins of punishment from such a theory, and may come to appreciate the deep urges satisfied by this social institution, but the theory does not make clear why a practice with so much to be said against it is nevertheless not wrong.

There is, however, a justificatory posture that this theory might assume. Private vengeance is a source of injustice and inhumanity as well as of social disorder, since the wrong person may often be seized as the guilty party, and whoever is seized is likely to be treated according to the dictates of a vengeful passion instead of in a way prescribed by dispassionate and principled mandates of the law. The very possibility that this might happen would have a profoundly antisocial effect in the community, and violence in response to acts of vengeance or even in anticipation of them would become no less common than the acts of vengeance themselves. Criminal liability conceived as orderly public vengeance is therefore an improvement over more primitive responses to crime, and if there were no other choice it could certainly be justified as a measure to prevent private vengeance.

Public vengeance is not the only way to deal with the evils of private vengeance, however, and in fact the system of criminal liability that we have provides a way that is superior to public vengeance. Acts of private vengeance are made punishable as crimes by the criminal law as are any other criminal acts. As a means of preventing acts of private vengeance this alternative is preferable to a system of public vengeance, since it does not require us to inflict suffering upon criminals in a measure sufficient to satisfy the appetites of victims and others who seek vengeance on their behalf. Instead it allows us to pursue the more enlightened paths that our legal system provides while preventing acts of private vengeance just as we prevent other criminal acts. Since there is this preferable alternative to public vengeance, punishment once again on this account is needless, and so not justified.

THE INTIMIDATION VERSION OF DETERRENCE

Deterrence is the purpose most frequently invoked in support of a system of criminal punishment. Since the notion of deterrence is itself somewhat slippery, however, more than one version of deterrence theory has to be considered. It is agreed that a standing threat of punishment for crime is proper, and that the threat would soon be perceived as empty if it were not made good when a crime is committed. But having an effective threat on the one hand, and carrying it out on the other, gives rise to two different ideas of deterrence, one stressing the effect of the threat upon those who are amenable to it, the other stressing the effect of punishment upon those who are not.

The first version of deterrence theory regards the intimidation of those who are tempted to commit a crime as being a social necessity that justifies the intimidating threat, and views the need to keep the threat effective as the justification for carrying it out. Creating and imposing liability to punishment each have separate grounds of justification, then, and each must be justified in order to justify criminal liability as a social practice that embraces both phases. But there are difficulties with both.

In order for temptation to crime to be deterred by the threat of dire consequences it is necessary that there be a temptation in the first place. No doubt some crimes would be committed by persons who for a time are inclined to act criminally because of some attractive prospect or some surge of

desire within, but dread of punishment corrects these untoward inclinations, leaving the person finally disinclined. It is
like other decisions not to act that we all make when finally
the risk makes it seem not worthwhile. But not all things that
we do were we tempted to do, and not all crimes that we commit were we tempted to commit. In many cases there simply
was no temptation and so no opportunity for thoughts of dire
consequences to exert their countervailing influence. When
we are single-mindedly caught up in our continuing effort
without time for consideration, or when we are driven by
feelings that leave no opportunity for us to see ourselves as
we may be at a later and sorrier time, we do not then act
from temptation and do not take a course that prospects of
punishment might cause us to abandon.

Most murders, for example, are not committed by people
who are tempted and succumb to temptation, but by people
ruled by strong emotions that remain sovereign over their
actions at the time, even though in many cases they could
have chosen to act differently either by controlling their emotions or by controlling themselves in spite of their emotions.
The law, however, punishes such murders as it punishes
those that the murderer is tempted to commit. If it is to
deter such homicides that we threaten to punish them, we are
engaged in a futile exercise. If, on the other hand, we punish
them to preserve the credibility of the threat for others, we
are engaged in a needless exercise, for the credibility of a
threat would not be impaired if we fail to carry it out when
circumstances made the threat meaningless in the first place
and that fact is made known.

Besides the many homicides that are crimes of passion,
there are a great many other crimes in which there is no
temptation to crime, and the same holds true for all these
other crimes. They include crimes that are committed routinely in the course of conducting some enterprise of organized crime, or are committed by professional criminals and

others who off-handedly engage in criminal practices as part
of the life of crime to which they are dedicated. In these instances the perpretrator has already become impervious to
the admonitory force of the law and has assimilated what it
threatens as part of the ongoing risks of his criminal occupa-
tion. Since in imposing (and in creating) criminal liability no
distinction is made between those instances in which intimidation might work and the many in which it could not,
intimidation does not serve to provide a general justification for criminal punishment, for without that distinction
as a basis of exemption from liability many instances of
punishment for the sake of intimidation are useless or
needless.

There is another objection to the intimidation theory, one
based on the severity of penalties prescribed. It is intuitively
clear that crimes for which the heaviest punishment is laid
down on the whole are not crimes in which temptation is
either particularly strong or especially common. Murder is
punished most severely, but, as we just noted, it is often not
a result of temptation at all. Crimes are punished most severely because they are the most serious, which is to say that
the harm done or threatened when such crimes are committed is most serious and the risk in what is done intentionally is especially great. Yet only when temptations are strongest is there a need for threats of the most dire consequences
in order to deter through intimidation, for only then is it
especially difficult to overcome the temptation. Since in our
system of criminal liability much punishment is far in excess
of the requirements of intimidation, from the standpoint of
intimidation such punishment is needless and so not justifiable on those grounds.

The law with its promise of punishment may intimidate
only irregularly, but the known presence of a policeman or
even of an ordinary citizen will often deter those who might
otherwise commit crimes. So, often, will the likelihood of an

appearance on the scene of some such person during the crime. The very presence of others has a powerful deterrent effect because it threatens apprehension by the authorities, either immediately or afterward when the police are called and information is provided. But the deterrent effect of this presence depends ultimately upon the awesome threat of the law. If mere arrest and adjudication as a lawbreaker were all that need be feared, many who are tempted to commit crimes would do so even with a policeman at their elbow when the satisfaction or gains in prospect overshadow the mere inconveniences that may be expected from a denuded criminal process. It can therefore be argued with much weight that even if the threat of punishment often does not itself intimidate, it still is necessary if the presence of a policeman or anyone else is to have its deterrent effect.

There is no question that the presence of police or other persons often does intimidate and inhibit in just this way, and diverts those wishing to engage in crime to safer opportunities that are thought to be free of such a hazardous presence. Certainly punishment for crimes knowingly committed in the presence of others is neither useless or needless, and if punishment under the law were limited to such cases and to those cases in which others come on the scene during the crime, punishment would be justifiable on a theory of intimidation. But the law has no such limitation, and it provides punishment for the many crimes committed when no police or other persons are present as well as for crimes committed in the presence of others. Since in this perspective only those who are present or are likely to appear can threaten punishment vicariously on behalf of the law, and since there is no threat of this sort on many occasions of crime, the threat of punishment made by the law is useless as an instrument of intimidation in such situations. Creating a threatening presence cannot, therefore, be the *general* justifying purpose of criminal punishment that we seek.

THE PERSUASION VERSION OF DETERRENCE

Another version of deterrence stands in contrast to mere intimidation. When a threat has failed to deter, that is not the end of the matter. The threat must be kept generally effective by carrying out what was threatened, and this feature is taken account of in the intimidation version. But there is also the matter of making the threat effective in the future for the person whom it failed to deter this time, and the way to do this, it is thought, is by bringing home the consequences to him. It is one thing, after all, to contemplate in the abstract what is generally regarded as a very undesirable experience. It is quite another thing to experience it so that one can remind oneself of the suffering and imagine enduring it again as a possible consequence of further criminal activity. Accordingly, on this theory those who have disregarded the threat and broken the law are persons who need a more meaningful threat, and this is provided by an occasion of its fulfillment which they may contemplate in the future.

On its face, the persuasion version of the deterrence theory is not without plausibility. It does rest on an assumption, as does the intimidation theory, that persons are in general mindful of the unpleasant consequences they may expect should they commit a crime and be apprehended. As we know from our discussion of the intimidation theory, the circumstances of many crimes bring that assumption into question, and so pose an objection to either of these versions of the deterrence theory. But passing that objection, there is a further assumption made by the persuasion theory that is not entirely unreasonable. It is thought that threats of unexperienced punishment are in general meaningful to most people—the law-abiding element—while among the others—the criminal element—there is a higher threshold of intimidation which the bare threat of unexperienced suffering can not cross. Perhaps those who are law-abiding have more at stake, perhaps they are simply less bold; whatever the reason, they are likely to take the bare strictures of the criminal law more seriously. When a law-abiding person commits a crime, however, he shows himself to be something of an exception who may be suspected of having some deficiency in sensibility or awareness that calls for correction through the heightened stimulation that the rigors of punishment when recalled will thereafter impart. Those not law-abiding are thought to be naturally deficient in such sensibility, and so in the same way require correction.

The reason that punishment cannot be justified as a means of deterring lawbreakers from further crime is that it fails to do that. Though the harshness of the law is made manifest to scoffers and doubters, the effect of such a revelation is at most to persuade them that crime does not pay if one is punished for it. It leaves untouched a quite realistic notion that one has a good chance of getting away with crime, in which case crime does pay. Even more important, punishment has other effects that make its lesson a matter of little importance. A prisoner is stigmatized by being sent to prison, and because the stigma remains he is thereafter deprived of the full benefits of life in a law-abiding community when he returns to one. Even before he suffers from the effects that his stigmatization has on others, he experiences its baleful effects on himself. There is a profound loss of self-respect, which normally results in his being even less inclined than before to pursue whatever opportunities for a decent life are available to him within the law. In the prison community of criminals, the values, methods, and ambitions of those who live without respect for the law prevail, and only a minority who have real hope of redeeming themselves in spite of their shame and loss of status can be expected to resist these constraints toward a life of crime.

There is because of all these things a new configuration of motives and goals developed in the very process of punishment that tends to weaken the influence of fear of punishment; and so on balance punishment in its total effect weakens rather than strengthens the deterrent force of the prospect of further punishment. If the failure were attributable to factors that could be changed without changing what is essential for punishment, then even universal failure would not mark punishment as useless in this regard. But it is clear that stigmatization and its attendant evils are part and parcel of criminal punishment no matter what its form. Since punishment is not successful in what on the persuasion theory it purports to accomplish, and since the failure is attributable to features of the practice that cannot be expected to change, punishment on this account is useless and cannot be justified as an attempt to make the threat of the law more credible.

III. A PREFERRED THEORY

STATEMENT OF THE THEORY

There is a third version of deterrence, one that places no stock in considerations of intimidation and makes no claim that the law has a general tendency to scare off would-be wrongdoers by its threat. In this version stress is still placed on the threats made by the law, and for that reason it can be called a deterrence theory. But the threats made by the law play a different role than the one assigned to it in the other versions of deterrence, and those who are fond of labels may wish a special designation. "Anti-impunity" captures its distinctive feature, though so graceless a name cannot hope to be widely adopted.

According to this theory, punishment for violating the rules of conduct laid down by the law is necessary if the law is to remain a sufficiently strong influence to keep the community on the whole law-abiding and so to make possible a peaceable society. Without punishment for violating these rules the law becomes merely a guide and an exhortation to right conduct. No doubt even without liability to punishment an appreciation of the consequences of crime would itself encourage many to forbear in the face of temptation. But most of us would sometimes succumb on occasions when the urge was particularly strong if getting away with it was a certainty because liability for crime was something unknown in the community. Only saints and martyrs could be constantly law-abiding in a community that had no system of criminal liability, for at the very least in acts of retaliation and of self-preservation everyone else would occasionally do what the law prohibited. The threats of the criminal law are necessary, then, only as part of a system of liability ensuring that those who commit crimes do not get away with them. The threats are not laid down to deter those tempted to break the rules, but rather to maintain the rules as a set of standards that compel allegiance in spite of violations by those who commit crimes. In short, the rules of conduct laid down in the criminal law are a powerful social force upon which society is dependent for its very existence, and there is punishment for violation of these rules in order to prevent the dissipation of their power that would result if they were violated with impunity.

According to this theory, then, having a system of criminal liability is justified because (but only if) it is useful and preferable to any workable alternative as a means of keeping effective the rules of conduct set forth in the criminal law. As the other theories have had to face the objection that criminal liability is useless or needless for the purpose they favor, so must this theory face these objections in advocating its justifying purpose.

OBJECTIONS BASED ON USELESSNESS

The first objection is that criminal liability to keep the law effective is in any case a useless measure, since criminals are in general heedless of the rules. Indeed, it is this very lack of concern about what the law says that distinguishes a person who is not law-abiding from one who is. If a law-abiding person is told that what he proposes to do is against the law, that bit of intelligence will by itself weigh heavily against his going ahead. What the law says will matter a great deal to him just because the law says it. But those who are not law-abiding feel no such constraint and are not impressed by the simple fact that something is against the law. Their concern is only with evading the consequences of a particular violation. Society's concern in preventing crime is, however, mainly with the activities of the criminal rather than the law-abiding portion of the population, and since the rules as such do not matter to the criminal in any case, punishment so that the rules are taken seriously is said to be useless.

There is much merit to this argument when taken as an objection to justifying criminal punishment as a measure of crime prevention in the ordinary sense. Arrests, prosecutions, convictions, and sentences are often thought to be stages in a crime-reducing process aimed at making the community more law-abiding, so that there will be fewer crimes in the future than there have been in the past. If this view of the process were correct, the objection would indeed be a good one. But in spite of widespread belief to the contrary, the process is in fact not one of crime reduction either in its aim or in its effect. Only when for some reason there is a radical disintegration of the social order and normally law-abiding people incline toward crime can the process be viewed as a program of crime prevention in the short run, for only then is the buttressing of the rules accomplished by the process a matter of immediate concern to prevent crime in the short run. Normally, criminal liability has only the long-run aim of preventing a disintegration of the social order through a loss of respect for the rules, ensuring that the normally law-abiding will remain that way and that the community will remain on the whole law-abiding. Short-run crime prevention that reduces crime rates can be expected only from measures that make the satisfactions of a law-abiding existence more readily available to those who now find a life of crime more appealing, or from measures that make the successful commission of crimes more difficult. We cannot punish away crime, but we can contain it through rules that are kept effective by punishment of violations so that in general only those who disclaim allegiance to prevailing social standards are its regular perpetrators.

A corresponding argument can be made with reference to law-abiding citizens, and this gives rise to a second objection. The law-abiding are concerned with whether a course of action is against the law, not with the prospect of punishment. Since whether a course of action is against the law does not depend upon whether those who violate the law are punished, we need not punish in order for the law-abiding to keep the law. For those among the law-abiding who will violate the law in spite of its restraining influence, the provision for punishment is useless, so runs this argument. And for those who are law-abiding and do keep the law, it is needless. Hence punishment cannot be justified as a measure to keep the law-abiding from committing crimes.

In support of its premise that the law-abiding are deterred by the law itself and not by its threat of punishment, this argument would remind us of the usual demurrer to a suggestion of crime that may be expected from the law-abiding even when there is a tempting opportunity with little risk of detection, and of the continuation of law-abiding habits that is usual among the law-abiding when there is a temporary breakdown of law enforcement. The internal constraint of the law among the law-abiding, which follows simply from a recognition that the course being contemplated is against the law, keeps the law-abiding in the path of the law even when the law is only a bare pronouncement.

Once again, the objection is valid on its own assumptions, but is misconceived because of a mistake about the proposed grounds of justification. It is not the case that, according to the theory being proposed, liability to punishment is necessary in order to prevent an increase in the current crime rate that supposedly would result if the law-abiding resorted to crime, just as it is not the case on this theory that criminal liability is designed to reduce that crime rate by enhancing the restraining influence of the law on the criminal population. The theory simply proposes that if forbearance from crime were made to depend only upon whatever satisfaction there might be in voluntarily conforming one's conduct to the law rather than upon the influence of an obligation to obey enforceable laws, the influence of the law among a very large part of the law-abiding population would not be sufficient to keep that part of the population law-abiding. Unless it is shown that unenforceable declarations by a legislature are sufficient to preserve the law-abiding habits of the law-abiding, the liability required to make law enforceable has not been shown to be unjustified—which is what this objection purports to show.

At this point it may be observed that though a very rough division of the entire population into law-abiding and criminal may be made in any community, there are persons in any community who are only marginally members of one group or the other. A person of this sort is prone to seize an opportunity regardless of whether it is criminal when impunity seems assured by the circumstances, though otherwise he will desist out of regard for the law just as do the law-abiding. As with law-abiding types but not with true criminals, it matters to him that the law forbids certain conduct;

but unlike the case of the truly law-abiding, it does not matter enough to deter by itself. Whether such person would normally be classified as marginal among the law-abiding or marginal among the criminal population seems largely a matter of his circumstances and associations in the community. But whichever side of the great divide he belongs on, he is the type of person for whom the existence of a system of criminal punishment is most important, since unlike the truly criminal he is amenable to its deterrent influence, and unlike the truly law-abiding he is likely to turn to crime immediately in the absence of such a system.

OBJECTIONS BASED ON NEEDLESSNESS

There are objections to this theory based on the claim that punishment is needless, and their gist is that the suffering entailed by criminal liability as we know it could be reduced or avoided by adopting some alternative scheme.

The first objection turns initially to the essential and indispensable element of criminal punishment as it is practiced under a morally enlightened and modern system of penology. That element appears to be the emphatic condemnation, carried on under the auspices of the state, of a person who has broken the law for the act that has broken it. Mental and even physical suffering in some small degree may still inevitably accompany these measures of condemnation, but in civilized societies of the modern world there are strong moral constraints against deliberate infliction of any kind of suffering in order to punish for crime. Instead, modern penology designs its programs and facilities to alleviate suffering as much as possible and even provides a life in which many of those convicted of crime experience less discomfort than they did when they were free men. But surely, it is said, the condemnation necessary to ensure that the law is taken seriously can be carried on in a way that eliminates much of the remaining suffering that torments needlessly not only the one who committed the crime but innocent members of his family who deserve none of the great misfortune spilling over into their lives.

Newspaper editorials, sermons, and group resolutions commonly contain condemnation of conduct as well as of those who engage in it. Though it may cause some incidental suffering, the condemnation is accomplished through its very expression without more, and no one need suffer. Can we not then in the legal system condemn any crime that has been committed through some device that operates in a similarly humane fashion but still is effective to preserve the law?

Suppose a public registry of convictions were established, and with suitable publicity and solemnity entries were made of each crime and its perpetrator. It could not be said that under such a system all who committed crimes were getting away with them. For many law-abiding persons, public humiliation and loss of reputation would result from their registration, and might even equal in condemnation what they would suffer by imprisonment. But for many among the law-abiding who commit crimes, and certainly for criminals, such a system is deficient. It does not necessarily cause the one convicted to suffer condemnation, but only to suffer certain disabilities that follow from condemnation depending upon the circumstances of the person condemned. In such a system, unlike the one we now have, a person who can shield himself against these undesirable consequences *does* get away with his crime. What is required is a system in which all who stand condemned suffer the kind of condemnation that makes the law's threat meaningful as an effective declaration against crime with impunity. For that, mere condemnation is not enough.

Though a person who breaks the law must suffer condemnation, there is no reason to expect of criminal punishment that it cause him to condemn himself and to suffer remorse for what he has done. And though *he himself* must suffer condemnation, it is condemnation not of his person but rather of his conduct. *He* suffers condemnation for what he has done, but not for what he is in view of that. In our more primitive moods we feel tempted to condemn the person as a criminal, and mean by that to condemn him as a kind of person. But the state has no business criticizing its wayward citizens in that way, since condemnation of the person for what he is contributes nothing to keeping the law effective. Condemnation for his conduct does.

Yet another objection to this theory questions the justifiability of punishing everyone who deserves it. Surely it must be the case—so runs this objection—that if only some substantial portion of all those who commit crimes had liability imposed, the point would still be made that one cannot expect to get away with crime. Accordingly, a system that imposed liability more sparingly might be devised. It would have to be designed so as not to offend against justice through unequal treatment. It might, for example, designate by lottery or by some other means of random selection who among those accused are to be prosecuted or who among those convicted are to be punished. True enough, the chances of anyone's getting away with a crime would then be somewhat greater. But so many uncertainties now stand between the commission of a crime and the apprehension, much less conviction, of the one who commits it that the additional uncertainty under the proposed system seems in itself no obstacle. If imposing liability only for some part of all the crimes committed would indeed be enough to secure the general observance of the rules, the portion that can be dispensed with represents needless human suffering under our present system, and this portion is for that reason not justifiable.

It is hard to imagine such a system's failing to diminish the condemnatory force of criminal liability to a point where it is largely defeated in its purpose. If exemptions were granted in this way simply to make the system more humane, the ele-

ment of bad luck in failing to gain exemption would loom
even larger than the condemnation when punishment was
imposed, and the rules of conduct set out in the criminal law
would be regarded more as hazards in a game than as standards of socially acceptable conduct to which members of the
community owe an allegiance. Though hard to imagine in
this form of random selection, it might, however, be possible
to devise a scheme of exemptions in some form that did not
have this subversive effect—in which case the objection must
be accepted as perfectly valid. In fact, such a scheme does exist
not only in theory but in practice, and so, even though the objection is in principle a valid one, the reform it proposes is not
necessary.

If everyone who broke the law were prosecuted and punished, quite clearly there would be criminal liability in excess
of what is required to keep the law effective. But in our system of criminal justice as it is presently constituted, there
are both partial and complete dispensations from punishment
or prosecution even though liability has been determined, or
likely could be. Sometimes it is a matter of humane regard
for the convicted person and for others who would be
affected by his imprisonment. In other cases those who enforce the law make use of dispensations to induce cooperation
in bringing others to justice, or in avoiding the time and
expense of a trial when the guilt of the accused seems a fore-
gone conclusion. In still other cases the accused is simply
given another chance on the theory that apprehension this
time will itself serve to deter misconduct in the future. The
effect of these dispensations is to lessen considerably the total
amount of punishment inflicted by the state. With the same
effect, prosecution is often not even undertaken when violations are merely technical in the sense that the person in violation of the law did not intend to get away with anything,
for it is then frequently the case that there is no need to
prosecute to prevent him from getting away with his viola-

tion. Here the point is that not every technical violation need be prosecuted to uphold the law, since mere technical violations are normally not instances of acting against the law, but as violations they are only accidental in a course of law-abiding conduct.

By dispensations from punishment and by forebearance from prosecution the total suffering created in the course of preserving the law is considerably less than it might be. Even so, the question remains whether there is still not an unjustifiable excess after all these reductions are accounted. The answer is that without good reasons for desisting from prosecution or punishment in a particular case, a person who has acted against the law but has been exempted from liability has got away with breaking the law; though when there are good reasons for dispensation, quite apart from those that affect determinations of liability, the law is upheld when these reasons are taken into account and there is a decision to grant dispensation. Considerations that support liability and normally warrant its imposition must be weighed against other considerations that furnish good reasons for not imposing it, and a decision made on balance. Since the criminal law provides a way of determining whether liability exists, but not a way beyond that for determining whether it ought to be imposed, there is no weakening of the law through impunity when it is decided upon full consideration for good and sufficient reasons that liability ought not to be imposed.

PUNISHMENT OF THE INNOCENT

No issue concerning punishment has more vexed philosophical controversy than the justifiability of punishing the innocent, and it is useful at this point to notice the implications of what we have said for this question.

Some critics of utilitarian theories of punishment have alleged that under certain conditions punishment of an innocent person could be countenanced on utilitarian grounds.

On the supposition that the innocence of the person punished would never be discovered, it is said that the benefits of apparent punishment for a crime that has been committed might serve to justify in a utilitarian balance those official acts that would have the appearance of being punishment for the crime. But under our analysis, imposing liability even on the guilty may be dispensed with when there is good reason to do so. When someone is not punished because he is innocent, there is the best of all possible reasons for not punishing him, and the fact of his innocence alone assures that his impunity does not mean that he is getting away with breaking the law.

The point may be put this way. No innocent person need be misrepresented as guilty and then punished, since without that no one will be regarded as having been *allowed* to get away with the crime, which is all that need concern us, even though it may indeed be the case that ultimately someone will have got away with it. More than that, there often must be some element of social disutility in knowingly punishing an innocent person, for those (including the guilty person) who know the truth know that the guilty person, whoever he may be, has been *allowed* to get away with his crime.

Philosophers sometimes debate whether the taking of an innocent life in some worthy cause—the saving of other innocent lives, for example—can be justified. If it should turn out that the sacrifice of some innocent life is justified to save others, the sacrifice might take place in the form of a criminal execution. One can imagine, for example, the execution of a single innocent scapegoat to appease those who hold many other innocent persons hostage and threaten them with certain death. Similarly, some lesser sacrifice also in the form of criminal punishment inflicted on an innocent person might be justifiable when it is the only way to avert some greater evil. But even if in the extraordinary circumstances of these cases punishment of the innocent should turn out to be justifiable, it is not the practice of punishing an innocent person that is justified, but only the sacrifice of an innocent life or the infliction of suffering upon an innocent person in whatever form that may be done.

OBJECTIONS BASED ON UNDESIRABLE FEATURES

There is a further objection to the justifiability of criminal punishment as we know it, this one based upon the enduring undesirable features that it bears. Some of the anguish and humiliation that prisoners seem almost universally to endure, and some of the hard treatment that is often their lot, seem unnecessary for the purpose of upholding the law through condemnation of lawbreaking. To the extent that this is so, and to the extent that such features may be said to be part of the system of criminal liability and not simply a constant aberration within it, punishment is, according to this objection, unjustifiable.

The objection is unexceptionable. It stands as the principal mandate for prison reform, and more, for a system of criminal liability that does away with such institutions except to the extent required to satisfy the social needs that make criminal liability necessary in the first place. There are certain features of a correctional system that shock our conscience, and we must do away with them whenever and wherever we discover them. Incarceration itself, even when humane, gives us cause for regret though it does not shock us, and to the extent that it is not required we are bound to do away with it as well. In principle it is a matter of punishing by incarceration only when that is necessary to prevent the guilty from getting away with their crimes according to *considered views* in the community. A system of criminal liability that neglects this principle and is not constantly striving toward elimination of needless suffering is not a justifiable system of liability. But so long as the principle is given effect through diligent effort at reform, the *system* with the self-reforming process is not—because of the needless suffering that can be found in it at any time—unjustifiable. Because our practices are inevitably imperfect, some allowance must always be made for suffering that in principle is needless. But such suffering can be countenanced only so long as there is active concern and steady effort to minimize it, rather than smug toleration of its inevitability.

Carrying this further, we must conclude that if a workable alternative to criminal liability itself can be found, one that does not require the suffering that is unavoidably part of any system of criminal punishment, and is preferable, all things considered, to what we have, then we would be bound to regard criminal liability itself as needless and so unjustifiable. Furthermore, if it can be demonstrated that when those who commit crimes are regularly allowed to get away with them the community still remains on the whole law-abiding, once again criminal liability would be shown to be needless and therefore not justifiable. The burden of establishing these propositions is very heavy, and it comes as no surprise that hardly anyone has seriously attempted to shoulder either of them.

CHAPTER TEN

Liability, Culpability, and Punishment

Questions of criminal liability and of culpability have remained inseparable throughout this book, and in this final chapter the basis and some of the consequences of this intimate association receive further examination.

In the first section some points from previous discussions are collected and amplified to provide a comprehensive statement of why it is that criminal liability is right only if it is for culpable conduct. More limited problems are then considered.

The first of these arises when the strongest accusation to be made is one of mere negligence and there is uneasiness about punishment at this low blame level. In the third section a more difficult problem of a similar kind is investigated. It is usual for the law to provide less punishment for crimes of attempt than for completed crimes. If that is as it should be, what is the reason for punishing the two differently? If the difference cannot be justified, at what level should parity of punishment be established? This prompts consideration of the more general problem of parity between crime and punishment, which is pursued in the fourth section.

Punishment is wrong if it does not fit the crime. But it is far from clear what the principles of fit punishment are. Once the primitive idea of a harm for a harm is abandoned, the best measure of punishment seems to be the blameworthiness of the conduct that is the basis of liability. Yet considerations other than culpability regularly enter into sentencing decisions, and some of them, at least, seem the sort of thing that ought to weigh in sentencing deliberations. Setting admissions standards for these other considerations and deciding what weight ought to be given to them is important if sentences are to be just.

Avoiding talk of punishment has long been the fashion among designers and administrators of correctional systems. Various modes of nonpunitive treatment are recommended for those who commit crimes, and it is thought that such treatment is a desirable substitute for punishment. Yet hardly ever is it denied outright that crime deserves to be punished, and rarely is consideration given to whether punishment can take place within a program of nonpunitive treatment. In the final section, a scheme of reconciliation is proposed so that enlightened forms of criminal liability that still serve the purposes of punishment may be put into practice with neither intellectual nor moral embarrassment.

I. CULPABILITY AND LIABILITY

THE OBJECTION TO LIABILITY WITHOUT CULPABILITY
IN THE LAW AS IT IS

The unseemliness of subjecting a person to criminal liability for blameless conduct is by now a familiar theme. Condemning one who is blameless is universally abhorred as an injustice, and it is astonishing that those who advocate criminal liability regardless of culpability do not perceive this abhorrence as an insurmountable obstacle to the adoption of their program. The reason for this is not hard to find. Those who would ignore blameworthiness when considering who should be put away have the safety of the community as their exclusive interest. They fail to appreciate that a system of criminal liability according to law works only through the medium of rules, and imagine it rather to be a system of social engineering whose corrective measures purify the social environment and render innocuous the dangerous elements in it.

Apart from its injustice, criminal liability on these terms is deeply degrading, since it must be borne regardless of whether one has chosen to do the thing for which liability is imposed. Those who propose such liability are not insensitive to concerns of human dignity. In other settings they may be depended upon to appreciate that it is a most extreme indignity to refuse to consider what a person intended to do when he acted as he did. The exceptional indifference when criminal conduct is being judged is perhaps best explained by fears of harm so strong that a judgment of harmful yet innocent is psychologically unacceptable.

Beyond justice and personal dignity, there is a practical reason for requiring culpability. If conduct is not culpable, condemnation of it is meaningless. A law creating liability for acts that are blameless will not be given support by condemnation of those acts, and liability without culpability is therefore law enforcement that does not serve the purpose that justifies it in the first place. Explaining why this is so requires us to take a closer look at culpability.

It seems clear that of the four dimensions of culpability distinguished in Chapter Three, there are two that would still be heeded in a community whose criminal jurisprudence allows liability without culpability. How serious was the harm that the act threatened, and how great a risk there was of its occurring because of what was done, are both matters that would enter into determinations of liability. The fate of considerations bearing on the legitimacy of what was done is uncertain in this new jurisprudence, for the social engineers responsible for its design may regard the question of whether under the circumstances one man had a right to harm another as irrelevant and an impediment to the advancement of social safety; or, on the other hand, they may see it as a harmless indulgence that can be allowed to those who have some sentimental attachment to traditional views.

There is, however, one dimension of culpability—the dimension of intentionality—which must surely be ignored under this new scheme of liability. It would not matter what, if anything, was done intentionally, nor would *any* excuse which normally relieves from blame matter then. This would be the case for excuses that relieve from blame indirectly by denying that the accused was a responsible agent, as well as for excuses that are aimed straight at culpability and deny that his act was intentional. Under such a system, it would not matter that a person did his best to heed the law and in spite of that the law was violated by him. True, liability under such a scheme for those who did not attempt to heed the law and broke it might still have the effect it is designed to have under the present scheme. But in other cases, liability would not serve the purpose it now does, and would almost certainly have very bad effects. Dread of punishment and of the law imposing it would be increased, and so presumably would precaution against allowing oneself to do harm unintentionally or because one could not help oneself. The cost in liberty of such precaution would be appalling, for the only way to protect against mishaps that are purely a matter of chance in the course of some legitimate activity is not to engage in the activity. No less important in terms of practical consequences would be the loss of respect for the law which such a scheme is sure to engender. A system that routinely disregards the rudiments of exculpation insisted upon by common justice can no longer preserve the effectiveness of the law as a force for social control, since allegiance to its rules is bound to disappear and is certain to be replaced by artifice and guile as citizens make every effort to protect themselves against the hazards of the law.

OBSTACLES TO A SYSTEM OF LIABILITY WITHOUT CULPABILITY

This argument assumes that the reason for having criminal liability is to keep the rules of conduct effective, thereby maintaining a community that is on the whole law-abiding and able to offer the benefits of life in society to its members. It was argued in the preceding chapter that only such a purpose can serve to justify criminal liability as we know it. But we might suppose a radical change in which modification of behavior were substituted as a goal. In fact it is a goal much talked about at the present time and even pursued within narrow limits on an experimental basis. Liability would then exist to provide the opportunity for changing dispositions toward antisocial behavior of a criminal sort. For this, condemnation has importance only to the extent that it is found to be a useful technique for conditioning the future behavior of the one made to suffer condemnation. Since liability would not entail condemnation, blameworthiness would then no longer be a requirement for liability, but would merely be an incidental consideration providing grounds for believing that condemnation would be effective as a technique to bring about desired changes. Blameworthiness and condemnation would have only an instrumental part to play then, and as a consequence the law would have an altogether different role.

At present we rely on the law to exert a powerful influence when a course of conduct is being freely decided upon, and expect that influence to prevail quite regularly among the law-abiding. But under the proposed system, behavior giving rise to criminal liability would be avoided not as a matter of choice but because of an aversion to it that pre-empts the need for choice. The law does not then exercise an influence over choice, but only mandates an opportunity for changing those persons who are presumed by their deeds to have shown themselves in need of change.

Though culpability is not required for liability in such a system, the question remains whether liability is justifiable without it. Though refusing to take into account good excuses that wrongdoers may have is a thoroughly demeaning way of treating them, under certain circumstances such treatment might be justifiable. The burden of justification, however, is a formidable one, and here it is necessary only to indicate how formidable it is.

Since in such a system the purpose of making a person liable is to change him in ways that remove his disposition to do what the law prohibits, it is necessary that those in whose hands he is placed be able to diagnose correctly and treat effectively. Imposing liability is a futile act without that, and as with every practice in need of justification its futility would be its undoing. Furthermore, rendering a person incapable of undesirable behavior by techniques that also deprive him of his ability to engage in acceptable activities is in any case not justifiable if there are methods of achieving social safety that do not work such debilitation. Thus far the very limited success with techniques of behavioral conditioning has been achieved at a tremendous cost in debilitation, and it is doubtful, in view of the very modest gain in social safety that such a program represents, that it can be justified as an alternative to the less objectionable, if no more successful, system of liability that we now have.

Finally, one may again question the usefulness of a system of liability that subjects to corrective treatment all and only those who have broken the law. The unreasonableness of inferring dispositions from acts has been noted in our earlier discussions, and while that point is again relevant here, the converse is even more important. At any given time there are many persons with a disposition to act in criminally harmful ways who have not yet acted, but who will act in accordance with that disposition at some future time. It is therefore a matter of considerable doubt whether a program of corrective conditioning *that is limited to those who have already acted criminally* is sufficiently useful in achieving social safety to justify it in spite of its highly objectionable features.

II. LIABILITY FOR NEGLIGENCE

As we noted earlier, in some quarters there are strenuous objections to laws punishing conduct that is merely negligent; moreover, theorists of the law feel bound generally to take seriously the misgivings that punishment for conduct at a low level of blame inevitably produces. All legal systems of course tolerate some criminal liability of this sort, though in different countries there are important differences in the kind of harm that must be threatened by the negligent activity before the criminal law takes notice. Strict liability as well as liability for negligence of the more obvious type is brought into question, since in both instances conduct merits relatively little blame, and part of what is to be said here about liability for negligence has been anticipated earlier in the discussion of strict liability. The objection to punishing such conduct rests on certain mistaken notions about culpability, and on certain views about the propriety of punishment in general that argue against punishment in such cases.

NEGLIGENCE AND CULPABILITY

All crimes of negligence consist of conduct that is blameless in one aspect but quite blameworthy in another. If the acts of the accused are merely negligent, the activity in which he was engaged could not in itself be condemned as wrong. Much of our life is taken up in activities that are done openly and need no explaining away, but some of these activities have attendant dangers, and for that reason we are not free to carry them on in any way we might choose. If we carry on these activities as we should with due regard to the danger, our conduct remains blameless. But if we are heedless of the hazards in what we do, or even insufficiently attentive, our conduct merits blame according to how heedless or inattentive it is.

Sometimes the dangers are not present but are only prospective, and in that case the activity is not thought of as dangerous but rather as an activity that can be dangerous, or that can create dangers. Driving on an icy road *is* dangerous, while driving under normal conditions *can be*. Either kind of activity requires that the risk be borne in mind when the activity is engaged in, though when the risk is greater, so too is the precaution required. When dangers already present are ignored, there is negligence of a higher degree of culpability than when dangers not yet present are created in the course of the activity. The reason for this difference is the greater threat of harm that dangers already present represent. Within these higher and lower ranges of negligence there are degrees of culpability determined by other factors. In both ranges these finer determinations depend on how manifest the danger is; how imminent the harm of which there is danger; how serious that harm is; the importance of the interests that legitimate the activity; and the feasibility of adequate precaution against the harm.

In contrast to crimes of negligence, crimes higher on the scale of culpability all consist of activities that are in themselves wrong. As we know from previous discussions beginning in Chapter Three, conduct higher on the scale of culpability is more dangerous and for that reason, in the absence of some redeeming consideration, it is not tolerated as legitimate activity.

Sometimes those who object to criminal liability for negligence suggest in effect that built into the very imputation of negligence there are exculpatory claims that defeat liability. Two such purported exculpatory claims are brought to mind by the phrase *"mere* negligence." For one thing, in cases of mere negligence there is no intention to do harm. For another, when there is mere negligence there is thought to be only some inadvertence or other slackness of mind to which all of us are subject from time to time and which we cannot avoid, poor imperfect creatures that we are.

In cases of mere negligence no harm is intended. But that fact cannot provide the substance of an exculpatory claim of interest to the criminal law, for as we now well know, intending to do harm is never a necessary condition for criminal liability.

The other purported claim of exculpation would in effect invoke the responsibility principle and argue that the presumed mental lapse that makes our conduct negligent is not something we could help. If negligence were indeed just a matter of an innocently wandering mind we should certainly give credit to this excuse. As we have just seen, however, negligence involves *choosing* to carry on an activity in one way rather than in another, and so, in spite of any mental lapses that may have occurred, the requirements of the responsibility principle are fully satisfied.

NEGLIGENCE AND PUNISHMENT

Quite apart from special considerations that apply to *criminal* punishment, when conduct is in itself wrong and cannot be justified by some special circumstance, there is a warrant for punishing it just because it is wrong. But negligent conduct is not in itself wrong, and this presents special problems.

Those who take a narrowly retributivist line about punishment in general will of course have difficulty unless they disagree and find negligence to be in itself a species of wrongdoing. What has been said about strict retributivism in the preceding chapter will allow us to pass such an objection here. There is, then, an array of consequentialist theories posing objections to punishment for negligence.

Those who regard the justifying purpose of punishment to be the working of changes in wrongdoers naturally object to punishment for negligence. Since there is no wrongdoing, there is no evidence of a disposition to do wrong, and so no evidence of a person in need of change. There are those who see criminal liability as a measure of social defense to remove from circulation those people who are dangerous because they are not committed to abiding by the law. But since law-abiding members of the community no less than others commit acts of negligence, once again on this view, criminal liability for negligence is insupportable. Finally, there is the view that criminal liability represents a threat of punishment which intimidates and so deters many who are tempted to commit crimes. But since no one is tempted to be careless, it is thought that on occasions of negligent conduct there is no temptation to be counteracted by the law's awesome threat.

All these arguments rest upon a general misconception about criminal liability. Liability for negligence, like all other criminal liability, is to keep the law effective. It is socially desirable to require that activities be carried on in a safe way if they are dangerous or may become so. Sometimes this is done by prohibiting certain practices that enlarge the hazards of a dangerous activity, and sometimes by imposing precautionary requirements on those who engage in such activities. In either case, the law demands compliance in order to prevent harm, just as it does when more serious crimes are put on the books. When the law is violated, there is punishment, just as there is for more serious crimes, in order to keep the law's demand effective. When negligence is made criminal it is no more difficult to conform one's conduct to the law than when a more serious crime is put on the books, for in general it is just as easy to do something in the right way as it is to do only what is right. True, unfairness is more likely when restrictions are directed to legitimate activity. Since the activity is allowed, it cannot be burdened unreasonably with restrictions having the effect of defeating it or of making its very pursuit not worthwhile. But if a law creating liability for negligence is not unfair and deserves to be on the books, like all other criminal laws it can be kept from becoming a dead letter only if violation with impunity is not allowed.

III. PUNISHMENT OF ATTEMPTS

THE PROBLEM

How should attempts be punished? This question must be answered by theorists who seek to provide policy guidance for the criminal law, though surely it is among the most puzzling. It is usual for the law to prescribe a lesser penalty for the attempt than for the completed crime. The reason is plain enough. Doing harm is a more serious matter than simply doing what might have ended up as that but didn't. It seems therefore that one who does harm does something that is more wrong than one who does something harmful but with no one harmed. Doing harm, we might say, appears to be more culpable than merely presenting a threat of it.

This naïve though robust moral intuition reflected by the law is confronted by objections that have philosophical as well as policy footings.

In many cases of attempted crime the nonoccurrence of harm is purely fortuitous, and this prompts doubts about the justice of punishing more moderately simply because the harm has not occurred. In an assassination, for example, the difference between a completed crime and an attempt might well depend on some slight movement of the victim at the instant the shot was fired or on what he happened to be carrying in his pocket. Examples can be multiplied in countless numbers for almost any crime to provide cases in which harm occurred or failed to occur only because of something over which the accused had no control at all. In these cases the conduct of the perpetrator is equally culpable whether or not harm occurs, since either way the conduct is exactly the same. Those who object to the disparate liability to be found in the law consider it a result of unenlightened notions of retribution, even vengeance. According to more primitive moral views, when harm occurs and a person is responsible for it, his culpability is measured by the harm he has done. What he must pay to restore the moral balance must therefore take the harm he has done into account. But those who object to this ask whether culpability—and so punishment as well—should be measured at all by the harm for which the accused is responsible when its occurrence is only a matter of chance.

There is also a policy objection to different penalties that rests upon an assumption about the purpose of criminal liability. If only because of the great vogue it currently enjoys, this objection deserves to be noted. In legal circles the elimination of different punishment for the attempt and for the completed crime is now favored on the theory that in either case the perpetrator is equally bent on doing harm, and so is equally dangerous whether or not harm actually occurs. It is assumed that criminal liability exists to deal with dangerous persons, and often it is suggested that with regard to attempt liability this purpose is paramount. Since perpetrators both of attempts and of completed crimes may engage in the same conduct, it is concluded that the same range of penalties ought to be prescribed for both, for when their conduct is the same both are equally dangerous. If it turns out that they are not equally dangerous, that fact would be reflected in the sentences actually imposed in particular cases.

Our previous discussions require a rejection of such questionable assumptions about the purpose of criminal liability. The case, then, for liability that is the same and the case for liability that is different both seem very strong. In fact both are very strong but (as we shall see) they are not cases in opposition, as they appear to be. It is usual in discussing this question to proceed on the assumption that all attempts are related in the same way to the completed crimes of which they are an incomplete version. If that were so, it would indeed be inconsistent to advocate the same sentences and different sentences as well. But in fact attempts and completed crimes are not all related in the same way one to the other.

It is true that all attempts are incomplete versions of the crime, since the harm required for the completed crime did not occur. But some conduct puts the harm more immediately in prospect and is more dangerous. Because of that it is more culpable, and liability ought then to be greater according to a general principle of criminal justice (discussed at length in the next section) that requires liability to be proportionate to culpability. Conversely, since less dangerous conduct is less culpable, under the same principle there ought to be less liability for it. In some cases, then, attempt liability will be as extensive as liability for the completed crime, and may even be greater, for sometimes, even though harm does not occur, the conduct of the accused was more dangerous than in a case in which harm does occur. In other cases of attempt the conduct is less dangerous and so liability is less extensive.

"ABORTIVE" ATTEMPTS

Starting with two species of "abortive" attempts, several varieties of attempts must be distinguished and classified according to differences in culpability.

When a course of criminal conduct has not proceeded far enough for harm to occur, there is (what we shall call) *abortive conduct*. Though the actor is not yet able to do harm, what he has done may still pose a threat of harm substantial enough to merit recognition as an attempt. In that case, the abortive conduct should have liability assigned to it as an attempt, though a lesser degree of liability for the particular crime should be assigned, since the threat of harm is less than it might be.

Among attempts in which the conduct is abortive, two species can be distinguished.

For some crimes the law requires that the act of the accused have a certain result. When that requirement is not met, the harm has not occurred and so neither has the completed crime. If a person engaged in committing a crime has his activities brought to an end before they have gone far enough to make the result possible, the activities he has engaged in are properly regarded as abortive conduct. An assassin lying in wait with everything in readiness may be apprehended moments before the victim comes into view. What he has done is enough for attempt liability, since there is a present danger of the harm in what he has already done. But since not enough has been done for death to occur, the conduct is not *harmful* but simply *dangerous*.

Other crimes are committed when certain acts are done, and require no result. These are crimes in which the harm is constituted by the very doing of the prohibited act. In such crimes part of the required act may be done and part not yet done when the activity is brought to an end, in which case we have abortive conduct of the other variety. When part of the act required for the crime remains undone, the harm has not occurred, and so neither has the completed crime. But if enough has been done to constitute a present danger of it, there is enough for attempt liability. A burglar might be apprehended while still working on the lock, though the crime he is engaged in committing requires that he break in. A rapist may be successfully resisted or frightened off before he can penetrate his victim, though his penetration is part of what the law requires for rape. Once again, conduct is *dangerous* to a degree that makes attempt liability appropriate; and yet because part of what the law requires remains undone, the harm could not occur and so once again with reference to what is necessary for the completed crime the conduct cannot be regarded as *harmful*.

THE NOTIONS OF DANGEROUS CONDUCT AND OF HARMFUL CONDUCT

Dangerous conduct and *harmful* conduct are contrasting notions of crucial importance that again need to be made clearer at this point, though some of these matters have been taken up already in the course of discussing degrees of culpability in Chapter Three.

Of the two, *dangerous* conduct is the less confusing notion, but it is vague enough to work mischief. In order to meet the minimum requirement for attempt liability the danger represented by what was done must be a *present* danger. A present danger is a real danger but it is something more than that. A present danger calls for measures to be taken against what is threatened, and the call is so urgent that neglect of it would be irresponsible. Real dangers that are not yet present require us as prudent people to be on the alert, but leave us the option of watching and waiting if we do not wish to act now. Conduct in which the danger is not yet a present danger is insufficiently dangerous to be the basis of criminal liability. Examples of this we saw earlier in Chapter Six in our discussion of what the law regards as mere preparation.

Sometimes conduct is more dangerous than is necessary to
meet the minimum requirement for liability. Not only is its
danger present, but that danger is *imminent*. Unless effective
measures are taken, harm then will almost certainly occur in
the normal course of events. Normally when danger is imminent a deliberate failure to take action against it is irrational and not merely irresponsible. Since imminently dangerous conduct represents a more serious threat, its culpability
is greater.

One has little difficulty in appreciating that conduct can be
more or less dangerous according to just how imminent is
the harm that it threatens. In grading dangerous conduct,
as well as in recognizing it, common sense is our principal
resource. In any community one finds on these matters a
wide range of common beliefs that derive largely from a common experience in suffering harm and seeking to avoid it.
When something questionable is done, we turn to these beliefs to determine whether harm was in the offing and how far
off it was. But common sense is not the final arbiter. Armed
with new facts and with a new appreciation of what we already know, our critical intelligence stands ready always to
show us that our fears are empty, or that the harm threatened
by a particular act is rather more remote than we had supposed.

Harmful conduct is a more elusive notion than dangerous
conduct, though it is less troublesome when captured and put
to work. Harmful conduct can take place when harm does not
occur as well as when it does, though unfortunately this fact
about conduct is often overlooked. If the *occurrence* of harm
(and not merely its danger) is imminent, the conduct to which
that harm would be attributable if it occurred is harmful
conduct, and this is so whether or not the harm actually does
occur. Consider the assassin with his victim fixed in his sights
and his finger slowly squeezing the trigger until the shot is
fired. His act is a harmful act whether or not the bullet hits

its mark. It is a more dangerous act than simply pointing a gun and firing, for once the shot is fired it is only chance that can avert the harm. For this reason, the conduct is as dangerous as can be. But if the assassin is apprehended a moment before he would have fired, we would regard his conduct as imminently dangerous, though not harmful. Then it is not simply by chance that the victim is not killed; and normally a deliberate failure to intervene in those circumstances to remove the danger would be irrational.

What distinguishes harmful from imminently dangerous conduct, then, is the fact that only when conduct is harmful is it the case that harm is avoided only by chance. But one ambiguity remains to be resolved. It is common enough to say that Smith's act *was* harmful, in which case a report is given to the effect that harm occurred and that something that Smith did was responsible for it. If no harm occurred, that statement would be false. But it is also commonly said (this time in a tenseless way) that Smith's act *is* harmful, in which case a statement is made about the kind of act it is, and more particularly that it is an act of the most dangerous sort. Even though no harm occurs as a result of Smith's act, this statement may nevertheless be true. It is not redundant, furthermore, to say that Smith's harmful act did indeed (bad luck) result in harm; nor is it a contradiction to report that, happily this time, the harmful act (by a stroke of luck) caused no harm. Sometimes, of course, in deciding how dangerous an act was we are helped by what we know of the outcome. This is the case when our experience with acts of this sort is meager and so we know little about what is likely to happen as a result—though usually we are familiar enough already with the dangers of what was done and need not consult the outcome to acquaint ourselves further. We are in any case free to conclude that in view of the character of the act the outcome was an anomaly.

The three grades of dangerous conduct for which there is

liability can be conveniently illustrated by a burglar at work. We might first imagine him walking down the hallways in an elegant apartment house trying the knob on the door of each apartment in the hope of finding one that is unlocked. With regard to the risk that this presents, it would be irresponsible not to take what measures one could to prevent the harm that is threatened, and for that reason the activity is rightly regarded as a *present danger*. But if, failing to find an unlocked door, the burglar proceeds to try to pick a lock on one of them, what he then does is *imminently dangerous,* for unless he is stopped he will almost certainly gain entry. It is irrational and not simply irresponsible to ignore the risk and leave to fate the security of the occupant and his possessions. The burglar may remain undetected and his lock-picking efforts may finally be crowned with success. He opens the door and rushes in only to find that the dwelling he expected on the other side has just been demolished to make way for a doctor's office, so that no longer could the premises be considered a dwelling place. What he has done is then rightly regarded as *harmful* conduct, though the harm of ordinary burglary does not occur in these legally unsuitable premises. It is harmful conduct, since only by chance did the harm not occur.

"COMPLETED" ATTEMPTS AND THE VARIETIES OF IMPOSSIBILITY

Standing in contrast to "abortive" attempts, there is another variety of attempt liability in which conduct is less dangerous than it might be, and for that reason it warrants a lesser liability. Unlike cases of abortive conduct, the activity that threatens harm in these cases has not ended prematurely but in fact has been completed. Harm, however, has not been brought about but has only been threatened. Though everything necessary for the completed crime had been done, something was wrong, or went wrong. But something further is required to warrant lesser liability for the attempt. In all these cases of lesser liability it is impossible for the harm to occur, and the impossibility is *overt*. These cases of overt impossibility stand in contrast to cases of two other kinds in which the harm also is impossible.

The first are cases of what we might call *manifest impossibility*. In Chapter Six we saw that proper grounds for criminal liability are lacking altogether when there is no reason for the actor to believe that harm would occur, and it is in these cases that the impossibility is manifest. At the other extreme are cases of *covert impossibility*. In these cases, though in fact the harm cannot occur, there is reason in general to believe that it will; and there is reason, furthermore, for the actor to believe that it will. In such cases his conduct is no less culpable when the harm does not occur, and thus there is no warrant for lesser liability when harm does not occur. *Overt impossibility* stands in the middle. Though the actor has reason to believe that harm can occur, there is no reason to believe that it will.

To illustrate these different varieties of impossibility, one might imagine three different cases of attempted assassination.

In the first case the assassin holds in his hand a toy gun which he quite irrationally believes to be a weapon capable of killing. Though careful aim is taken and the trigger is pulled, the death of the intended victim is *manifestly impossible*. The actor believed that it was possible. But there was no reason to believe it, since normal attention to those matters of ability that necessarily concern anyone truly engaged in performing the act would disclose the impossibility. More than that, in this case not only was there no reason to believe that it was possible, but the actor himself had no reason to believe it was. It was sheer indifference or perhaps some delusion that caused him to attempt an assassination with a toy gun, rather than simply a failure to give normal attention to matters bearing on his ability to do the job. When the actor neglects altogether these matters of ability and is utterly unequipped to accomplish his purpose, we naturally do not consider what he does as a serious threat at all, and certainly no present danger. A person who knew what the would-be assassin was doing but chose to ignore it could hardly be called irresponsible.

In a second case we might suppose that the assassination attempt consisted of a shot fired at the intended victim after careful aim had been taken. Unknown to the actor, however, the weapon is notoriously inadequate since its range is about a hundred yards and the target is many times that distance. The outcome intended by the actor is again impossible, but this time it is an *overt impossibility*. Once again, there was no reason to believe that the victim's death was possible, since, in this case as in the first, normal attention to matters of ability would make clear the impossibility. Unlike the first case, however, in this one the actor had reason (though not good reason) to believe that what he intended was possible. Though he failed to pay attention as one normally would to his ability to do the job, still he was only careless and not indifferent or a victim of some delusion. Unlike the man with a toy gun, he armed himself with a deadly weapon, which is sufficient attention to ability to make his act truly dangerous. In this case others normally would be concerned with something more than what it was that the actor had in mind as he acted. Their concern would be with what he was doing, and ignoring it would be a measure of irresponsibility on their part.

The third case is one of *covert impossibility*. The weapon now is the right one for the job, but the assassin fires a round with a hidden defect, and because of that the bullet fails to reach its target. Not only did the actor have reason to believe that what he intended was possible, but there was in fact reason to believe it, for in this case even though, once again, he lacked ability he had not been deficient in enabling himself to do the job. It is fair to say that in this case the conduct was as dangerous as could be and that it is a case of harmful conduct, for even though what was done could not bring about the victim's death, his death was averted only by chance.

Overt impossibility, then, makes conduct less dangerous and so less culpable; and because of that it warrants a lesser liability. Covert impossibility, on the other hand, has no exculpatory value, for it gives rise only to the barren argument that it was by chance that harm did not occur.

ADJUSTMENT OF LIABILITY

The principle underlying equal liability for the attempt and for the completed crime in cases of covert impossibility is simple enough, and has general application beyond cases of covert impossibility. When it is only by chance that harm does not occur, there is no reason to deem what was done less dangerous. But there are many cases in which harm *was* possible and in which similarly it did not occur only because of some chance event or condition; and in these cases as well there is no reason to deem the conduct less dangerous than if harm had occurred. The victim's cigarette case or momentary nod may save his life, but what the assassin has done is harmful conduct nonetheless.

When conduct is harmful, liability for it must be the same whether or not the crime is completed. This confronts us with the question of whether liability is to be the lesser liability that is now normally prescribed for the attempt or the greater liability normally prescribed for the completed crime. There can be no uniform answer. Liability ought always to be for conduct according to its culpability, and differences that the occurrence of harm might make—such as feelings to be assuaged, or injury to be compensated—never have a place in determining the extent of criminal liability. Adjustment of penal provisions that now punish the attempt and the completed crime differently will at times call for upgrading the attempt and at other times for downgrading the completed crime to achieve parity of punishment for the same conduct.

It is simply a matter of taking into consideration all elements that determine culpability and then adjusting the penalty so that the conduct in question is assigned a correct position relative to the culpability of other crimes on the scale of penalties that one finds in a penal code.

Not only harmful conduct but imminently dangerous conduct as well sometimes receives unequal treatment in the attempt and in the completed versions of a crime. Consider now not the cool and deliberate act of the distant assassin but instead violent homicidal assaults in which the assailant attacks his victim with deadly force. Some of these assaults will again be cases of harmful conduct. Methodical strangulation of the victim by practiced hands or even repeated and deliberate stabbing at vital parts are cases of harmful conduct, for there can be no doubt about what the outcome normally will be if the actor is allowed to proceed. But there are other cases of homicidal assault in which the attack is sudden and the blows are sporadic—cases in which there is not methodical violence aimed at killing. In such a case there is sufficient doubt about the normal outcome of what is done to warrant the conclusion that a danger of death was imminent, but its occurrence was not. Once again, in such a case it should make no difference whether death results or the victim survives. Whether the victim lives or dies, the conduct of the one who attacked him was imminently dangerous, and so equally blameworthy in either case. The law as it now stands, however, is disposed to treat any homicidal assault resulting in death as though it were harmful conduct, and the direction of law reform for such cases should therefore be toward lesser liability for the completed crime.

LEGISLATIVE FORMULATION

How shall legislation manage a scheme of liability to take proper account of the complications uncovered here? For crimes in which culpability turns out to be the same for the attempt and for the completed version, liability may be made the same by redefining the crime so that the conduct itself constitutes the completed crime. Under such a scheme of legislation, there would still be cases of abortive conduct, and only these cases would then be cases of attempt. The assassin whose bullet missed the mark only by chance would be subject to the same punishment as the assassin who succeeds, but not the assassin apprehended while waiting for his victim to appear. When the conduct is dangerous, rather than harmful, liability would follow a similar pattern. The deadly assault whose probable outcome is a matter of speculation would be treated the same whether death occurs or not. If the same deadly assault is arrested at the outset when conduct is still incomplete, it would be treated as an attempt, and since it is then less culpable than if it were completed, it would warrant a lesser liability.

In order to designate conduct that is harmful or conduct that is imminently dangerous as part of the definition of the crime in its completed version, legislation would make reference to general standards of dangerousness. Accordingly, for deadly assault the conduct of the accused must place the victim in imminent danger of death, and for murder the act must make the occurrence of death imminent. Wide discretion is then left to those who must decide about the character of the conduct in particular cases. But such discretion has abundant precedent in the criminal law where such crucial issues as due care or reasonable cause, for example, are regularly left to be decided under standards no more certain.

Under the proposed legislative scheme the lesser liability of an attempt would be managed along the same general lines. When the attempt is "abortive," or when the required harm is overtly impossible, there is either imminently dangerous conduct or, less than that, conduct that represents a present danger but no more. The definition of the attempt (for specific crimes or for general categories of crime) would make use of these standards of dangerousness. When the completed crime is a matter of harmful conduct, either of the lesser degrees of dangerousness will do for the attempt, and the extent of liability for it will then be assigned according to which degree it is. Crimes in which conduct is imminently dangerous in the completed version would have conduct representing (merely) a present danger in the attempt version. Conduct that is only a present danger may still be the stuff of a completed crime. But such a crime can have no attempt version that calls for lesser liability, since conduct posing a threat of harm that is not even a present danger must inevitably fail to concern the criminal law.

IV. PROPORTIONAL PUNISHMENT AND JUSTIFIABLE SENTENCES

DESERT AND SENTENCE

Our conclusions about attempt liability rest on the still unexamined premise that liability ought to match culpability. This general principle of proportion between crime and punishment is a principle of just desert that serves as the foundation of every criminal sentence that is justifiable. As a principle of criminal justice it is hardly less familiar or less important than the principle that only the guilty ought to be punished. Indeed, the requirement that punishment not be disproportionately great, which is a corollary of just desert, is dictated by the same principle that does not allow punishment of the innocent, for any punishment in excess of what is deserved for the criminal conduct is punishment without guilt.

The criminal law adheres in general to the principle of proportionality in prescribing liability according to the culpability of each kind of criminal conduct. It ordinarily allows some significant discretion to the judge in arriving at a sentence in each case, presumably to permit sentences that reflect more subtle considerations of culpability that are raised by the special facts of each case. Judges and those from whom they take advice affirm that punishment ought always to fit the crime; yet in practice sentences are determined largely by other considerations. Sometimes it is the correctional needs of the perpetrator that are offered to justify a sentence, sometimes the desirability of keeping him out of circulation, and sometimes even the tragic results of his crime. Inevitably these considerations cause a departure from just desert as the basis of punishment and create cases of apparent injustice that are serious and widespread.

The appearance of injustice may be misleading, however, for in general wrongdoers need not receive as punishment what they deserve in order for justice to be done. They may without injustice be given more than they deserve if they have agreed to that under the general social arrangement of rules and penalties for their violation. If it is reasonable to suppose that morally conscientious persons would include as a provision of the social contract penalties in excess of those warranted by culpability, even though it would still be undeserved the excess portion of a sentence would then be justifiable by virtue of a contractual obligation to serve such a sentence that is binding on each member of society who commits a crime. Such an arrangement would not be unreasonable if the general welfare of the community depended upon it, and it would be eminently reasonable if not only the general welfare but the very survival of civil society made it necessary.

Similarly, punishment that is less than deserved may nevertheless be just. This might again be the case because of a general agreement that lies at the foundation of society, but there is a more plausible argument to be made. Criminal punishment according to desert may not be needed to keep the law generally effective, and since this is the purpose that justifies punishing in the first place, the unneeded punishment would then not be justifiable.

What we shall argue here is that liability according to desert is always sufficient to serve (and normally to serve successfully) this purpose of preventing the rules from becoming ineffective because of violation with impunity, and so punishment more than deserved is always needless and never justifiable. Furthermore, liability according to desert is sometimes necessary to keep the rules effective, but not always. When there are certain reasons why a person who is punished more moderately for his crime will not get away with his crime, such punishment less than what he deserves for what he has done is justifiable, and punishment in excess of that is not. But when special conditions favoring the perpetrator are absent and he will get away with his crime to the extent that he is punished less than he deserves to be, punishment less than he deserves is useless and for that reason alone it is not justifiable, though certainly there are other important things to be said against it as well.

PROPORTIONAL PUNISHMENT

Punishment that fits the crime is punishment in proportion to the culpability of the criminal conduct and it is what the perpetrator deserves for his crime. We know already how culpability is to be determined, and it is easy enough then to decide on greater or lesser punishment according to greater or lesser culpability and to assign penalties on a scale that reflects relative culpability among crimes, both for different kinds of crimes and for different instances of the same kind of crime. But that is only the first step in keeping crime and punishment in proportion. The scale itself must be pitched at a level neither too high nor too low, for otherwise even though punishments for different crimes might not be out of proportion to one another on the scale, the scale itself might be generally out of proportion as uniformly excessive or uniformly deficient.

In a morally primitive society this difficulty need not arise, for punishment can be calculated to cause suffering which is equivalent to the suffering caused by the crime. But in a morally advanced society no such common element in crime and punishment is available as a basis of calculation. Instead, according to our theory of criminal punishment it is a matter of not allowing those who break the law to get away with their crime, and punishment is proportional to crime when it is enough, but not more than enough, for that purpose. It has been suggested that the minimum punishment sufficient to ensure against crime with impunity can be determined by reference to considered judgments in the community, but this without more leaves the matter unacceptably obscure. The idea of fair market value that is commonly made use of in appraising property is illuminating here.

It is universally agreed that proper judgments of fair market value are rational judgments based on considerations generally accepted as determinants of worth in the market community. Some such notion as the price at which a willing buyer and a willing seller will engage in a transaction is used, and fair market value can thus be seen to depend on the normal dispositions and attitudes of those who make a market in a community at a given time.

Several things are important here. Though the criteria of value make reference to presumed dispositions of members of the community, they are objective criteria and make reference only to dispositions that can be rationally defended. Though these dispositions change and valuations change with them, the changes are not mercurial and are sufficiently stable to allow for judgments of value that seem settled at any given time. And though market value ultimately depends upon subjective factors, it does not depend upon what those who make up some representative cross-section of the community would in fact be disposed to offer or accept, but rather upon what any member of the community would be bound in good conscience to admit is a fair price once he has considered carefully all those things that bear on it. And finally, though judgments of fair market value express opinions that within limits will inevitably differ depending on who is making the judgment, there are ways of criticizing and defending opinions by appeal to reasons, and so there are ways of deciding which opinion is best.

Proportional punishment bears marked similarities to fair market value. Though reference must be made to what is minimally sufficient in the light of culpability to prevent the appearance of crime with impunity in the eyes of the community, the standard of punishment is an objective one, for it depends not on what most people feel like seeing the perpetrator suffer, but rather upon what is defensible through reasoned argument. It is not then the bare opinion of some majority that prevails, but a considered judgment that anyone may arrive at. Often there will be some disagreement even among those who have arrived at considered opinions, but this is no cause for despair or for fear that unjust sentences will often result. In cases of enlightened disagreement a reasoned choice can be made among the opinions offered, and justice can be done by adopting the opinion that finally seems best after each considered opinion has been critically scrutinized in an open-minded way. Furthermore, the best opinion of what a particular crime deserves is different now from what it was some time in the past, and certainly it is bound to be still different in the future. Social attitudes change and the threshold of impunity is therefore a shifting one. But this does not mean that we are doomed to perpetual injustice in sentencing, for as long as sentences reflect considered judgment at the time they are given, the requirement of proportionality is satisfied.

DISPROPORTIONATELY SMALL SENTENCES

Considerations apart from culpability that weigh toward a reduction of sentence we shall consider later. First we shall want to look at cases in which such considerations are absent and see why it is that sentences must then be determined by culpability alone.

Disproportionately small liability is useless because it cannot maintain respect for the law among the law-abiding. Under prevailing views, a year in jail for murder would be regarded as inadequate condemnation of the crime unless such a sentence were warranted by special mitigating considerations. The effect of such a sentence would be much the same as a failure to enforce the law altogether, for in either case the perpetrator has got away with his crime. Since punishment that is markedly deficient fails to preserve respect for the law and even encourages a measure of contempt, the sentence that mandates such punishment is unjustifiable, for it is an exercise in futility, and even more, a subversive influence on the law.

It might be objected that token punishment is better than no punishment at all and that it is wrong therefore to speak of it as unjustifiable. True enough, the objection concedes, a year in jail for ordinary cold-blooded murder would be getting away with murder, but even that is better than nothing at all, since at least the murderer then is not getting away with his crime completely. If we ignore known violations of the law, the objection continues, there will be a rapid disintegration of law-abiding attitudes. But enforce the law, even though with sentences that are unconscionably lenient, and law-abiding attitudes will then only weaken and crumble slowly.

The objection seems sound enough in its premises, for surely the simple fact that the law is in some way enforced makes a great difference. A system of grossly inadequate sentences is to be preferred to a system that fails altogether to enforce the law; and if no enforcement at all or grossly inadequate sentences were the only alternatives available, then grossly inadequate sentences would be justifiable. But the argument against these sentences is that they allow the destruction of law-abiding attitudes when yet another available alternative would not. Since sentences commensurate with the crime can be passed, and since that alternative does not undermine respect for the law, sentences so slight that they are altogether out of proportion are not justifiable. Because they do not preserve the law among the law-abiding, these sentences are useless and, with reference to the purpose that justifies criminal punishment, a pointless infliction of whatever suffering they cause, though admittedly they cause less suffering than a proper sentence that *does* serve the justifying purpose of punishment, and though the suffering they cause is (to say the least) well deserved.

DISPROPORTIONATELY LARGE SENTENCES

Similarly, liability in excess of blameworthiness is not justifiable. Though it cannot be objected to as a useless infliction of suffering, it represents needless suffering. To keep the law effective as a rule for the law-abiding, we need give those who break the law no more than they deserve for breaking it, and what they deserve is measured precisely by the culpability of the conduct that violated the law. Just desert is, once again, a matter of conscientious and considered judgment based on what is generally viewed in the community as necessary to prevent the lawbreaker from getting away with his crime in view of its culpability.

Courts and legislatures both indulge liberally in excessive punishment. Nowhere in the law are legal standards that a judge must respect less developed, yet nowhere are the consequences of the judge's decision more momentous. It is a commonplace that different judges in like cases will sentence very differently, and over such a great range that though some sentences must be excessively lenient many other must be excessively harsh. There is little uniformity among the notions—one hesitates to call them theories—upon which sentences rest. When a judge thinks that the good of society is served by a stiff sentence, or that it is good for the person found guilty who stands before him, or when he thinks that it is deserved (for whatever reason), he implements his views without any firm guidance from the law and so enjoys autocratic license to an extent unknown elsewhere in the law. The abuse of power allowed to a sentencing judge by the legal system is concealed to some extent by the administrative facilities of a modern criminal justice system. Reports and recommendations are provided to the court and are used to create an appearance of regularity and even principle in sentencing, though in any jurisdiction there is shocking inconsistency and a regular disregard of uniform standards grounded in principles of justice.

In legislation, excessive liability is somewhat less frequent, but since laws are uncluttered by the facts of a case each instance is more visible. Most often such legislation represents a draconian response to gratify a fearful and angry public when a particular crime or some general problem of crime arouses strong feelings. The form which modern legislative excess most often takes is a mandatory minimum sentence that precludes moderation even when there are weighty exculpatory considerations. In addition, there are some older laws on the books that startle us by their harshness and in some cases even shock our conscience, particularly when the penalty of death is provided for a crime in which no life is taken. We are reminded of a still earlier time of unbridled excess when every crime that was deemed at all serious was treated as a capital offense. Apart from these drastic measures taken on the tide of strong emotion, the modern indeterminate sentence coolly allows for punishment that is far greater than deserved, on the theory that it is the criminal and not the crime for which a sentence is imposed. As a variety of sentencing injustice this form of disproportionate sentence is especially insidious, for it appears benignly in the guise of enlightenment.

But the passions of the judges, of legislators, and of the public, together with the sophistications of penology, do not give full account of why we have punishment in excess of culpability. A thoughtful argument may be made which in effect relies on the theory of justification that we found acceptable in the last chapter. The gist of the argument is that the strength of the law is greater when punishment for breaking it is more severe. It is not a matter of greater intimidation produced by a greater threat, but of a more solemn attitude of respect and obedience which in cases of extreme temptation or provocation will cause inhibition to prevail when otherwise it would not. The argument has a special appeal when used to justify capital punishment for murder. It is said that the extreme penalty makes the prohibited act seem a more awful one. This in essence was the view expressed by J. F. Stephen when he suggested that murder is regarded as it is because the law hangs a man for it. The argument, then, is one of social utility that bypasses the question of what punishment is *deserved,* and stresses instead the presumed enhancement of the law as an instrument of restraint. It is an argument that purports to meet the objection that disproportionately great punishment is needless and therefore unjustifiable.

But the argument turns out to have less merit than first appearances suggest. Consider the time when all felonies were punishable by hanging. Neither those who committed crimes nor those who sat in judgment regarded larceny and murder as equally serious, though both offenses were punishable by hanging. Nor is there reason to believe even that larceny was regarded as a very grave offense. Two well-known items of legal history attest to these conclusions. Pickpockets, whose crime might be punished by hanging, are said to have been especially active among crowds at public executions. And when they (or other thieves) were caught and tried, it was usual for juries to acquit them of the capital charge even in the face of the clearest evidence of guilt.

In modern times there are many examples of unduly harsh laws that are self-defeating in the same way. A contemporary favorite is drug laws born of regulatory impotence that seek to terrorize traffickers and even users by requiring savage penalties. Police, juries, judges, and even prosecutors are all reluctant to bring about the unduly harsh punishment that the law requires. Instead of strengthening the law, its penalties deter its enforcement and so cause the law to become weaker than a more moderate law would be. In harsh laws, then, there is not the social utility that is supposed, but on the contrary a disutility resulting both from loss of respect for laws when they are unjust and from a disinclination to work injustice by enforcing them. There is something in Stephen's observation that does seem right, however, and it becomes clear when a different interpretation is placed on what he says. If capital punishment is deserved for murder, standard punishment somewhat less than that would likely result in somewhat less aversion to the crime; though, as we shall soon see, there may be good reasons in spite of that to reject capital punishment.

DISPROPORTIONATE UNIFORMITY

Proportion between crime and punishment is a goal respected in principle, and in spite of errant notions it remains a strong influence in the determination of sentences. The practice of punishing all serious crimes with equal severity is now unknown in civilized societies, but such a radical departure from the principle of proportionality has disappeared from the law only in recent times. Even now there are public moods of repression when all serious crime is viewed as a single grave affliction that is thought to call for uniformly drastic measures. Anything less than a penalty of the greatest severity for any serious crime is thought then to be a measure of toleration that is unwarranted and unwise. But in fact quite apart from those considerations that make punishment unjustifiable when it is out of proportion to the crime, uniformly disproportionate punishment has some very undesirable practical consequences.

Criminal punishment represents condemnation of a criminally wrong act. But if we condemn all wrong acts equally without regard to how wrong each is, we invite serious troubles. In the first place, if right or wrong *tout court* were all that mattered, we would find the entire world divided starkly and simply into saints and sinners. Without greater and lesser punishment those who commit crimes would all be condemned simply as criminals; and since all would bear a stigma no different than that of the worst, all would be regarded as the worst. Under such a system we might also expect a deterioration of our moral sensibilities. Our sense of right and wrong is not unlike our sense of light and dark. If day or night alone mattered we should lose our ability to discriminate the flushes and shadows that fall between; and if only right or wrong mattered—never mind how wrong—we should be unable to perceive the moral world except in terms that are similarly stark.

Even more important than loss of moral sensibility, our conduct would be different with only a single simple moral alternative to guide us. Now when we plan a course of action we choose among possibilities that present different risks of harm, and along the way we alter our course when necessary to avoid harm. But if at a time of reckoning it would not matter what harm we have done so long as we have done harm, we then have no reason to avoid any harm that it would be inconvenient to avoid. If it seems easier or safer to murder for money, we would do that and not try to steal it discreetly. Though now all but wanton criminals avoid unnecessary harm, forbearance and avoidance of harm would then be abandoned as meaningless impediments to success. No doubt concern about harm would survive among many law-abiding citizens even though the law refused to recognize degrees of wrongdoing; but that is small consolation since the concern would then exist only among those members of the community who in any case are least disposed to commit crimes. In short, a great deal more harm is bound to be done in a world that does not care, when accounts are settled, how wrong an act is; and this is so whether settlement is made uniformly on the harshest or on the easiest terms.

INEQUITABLE DISPARITY

The principle of proportional punishment may be adhered to only some of the time, and there is then an appearance of injustice, since crimes that are alike in all respects relevant to punishment are punished differently. Inequality of treatment is a standing concern of criminal justice and has recently been given great prominence as a matter of public concern in the United States and elsewhere. Two classes of complaint are commonly made.

The first is that inadequate legal representation puts poor people at a relative disadvantage when sentences are decided upon. Because no effort is made on their behalf to create an attitude toward them more favorable than the evidence in the case alone warrants, they are given harsher sentences than others who commit the same crime but whose resources permit a more hopeful and appealing picture to be presented to the sentencing judge. There can be no question that inadequate financial resources often results in legal representation that is unacceptably weak, and that inequality of treatment by the sentencing judge is in some measure attributable to

unequal representation in court of those who have been convicted. As an offense to criminal justice this is second only to
unjust convictions; and like that evil it confronts us with an
urgent demand for reform to provide better legal services for
all who are subject to the criminal process.

The other complaint is of greater interest here. Some convicted persons, it is said, are sentenced according to their
wrongdoing, while others are given sentences according to
the judge's idiosyncratic notions which have no sound foundation in principle. Among these notions are ideas about what
kind of person the defendant is, what his crime represents,
the social needs to be served by his punishment, and what
serving a sentence will do for (or to) him. Unduly lenient as
well as unduly severe sentences are said to be attributable to
the biases and insupportable theories influencing those who
pass sentence.

To meet this complaint, reform must take an altogether
different direction. The remedy is not a more ample and discriminating presentation of facts by competent lawyers. What
is lacking that must be supplied is a uniform set of sentencing
standards that conform to principles of criminal justice; that
prevent any exercise of discretion not supportable under
those principles; and that, like any proper body of legislative
provisions, is law formulated with sufficient clarity to allow a
higher legal authority to tell, on appeal, whether or not the
law has been followed.

THE PRINCIPLE OF MITIGATION OF SENTENCE

Disparity among sentences is inequitable when it cannot be
justified in principle, which is just the case when it results
from disregard of the principle of proportion between crime
and punishment. For this reason, biases and theories of criminal liability whose influence subverts considerations of culpability and frustrates the principle of proportionality have no
proper place in sentencing deliberations. But there is an-

other principle that must also be observed upon pain of inequitable disparity. Sometimes there are good reasons for reducing the sentence which the principle of proportional punishment would otherwise warrant, and what we might call the principle of mitigation of sentence requires us to give them effect. The principle is founded, once again, on considerations of justifiable punishment and involves certain humane considerations as well as certain practical requirements of sound policy. Disregard of this principle is therefore morally wrong and may also turn out to be imprudent administration of a system of criminal justice. If the principle is disregarded some of the time but not all of the time, there are inequitable disparities among sentences that stand independently as instances of injustice.

When a convicted person is seriously ill, or his imprisonment will work unusual hardship on innocent persons, or when he has made amends for the harm he has done, or cooperates with the authorities as an informer or a witness, it is customary to take these things into consideration when deciding on a sentence, and to allow them to weigh toward leniency. These are only a few of the many items usually thought to count in favor of mitigation of a sentence, though it is plain enough that none of them have any bearing on how culpable was the criminal conduct for which punishment is to be imposed. They are thought to be good reasons for a lesser sentence, and they have the effect of lessening punishment even though they are not grounds for less punishment according to the principle of proportional punishment. The punishment *deserved* for the crime is no less when these things are taken into consideration, but since what is deserved is not all that matters in deciding what sentence is right, there is good reason for a lighter sentence in spite of that.

Good reasons of this sort count in mitigation of sentence, and so in effect in mitigation of punishment, but they do not count in mitigation of the offense. Just as disregard of exculpatory matters that count in mitigation of the offense would result in punishment that is not justifiable, disregard of good reasons that are not exculpatory would result in an unjustifiable sentence. If there is a good reason for a lighter sentence than fits the crime, the heavier sentence in spite of that is unnecessary, and so it is unjustifiable punishment. This is so because no one would be deemed to have got away with his crime if under these circumstances he were given the lighter sentence. Condemnation for the crime would be no less, though it would be accomplished by less severe measures.

The principle of mitigation, like the principle of proportion, has both legislative and judicial applications. Discretionary dispensations can be granted by a judge in order to make sentences right with regard to these other things after he has first arrived at a presumptive sentence based on desert according to culpability. Probation and low minimum sentences allow mitigation when circumstances that have no bearing on the crime provide a good reason for moderating a sentence.

The principle of mitigation has what is probably its most important legislative application when abolition of capital punishment is debated. It is said by defenders of the death penalty that the most serious crimes that involve taking a life deserve punishment in kind, for anything else will leave the perpetrator a person who in some measure has got away with his crime. Appeals to intuition produce support for this. Unless the lifelong torment of prison is assured as a substitute for execution, it seems even to those who take a dispassionate view of the matter that the most serious crimes of all have not been visited with adequate punishment. But even if the principle of proportion calls for capital punishment or hopeless incarceration for life, the principle of mitigation of sentence requires us to give heed to those humane and other moral considerations *that apply in every case* and that militate strongly against such punishment. When those reasons are made clear and their force is generally appreciated, there can be no claim that those who are not made to pay with their lives—whether by the death penalty or through a living death—have got away with their crime. Under such circumstances we condemn the crime adequately by punishment that is something less than deserved.

It is no easy matter to decide what shall count as a good reason in mitigation of sentence once the relatively certain elements of culpability have been weighed and more general moral or prudential considerations are taken up. Because we are civilized—indeed, because we are human—our moral life includes many different sorts of things, and in meting out punishment for crime we need to go beyond the simple justice of desert and show respect as well for other things of value.

In the first place there are sometimes larger considerations of justice whose influence makes itself felt. In fairness to him, what a man has done that redounds to his credit ought sometimes to be admitted to counterbalance the crime that now redounds to his discredit. The acts of a good citizen and even of a virtuous human being often have a proper place and count in his favor in deciding on his sentence. Still, not every kind of creditable activity is properly taken into consideration, and we find it difficult to decide where to draw the line.

Apart from justice, there is mercy. If justice is without rigor, justice is undone; and yet the harshness often accompanying rigorous justice may be tempered without causing justice to be undone. But merciful dispensation is not available on the easiest terms. Mercy is always given without there being a claim of right to it, and so it is exceedingly difficult to distinguish the compassion of common decency that ought to influence a sentence from the tender regard that is a precious human sentiment but has no place in the deliberations of a sentencing judge.

Sometimes compassion is not a matter of mercy but a matter of right. When suffering would be cruel, the sentence must be mitigated to prevent that. When compassion founds a claim of right, the issue, again, is a difficult one, since it is not easy to mark the point where cruelty ends and humane suffering begins.

' Finally, there are reasons of expediency that seem to warrant mitigation. We wish to encourage those apprehended to cooperate in bringing others to justice, and so we reward their cooperation with lighter sentences than they would otherwise receive. But mere expediency cannot alone establish that a concession is right, and we are constantly reminded by bargains made only for administrative convenience that there are difficult questions to be answered in deciding just what kinds of sentencing bargains are proper.

In contrast to these seemingly right, though admittedly perplexing, considerations there are others that clearly are not good reasons for a reduced sentence, but are commonly given weight as though they were. The most important class of bad reasons are those pointing to the goodness (or badness) of the convicted person. Even assuming that irrational biases are avoided and that a fair appraisal of each convicted person is made, the appraisal itself is out of place, for it is not part of the proper administration of criminal justice to make judgments about who is truly a bad person and who is really not so bad. Nothing in the design of the judicial process or in the method of selecting those who exercise sentencing power suggests that judges are meant to possess a competence to render such awesome judgments about persons; and no less is this true of prosecutors and others who advise judges. It is not at all surprising or distressing that this competence should be lacking, for the purpose of imposing criminal liability is in no way advanced by an administration of punishment according to character or reputation.

MITIGATING CONSIDERATIONS

Because standards are uncertain, good reasons turn out to be problematic and considerations that ought not to be admitted at all often influence the sentencing judge toward a more lenient sentence. Two general exclusionary conditions for mitigating considerations provide a foundation for suitable sentencing standards.

In the first place it is important to decide whether a proposed mitigating consideration would impair the utility of the sentence. Would what seems a good reason for reducing the sentence, if given weight, allow the guilty man in some measure to get away with his crime? If so, it is not really a good reason since the lighter sentence is then futile as a measure in support of the law. But in fact sentences that promote the evils of impunity are now commonplace in American courts, for it is usual to give lighter sentences to those who plead guilty only because they then relieve the court and the prosecutor of the burden of a trial. It is the very essence of a fair bargain between prosecutor and the accused that the accused get away in some measure with his crime. If in the end he gets what his crime deserves, he has been cheated by the bargain, for he has given up his opportunities for gaining an acquittal and has received the sentence that would have been proper had he been tried and convicted. Paradoxically, only when improper bargaining tactics are employed by the state to coerce a guilty plea can a proper sentence be arrived at. When a heavier sentence than the crime deserves is threatened if there is a trial resulting in conviction, and the lesser sentence that the crime deserves is then offered to force a plea of guilty, the bargain struck through such abuse of power results finally in a sentence that is fully deserved and yet does not allow any measure of impunity.

If plea bargaining is on the whole a regime of inducement

rather than coercion, as those in charge claim it is, it results in a pattern of sentences that allow those who plead guilty to go partly (and sometimes wholly) unpunished. No one knows better than the person who pleads guilty that he has been allowed to get away with something for the sake of administrative convenience. If he is not law-abiding to begin with, his lack of respect for the law quickly ripens into cynical contempt when he sees himself as nothing more than an item in a market place. The truth is not restricted to participants in the process, and among members of the community at large respect for the law is gradually replaced by faith in bargain-mongering lawyers when punishment is perceived as a matter of negotiation rather than desert.

Besides impairing the utility of punishment, leniency might be inequitable. When that is the case, whatever consideration it is that has dictated leniency cannot be a good reason for reducing the sentence. Inequitable disparity results when there is special treatment for some that cannot be justified by principles that apply to all, and since everyone is entitled to equal standing before the law, such treatment cannot be tolerated. Respectability of the person to be sentenced is an example of the sort of thing that regularly tempts those who pass sentence to be lenient, and particularly is this so when the crime is one that law-abiding citizens do not usually commit. Perhaps indulgence is prompted by sympathy for what is seen as merely a lapse, or perhaps it is a matter of reserving the unrelieved brunt of punishment for those who are perceived as hostile and outside the law. In any case, there is no acceptable principle according to which punishment may in part depend on the character or reputation of the person punished, and dispensation based on respectability is therefore always wrong.

Everyone who is sentenced has in the eyes of the law committed a crime. The principle of proportional punishment therefore applies equally to all. But not everyone sentenced is fortunate enough to have available some mitigating consideration to weigh in his favor, or to have one that weighs as heavily as the one that is available to another man; hence it might be said that the principle of mitigation of sentence does not affect equally all those to whom it applies. That is clearly so. A healthy young man cannot make claim to the infirmities of old age, and a person who has acted alone does not have accomplices against whom he can testify. But the principle of mitigation is equally available to everyone, and for that reason it would be wrong to conclude that application of the principle works injustice. It is of course true that a man who has little or nothing to offer in his behalf may complain of a kind of cosmic injustice, and certainly of bad luck. But that is an objection against the way of the world and not against the human effort to avoid unnecessary suffering which the principle of mitigation represents.

SENTENCES IN EXCESS OF CULPABILITY

Various considerations dictate a more lenient sentence than culpability alone would indicate. But are there also good reasons for a heavier sentence than would be warranted by culpability alone? Are there sometimes reasons for punishing more severely than is necessary to prevent the perpetrator from getting away with his crime? Certain features of everyday sentencing practice and of laws prescribing sentences appear to rest on purported good reasons for increased punishment that have nothing to do with the blameworthiness of what the perpetrator did. Unfavorable items in his personal history, and information about his circumstances and prospects in life, appear regularly in sentencing reports, and particular attention is given to items supposed to be evidence that he is or may become dangerous. In addition, previous convictions are regularly given the greatest weight in decid-

ing on a sentence. The importance of a man's criminal record
is codified in recidivist and habitual-offender provisions. It
would seem then that the guilty person is subject to punishment not only for the crime for which he is being sentenced,
but also in some measure for previous crimes for which he has
already been punished, and for being a certain sort of person
as well. Such laws seem to be in sharp conflict with the principle of proportional punishment.

Whenever it is the criminal and not the crime that measures punishment, the principle is indeed violated and the
sentence is unjustifiable. Yet in principle at least, heavier
punishment based on a record of previous crime might be
justified. Normal sentences may reflect an implicit optimism
about future conduct, for there is good reason for punishing
less severely than culpability would warrant those persons
who are first offenders and others who have not yet shown
themselves to be dedicated to crime. It is a matter of giving
them the benefit of the doubt so long as there is a reasonable
doubt about their intentions. But when the record dispels
any grounds for optimism there no longer is good reason to
mitigate the sentence, and a sentence without dispensation is
imposed based on untempered considerations of culpability.
Such a record may include not only past crime but active
criminal association that marks a man's life as a life of crime.
Reference to a record of crime or active criminal association
might be for the proper purpose of preventing a mitigation
of sentence that otherwise would be right; or it might be for
the improper purpose of imposing a heavier sentence than
the crime deserves. We can only know whether or not the
proper purpose is being served after we have first decided
what sentence the crime deserves, and after we then decide
what sentence is necessary to prevent the perpetrator from
getting away with his crime in view of any other mitigating
considerations that might be available to him.

V. PUNISHMENT AND LIABILITY

DISTINGUISHING AND RELATING THE CONCEPTS

At many points throughout our discussion the terms *criminal liability* and *punishment* have been used interchangeably in a way that might well make a careful reader uneasy. Punishment is generally understood to be the intentional infliction of suffering for wrongdoing, but that seems a very misleading conception of criminal liability as we know it in a modern system of criminal justice. Certainly it would be ludicrous to describe in this way the main features of a modern correctional regime, for intentional infliction of suffering is generally considered a barbarism and is hardly to be found at all, even euphemistically, in the standard curriculum of modern penology. Moreover, once sentence is passed, scant attention is given to the crime for which liability has been imposed and no effort is made to connect the unpleasant aspects of life in prison with the crime that brought it about. Yet, even though criminal liability is now meant to be beneficent as well as beneficial, its imposition is still meant to be a condemnation of what was done, and punishment is precisely the instrument of such condemnation. Even avoidance of the term *punishment* in the vocabulary of modern penology is only to soften traditional attitudes and stress brighter opportunities, but without any conviction that the essential nature of criminal liability is now different. But more than correct names and accurate characterizations are at issue. It is necessary to reconcile punishment with enlightened correctional programs so that criminal liability can remain true to the aim of upholding the law while at the same time remaining true to the progressive ideals of correctional reform that reflect the civilized values of our society. This calls first for an examination of the very idea of criminal punishment, especially in its relation to the ideas of liability and of treatment.

What plagues us is a conceptual difficulty that makes punishment of those who commit crimes seem at odds with humane regard for them. The difficulty is rooted in a view that equates punishment with punitive treatment, or at least regards as nonsense a notion of punishment that does not entail punitive treatment. Since punitive treatment does imply intentional infliction of suffering, it is difficult to reconcile this view with measures that aim at the alleviation and elimination of suffering for those we punish.

But criminal liability, which *is* liability to punishment, need not involve punitive treatment, and in fact enlightened modern penology aims to treat people liable to criminal punishment in nonpunitive ways so long as they cooperate to make that possible. Programs of therapy, education, recreational activity, and vocational training are not punitive treatment when carried on for the benefit (and even the enjoyment) of prisoners, any more than when they are carried on for citizens whose liberty is unrestricted. But neither is it the case that prisoners are no longer subject to punishment while they are in these programs. It is not the case that their day consists of punishment when they are locked in their cells but not when they are sitting in a history class. Punishment is a mode of legal liability, not a mode of treatment. This logical point is captured in the observation that convicted persons are sent to prison *as* punishment, not *for* punishment. Common confusion springs from an ambiguity in the term *punishment,* and it can be avoided by using the term *punitive treatment* to refer to such things as life in a traditional prison cell, while reserving *punishment* to refer to what criminal liability inevitably entails regardless of the sort of treatment given to those who are liable.

Distinguishing *punishment* and *punitive treatment* is only the first of two steps in clarifying the idea of criminal punishment. *Criminal liability* and *punishment* still need to be distinguished. The two terms may be used interchangeably in many characteristic contexts, but when we speak of *punishment* rather than *criminal liability* we direct attention to the feature of criminal liability that makes it the kind of legal liability it is. A helpful analogy is found in civil liability, with its corresponding notion of a remedy. Civil liability that does not provide a remedy is civil liability in name only. The purpose for which civil liability exists cannot be served if remedies are not provided for injuries suffered or threatened. Similarly, without punishment there cannot be the kind of condemnation necessary to uphold the law when it is broken; and so without punishment the purpose for which criminal liability exists cannot be served.

We might imagine a system of criminal justice in which obligatory benefits are conferred upon those who break the law for the first time, since it is found that there is less likelihood of repeated criminal activity if those who break the law are in the first instance made to feel grateful and indebted to society, instead of being made to pay what seems a debt of suffering that fills them with resentment. Though encouragement to crime would surely be a problem, there is in fact good reason to believe that such a system would be an improvement over the one we now have in forestalling a life of crime for many who are convicted. But liability to such mandatory benefits that ordinarily we regard as a reward would not be liability to punishment. It would in fact be a clear alternative to punishment whose very purpose is to avoid the undesirable consequences that attend punishment. And because this alternative does not serve to vindicate and uphold the law as punishment does, liability to it cannot be criminal liability except in name.

Less fanciful forms of legal liability are similarly not punishment, even though the liability is imposed because of the

commission of a crime. Consider the case of an alien who is
deported as a result of his conviction, or of a lawyer who is
disbarred. The alien is not punished twice, once by his sentence, and again by deportation; nor is the lawyer given a
double portion of punishment, the first consisting of the loss
of his profession and the second the loss of his freedom, even
though others receive only a prison sentence for the same
crime. These measures are not punishment and serve purposes other than those of the criminal law—ridding the country of people who are thought undesirable and do not have a
citizen's right to remain, or protecting the community from
legal practitioners who have put in doubt their suitability
for the trust that must be reposed in them. But there is lack
of reprobation in these measures, and they do not represent
condemnation of the crime that has been committed. If in-
competence were the grounds of disbarment, or disease the
grounds of deportation, no one would think that these acts
of the state were acts of condemnation, and neither is there
reason to think so when the grounds are criminal conviction.
For this reason these measures are not punishment.

Conversely, a measure *is* punishment so long as it is reprobation for wrongdoing to serve the purpose of criminal liability, even though some other purpose also is served by it. In
times past, convicts worked mines and rowed galleys, and in
more recent times colonial powers found in the prison population a source of cheap or even free labor to sustain agri-
cultural and other economic enterprises that otherwise could
not exist. In modern times convict road gangs in the United
States have provided a work force which state highway
budgets would otherwise have found a considerable burden.
Even military service has at times been used as a form of
penal servitude. In all these cases it is clear that the forced
service is criminal punishment. What reasons there are for
the choice of a particular regime of treatment for those who
are being punished as criminals is immaterial to the question

of whether their treatment really is punishment. If, however, those found guilty of crime simply become liable under the law to benefit the public good or to be benefited by it and are required to leave the country, join labor battalions, do military service, or undergo a course of therapy, but without reprobation for the crime they have committed, then punishment has been abandoned. Their liability then is *because of* what they have done, and not *for* it.

NONPUNITIVE TREATMENT

Modern criminal punishment is in essence a change of status. It is marked by a loss of autonomy so great that, as wards of the state, convicted criminals are their own masters even less than children and incompetents. The change of status is worked when liability is imposed, and the form that the liability takes is not of the essence of punishment. The treatment that those being punished receive is not the means of punishing them, but is only the way in which their punishment is carried on. Though their suffering will be greater or less depending upon how they are treated, their punishment is the same. Ways of treating those who are being punished are therefore not to be judged good or bad according to whether they are suitably punitive, nor even more generally according to whether they further the aims of punishment. Those aims are sufficiently served by subjection to punishment itself and need no enhancement by punitive treatment.

It is, however, a constant source of concern among the law-abiding that prisoners may be treated too well. Some legislators and many in the community at large admonish that our prisons not be made into country clubs. Behind a reluctance to spend money for better facilities there are often reservations about pampering prisoners and providing them with experiences they may happily endure. The same attitude prompts complaints that it is unfair to treat criminals so well while their victims continue to suffer, or while unfortunates in the community who have remained law-abiding are objects of lesser governmental solicitude.

There are genuinely difficult questions about how much money in a government budget ought to be allocated for improvements in the correctional system while other social needs remain unsatisfied, and about what programs and amenities ought to be provided even if money were no object. The problems are usually presented in an enlightened way and made to appear no different than the problems that must be faced when education or medical care budgets are the issue, and everyone is in agreement that so long as the public treasury can afford it, the more spent, the better. Beneath the surface, however, there is often a will to penury aimed at maintaining a high enough level of misery among the prison population on the twin assumptions that only if the penal experience is on the whole punitive will justice be done, and, even more important, that only then will prison strike terror in the hearts of those who contemplate crime.

It may be that justice is done only when those who do wrong are made miserable. When the motive is not vengeance but simple recompense for evil this view of punishment enjoys great popularity even among moral theorists. But even if there is great moral merit in punitive treatment as recompense for evil, the state has no business administering punishment for that reason. We should remind ourselves again that while the state is bound to act in morally right ways, it has no warrant to do whatever can be shown to be in general morally right. The state is very powerful and very dangerous, and for that reason it must be kept on a very short leash. The state is obligated to maintain a social order in which persons and property are secure, and while it must act justly in doing its job, it is not free to carry on a crusade of retribution simply for the sake of doing justice. For this reason, even if deliberate repayment of evil with evil is morally justifiable in the context of moral concerns generally, it is wrong as a political excess if practiced by the state.

Dereliction of a moral duty, however, is not the most common complaint against abandonment of punitive treatment. It is widely thought that if comforts and amenities are allowed to prisoners, the deterrent effect of punishment will be weakened or lost altogether. Many in the community who are likely to commit serious crimes live without these amenities, and it is thought that a prison concerned mainly to keep its inmates happy would make crime seem even more worthy of serious consideration.

These fears are evoked only when it is imagined how the prospect of a more comfortable prison experience will seem to those downtrodden members of the community who are not law-abiding. For those members of the community whose circumstances are equally miserable but who nevertheless are law-abiding, the shame and degradation associated with going to prison is normally very powerful, and this preserves prison as a dreadful prospect. One reason for this may be that respectability among the law-abiding poor is destroyed, not simply marred, by a prison sentence. Another reason may be that temptation to crime is much stronger because noncriminal opportunities are scarcer, and those who do not abide the strong inhibitions that are developed among the poor to thwart temptation are condemned with special force by those among them who remain law-abiding.

For those who live their lives in great hardship but without allegiance to the law it is a different matter. Though they are not indifferent to restraint on their freedom, it is likely that punishment would have a different meaning for them if a prison sentence were no more disagreeable than a term of service in the army. Since they regard themselves as living outside the law, they do not suffer the stigma of punishment for breaking it, and some among them would think the loss of freedom in prison well compensated by a life easier and more pleasant than any they have ever before known. If, therefore, punishment existed to deter those who would commit crimes by confronting them with a thoroughly distasteful prospect as the wages of crime, the argument against nonpunitive treatment and for punitive treatment instead would have much to recommend it. But since deterrence through intimidation does not serve as a general aim of punishment, elimination of the punitive elements that intimidate need give us no cause for concern.

Admittedly, at some point the consequences of getting caught might become so attractive that some among the downtrodden who live a life of crime will prefer inside to outside. History furnishes examples of such a preference, and even so recently as a century ago prison was preferred to the workhouse, and the workhouse to starvation on one's own. But nowhere today do even the most comfortable correctional institutions attract those who live as free men. Doubts on this point are easily dispelled by consulting those who have been living in conditions of great deprivation, but as free men, and who now face imminent introduction into such a correctional program.

An enlightened penal policy that is not based on punitive treatment does no harm to law and order. But more than that, the consequences of punitive treatment argue strongly against punishment in that form. It is universally recognized that prisons are breeding places for crime, and that of those committed to prison many more are hardened than are softened by their experience. Loss of self-respect, alienation, and despair all conspire to make only criminal opportunities seem both attractive and possible for the future. Punitive treatment is bound to have this effect on many among the marginal portion of the population who have run afoul of the law but who might either be redeemed as law-abiding or confirmed as criminal, for punitive treatment adds gratuitous psychological insult to the necessary social injury of punishment itself. Nonpunitive treatment, on the other hand, if intelligently conceived and administered, will at least allow self-esteem to survive and will preserve healthy ambition and realistic expectations of a good life for those among the marginal portion of the population who have been found guilty of a crime.

THE DANGERS OF BENEVOLENT TREATMENT

Benevolence too has its dangers, and never are they greater than when the benevolence is enforceable. Treatment as part of criminal punishment is under the authority of the state, and the power to determine what treatment there shall be and on what terms it shall be given remains always with the state. There is constant temptation to abuse the power by illicitly using the person treated as a means to some good end. Not infrequently the one supposed to be benefited is the prisoner himself when he is offered some treatment aimed at his improvement and is induced to undergo it by an assurance that in his improved condition he will be more eligible for early release. At other times the intended beneficiary may be all mankind. Medical and other experiments are performed using those prisoners whose cooperation can be obtained by bland promises of more favorable consideration of applications for early release; or even worse, by devious threats of unsympathetic consideration leading to prolonged incarceration for refusal to cooperate. Restraints upon benevolent treatment are always necessary when those who treat have an advantage over those who are treated, and this becomes an urgent matter when those who are treated have been put at a serious disadvantage by a massive incursion upon their autonomy. Three points must guide us in devising restraints upon benevolent treatment.

In the first place, it is wrong to treat persons subject to criminal punishment as means merely to some end if it would be wrong to treat citizens who are free of criminal liability in that way. As a person, someone who has committed a crime is entitled to the same respect for his person as anyone else. The most disturbing departures from this mandate are found in medical or quasi-medical procedures in correctional institutions undertaken with such poor expectations of success that pursuit of these procedures among the population at large would be unthinkable. Though diagnosis is too uncertain or therapy too dangerous to be countenanced under normal standards of proper medical practice, prisoners are nevertheless considered fair game for experimental procedures aimed at changing them. A gloss is put upon what is plainly unethical and even inhumane.

In various ways it is suggested that desperate cases require desperate measures, and that a principle which measures the justifiable risk by the urgency of the need for a remedy allows what otherwise would be questionable procedures. The dangerous-man fallacy encourages this, for it is assumed that crimes regarded with revulsion and fear by normal men must have been committed by persons who are abnormal, dangerous, and much in need of corrective treatment. One method of treatment is inducing or increasing feelings of aversion so that violence will be shunned in the future. Another method is debilitation so that further harmful acts become unlikely if not altogether impossible. Standards of personal dignity and humane regard that are respected generally in our society do not allow such procedures, though behind prison walls these standards, like many others, are easily disregarded.

The second point has already been touched on earlier at several places in our discussion. Benevolence has throughout history had no more ardent advocates than those who wish to work the moral correction of others. It is universally assumed that those convicted of crime need moral correction, though many think that this is not enough. There can hardly be a more hospitable place than prison for the practice of unwanted benevolence, and nowhere are there more inviting opportunities for some to impose on others their notions of how men ought to live. It is surely important that the state provide facilities in prison for education and opportunities for cultivation of good moral character through healthy personal relations. But the state has no business doing more than that inside prison or outside. We are reminded of the dangers by recalling the acts of wanton cruelty that are regularly performed throughout history in the name of benevolent moral correction by those who enjoy absolute power over others.

There is a third point that touches both the first and the second. It is commonly assumed that a person who commits a crime most likely has something wrong with him, and that what is wrong explains why he committed the crime. The myth is venerable, yet no less hearty now than in earlier times. Of course many who commit crimes do have abnormalities to which their socially unacceptable behavior is attributable. But many others do not. It cannot be inferred from a breaking of the law that the lawbreaker has something wrong with him, for criminal laws are formulated to prohibit what is harmful and not to test for socially defective persons. Nor can it be said even of the person who has no respect for the law and violates it that he is abnormal and so has something wrong with him. True, there is something *about* him that ought to change—namely, his attitude toward the law and the social allegiance that that implies, but such things are not changed by any course of treatment. Since it is incorrect to assume that almost certainly something must be wrong with anyone who commits a crime, it is wrong to subject everyone who commits a crime to a regime of treatment directed to curing a presumed abnormality. Only when it is established on independent grounds that there is some abnormality may treatment be administered. Indeed it then becomes mandatory to provide whatever treatment is proper to those for whom the state has assumed the responsibilities of a custodian.

Finally, when all we should not do is clear, we must turn to the even more urgent questions of what we should do. There is, after all, a great void to fill which consists of months and years in the lives of our fellow human beings. The punitive tradition would have us keep the inmates of our prisons constantly deprived to a point just short of inhumanity, so that the life of the prisoner becomes a routine of minimum subsistence for mind and body in which the meanness of what is provided figures more prominently than the satisfactions it affords. Once we recognize that treatment is not for the sake of punishment we must take up the challenge of providing a nonpunitive life for those who are being punished. It is an awesome responsibility, for since the disappearance of slavery nowhere in human society is there such complete control by some over others. In meeting that challenge we cannot easily forget the observation that a civilization is judged by the way it treats its criminals. Many other things have been offered as the touchstone of civilization for the awesome judgment of history, but none tests more searchingly the moral development that civilization itself represents.

Notes

Since nothing appearing in the notes is required to follow the argument in the text, readers may wish to consult the notes only after completing each section of the text.

CHAPTER ONE
Conceiving Criminal Justice

Pages 7–9. The purpose of rules established by the criminal law. Rules of the first kind are to a great extent similar in every developed society, though rules of the other two sorts tend to be quite different from one society to another. Rules of the first group (but not of the second and third) make society possible at all by reducing to an acceptable level the *danger* of serious harm and preserving an environment that is safe enough for life to be lived in society. This environmental aim is of paramount importance as a reason for having a body of criminal law in the first place, and certainly in serving this purpose the criminal law meets with greater success than it does when it seeks to prevent isolated acts of violence and theft.

Pages 11–12. Punishment is needless in cases admitting of excuse or justification. The argument here is a moral argument against the needless infliction of suffering; it is developed more generally in Chapter Nine. One might refer to H. L. A. Hart's discussion of this question in "Legal Responsibility and Excuses," which appears at pages 40–44 in *Punishment and Responsibility;* and in "Prolegomenon to the Principles of Punishment," in the same volume at pages 18–20. In the first of these, the utilitarian views of Bentham and Glanville Williams are criticized because they ignore the injustice and unfairness of punishing those who have excuses; and because they assume that such a draconian regime would be useless in failing to deter, when in fact it might be that the unavailability of excuses in the law might discourage those who otherwise would commit crimes with the hope of escaping punishment by successfully presenting a fraudulent claim of excuse, should they be caught. This latter point of criticism by Hart seems to rest on certain assumptions about deterrence that are shared by those whom Hart criticizes but are rejected here in Chapter Nine. Another notable discussion on this general point of deterrence and excuse is found in Michael and Wechsler, "A Rationale of the Law of Homicide I," 37 *Columbia Law Review* 701 (1937).

Pages 13–14. Crimes that are basic moral wrongs. Though it is the social consensus about rights that makes the wrong a moral wrong, it is the recognition of their harmfulness that makes such crimes basic wrongs. A social consensus differs from a political consensus in that it places the burden upon dissenters to show that conduct of a certain kind (e.g., one of the common crimes) is not really wrong. But mere social consensus is not enough to estalish a wrong as a common crime. That designation depends upon the general recognition of clear, immediate, and serious harm residing in what is done, and not simply upon the existence of a general, even universal, condemnatory attitude toward it.

Page 19. The moral imperative to punish crime. The best known expression of this view is to be found in Kant's *Rechtslehre,* Part II.

Pages 19–20. A moral obligation to punish crime. Such a view, in which men give up their right to enforce natural laws in a state of nature, is found in Locke's *Second Treatise,* Book II.

Pages 22–23. The moralistic conception of mens rea. The misconception about *mens rea* is entertained by many who do not take a moralistic view of the criminal, as well as by those who do hold such views. It is no surprise to find in Book IV of Blackstone's *Commentaries* the statement that the "overt act" is necessary "to demonstrate the depravity of the will"; or that ". . . to constitute a crime against human laws, there must be, first, a vitious will." But the mistaken moralistic premise is perpetuated by so eminent a critic of moralism in the criminal law as Barbara Wootton. In Chapter 2 of *Crime and the Criminal Law,* in arguing against *mens rea* as a requirement for criminal liability, she writes, "No guilty intention, no crime, is the rule. Obviously this makes sense if the law's concern is with wickedness: where there is no guilty intention, there can be no wickedness."

Pages 27–28. The social commitment to Good Samaritan laws. In societies in which private interests and privacy itself are less highly valued, and in which cooperation and reliance on one another are deemed more important, there is a greater commitment to duties of rescue. Such commitment exists in many advanced societies with socialist ideals as well as in many primitive societies. It seems reasonable to say even for those societies, however, that what we would regard as Good Samaritan laws normally impose an obligation only to do what in those societies is deemed one's business as a member of society. People are deemed to be each other's keepers under prevailing social views; they are not made to act as keepers in spite of prevailing social views simply because it is the morally superior course.

Page 29. Attention to the accused's moral standing. A recent account of the workings of the American plea-bargaining system makes clear how much attention is paid to these matters in practice. See Rosett and Cressey, *Justice by Consent* (1976).

Pages 29–30. Objection to imposing liability according to a person's moral worth. At earlier periods in history the authority of the state was not purely political, and its responsibilities included enforcement of many religious precepts that were (and are) intensely person-regarding, as well as the paternalistic enforcement of prevailing moral views in a secular context in which the sovereign (or its collective surrogate) acted as head of a national family whose members were thought in need of chastisement when they showed themselves to be bad. Though these roles are no longer professed, such ideas do survive and still show themselves anomalously from time to time.

Page 39. Indeterminate sentences. An illuminating source of information about indeterminate sentences is the background paper by Alan M. Dershowitz that appears at pages 69–142 in *Fair and Certain Punishment* (Report of the Twentieth Century Fund, McGraw-Hill, 1976).

Pages 43–44. Statistically determined group of criminally dangerous people. Without statistical refinements such a program might be equally effective, though even more offensive to libertarian values. The suggestion (not endorsed by its author) that all Black males in New York City between 18 and 29 be subject to special rules for search by the police is engagingly discussed by Andrew Hacker in a piece titled "Getting Used to Mugging," which appeared in *The New York Review* in April 1973.

Page 44. Behavioral control. An unusually vivid, though selective, account of correctional practices and ambitions in this line appears in

Jessica Mitford's book, *Kind and Usual Punishment* (1973), particularly in Chapter 8.

CHAPTER TWO
Conceiving Criminal Conduct: Acts

Page 49. The orthodox view of conduct. The law has no special claim on the notion of acts as bodily movements, and in the literature of theory of action one finds philosophers regularly occupied with bodily movements in speaking about what one would suppose were acts. In legal material one finds in statutory definitions no less than in theoretical explanations a universal reliance on the physical model to make sense of the idea of an act. One may convince oneself of this by consulting any penal code or any standard work of criminal law theory.

Page 50. Liability for arson in New York. The first case is arson in the third degree under New York law (N.Y. Penal Law [1967] sec. 150.05); the second, arson in the second degree (N.Y. Penal Law sec. 150.10) or in the first degree (N.Y. Penal Law sec. 150.15).

Page 50. Eliot quotation. From *The Hollow Men* (1925).

Pages 53–54 Bodily movements and criminal acts by corporations. The notion dies hard, and *in extremis* it gropes for metaphors, as we are reminded by Lord Denning's opinion in *H. L. Bolton (Engineering) Co. Ltd. v. P. J. Graham Sons, Ltd.,* [1957] 1 Q.B. 159 at 172; [1956] 3 All E.R. 624.

> A company may in many ways be likened to a human body. It has a brain and nerve centre which controls what it does. It also has hands which hold the tools and act in accordance with directions from the centre. Some of the people in the company are mere servants and agents who are nothing more than hands to do the work and cannot be said to represent the mind or will. Others are directors and managers who represent the directing mind and will of the company, and control what it does. The state of mind of these managers is the state of mind of the company and is treated by the law as such.

It seems extraordinary (and, if true, a great stroke of good fortune for the orthodox) that all those entities to which responsibility may be ascribed under the law should turn out to have a human psychophysical design.

No less marvelous is a judicial power of the opposite sort by which a corporation is transformed into some ordinary flesh-and-blood person whose criminal acts are then the criminal acts of the corporation. Lord Reid performed this feat in *Tesco Supermarkets, Ltd. v. Nattrass*, [1972] A.C. 153 at 170; [1971] 2 All E.R. 127 at 131–32.

> A living person has a mind which can have knowledge or in-tention or be negligent and he has hands to carry out his intentions. A corporation has none of these: it must act through living persons, though not always one and the same person. Then the person who acts is not speaking or acting for the company. He is acting as the company, and his mind which directs his acts is the mind of the company. There is no ques-tion of the company being vicariously liable. He is not acting as a servant, representative, agent or delegate. He is an em-bodiment of the company, or, one could say, he hears and speaks through the *persona* of the company, within his appro-priate sphere, and his mind is the mind of the company. If it is a guilty mind then that guilt is the guilt of the company.

Page 55. Spastic movement not part of an act. It should be noted that under orthodox theory as well, this kind of movement would not be regarded as part of an act, since the movement is not—in orthodox terminology—*voluntary*. But the central importance of bodily move-ments in the orthodox conception is unaffected by this requirement, as one may see in the discussion of voluntary and involuntary acts in sec-tion 3 of this chapter.

Pages 62–63. The notion of a negative act. This appears in *Perkins on Criminal Law* (2nd ed., 1969) at page 591.

Pages 65–66. Orthodox ways of dealing with difficulties presented by crimes of possession. Even the Model Penal Code has not freed itself of the lingering need to have as the gist of possession an independent act of acquiring or of retaining (though the latter requirement is more ambiguous than the former). See Proposed Official Draft, sec. 2.01(4).

Page 72. Committing murder against one's will. In the philosophical literature much is made of difficulties in the idea of acting willingly against one's will. But sometimes we *are* at war with ourselves and finally choose quite freely to do something which we are (and remain) dead set against doing. If this fact about people makes some favorite notions seem incoherent, so much the worse for the notions.

CHAPTER THREE
Conceiving Criminal Conduct:
Culpability, Intention, and Motive

Pages 83–88. Culpability in the first dimension. One of the most controversial homicide cases to come before English courts in recent times serves to test the analysis presented here. *In D.P.P. v. Smith*, [1960] 3 W.L.R. 546, the defendant was driving a car with sacks of stolen scaffolding clips in the back. Noticing the sacks, a police constable ordered the defendant to stop. Instead, he accelerated his car, and when the constable clung to the side of the car the defendant drove in a zigzag course in an evident attempt to shake off the policeman. He was successful in this, and the policeman was killed when run over by a vehicle coming from the opposite direction. The House of Lords ultimately upheld a murder conviction after this had been overturned by the Court of Criminal Appeal. That court had held that there was error in the trial judge's failure in his direction to the jury to draw a distinction between harm that was *certain* to result and harm that was *likely* to result; even more important in their view, he had not directed the jury to consider whether the defendant at the time had actually contemplated the likely results of what he was doing, for without that the mental element necessary for murder would be lacking. The House of Lords saw no warrant here for the distinction between harm "certain" to result and harm "likely" to result. More important, it disagreed that the defendant must actually contemplate the harm in prospect so long as he is capable of doing so and was not mentally abnormal in a way that would provide him with a defense. What the ordinary responsible man would have contemplated as the natural and probable result is all that matters then.

The House of Lords decision is profoundly disturbing because it seems that what the driver did (intentionally) seriously endangered the life of the policeman; but still, if the policeman survived *in view of what the driver did,* we would be unwilling to say that he survived *only by chance.* The driver's conduct was not aimed at killing the policeman, nor did it even put him in imminent danger of death. That would have been the case if, for example, the driver had deliberately run over the policeman or if he had deliberately slammed the side of his car against a wall to get rid of the clinging policeman. One can multiply cases in the imagination. In all of them one must consider *to what degree* life was endangered by what was done intentionally.

In making that judgment, one must consider *what the actor had reason to believe* about the dangers of his conduct. This very important consideration is discussed elsewhere in this book under the heading of *expectability*. In *Smith* there seems to be no difference between what the defendant had reason to believe and what a juryman or anyone else viewing the situation objectively would say there was reason to believe, though from the fragmentary details of evidence in the report one cannot be sure.

It seems likely that Smith was not in some curious position of disadvantage that did not allow him to appreciate fully the dangers in what he was doing. If (because of no fault of his own) he was in such a position of disadvantage, he should have had his disadvantage available as the basis of a defensive claim that would exonerate, viz., that *he* had no reason to expect that the policeman would be or could be killed (almost certainly, or quite likely, or very possibly). If Smith had been terribly confused about what he was doing or about what was going on, that might give him grounds for claiming either that *he* had no reason to believe he was endangering anyone's life to the extent necessary to support the charge, or that those parts of his activity that made it dangerous to that degree were unintentional—either sort of claim having great exculpatory power.

What the defendant actually contemplated or foresaw or intended at the time is obscure and ultimately irrelevant to the question of his liability. What the ordinary reasonable man must have contemplated as the natural and probable consequences may be plain enough but it will not alone suffice, since it tells only what there was reason to expect ordinarily, not what the defendant in his (special) circumstances had reason to expect. It is true that under this analysis a person in Smith's position might try to get rid of the policeman by crushing him against a wall and yet not appreciate what a ghastly thing he does: he might be thinking only of freeing himself of his hindrance. But such a failure of appreciation would not help and would still leave his homicidal conduct culpable in a very high degree.

The great theoretical interest of *Smith* as well as its appeal to conscience has resulted in a considerable literature that includes as one of its most unusual items a lecture by a distinguished judge, Lord Denning, who considered the case in the House of Lords. ("Responsibility Before the Law," Lionel Cohen lecture, January 1961, at the Hebrew University of Jerusalem; published by The Hebrew University Press, 1961.) The criticism of the decision, which he summarizes in the lecture, and his answers to his critics are both illuminating.

The decision in *Smith* is thought to have been overruled by section 8 of the Criminal Justice Act 1967, according to a majority of those giving opinions in an interesting case that more recently came before the House of Lords and that raised similar questions—*Hyam v. D.P.P.*, [1974] 2 W.L.R. 607. The Act is taken to establish a "subjective" standard requiring more attention to the actual mental state of the accused at the time.

Page 91. "Subjective" and "objective" theories of intention. The classic statement of the objective theory is that of Oliver Wendell Holmes in Lecture II of *The Common Law*. Holmes presents a very insightful theory of criminal liability, stressing dangerous conduct and making the required culpability depend largely on the dangerous tendencies of acts. But because Holmes operated with the usual mentalistic assumptions, he (needlessly) rejected certain claims of exculpation in spite of their moral force because in his view their toleration would place too great a burden on the law in requiring it to deal with obscure matters of the mind as it labored to satisfy social needs. Much light is cast on Holmes's "objective" theory by H. L. A. Hart in a note appearing in *Punishment and Responsibility* at pages 242–44.

Page 93. Self-deception. Though it does not matter that one deceives himself into or out of believing he is committing a crime, self-deception *does* matter when one claims one's mistake about some matter of fact as an excuse and the mistake turns out not to be an honest one because of self-deception. This is discussed in Chapter Seven, section 1.

Page 93. Causal accompaniment. An illuminating discussion of the required relation between state of mind and conduct is presented by G. Marston in "Contemporaneity of Act and Intention in Crimes," 86 *Law Quarterly Review* 208 (1970), and especially at 211–14 with regard to the matter of causal accompaniment.

Pages 96–98. Having an intention. It is wrong to think of having an intention as a state of mind that presents itself as *thoughts* of what (with a certain commitment) one anticipates doing. As I stand here talking to you this morning, I may intend to go to dinner at my friend's house this evening and to travel to Morocco next summer, though thoughts of doing either never once enter my mind during the entire conversation.

Pages 96–98. Confusion regarding intention. A recent case that well illustrates the hazards for judges (and for the lives of those who are being judged) in undiscriminating use of the "intention" terms, is *Hyam v. D.P.P.*, [1974] 2 W.L.R. 607. It is useful to take the trial judge's direction and the appellate opinions that discuss it and to consider to what extent the controversy about the "necessary intent" for murder is simply terminological, and to what extent it is a controversy about what is necessary for liability for homicide of that degree.

Page 98. The significance of having an intention. Though acting intentionally is not acting in fulfillment of an intention, it is true that having had an intention to do what one subsequently did may serve as evidence that one acted intentionally in doing it. Though in spite of having had the intention one might still have acted unintentionally, the burden of establishing that is obviously a heavier one if there was an intention whose fulfillment the act might be. This is because intentions often are fulfilled by acts designed and performed to fulfill them, in which case the actor must exercise the sort of control that means that he is acting intentionally.

Pages 99–100. Wicker excerpt. From the *New York Times*, January 22, 1970, p. 36, col. 8.

Page 102. The doctrine of transferred intent. The doctrine in its conventional form is illuminatingly presented by Glanville Williams in his *Criminal Law: The General Part* (2nd ed., 1961), secs. 44–49.

Page 104. Agnew statement. The statement was made by Mr. Agnew on October 29, 1972, in the TV program "Issues and Answers," and was reported in the October 30, 1972, issue of the *New York Times* (p. 22). As reported there, Mr. Agnew's remarks began, "I still don't see a connection between the President of the United States and the Watergate case."

Pages 107–8. The orthodox conception of motives. In the legal literature, ready examples are to be found in Glanville Williams *Criminal*

Law: The General Part (2nd ed., 1961), sec. 21; *Perkins on Criminal Law* (2nd ed., 1969), 828–33.

Page 108. Austin's description of motives. John Austin, *The Province of Jurisprudence Determined* (1832), Lecture IV.

Page 112. New York kidnapping law. The provisions for kidnapping in the first degree are found in N.Y. Penal Law (1967), sec. 135.25.

Page 113. Affirmative defense to a charge of unlawful imprisonment. N.Y. Penal Law (1967), sec. 135.15.

CHAPTER FOUR
Conceiving Criminal Conduct:
Harm and Attempts

Pages 119–20. Offenses to sensibility. There is a constant danger (suggested by some of the examples in the text) that having laws on the books to protect sensibilities will encourage the growth of laws that suppress some activity simply because it is inimical to prevailing tastes and moral ideas. In any political community there are some who will act as leaders in the cause of sensibility, and many others who will happily endorse prohibitions that accord with their own sensibilities, quite heedless of the rights of those who do not share them or who cannot afford them. In spite of these dangers, there must be laws to protect against those offenses to sensibility which are profound in their consequences, and which if allowed to occur freely would make whole stretches of the social environment uncongenial, even unusable, and a harrowing experience for those who choose (or are forced) to brave such an environment.

Page 132. Attempt liability to apprehend dangerous persons. This view is presented, for example, in Glanville Williams, *Criminal Law: The General Part* (2nd ed., 1961), sec. 207; and in the Model Penal Code comment on sec. 5.01 (in Tentative Draft No. 10 at pages 26–39).

Pages 142–43. Ambiguity surrounding "responsibility." This ambiguity is discussed with much illumination by H. L. A. Hart in *Punishment and Responsibility*, pages 211–30.

CHAPTER FIVE
Exculpatory Claims

Page 146. Liability for narcotics addiction. This case is *Robinson v. California*, 370 U.S. 660 (1962). The California statute provided that "No person shall use, or be under the influence of, or be addicted to the use of narcotics . . ." except when administered by or through a duly licensed person. The U.S. Supreme Court found this to be constitutionally objectionable under the Eighth and Fourteenth Amendments as cruel and unusual punishment, since it made the "status" of narcotic addiction a criminal offense in which "a person can be continuously guilty . . . whether or not he has ever used or possessed any narcotics within the State, and whether or not he has been guilty of any antisocial behavior there."

Page 146. Liability for being intoxicated in a public place. The case is *Powell v. Texas*, 392 U.S. 514 (1968). The Texas statute provided that "Whoever shall get drunk or be found in a state of intoxication in a public place, or at any private house except his own, shall be fined not exceeding one hundred dollars." In distinguishing this case from *Robinson,* the U.S. Supreme Court stressed that conviction here was not for being a chronic alcoholic but for being in a public place while drunk on a particular occasion. Merely being in a place (as we know from discussions in Chapter Two) *can* be conduct.

Pages 150–51. Infancy. At an earlier stage in its development, the common law postponed punishment of children who committed crimes even though they were of an age when they were presumed to have discretion, arguably on the theory that punishment at a tender age would be inhumane and the requirements of justice could be satisfied later. Indeed, there is no reason to assume that considerations of humanity and of justice both point to the same moment in personal development as the right one to separate those who are legally under-age from those who are not. There are, nevertheless, good reasons for not punishing a person only later on when he is older for what he has done earlier, since in the meantime he suffers the malignant effects of the fate that hangs over him, and is later made to endure his punishment after a lapse of time that may make his acceptance of it difficult or impossible.

The age of discretion was itself not so firm a barrier in earlier times, and the notion of a "mischievous discretion" that makes up for want of age found its way into the law in the form of the maxim *malitia supplet aetatem*. Contemporary concern about particularly vicious juvenile crimes often reflects such an idea.

Page 158. Impossibility of compliance. One is reminded by the notorious English case of *Larsonneur* that courts may disregard even the plainest principles of exculpation, and so work stark injustice. The alien in that case was unable to comply with the law (which made mere presence without permission an offense), but was nevertheless found guilty. 24 Cr. App. Reg. 74 (1933).

Page 160. "The thought of man is not triable. . . ." The author of this oft-quoted line is the medieval judge Chief Justice Brian of the Common Pleas. Y.B. 17 Ed. IV, page 2.

Pages 163–64. A claim that no such law exists. In operating the complex machinery of modern bureaucratic government, much depends upon success in effectively communicating changes in the law to all those who must keep current, and on occasion a failure of communication can result in prosecution's being undertaken for violation of a law that had been repealed; or for violation of what is only a prospective law that is pending as a bill not yet enacted, or not yet signed into law, or according to its terms not yet effective even though all formal requirements have been satisfied. Interesting examples of jurisdictional uncertainty are sometimes provided when jurisdiction rests on treaty between sovereign states or upon a constitutional allocation of jurisdictional powers within a federal system. American lawyers are familiar with problems of uncertain legislative jurisdiction in a federal system; and in Britain there are emerging uncertainties about both legislative and judicial jurisdiction as a result of Britain's membership in the European Community, since Community law might supercede and in effect nullify Acts of Parliament or other law in Britain, and might even curtail the jurisdictional powers of British courts.

Page 166. Renunciation defense in the Model Penal Code. The comment appears in Tentative Draft No. 10 at pages 69–74.

Page 173. Responsibility of military superiors. The principle of command responsibility is discussed in Chapter Eight as a principle of strict liability, and the case of General Yamashita provides a most striking instance of its effect.

Pages 174–75. Provocation. A provision reflecting these considerations appears in the Model Penal Code, Proposed Official Draft sec. 210.3(1)(b). Illuminating comment is provided in Tentative Draft No. 9 at pages 46–48.

Pages 178–84. Model Penal Code justifications for the use of force. The Model Penal Code provisions in the Proposed Official Draft are sec. 3.04 (self-protection); sec. 3.05 (protection of others); sec. 3.06 (protection of property); sec. 3.07 (law enforcement); sec. 3.08 (special responsibilities). Discussions are in Tentative Draft No. 8.

Page 184. The use of force in the execution of a public duty. The Model Penal Code provision in the Proposed Official Draft is sec. 3.03, and discussion of it is found in Tentative Draft No. 8.

Page 185. Violation of property rights. The Model Penal Code provision is sec. 3.10 of the Proposed Official Draft, and commentary appears in Tentative Draft No. 8.

Page 190. Historical perspective. Oliver Plunket is now generally thought to have been falsely accused by the infamous Titus Oates of conspiring with the French against England. But in the anti-Catholic climate of the times, the primate of Ireland would have remained a criminal danger in the eyes of the English even had he been able to establish his innocence.

CHAPTER SIX
Conduct-Regarding Exculpation

Pages 199–200. Two hypothetical cases discussed by Glanville Williams. The cases and Glanville Williams's conclusion appear in sec. 12 of *Criminal Law: The General Part* (2nd ed., 1961).

Pages 200–201. People v. Jaffe. The rather meager New York Court of Appeals opinion is reported at 185 N.Y. 497, 78 N.E. 169 (1906). The New York statute changing the law is N.Y. Pen. Law, sec. 110.10 (1967). The Model Penal Code rejection of the *Jaffe* rule is in sec. 5.01(1)(a), and commentary on this appears in Tentative Draft No. 10 at pages 30–38. A more recent case, *Haughton v. Smith,* [1974] 2 W.L.R.1., presented precisely the same problem to English courts, and a well articulated decision consistent with *Jaffe* was reached by the Court of Appeal and the House of Lords in overturning a conviction.

Page 202. Statute under which Jaffe was prosecuted. According to the report of the case, it "provides that a person who buys or receives any stolen property knowing the same to have been stolen is guilty of criminally receiving such property."

Page 204. The two umbrella cases. The cases appear in J. C. Smith and B. Hogan, *Criminal Law* (1965), at pages 157–58. Fascination with stealing one's own umbrella has earlier origins, however, and the question is posed by Baron Bramwell in *Regina v. Collins,* [1865] 169 E.R. 1477.

Pages 208–9. Picking an empty pocket. The leading case is *Regina v. Collins,* [1865] 169 E.R. 1477. A useful discussion of this problem is found in Jerome Hall's *General Principles of Criminal Law* (2nd ed., 1960) at pages 587–91, in which the parallels in French law are pointed out.

Page 209. The Lady Eldon cases. The original case appears in Wharton, 1 *Criminal Law* 304 n.9 (12th ed., 1932). The variation appears in Kadish and Paulsen, *Criminal Law and Its Processes* (3rd ed., 1975) at page 365.

Page 213. Dangerous beliefs and attempt liability. The Model Penal Code comment and Professor Glanville Williams both take this view of the basis of attempt liability. See Model Penal Code T.D. No. 10, pages 26–39; Williams, *Criminal Law: The General Part,* sec. 207.

Page 213. "On the job." This vivid description appears in *Rex v. Osborn* 84 J.P. 63 (1920).

Pages 219–20. Death from diluted whiskey. I am indebted to Dr. Nathan Lane for this example.

Page 220. Quotation from Glanville Williams. Criminal Law: The General Part (2nd ed., 1961) page 652.

Pages 242–43. The case of the three men in the desert. This intriguing case appears in Glanville Williams *Criminal Law: The General Part* (2nd ed., 1961) at page 26. My own recollection is of first hearing it discussed in the seminar on excuses given at Harvard by J. L. Austin in 1954–55. George Pitcher confirms this recollection in "Austin: a personal memoir," published by Oxford University Press in the collection entitled *Essays on J. L. Austin* (1973).

Page 243. The argument against liability for murder. The analysis given by Glanville Williams, for example, is apparently of this kind. *Criminal Law: The General Part* (2nd ed., 1961) at page 26.

Pages 248–49. Intervening voluntary acts. This is discussed in Hart and Honoré, *Causation in the Law,* at pages 129–51. The principle is made subject to certain exceptions by the authors, but these exceptions do not appear to cover the case suggested here. Though this voluntary intervention principle is discussed by Hart and Honoré in the context of tort liability, there is no reason why it should not be taken as a limitation on criminal liability as well.

CHAPTER SEVEN
Actor-Regarding Exculpation

Page 265. The case of forcible intercourse. In its essentials, this is the case of *D.P.P. v. Morgan,* [1975] 2 All E.R. 347.

Pages 268–69. Relief when there is ignorance or mistake of law. The Model Penal Code provision that shows the way for such relief is sec. 2.04, and comment on it is found in Tentative Draft No. 4.

Page 286. "Choice of evils" test. Model Penal Code sec. 3.02.

Page 287. Model Penal Code defense of duress. Model Penal Code sec. 2.09. The comment quoted appears in Tentative Draft No. 10 at page 6.

Pages 293–94. Making oneself dangerous through self-induced loss of control. A case of unusual interest here is *A.-G. for Northern Ireland v. Gallagher,* [1963] A.C. 349, in which in an opinion by Lord Denning it was held that deliberate self-intoxication to produce "Dutch courage" would not provide a defense to a charge of murder. This seems sound in principle since (presumably) the defendant was not debilitated to a point at which he could not choose whether or not to kill his wife after he had intoxicated himself to overcome his normal inhibition.

Uninhibited acts are no more excusable than those done only by over-coming feelings of reluctance as one acts. One wants, however, to be sure that there was not extreme intoxication rendering a person incapable of choosing whether or not to kill at a time when there still was opportunity for powers of choice to be effectively exercised by a normal person.

Page 296. The M'Naghten rules. In 1843, Daniel M'Naghten shot and killed the private secretary of Sir Robert Peel, believing his victim to be the Prime Minister himself. M'Naghten evidently suffered from paranoid delusions and thought that his life was in danger as an object of Tory persecution. He was acquitted on grounds of insanity, and in the wake of widespread public concern the House of Lords took the unusual step of asking the judiciary certain specific questions regarding insanity as a defense to a criminal charge. The judges' answers provide the full substance of the M'Naghten rules, though a single passage in the report is generally taken to state the rules in their essential form.

> To establish a defense on the ground of insanity it must be clearly proved that, at the time of committing the act, the party accused was labouring under such a defect of reason, from disease of the mind, as not to know the nature and quality of the act he was doing, or, if he did know it, that he did not know he was doing what was wrong.—*M'Naghten's Case, 10 Clark & Fin. 200 (1843).*

Page 297. M'Naghten and irresistible impulse. This version of the insanity defense is found in almost a third of the states in the United States and is the rule generally recognized in the Federal courts. The Model Penal Code version is found in section 4.01(1), which speaks of a lack of capacity to conform conduct to the requirements of law.

Pages 297–98. The Durham rule. This rule takes its name from a 1954 District of Columbia case. In 1972 in the *Brawner* case the same Federal court that had adopted the rule decided to abandon it in favor of the Model Penal Code version of the insanity defense.

Page 298. Derangement or deficiency, without more, as a defense. The Code of Napoleon of 1810 simply made severe mental disorder (*démence*) at the time of commission of the crime a sufficient condition for exemption from liability, and many Civil Law countries still follow this rule. An excellent account of the history of the insanity defense in English law before M'Naghten is provided by Nigel Walker's *Crime and Insanity in England,* vol. 1 (1968). A most important recent development in the direction of simplified exemption is the *Report of the Committee on Mentally Abnormal Offenders* (the Butler Committee report), which was presented to Parliament in 1975 and which recommends exemption if there is severe mental illness, or severe subnormality, as defined in the Report. (See particularly recommendation 50 and paragraph 18.35.) The Report (in paragraph 18.29) notes that "it is theoretically possible for a person to be suffering from a severe mental disorder which has in a causal sense nothing to do with the act or omission for which he is being tried: but in practice it is very difficult to imagine a case in which one could be sure of the absence of any such connection."

Page 299. Blackstone's explanation. This is found in Chapter 2 of Book IV.

Pages 302–3. Insanity defense made to depend upon deterrability of conduct. See Bentham's *Introduction to the Principles of Morals and Legislation* Chap. XIII; and H. L. A. Hart's comments to be found in his *Punishment and Responsibility* at pages 19–20.

Pages 307–8. The discarded part of M'Naghten. The original statement by the court on this point made a distinction between killing under a delusion of self-defense (justifiable homicide), and killing under a delusion of revenge for some injury suffered (not justifiable homicide). One of the curious features of the case is that, if things were really as M'Naghten thought them to be, that would not furnish him with a good defense under the rule, since apparently he believed himself to be persecuted and generally in danger, but not threatened with imminent death on the occasion and left with no reasonable alternative but to kill someone who was about to kill him.

Pages 308–9. The meaning of "wrong" under the M'Naghten rules. Model Penal Code, sec. 4.01, and comments on this question appearing in T.D. No. 4 at pages 156–92, *passim.* Further interesting discussion on this point is found in Devlin, "Criminal Responsibility and Punishment," [1954] *Criminal Law Review* at pages 680–82; and in N. Morris, " 'Wrong' in the M'Naghten Rules," (1953) 16 *Modern Law Review* 435.

Page 310. Irresistible impulse. Persons handicapped by irresistible impulse may break the law in simple and immediate ways—the momentary act of violence or of shoplifting as one succumbs to an urge on the occasion. But the more elaborate activities required to attain remote criminal objectives are untrue to the psychological facts of irresistible impulse, hence bank robbers and counterfeiters are most unlikely to be victims of such an abnormality.

Page 313. Diminished culpability. The Model Penal Code provision is section 4.02.

CHAPTER EIGHT
Limits of Excuse

Pages 323–27. Varieties of determinism. Solutions proposed for the problems of determinism and free will tend to acquire labels and to be arranged as members and affiliates in contending groups. I have no interest in classifying particular views or in imputing a thesis to anyone who may already find himself (willing or not) classified in some way on this issue. Distinctions among determinist positions are made in the text only to point out some alternative possibilities, but not to attribute views to anyone.

Pages 325–27. The actor must have acted as he did because he could not do otherwise. This point is made by Harry G. Frankfurt in "Alternate Possibilities and Moral Responsibility" in *The Journal of Philosophy,* vol. 66 (1969), and the example here is an adaptation of Frankfurt's illustration.

Page 330. Hart's "Changing Conceptions of Responsibility." These arguments appear in *Punishment and Responsibility* (1968) on pages 206–9.

Page 333. Hart's "Punishment and the Elimination of Responsibility." These arguments appear in *Punishment and Responsibility* (1968) on pages 180–83.

Page 336. Wootton's Crime and the Criminal Law. Lady Wootton's arguments appear in Chapter 2 at pages 40–57.

Page 338. Crime of custodial interference in New York. N.Y. Penal Law, sec. 135.45 (1967). Emphasis in text is added.

Page 345. Case of General Yamashita. Matter of Yamashita, 327 U.S. 1 (1945).

Page 352. Loss made to fall on the guilty party. The opinion of the Court in *United States v. Dotterweich,* 320 U.S. 277 (1943), takes a position of this sort. In this case of innocently mislabeled mail-order pharmaceuticals, Mr. Justice Frankfurter said:

> Hardship there doubtless may be under a statute which thus penalizes the transaction though consciousness of wrongdoing be totally wanting. Balancing relative hardships, Congress has preferred to place it upon those who have at least the opportunity of informing themselves of the existence of conditions imposed for the protection of consumers before sharing in illicit commerce, rather than to throw the hazard on the innocent public who are wholly helpless.

Page 353. Civil liability for blameless but hazardous activity. A fountainhead of law and theory is the English case of *Rylands v. Fletcher,* [1868] L.R. 3 H.L. 330. In the development of this principle of liability, some cases stress the gain to those who create risks, and others emphasize the unusual character of the hazardous activity.

Pages 358–59. Mail-order pharmaceuticals case. This case (somewhat simplified) is *United States v. Dotterweich,* 320 U.S. 277 (1943).

Pages 359–60. Marijuana smoking case. Sweet v. Parsley, [1970] A.C. 132.

Page 360. Registration case. Lambert v. California, 355 U.S. 225 (1957).

Pages 360–61. Inspection sticker case. Kilbridge v. Lake, [1962] N.Z.L.R. 590.

Page 364. Regina v. Prince. [1875] L.R. 2 Crim. Cas. Res. 154.

Pages 366–67. Model Penal Code treatment of intercourse with underage females. The comments are on sec. 207.4, and appear in T.D. No. 4 at page 253.

Page 369. Model Penal Code treatment of felony murder. The relevant provision is sec. 210.2(1)(b). It creates a presumption of the requisite conduct for cases that traditionally would be regarded as clearly warranting a felony murder rule.

Page 369. Case of "knowingly converting" Government property. Morissette v. United States, 342 U.S. 246 (1952).

CHAPTER NINE
Justification of Criminal Punishment

Page 376. Bentham quotation. An Introduction to the Principles of Morals and Legislation, ed. W. Harrison (Oxford, 1948), page 281.

Page 378. Kinds of retributivist theories. Kant must be taken to be the paradigm among theorists who view punishment for crime simply as a good in its own right (though even in Kant's writings there are some passages that seem to be arguments of justification). His well-known view that crime *must* be punished (which makes his version extreme even among good-in-its-own-right theories) is not a view that need be adopted by a retributivist for his theory to deny, in effect, that there is any need for punishment to be justified. It need only take punishment to be morally unblemished and so not at all in need of careful philosophical examination before a clean bill of moral health is forthcoming.

Those retributivist theories that do see some evil in punishment but find in desert a justification for it do not all rely on the same reasons. Some stress the settling of a moral account in which the victim appears as creditor; some attach great importance to matters of fairness in not letting one who breaks the law get away with it when other members of society have exercised self-restraint to keep themselves law-abiding; and not giving the criminal the punishment he deserves is regarded by some as a neglect that deprives him of what he is owed in a moral accounting in which he appears not as a debtor but as a creditor entitled to be made morally whole through punishment for wrongdoing. The last reason, unlike the other two, is a matter of moral concern pure and simple, without any suggestion of a social need lurking in the background. It is therefore not considered in the text as grounds of a justificatory argument, for the same reason that the good-in-its-own-right position is ignored.

Page 382. The Kantian conception of the law. Kant speaks of the penal law as a categorical imperative in the *Rechtslehre,* and a good deal is made to depend on that idea in his theory of punishment.

CHAPTER TEN
Liability, Culpability, and Punishment

Page 444. J. F. Stephen on capital punishment for murder. In his *A History of the Criminal Law of England* (1883), Stephen said,

> Some men, probably, abstain from murder because they fear that if they committed murder they would be hanged. Hundreds of thousands abstain from it because they regard it with horror. One great reason why they regard it with horror is that murderers are hanged.

Page 464. Preference for prison. This, and much else of importance in the background of present concerns, is made clear in J. J. Tobias's excellent study *Crime and Industrial Society in the Nineteenth Century* (1967). On the present point, see pages 240–43 of the Pelican Books edition (1972).

Page 468. "A civilization is judged by the way it treats its criminals." The person to whom this observation is usually attributed is Winston Churchill.

Bibliography

The items in this bibliography are meant to provide a background and to supplement particular discussions in the book. The relevance of each item to the topics in the book is indicated by a list of items according to the item number under chapter and section headings. Many items (especially books) are relevant only in part. No attempt has been made to include all work of importance on any topic, and some items that appear in the Bibliography are included only because they present a point of view that the reader may particularly wish to take account of in connection with present concerns.

1. Acton, H. B., ed. *The Philosophy of Punishment* (1969).
2. Allen, F., "Legal Values and Correctional Values," 18 *U. Toronto L. J.* 119 (1968).
3. ———. *The Borderland of Criminal Justice* (1964).
4. Alschuler, "The Prosecutor's Role in Plea Bargaining," 36 *U. Chi. L. Rev.* 50 (1968).
5. American Friends Service Committee, *Struggle for Justice—A Report on Crime and Punishment in America* (1971).
6. American Law Institute, *Model Penal Code* (1962).
7. Andenaes, J., "Choice of Punishment," *Scandinavian Studies in Law* vol. II (1958).
8. ———. "General Prevention," 43 *Crim. Law, Crim. & Police Sci.* 176 (1952).
9. ———. "The General Preventive Effects of Punishment," 114 *U. Pa. L. Rev.* 949 (1966).
10. ———. "The Morality of Deterrence," 37 *U. Chi. L. Rev.* 649 (1970).
11. Anscombe, G. E. M., *Intention,* 2nd ed. (1963).
12. Arens, Richard and Lasswell, Harold D., "Toward a General Theory of Sanctions," 49 *Iowa L. Rev.* 233 (1964).
13. Aristotle, *Nicomachean Ethics,* Book V.
14. Armstrong, K. G., "The Retributivist Hits Back," *Mind,* vol. 70 (1961). Reprinted in *The Philosophy of Punishment,* ed. H. B. Acton (1969).

15. Arnold, T. W., "Criminal Attempts—The Rise and Fall of an Abstraction," 40 *Yale L. J.* 53 (1930).

16. Arnolds and Garland, "The Defense of Necessity in Criminal Law: The Right to Choose the Lesser Evil," 65 *J. Crim. L. & Crim.* 289 (1974).

17. Ashworth, A. J., "Excusable Mistake of Law," (1974) *Crim. L. Rev.* 652.

18. ———. "Reason, Logic and Criminal Liability," 91 *Law Q. Rev.* 102 (1975).

19. Atkinson, Max, "Interpreting Retributive Claims," *Ethics*, vol. 85 (1974).

20. ———. "Justified and Deserved Punishments," *Mind*, vol. 78 (1969).

21. Austin, John, *The Province of Jurisprudence Determined* (1832), Lecture IV.

22. Austin, J. L., "A Plea for Excuses," 57 *Proc. of The Aristotelian Soc.* (1956–57).

23. Bacon, F., "Of Revenge," *Essays* (1625).

24. Baier, K., "Is Punishment Retributive?" *Analysis*, vol. 16 (1955–56).

25. ———. "Responsibility and Freedom," in *Ethics and Society*, ed. R. T. de George (1966).

26. Baker, Brenda, "Acting Under Duress," *Canadian J. Phil.*, vol. 3 (1974).

27. Ball and Friedman, "The Use of Criminal Sanctions in the Enforcement of Economic Legislation: A Sociological View," 17 *Stan L. Rev.* 197 (1965).

28. Bazelon, D. L., "The Concept of Responsibility," 53 *Georgetown L. Rev.* (1964).

29. Beale, J. H., "Consent in the Criminal Law," 8 *Harv. L. Rev.* 317 (1895).

30. ———. "Recovery for Consequences of an Act," 9 *Harv. L. Rev.* 80 (1895).

31. Beardsley, E. L., "A Plea for Deserts," *Amer. Phil. Quart.*, vol. 6 (1969).

32. ———. "Determinism and Moral Perspectives," *Phil. & Phenom. Res.*, vol. 21 (1960.

33. ———. " 'Excusing Conditions' and Moral Responsibility," in *Determinism and Freedom in the Age of Modern Science*, ed. S. Hook (1958).

34. ———. "Moral Worth and Moral Credit," *Phil. Rev.*, vol. 66 (1957).

35. Beardsley, Monroe C., "Actions and Events: The Problem of Individuation," *Amer. Phil. Quart.*, vol. 6 (1975).

36. Beccaria, C. B., *An Essay on Crimes and Punishments* (1764).

37. Beck, L. W., "Conscious and Unconscious Motives," *Mind,* vol. 75 (1966).

38. Becker, Lawrence C., "Criminal Attempt and the Theory of the Law of Crimes," *Philosophy and Public Affairs,* vol. 3 (1974).

39. Benn, S. I., "An Approach to the Problems of Punishment," *Philosophy,* vol. 33 (1958). A revised version appears in S. I. Benn and R. S. Peters, *Social Principles and the Democratic State* (1959).

40. Bennett, Jonathan, "Shooting, Killing and Dying," *Canadian J. Phil.,* vol. 2 (1973).

41. Bennett, R. T., "Drug Addiction and Its Effect on Criminal Responsibility," 9 *Wake Forest L. Rev.* 179 (1973).

42. Bentham, J., *Introduction to the Principles of Morals and Legislation* (1789), Chaps. 7–17.

43. ———. *Principles of the Penal Law,* ed. J. Bowring (1843).

44. Berofsky, B., "Determinism and the Concepts of a Person," *J. Phil.,* vol. 61 (1964).

45. Binavince, E. S., "Ethical Foundation of Criminal Liability," 33 *Fordham L. Rev.* 1 (1964).

46. Bingham, J. W., "Some Suggestions Concerning Legal Cause at Common Law," 9 *Colum. L. Rev.* 16 (1909).

47. Blackstone, W., *Commentaries on the Laws of England* (1765), Book IV.

48. Blumenfeld, D., and Dworkin, G., "Necessity, Contingency and Punishment," *Philosophical Studies,* vol. 16 (1965).

49. Boggs, A. A., "Proximate Cause in the Law of Tort," 44 *Amer. L. Rev.* 88 (1910).

50. Bolgar, "The Present Function of the Maxim *Ignorantia Juris Neminem Excusat*—A Comparative Study," 52 *Iowa L. Rev.* 626 (1967).

51. Bosanquet, B., *The Philosophical Theory of the State,* 4th ed. (1923), Chaps. 7, 8.

52. Bradley, F. H., "Some Remarks on Punishment," *Int. J. of Ethics,* vol. 4 (1894).

53. Brady, J. B., "Abolish the Insanity Defense?—No!" 8 *Houston L. Rev.* 629 (1971).

54. ———. "Punishment for Negligence: A Reply to Professor Hall," 22 *Buff. L. Rev.* 107 (1972).

55. ———. "Strict Liability Offenses. A Justification," 8 *Crim. L. Bulletin,* 217 (1972).

56. Brand, Myles, "Danto on Basic Actions," *Nous,* vol. 2 (1968).

57. Branden, N., "Free Will, Moral Responsibility and the Law," 42 *S. Cal. L. Rev.* 264 (1969).

58. Brandt, R. B., "A Utilitarian Theory of Excuses," *Phil. Rev.*, vol. 78 (1969).

59. ———. "Blameworthiness and Obligation," *Essays in Moral Philosophy*, ed. A. I. Melden (1958).

60. ———. "Determinism and the Justifiability of Moral Blame," in *Determinism and Freedom in the Age of Modern Science*, ed. S. Hook (1958).

61. Brett, Peter, *An Inquiry Into Criminal Guilt* (1963).

62. ———. "Mistake of Law as a Criminal Defense," 5 *Melb. Univ. L. Rev.* 179 (1966).

63. Bridgman, P. W., "Determinism and Punishment," in *Determinism and Freedom in the Age of Modern Science*, ed. S. Hook (1958).

64. Buckle and Buckle, *Bargaining for Justice* (1977).

65. Butler, S., *Erewhon* (1872).

66. Camps, F. E., and Havard, J.D.J., "Causation in Homicide—A Medical View," (1957) *Crim. L. Rev.* 576.

67. Card, C., "On Mercy," *Phil. Rev.*, vol. 81 (1972).

68. Carpenter, C. E., "Concurrent Causation," 83 *U. Pa. L. Rev.* 941 (1935).

69. Charvet, J., "Criticism and Punishment," *Mind*, vol. 75 (1966).

70. Chisholm, R. M., "The Descriptive Element in the Concept of 'Action'," *J. Phil.*, vol. 61 (1964).

71. ———. "The Structure of Intention," *J. Phil.*, vol. 67 (1970).

72. Chopra, Y. N., "The Consequences of Human Actions," *Proc. of The Aristotelian Soc.* (1965).

73. Clark, Michael, "The Moral Gradation of Punishment," *Phil. Quart.*, vol. 21 (1971).

74. Clark, R. S., "Automatism and Strict Liability," 5 *Victoria Univ. of Wellington L. Rev.* 12 (1968).

75. ———. "Defence of Impossibility and Offences of Strict Liability," 11 *Crim. L. Quart.* 154 (1969).

76. Cohen, M. R., "Moral Aspects of the Criminal Law," 49 *Yale L. J.* 987 (1940).

77. Collings, "Negligent Murder—Some Stateside Footnotes to D.P.P. v. Smith," 49 *Cal. L. Rev.* 254 (1961).

Comments (unsigned)

78. "A Punishment Rationale for Diminished Capacity," 18 *U.C.L.A. L. Rev.* 561 (1971).

79. "LSD—Its Effects on Criminal Responsibility," 17 *DePaul L. Rev.* 365 (1968).

80. "The Law of Necessity as Applied in the Bisbee Deportation Case," 3 *Ariz. L. Rev.* 264 (1961).
81. "The Logic of Conspiracy," *Wis. L. Rev.* 191 (1970).
82. Comment on *Stephenson,* 31 *Mich. L. Rev.* 659 (1933).
83. Cook, W. W., "Act, Intention and Motive in the Criminal Law," 26 *Yale L. J.* 645 (1916).
84. Cooper, D. E., "Collective Responsibility," *Philosophy,* vol. 43 (1968).
85. ———. "Collective Responsibility—Again," *Philosophy,* vol. 44 (1969).
86. Cross, R., "Mental Element in Crime," 83 *Law Q. Rev.* 215 (1967).
87. Cuomo, Anthony A., "Mens Rea and Status Criminality," 40 *S. Cal. L. Rev.* 463 (1967).
88. Dahl, Norman O., "Ought and Blameworthiness," *J. Phil.,* vol. 64 (1967).
89. Danto, A. C., "Basic Actions," *Amer. Phil. Quart.,* vol. 2 (1965).
90. Davidson, D., "Actions, Reasons and Causes," *J. Phil.,* vol. 60 (1963), reprinted in *The Philosophy of Action,* ed. A. R. White (1968).
91. Davis, K. C., *Discretionary Justice* (1969).
92. Davis, Lawrence H., "Individuation of Actions," *J. Phil.,* vol. 54 (1970).
93. Davis, Philip E., "The Moral Content of Law," *Southern J. of Phil.,* vol. 9 (1971).
94. De Boer, C., "On the Nature of State Action in Punishment," *The Monist,* vol. 42 (1932).
95. Demos, R., "Some Reflections on Threats and Punishments," *Rev. of Metaphysics,* vol. 11 (1957–58).
96. Dershowitz, A. M., "Abolishing the Insanity Defense: The Most Significant Feature of the Administration's Proposed Criminal Code—An Essay," 9 *Crim. L. Bulletin* 434 (1973).
97. ———. Background paper for *Fair and Certain Punishment,* report of the Twentieth Century Fund (1976).
98. de Tarde, G., *Penal Philosophy* (1912).
99. del Vecchio, G., "Divine Justice and Human Justice," *Juridical Rev. N.S.,* vol. 1 (1956).
100. Densner, Edwin E., "The Doctrine of Impossibility in the Law of Criminal Attempts," 4 *Crim. L. Bulletin* 398 (1968).
101. Diamond, "Criminal Responsibility of the Mentally Ill," 14 *Stan. L. Rev.* 59 (1961).
102. Dietl, Paul J., "On Punishing Attempts," *Mind,* vol. 79 (1970).
103. Dix, "Psychological Abnormality as a Factor in Grading Criminal

Liability, Diminished Capacity, Diminished Responsibility, and the Like," 62 *J. Crim. Law, Crim. & Police Sci.* 313 (1971).

104. Downie, R. S., "Collective Responsibility," *Philosophy*, vol. 44 (1969).

105. Doyle, J. F., "Justice and Legal Punishment," *Philosophy*, vol. 42 (1967).

106. Dubin, Gary V., "Mens Rea Reconsidered: A Plea for a Due Process Concept of Criminal Responsibility," 18 *Stanford L. Rev.* (1966).

107. Durkheim, E., *The Division of Labour in Society* (1893).

108. Dworkin, G., and Blumenfeld, D., "Punishment for Intentions," *Mind*, vol. 75 (1966).

109. Dworkin, Ronald, "Jurisprudence," in *Taking Rights Seriously* (1977).

110. Dyde, S. W., "Hegel's Conception of Crime and Punishment," *Phil. Rev.*, vol. 7 (1898).

111. Eaton, M., "Punitive Pain and Humiliation," *J. Amer. Inst. of Crim. Law and Crim.*, vol. 6 (1915–16).

112. Ebersole, F. B., "Free-Choice and the Demands of Morals," *Mind*, vol. 61 (1952).

113. Edgerton, H. W., "Legal Cause," 72 *U. Pa. L. Rev.* 211; 343 (1924).

114. ———."Negligence, Inadvertence, and Indifference: The Relation of Mental States to Negligence," 39 *Harv. L. Rev.* 849 (1925).

115. Edwards, J. Ll. J., "Automatism and Criminal Responsibility," 21 *Modern L. Rev.* 21 (1958).

116. ———. "Automatism and Social Defense," 8 *Crim. L. Quart.* 258 (1966).

117. Elkind, Jerome B., "Impossibility in Criminal Attempts: A Theorist's Headache," 54 *Virginia L. Rev.* 20 (1968).

118. Elliott, D. W., "Frightening a Person into Injuring Himself," *Crim. L. Rev.* 15 (1974).

119. Elliott, I. D., "Responsibility for Involuntary Acts: Ryan v. The Queen," 41 *Austral. L. J.* 497 (1967–68).

120. Emmons, D. C., "The Retributive Criterion of Justice," *Mind*, vol. 79 (1970).

121. Enker, Arnold N., "Impossibility in Criminal Attempts—Legality and the Legal Process," 53 *Minnesota L. Rev.* 665 (1969).

122. Eser, Albin, "The Principle of 'Harm' in the Concept of Crime: A Comparative Analysis of the Criminally Protected Legal Interests," 4 *Duquesne Univ. L. Rev.* 345 (1966).

123. Ewing, A. C., "Punishment as a Moral Agency: An Attempt to Reconcile the Retributive and Utilitarian View," *Mind*, vol. 36 (1927).

124. ———. "Punishment as Viewed by the Philosopher," 21 *Canadian Bar Rev.* 102 (1942).

125. ———. *The Morality of Punishment* (1929).

126. Ezorsky, G., ed., *Philosophical Perspectives on Punishment* (1972).

127. Fain, Haskell, "Hart and Honoré on Causation in the Law," *Inquiry,* vol. 9 (1966).

128. Farmer, H. H., "The Notion of Desert Good and Bad," *Hibbert J.,* vol. 41 (1942–43).

129. Feinberg, Joel, "Action and Responsibility," in *Doing and Deserving* (1970) at 119–51.

130. ———. "Causing Voluntary Actions," in *Doing and Deserving* at 152–86.

131. ———. "Collective Responsibility," *J. Phil.,* vol. 65 (1968). Reprinted in *Doing and Deserving* at 222–51.

132. ———. "Crime, Clutchability, and Individuated Treatment," in *Doing and Deserving* (1970) at 252–71.

133. ———. *Doing and Deserving* (1970).

134. ———. "Harm and Self-Interest," in *Law, Morality And Society,* ed. Hacker and Raz (1977).

135. ———. "Justice and Personal Desert," *Nomos VI: Justice,* ed. C. J. Friedrich and J. W. Chapman (1963). Reprinted in *Doing and Deserving* at 55–94.

136. ———. "On Being 'Morally Speaking a Murderer,' " in *Doing and Deserving* at 38–54.

137. ———. "On Justifying Legal Punishment," *Nomos III: Responsibility,* ed. C. J. Friedrich (1960).

138. ———. "Problematic Responsibility in Law and Morals," *Phil. Rev.,* vol. 71 (1962). Reprinted in *Doing and Deserving* at 25–37.

139. ———. "Sua Culpa," in *Doing and Deserving* at 187–221.

140. ———. "Supererogation and Rules," in *Doing and Deserving* at 3–24.

141. ———. "The Expressive Function of Punishment," *Monist,* vol. 69 (1965). Reprinted in *Doing and Deserving* at 95–118.

142. ———. "What Is So Special about Mental Illness?" in *Doing and Deserving* at 272–92.

143. Fingarette, Herbert, "Addiction and Criminal Responsibility," 84 *Yale L. J.* 413 (1975).

144. ———. "Diminished Mental Capacity as a Criminal Law Defense," 37 *Modern L. Rev.* 264 (1974).

145. ———. "Insanity and Responsibility," *Inquiry,* vol. 15 (1972).

146. ———. "The Concept of Mental Disease in Criminal Law Insanity Tests," 33 *U. Chi. L. Rev.* 229 (1966).

147. Finnis, J., "Punishment and Pedagogy," *Oxford Rev.* (Trinity 1967).

148. ———. "The Restoration of Retribution," *Analysis*, vol. 32 (1972).

149. Fitzgerald, P. J., "Acting and Refraining," *Analysis*, vol. 27 (1967).

150. ———. "Crime, Sin and Negligence," 79 *Law Q. Rev.* 351 (1963).

151. ———. *Criminal Law and Punishment* (1962).

152. ———. "Real Crimes and Quasi Crimes," 10 *Natural Law Forum* 21 (1965).

153. ———. "Voluntary and Involuntary Acts," in *Oxford Essays in Jurisprudence,* ed. A. G. Guest (1961).

154. Fitzgerald, P., and Williams, G. L., "Carelessness, Indifference and Recklessness: Two Replies," 25 *Modern L. Rev.* 49 (1962).

155. Fletcher, George P., "Prolonging Life," 42 *Wash. L. Rev.* 999 (1967).

156. ———. "The Individualization of Excusing Conditions," 47 *S. Cal. L. Rev.* 1269 (1974).

157. ———. "Theory of Criminal Negligence: A Comparative Analysis," 119 *U. of Pa. L. Rev.* 401 (1971).

158. Flew, A. G. N., *Crime or Disease* (1973).

159. ———. "The Justification of Punishment," *Philosophy*, vol. 29 (1954). Reprinted with postscript in *The Philosophy of Punishment,* ed. H. B. Acton (1969).

160. Foot, P., "Freewill as Involving Determinism," *Phil. Rev.,* vol. 66 (1957).

161. ———. "The Problem of Abortion and the Doctrine of the Double Effect," reprinted in *Moral Problems,* ed. James Rachels (1971).

162. Fox, "Physical Disorder, Consciousness, and Criminal Liability," 63 *Colum. L. Rev.* 645 (1963).

163. Frankel, L. H., "Criminal Omissions: A Legal Microcosm," 11 *Wayne L. Rev.* 367 (1965).

164. Frankel, M. E., *Criminal Sentences—Law Without Order* (1973).

165. Frankfurt, H. G., "Alternate Possibilities and Moral Responsibility," *J. Phil.,* vol. 66 (1969).

166. Fried, Charles, "Moral Causation," 77 *Harv. L. Rev.* 1258 (1964).

167. Fry, E., "Inequality in Punishment," *Nineteenth Century,* vol. 14 (1883).

168. Gardiner, "The Purposes of Criminal Punishment," 21 *Modern L. Rev.* 117 (1958).

169. Geach, P. T., "Ascriptivism," *Phil. Rev.*, vol. 69 (1960).

170. Gendin, Sidney, "A Plausible Theory of Retribution," *J. of Value Inquiry*, vol. 5 (1970).

171. ———. "Insanity and Criminal Responsibility," *Amer. Phil. Quart.*, vol. 10 (1973).

172. Gerber and McAnany, *Contemporary Punishment: Views, Explanations, and Justifications* (1972).

173. Glazebrook, P. R., "Should We Have a Law of Attempted Crime?" 85 *Law Q. Rev.* 28 (1969).

174. ———. "The Necessity Plea in English Criminal Law," (1972) *Camb. L. J.* 87.

175. Glover, J., *Responsibility* (1970).

176. Glueck, S., *Crime and Justice* (1945).

177. Goldinger, M., "Punishment, Justice and the Separation of Issues," *Monist*, vol. 49 (1965).

178. Goldstein, A., *The Insanity Defense* (1967).

179. Goldstein, J., and Katz, J., "Abolish the Insanity Defense—Why Not?" 72 *Yale L. J.* 853 (1963).

180. Goodhart, A. L., *English Law and the Criminal Law* (1953).

181. ———. "Possession of Drugs and Absolute Liability," 84 *Law Q. Rev.* 382 (1968).

182. ———. "The Third Man or Novus Actus Interveniens," 4 *Current Leg. Prob.* 177 (1951).

183. Gotlieb, A. E., "Intention, and Knowing the Nature and Quality of an Act," 19 *Modern L. Rev.* 270 (1956).

184. Green, L., "Are There Dependable Rules of Causation?" 77 *U. Pa. L. Rev.* 601 (1929).

185. ———. *Rationale of Proximate Cause* (1927).

186. Green, T. H., *Lectures on the Principles of Political Obligation* (1885), reprinted as "The State's Right to Punish" in *J. Amer. Inst. of Crim. Law & Crim.* vol. 1 (1910–11).

187. Gregory, C. O., "Proximate Cause in Negligence—A Retreat from 'Rationalisation'," 6 *U. Chi. L. Rev.* 36 (1938).

188. Griffen, J., "Consequences," *Proc. of The Aristotelian Soc.* (1965).

189. Gustafson, D. F., "Momentary Intentions," *Mind*, vol. 77 (1968).

190. Hacker, A., "Getting Used to Mugging," *The New York Review*, April, 1973.

191. Hadden, T. B., "A Plea for Punishment," (1965) *Camb. L. J.* 117.

192. Haksar, V., "The Responsibility of Mental Defectives," *Philosophy*, vol. 38 (1963).

193. *Hale's Pleas of the Crown* (first published 1678), Chaps. 4, 5, 6, 8, 9.

194. Hall, J., "Analytic Philosophy and Jurisprudence," *Ethics,* vol. 77 (1966).

195. ———. "Criminal Attempt—A Study of the Foundation of Criminal Liability," 49 *Yale L. J.* 789 (1940).

196. ———. *General Principles of Criminal Law,* 2nd ed. (1960).

197. ———. "Negligent Behavior Should Be Excluded from Penal Liability," 63 *Colum. L. Rev.* 632 (1963).

198. ———. "Nulla Poena Sine Lege," 47 *Yale L. J.* 165 (1937).

199. Hall, J., and Seligman, S. J., "Mistake of Law and Mens Rea," 8 *U. Chi. L. Rev.* 641 (1941).

200. Hamilton, A., "Making the Punishment Fit the Crime," *J. Amer. Inst. of Crim. Law & Crim.,* vol. 12 (1921–22).

201. Hardie, W. F. R., "Willing and Acting," *Phil. Quart.,* vol. 21 (1971).

202. Harno, "Intent in Criminal Conspiracy," 89 *U. Pa. L. Rev.* 624 (1941).

203. Harring, Janet S., "Liability Without Fault: Logic and Potential of a Developing Concept," (1970) *Wis. L. Rev.* 1201.

204. Hart, H. L. A., "Acts of Will and Responsibility," in *Punishment and Responsibility* (1968) at 90–112.

205. ———. Book Review of Wooton, *Crime and Criminal Law* (1963), 74 *Yale L. J.* 1325 (1965).

206. ———. "Changing Conceptions of Responsibility," in *Punishment and Responsibility* (1968) at 186–209.

207. ———. "The Enforcement of Morality," in *The Morality of the Criminal Law* (1965) at 31–54.

208. ———. "Immorality and Treason," 62 *Listener* (July 30, 1959).

209. ———. "Intention and Punishment," in *Punishment and Responsibility* (1968) at 113–35.

210. ———. *Law, Liberty, and Morality* (1963).

211. ———. "Legal Responsibility and Excuses," in *Determinism and Freedom,* ed. S. Hook (1958). Reprinted in *Punishment and Responsibility* (1968) at 28–53.

212. ———. "Murder and the Principles of Punishment: England and the United States," in *Punishment and Responsibility* (1968) at 54–89.

213. ———. "Negligence, Mens Rea, and Criminal Responsibility," in *Punishment and Responsibility* (1968) at 136–57.

214. ———. "Postcript: Responsibility and Retribution," in *Punishment and Responsibility* (1968) at 210–37.

215. ———. "Prolegomenon to the Principles of Punishment," in *Punishment and Responsibility* (1968) at 1–27.

216. ———. *Punishment and Responsibility* (1968).

217. ———. "Punishment and the Elimination of Responsibility," in *Punishment and Responsibility* (1968) at 158–85.

218. ———. "Social Solidarity and the Enforcement of Morality," 35 *U. Chi. L. Rev.* 1 (1967).

219. ———. "The Ascription of Responsibility and Rights." Reprinted in *Logic and Language,* ed. A. Flew (1955).

220. Hart, H. L. A., and Hampshire, S., "Decision, Intention and Certainty," *Mind,* vol. 67 (1958).

221. Hart, H. L. A., and Honoré, A. M., *Causation in the Law* (1959).

222. Hart, H. M., "The Aims of the Criminal Law," 23 *Law and Contemp. Prob.* 401 (1958).

223. Hedman, Carl G., "On the Individuation of Actions," *Inquiry,* vol. 13 (1970).

224. Hegel, G. W. F., *The Philosophy of Right* (1821), §§ 90–103.

225. Hickey, "Preventive Detention and the Crime of Being Dangerous," 58 *Geo. L. J.* 287 (1969).

226. Hitchler, "The Killer and His Victim in Felony-Murder Cases," 53 *Dick. L. Rev.* 3 (1948).

227. Hobart, R. E., "Freewill as Involving Determination and Inconceivable Without It," *Mind,* vol. 43 (1934).

228. Hobbes, T., *De Cive* (1642), Chaps. 1, 13.

229. ———. *Leviathan* (1651), Chaps. 13, 14, 15, 26, 27, 28.

230. Hobhouse, S., "Retribution," *Hibbert Journal,* vol. 40 (1941–42).

231. Holland, T. E., *The Eelements of Jurisprudence,* 13th ed. (1924).

232. Holmes, O. W., The Common Law (1881), Lecture II.

233. Honderich, T., *Punishment: The Supposed Justifications* (1969).

234. Hood, R., and Sparks, R., *Key Issues in Criminology* (1970).

235. Houlgate, Laurence D., "Excuses and the Criminal Law," *Southern J. of Phil.,* vol. 13 (1975).

236. ———. "Ignorantia Juris: A Plea for Justice," *Ethics,* vol. 78 (1967).

237. Howard, C., "Automatism and Insanity," 4 *Syd. L. Rev.* 36 (1962).

238. ———. *Strict Responsibility* (1963).

239. ———. "The Reasonableness of Mistake in the Criminal Law," 4 *Univ. of Queensland L. J.* 45 (1961).

240. Hughes, Graham, "Criminal Omissions," 67 *Yale L. J.* 590 (1958).

241. ———. "One Further Note on Attempting the Impossible," 42 *N.Y.U. L. Rev.* 1005 (1967).

242. James, F., and Perry, R. F., "Legal Cause," 60 *Yale L. J.* 761 (1951).
243. Jenkins, J. S., "Motives and Intentions," *Phil. Quart.,* vol. 15 (1965).
244. Jennings, "The Growth and Development of Automatism as a Defense in Criminal Law," 2 *Osgoode Hall L.S.J.* 370 (1962).
245. Jensen, O. C., "Responsibility, Freedom and Punishment," *Mind,* vol. 75 (1966).
246. Johnson, E. H., *Crime, Correction and Society* (1964).
247. Johnson, P. E., "The Unnecessary Crime of Conspiracy," 61 *Cal. L. Rev.* 1137 (1973).
248. Kadish, S., "Some Observations on the Use of Criminal Sanctions in Enforcing Economic Regulations," 30 *U. Chi. L. Rev.* 423 (1963).
249. ———. "The Decline of Innocence," 26 *Camb. L. J.* 273 (1968).
250. Kadish, S., & Paulsen, M., *Criminal Law and Its Processes,* 3rd. ed. (1975).
251. Kahn, "Automatism: Sane and Insane," (1965) *N.Z. L. J.* 113.
252. Kant, I., *Rechtslehre* (1797).
253. Kasachkoff, T., "The Criteria of Punishment: Some Neglected Considerations," *Canadian J. of Phil.,* vol. 2 (1973).
254. Keedy, "Criminal Attempts at Common Law," 102 *U. Pa. L. Rev.* 464 (1954).
255. Keeton, R. E., *Legal Cause in the Law of Torts* (1963).
256. Kenner, L., "On Blaming," *Mind,* vol. 76 (1967).
257. Kenny, A., *Action, Emotion, and Will* (1963).
258. ———. "Intention and *Mens Rea* in Murder," in *Law, Morality, and Society,* ed. Hacker and Raz (1977).
259. ———. "Intention and Purpose in Law," in *Essays in Legal Philosophy,* ed. R. S. Summers (1968).
260. Kirchheimer, O., "Criminal Omissions," 55 *Harv. L. Rev.* 615 (1941).
261. Kleinig, John, "Mercy and Justice," *Philosophy,* vol. 44 (1969).
262. ———. "The Concept of Desert," *Amer. Phil. Quart.,* vol. 8 (1971).
263. ———. *Punishment and Desert* (1973).
264. Kneale, W., *The Responsibility of Criminals* (1967), in *The Philosophy of Punishment,* ed. H. B. Acton (1969).
265. LaFave and Scott, *Criminal Law* (1972).
266. Laird, J., "The Justification of Punishment," *Monist,* vol. 41 (1931).
267. Leigh, "Automatism and Insanity," 5 *Crim. L. Quart.* 160 (1962).
268. Lessnoff, M., "Two Justifications of Punishment," *Phil. Quart.,* vol. 21 (1971).

269. Lewis, C. S., "On Punishment: A Reply," *Res Judicatae*, vol. 6 (1952–54).

270. ———. "The Humanitarian Theory of Punishment," *Twentieth Century* (Australia), vol. 12 (1949). Reprinted in *Res Judicatae*, vol. 6 (1952–54) and in *Readings in Ethical Theory*, 2nd ed., ed. W. Sellars and J. Hospers (1970).

271. Lewis, H. D., "Collective Responsibility," *Philosophy*, vol. 23 (1948).

272. Livermore, J. M., and Meehl, P. E., "The Virtues of McNaghten," 51 *Minn. L. Rev.* 789 (1967).

273. Locke, J., *An Essay Concerning the True Original, Extent and End of Civil Government (Second Treatise of Civil Government)* (1690), Chaps. 2, 7, 8, 9.

274. Lofthouse, W. I., "Retribution and Reformation," *Hibbert J.*, vol. 41 (1942–43).

275. Longford, *The Idea of Punishment* (1961).

276. Louch, A. R., "Sins and Crimes," *Philosophy*, vol. 43 (1968).

277. Louisell and Hazard, "Insanity as a Defense: The Bifurcated Trial," 49 *Cal. L. Rev.* 805 (1961).

278. Lyons, D., "Is Hart's Rationale for Legal Excuses Workable?" *Dialogue*, vol. 8 (1969).

279. ———. "On Sanctioning Excuses," *J. Phil.*, vol. 66 (1969).

280. ———. "Unobvious Excuses in the Criminal Law," 19 *Wayne L. Rev.* 925 (1973).

281. Lyons, R., "Intention and Foresight in Law," *Mind*, vol. 85 (1976).

282. Mabbott, J. D., "Freewill and Punishment," *Contemporary British Philosophy*, 3rd ser., ed. H. D. Lewis (1956).

283. ———. "Punishment," *Mind*, vol. 48 (1939).

284. Macaulay and Other Indian Law Commissioners, *A Penal Code Prepared by the Indian Law Commissioners* (1837). *Notes on the Indian Penal Code*, in *Works*, ed. Trevelyan (London 1879), vol. 7.

285. Mackie, J. L., "The Grounds of Responsibility," in *Law, Morality, and Society*, ed. Hacker and Raz (1977).

286. Maitland, F. W., "The Relation of Punishment to Temptation," *Mind*, vol. 5 (1880).

287. Mallin, "In Warm Blood: Some Historical and Procedural Aspects of Regina v. Dudley and Stephens," 34 *U. Chi. L. Rev.* 387 (1967).

288. Mannison, D. S., "Doing Something on Purpose but not Intentionally," *Analysis*, vol. 30 (1969).

289. Mansfield, John, H., "Hart and Honoré Causation in the Law—A Comment," 17 *Vanderbilt L. Rev.* 487 (1964).

290. Marshall, J., "Punishment for Intentions," *Mind,* vol. 80 (1971).
291. Marston, G., "Contemporaneity of Act and Intention in Crimes," 86 *Law Q. Rev.* 208 (1970).
292. Martin, Rex, "On the Logic of Justifying Legal Punishment," *Amer. Phil. Quart.,* vol. 7 (1970).
293. McCloskey, H. J., "A Non-Utilitarian Approach to Punishment," *Inquiry,* vol. 8 (1965).
294. ———. "The Complexity of the Concepts of Punishment," *Philosophy,* vol. 37 (1962).
295. ———. "Utilitarian and Retributive Punishment," *J. Phil.,* vol. 64 (1967).
296. McCullagh, C. B., "The Individuation of Actions and Acts," *Australasian J. of Phil.,* vol. 54 (1976).
297. McDermott, T. L. "The Path of Automatism," 1 *Tasm. L. Rev.* 695 (1962).
298. McLaughlin, J. A., "Proximate Cause," 39 *Harv. L. Rev.* 149 (1925).
299. Michael J., and Wechsler, H., "A Rationale of the Law of Homicide," 37 *Colum. L. Rev.* 701, 1261 (1937).
300. Mill, J. S., *Utilitarianism* (1861), Chap. 5.
301. Miller, J., "The Compromise of Criminal Cases," 1 *S. Cal. L. Rev.* 1 (1927).
302. Mitford, J., *Kind and Usual Punishment* (1973).
303. Moberly, W. H., "Some Ambiguities in the Retributive Theory of Punishment," *Proc. of the Aristotelian Soc.,* vol. 25 (1924–25).
304. ———. *The Ethics of Punishments* (1968).
305. Monahan, J., "Abolish the Insanity Defense?—Not Yet!" 26 *Rutgers L. Rev.* 710 (1973).
306. Montesquieu, C.-L. de S. de., *The Spirit of the Laws* (1748).
307. Morris, Arval A., "Criminal Insanity," 43 *Wash. L. Rev.* 583 (1968).
308. Morris, C., "On the Teaching of Legal Cause," 39 *Colum. L. Rev.* 1087 (1939).
309. Morris, H., ed. *Freedom and Responsibility* (1961).
310. ———. "Guilt and Punishment," *Personalist* vol. 52 (1971).
311. ———. Ed. *Guilt and Shame* (1971).
312. ———. "Guilt and Suffering," *Philosophy East and West,* vol. 21 (1971).
313. ———. "Persons and Punishment," *Monist,* vol. 52 (1968).
314. ———. "Punishment for Thoughts," *Monist,* vol. 49 (1965).
315. Morris, N., "Prison in Evolution," in *Criminology in Transition* ed. Grygier, Jones, and Spencer (1965).

316. ———. "Psychiatry and the Dangerous Criminal," 41 *S. Cal. L. Rev.* 514 (1968).

317. ———. "The Felon's Responsibility for the Lethal Acts of Others," 105 *U. Pa. L. Rev.* 50 (1956).

318. ———. " 'Wrong' in the M'Naghten Rules," 16 *Modern L. Rev.* 435 (1953).

319. Morris, N., and Buckle, D., "The Humanitarian Theory of Punishment: A Reply to C. S. Lewis," *Res Judicatae,* vol. 6 (1952–54).

320. Morris, N., and Hawkins, G., *The Honest Politician's Guide to Crime Control* (1970).

321. Mueller, G. O. W., "Causing Criminal Harm," in *Essays in Criminal Science,* ed. G. O. W. Mueller (1961).

322. Mullock, Philip, "Responsibility, Propensity and Choice," 16 *Mercer L. Rev.* 1 (1964).

323. Mundle, C. W. K., "Punishment and Desert," *Phil. Quart.,* vol. 4 (1954). Reprinted with postscript in *The Philosophy of Punishment,* ed. H. B. Acton (1969).

324. Munkman, J., "Note on the Causes of an Accidental Occurrence," 17 *Modern L. Rev.* 134 (1954).

325. Murphy, J. G., "Involuntary Acts and Criminal Liability," *Ethics,* vol. 51 (1971).

326. ———. "Marxism and Retribution," *Philosophy and Public Affairs,* vol. 2 (1973).

327. ———. "Three Mistakes about Retributivism," *Analysis,* vol. 31 (1971).

328. ———. Ed. *Punishment and Rehabilitation* (1973).

329. Newman, D. J., *Conviction: The Determination of Guilt or Innocence Without Trial* (1966).

330. Newman, L., and Weitzer, L., "Duress, Free Will and the Criminal Law," 30 *S. Cal. L. Rev.* 313 (1957).

331. Nielsen, K., "When are Immoralities Crimes?" *Philosophia,* vol. 1 (1971).

Notes (unsigned)

332. "Amnesia, A Case Study in the Limits of Particular Justice," 71 *Yale L. J.* 109 (1961).

333. "A Rationale of the Law of Aggravated Theft," 54 *Colum. L. Rev.* 84 (1954).

334. "A Rationale of the Law of Burglary," 51 *Colum. L. Rev.* 1009 (1951).

335. "Conspiracy and the First Amendment," 79 *Yale L. J.* 872 (1970).

336. "Developments in the Law—Criminal Conspiracy," 72 *Harv. L. Rev.* 920 (1959).

337. "Justification for the Use of Force in Criminal Cases," 13 *Stan. L. Rev.* 566 (1961).

338. "Manslaughter and the Adequacy of Provocation: The Reasonableness of the Reasonable Man," 96 *U. Pa. L. Rev.* 1021 (1958).

339. "Negligence and the General Problem of Criminal Responsibility," 81 *Yale L. J.* 949 (1972).

340. "The California Supreme Court Assaults the Felony-Murder Rule," 22 *Stan. L. Rev.* 1059 (1970).

341. "The Conspiracy Dilemma: Prosecution of Group Crime or Protection of Individual Defendants," 62 *Harv. L. Rev.* 276 (1948).

342. "The Diminished Capacity Defense to Felony-Murder," 23 *Stan. L. Rev.* 799 (1971).

343. "The Use of Deadly Force in the Protection of Property Under the Model Penal Code," 59 *Colum. L. Rev.* 1212 (1959).

344. Nowell-Smith, P. H., "Freewill and Moral Responsibility," *Mind,* vol. 57 (1948).

345. Nozick, R., *Anarchy, State, and Utopia* (1974), Part I.

346. Oberdiek, Hans, "Intention and Foresight in Criminal Law," *Mind,* vol. 81 (1972).

347. O'Conner, D., "The Voluntary Act," *Medicine, Science and the Law,* vol. 15 (1975).

348. O'Doherty, E. F., "Men, Criminals and Responsibility," *Irish Jurist,* vol. 1 (1966).

349. O'Hearn, P. J. T., "Criminal Negligence: An Analysis in Depth," 7 *Crim. L. Quart.* 27, 407 (1964–65).

350. O'Regan, "Duress and Murder," 35 *Modern L. Rev.* 596 (1972).

351. Packer, H. L., "Making the Punishment Fit the Crime," 77 *Harv. L. Rev.* 1071 (1964).

352. ———. "Mens Rea and the Supreme Court," *Sup. Ct. Rev.* 107 (1962).

353. ———. *The Limits of the Criminal Sanction* (1968).

354. Paley, W., *The Principles of Moral and Political Philosophy* (1785), Book VI.

355. Passmore, J. A. and Heath, P. L., "Intentions," *Aristotelian Soc. Supp.,* vol. 29 (1955).

356. Paton, G. W., *A Text-Book of Jurisprudence,* 3rd ed. (1964).

357. Patterson, J., "How to Justify an Injustice," *Mind,* vol. 82 (1973).

358. Pears, D. F., ed. *Freedom and Will* (1963).

359. Peaslee, R. J., "Multiple Causation and Damage," 47 *Harv. L. Rev.* 1127 (1934).

360. Perkins, L. H., "Suggestion for a Justification of Punishment," *Ethics,* vol. 81 (1970).

361. Perkins, R. M., "Alignment of Sanction with Culpable Conduct," 49 *Iowa L. Rev.* 325 (1964).

362. ———. "An Analysis of Assault and Attempts to Assault," 47 *Minn. L. Rev.* 71 (1962).

363. ———. "A Rationale of *Mens Rea,*" 52 *Harv. L. Rev.* 905 (1939).

364. ———. "Criminal Attempt and Related Problems," 2 *U.C.L.A. L. Rev.* 319 (1955).

365. ———. *Criminal Law,* 2nd ed. (1969).

366. ———. "Ignorance and Mistakes in Criminal Law," 88 *U. Pa. L. Rev.* 35 (1939).

367. Pincoffs, Edmund L., "Legal Responsibility and Moral Character," 19 *Wayne L. Rev.* 905 (1973).

368. ———. *The Rationale of Legal Punishment* (1966).

39. Pitcher, G., "Hart on Action and Responsibility," *Phil. Rev.,* vol. 69 (1960).

370. Plamenatz, J., "Responsibility, Blame and Punishment," in *Philosophy, Politics and Society,* 3rd ser., ed. P. Laslett and W. G. Runciman (1967).

371. Plato, *Laws* 731, 859–62, 876, 921, 934.

372. ———. *Republic* 335, 409–10, 618.

373. Platt, A., and Diamond, B. L., "The Origins of the 'Right and Wrong' Test of Criminal Responsibility and Its Subsequent Development in the U.S.: An Historical Survey," 54 *Cal. L. Rev.* 1227 (1966).

374. Pollock, F., *A First Book of Jurisprudence,* 6th ed. (1929).

375. Pound, R., "Causation," 67 *Yale L. J.* 1 (1957).

376. Prevezer, S., "Automatism and Involuntary Conduct," *Crim. L. Rev.* 361, 440 (1958).

377. Puttkamer, "Consent in Criminal Assault," 19 *Ill. L. Rev.* 617 (1925).

378. Quinton, A. M., "On Punishment," *Analysis,* vol. 14 (1953–54). Reprinted in *Philosophy, Politics and Society,* 1st ser., ed. P. Laslett (1956).

379. Radzinowicz, L., *A History of English Criminal Law,* vol. 1 (1948).

380. ———. "Changing Attitudes Towards Crime and Punishment," *Law Q. Rev.,* vol. 75 (1959).

381. ———. *Ideology and Crime* (1966).

382. Radzinowicz, L., and Turner, J. W. C., "A Study of Punishment I: Introductory Essay," 21 *Canadian Bar Rev.* 91 (1943).

383. Rashdall, H., "The Theory of Punishment," *Int. J. of Ehics,* vol. 2 (1891–92).

384. Rawls, J., *A Theory of Justice* (1971).

385. ———. "Two Concepts of Rules," *Phil. Rev.,* vol. 64 (1955). Partially reprinted in *The Philosophy of Punishment,* ed. H. B. Acton (1969).

386. Rayfield, D., "Action," *Nous,* vol. 2 (1968).

387. Report of the Committee on Mentally Abnormal Offenders (The Butler Committee Report) (1975).

388. Rosett and Cressey, *Justice by Consent* (1976).

389. Rousseau, J.-J., *The Social Contract* (1762).

390. *Royal Commission on Capital Punishment 1949–1953: Report* (1953).

391. Rusche, G., and Kirchheimer, O., *Punishment and Social Structure* (1939).

392. Ryle, G., *The Concept of Mind* (1949), Chaps. 1, 3, 4.

393. Salmond, J. W., *Jurisprudence,* 12th ed. (1966).

394. Samek, "The Concept of Act and Intention and Their Treatment in Jurisprudence," *Australisian J. Phil.,* vol. 41 (1963).

395. Sayre, "Criminal Attempts," 41 *Harv. L. Rev.* 821 (1928).

396. Scheid, Don E., *Theories of Legal Punishment* (doctoral dissertation, New York University, 1977).

397. Schleifer, M., "The Responsibility of the Psychopath," *Philosophy,* vol. 45 (1970).

398. Schulhofer, S. J., "Harm and Punishment: a Critique of Emphasis on the Results of Conduct in the Criminal Law," 122 *U. Pa. L. Rev.* 1497 (1974).

399. Seavey, W. A., "Negligence—Subjective or Objective," 41 *Harv. L. Rev.* 1 (1927).

400. Seidman, R. B., "Mens rea and the Reasonable African: The Pre-scientific World-View and Mistake of Fact," 15 *Int. and Compar. L. Quart.* 1135 (1966).

401. Sen, P. K., *From Punishment to Prevention* (1932).

402. Shaw, G. B., *The Crime of Imprisonment* (1946).

403. Shuman, S. I., "Act and Omission in Criminal Law: Towards a Nonsubjective Theory," 17 *J. Legal Ed.* 16 (1964).

404. Siegler, F. A., "Lyons on Sanctioning Excuses," *J. Phil.,* vol. 67 (1970).

405. ———. "Omissions," *Analysis,* vol. 28 (1968).

406. Silber, J. R., "Being and Doing: A Study of Status Responsibility and Voluntary Responsibility," 35 *U. Chi. L. Rev.* 47 (1967).

407. Silving, "Testing of the Unconscious in Criminal Cases," 69 *Harv. L. Rev.* 683 (1956).

408. Sim, "Involuntary Actus Reus," 25 *Modern L. Rev.* 741 (1962).

409. Skinner, B. F., *Beyond Freedom and Dignity* (1971).

410. ———. *Science and Human Behavior* (1953).

411. Smart, A., "Mercy," *Philosophy*, vol. 43 (1968). Reprinted in *The Philosophy of Punishment*, ed. H. B. Acton (1969).

412. Smart, J. J. C., "Comment: The Humanitarian Theory of Punishment," *Res Judicatae* vol. 6 (1952–54).

413. ———. "Free-Will, Praise and Blame," *Mind, vol.* 70 (1961).

414. Smith, J., "Legal Cause in Actions of Tort," 25 *Harv. L. Rev.* 102, 223, 303 (1911–12).

415. Smith, J. C., "The Element of Chance in Criminal Liability," (1971) *Crim. L. Rev.* 63.

416. ———. "Two Problems in Criminal Attempts," 70 *Harv. L. Rev.* 422 (1957).

417. Smith, J. C., and Hogan, B., *Criminal Law* (1965).

418. Smith, L. M. G., "On Baroness Wootton's Larceny," *Social Theory and Practice*, vol. 1 (1970).

419. Snyder, O. C., "Criminal Responsibility," (1962) *Duke L. J.* 204.

420. Spinoza B., *Political Treatise* (1677). Trans. R. H. M. Elwes (1955), Chap. 3.

421. ———. *Tractatus Theologico-Politicus* (1670), Chap. 16.

422. Sprigge, T. L. S., "A Utilitarian Reply to Dr. McCloskey," *Inquiry*, vol. 8 (1965).

423. Squires, J. E. R., "Blame," *Phil. Quart.*, vol. 18 (1968). Reprinted in *The Philosophy of Punishment*, ed. H. B. Acton (1969).

424. Stephen, J. F., *A History of the Criminal Law of England* (1883).

425. ———. *Digest of the Criminal Law* (1877).

426. ———. *General View of the Criminal Law of England* (1863).

427. Stevenson, C. L., "Ethical Judgments and Avoidability," *Mind*, vol. 47 (1938).

428. Stigen, Anfinn, "The Concept of Human Action," *Inquiry*, vol. 13 (1970).

429. Stocker, Michael, "Intentions and Act Evaluations," *J. Phil.*, vol. 67 (1970).

430. Stuart, D., "Actus Reus in Attempts," (1970) *Crim. L. Rev.* 505.

431. ———. "Mens Rea, Negligence and Attempts," (1968) *Crim. L. Rev.* 647.

432. Sutherland, N. S., "Motives as Explanations," *Mind,* vol. 68 (1959).
433. Szasz, T., *Law, Liberty, and Psychiatry* (1963).
434. ———. *Psychiatric Justice* (1966).
435. Tao, L. S., "Alcoholism as a Defense to Crime," 45 *Notre Dame Lawyer,* 68 (1969).
436. Tay, A. E. S., "Moral Guilt and Legal Liability," *Hibbert J.,* vol. 60 (1961–62).
437. Taylor, C. C. W., "States, Activities and Performances," *Proc. of The Aristotelian Soc.* (1965).
438. Temkin, J., and Zellik, G., "Attempts in English Criminal Law," 1 *Dalhousie L. J.* 581 (1974).
439. Terry, H. T., "Negligence," 29 *Harv. L. Rev.* 40 (1915).
440. ———. "Proximate Consequences in the Law of Torts," 28 *Harv. L. Rev.* 10 (1914).
441. ———. *Some Leading Principles of Anglo-American Law Expounded with a View to its Classification, Arrangement and Codification* (1884).
442. Thalberg, Irving, "Hart on Strict Liability and Excusing Conditions," *Ethics,* vol. 81 (1971).
443. ———. "Remorse," *Mind,* vol. 72 (1963).
444. Thomas Aquinas, *Summa Theologiae* (1265–72), Parts I, IIa, IIb.
445. Thomas, D. A., "Sentencing—The Case for Reasoned Decisions," (1963) *Crim. L. Rev.* 243.
446. ———. "Theories of Punishment in the Court of Criminal Appeal," 27 *Modern L. Rev.* 546 (1964).
447. Tobias, J. J., *Crime and Industrial Society in the Nineteenth Century* (1967).
448. Toby, J., "Is Punishment Necessary?" *J. Crim. Law, Crim. & Police Sci.,* vol. 55 (1964).
449. Tulin, "The Role of Penalties in Criminal Law," 37 *Yale L. J.* 1040 (1928).
450. Tupin, J. P. and Goolishian, H. A., "Mental Retardation and Legal Responsibility," 18 *De Paul L. Rev.* 673 (1969).
451. Turner, J. W. C., "Attempts to Commit Crimes," in *Modern Approach to Criminal Law,* ed. Radzinowicz and Turner (1945).
452. ———. "Mental Element in Crimes at Common Law," in *The Modern Approach to Criminal Law,* ed. Radzinowicz and Turner (1945).
453. ———. "Towards the Deodand," (1960) *Crim. L. Rev.* 89, 168.
454. Ullmann, W., "The Reasons for Punishing Attempted Crimes," *Juridical Rev.,* vol. 51 (1939).

455. Urmson, J. O., "Motives and Causes," *Proc. of The Aristotelian Soc.* (1952), reprinted in *The Philosophy of Action* ed. A. R. White (1968).

456. Urowsky, "Negligence and the General Problem of Criminal Responsibility," 81 *Yale L. J.* 949 (1972).

457. van den Haag, E., *Punishing Criminals* (1975).

458. von Hentig, H., "The Limits of Deterrence," *J. Amer. Inst. Crim. L. & Crim.*, vol. 29 (1938–39).

459. von Hirsch, Andrew, *Doing Justice* (1976).

460. Waelder, "Psychiatry and the Problem of Criminal Responsibility," 101 *U. Pa. L. Rev.* 378 (1952).

461. Walker, N., *Crime and Insanity in England* (1968).

462. ———. "Crime and Punishment," *New Society,* March 12, 1964.

463. ———. "Punishing, Denouncing or Reducing Crime?" in *Reshaping The Criminal Law: Essays in Honor of Glanville Williams,* ed. P. Glazebrook (1978).

464. ———. *Sentencing in a Rational Society* (1969).

465. ———. *The Aims of a Penal System* (1966).

466. ———. "The Criminologist's Stone," in *Behavior and Misbehavior* (1977).

467. Walker, O. S., "Why Should Irresponsible Offenders Be Excused?" *J. Phil.*, vol. 66 (1969).

468. Wasserstrom, R. A., "H. L. A. Hart and the Doctrines of Mens Rea and Criminal Responsibility," 35 *U. Chi. L. Rev.* 92 (1967).

469. ———. "Strict Liability in the Criminal Law," 12 *Stan L. Rev.* 730 (1960).

470. ———. "Why Punish the Guilty?" *Princeton Univ. Mag.*, vol. 20 (1964).

471. Webb, P. M., "To Let the Punishment Fit the Crime: A New Look," 2 *N.Z. L. J.* 439 (1967).

472. Wechsler, H., "Sentencing, Correction and the Model Penal Code," 109 *U. Pa. L. Rev.* 465 (1961).

473. ———. "The Challenge of a Model Penal Code," 65 *Harv. L. Rev.* 1097 (1952).

474. ———. "The Criteria of Criminal Responsibility," 22 *U. Chi. L. Rev.* 367 (1955).

475. Wechsler, H., Jones, H., and Korn, H., "The Treatment of Inchoate Crimes in the Model Penal Code of the American Law Institute: Attempt, Solicitation, and Conspiracy," 61 *Colum. L. Rev.* 571 (1961).

476. Wertheimer, A., "Deterrence and Retribution," *Ethics,* vol. 86 (1976).

477. Wharton, *Criminal Law,* 12th ed. (1932).
478. White, A. R., "Carelessness, Indifference and Recklessness," 24 *Modern L. Rev.* 592 (1961).
479. Wilkins, B. T., "Concerning 'Motive' and 'Intention'," *Analysis,* vol. 31 (1971).
480. Williams, Bernard, "A Critique of Utilitarianism," in Smart, J. J. C., and Williams, Bernard, *Utilitarianism For and Against* (1973).
481. ———. "Deciding to Believe," in *Problems of the Self* (1973).
482. Williams, Glanville L., "Absolute Liability in Traffic Offenses," (1967) *Crim. L. Rev.* 194.
483. ———. "Automatism," in *Essays in Criminal Science,* ed. G. O. W. Mueller (1961).
484. ———. "Causation in Homicide," (1957) *Crim. L. Rev.* 429.
485. ———. "Causation in the Law," (1961) *Camb. L. J.* 62.
486. ———. "Consent and Public Policy," (1962) *Crim. L. Rev.* 74.
487. ———. "Criminal Law—Attempting the Impossible," (1974) *Camb. L. J.* 33.
488. ———. *Criminal Law: The General Part,* 2nd ed. (1961).
489. ———. "Police Control of Intending Criminals," (1955) *Crim. L. Rev.* 66.
490. ———. "Provocation and the Reasonable Man," (1954) *Crim. L. Rev.* 740.
491. ———. *The Mental Element in Crime* (1965).
492. ———. "The Proper Scope and Function of the Criminal Law," 74 *L. O. Rev.* 76 (1958).
493. Wilson, James Q., *Thinking About Crime* (1975).
494. Wittgenstein, L., *Philosophical Investigations* (1953).
495. Wootton, B., *Crime and the Criminal Law* (1963).
496. ———. "Neither Child nor Lunatic," *The Listener,* September 24, 1959.
497. ———. *Social Science and Social Pathology* (1959).
498. Woozley, A. D., "Legal Duties, Offences, and Sanctions," *Mind,* vol. 77 (1968).
499. Wright, R. A., "Causation and Responsibility in English Law," (1955) *Camb. L. J.* 163.
500. Zilboorg, G., *The Psychology of the Criminal Act and Punishment* (1954).
501. Zimring and Hawkins, *Deterrence: The Legal Threat in Crime Control* (1973).

REFERENCES FOR BIBLIOGRAPHY

CHAPTER ONE

Generally. 3, 12, 36, 176, 306, 320, 354, 379, 381, 382, 388, 389, 390, 421, 424, 426, 444, 448, 449, 457, 462, 463, 465, 472, 492.

Section 1. 8, 9, 68, 107, 136, 166, 186, 196, 208, 218, 228, 229, 232, 273, 299, 302, 331, 345, 384, 391, 401, 493, 498.

Section 2. 33, 34, 45, 47, 51, 59, 61, 73, 76, 88, 93, 99, 105, 108, 109, 138, 140, 149, 186, 207, 208, 210, 211, 218, 222, 232, 264, 273, 276, 284, 290, 313, 331, 332, 345, 367, 371, 372, 436, 443, 480, 491, 498.

Section 3. 2, 5, 97, 158, 166, 190, 222, 234, 246, 315, 316, 328, 386, 401, 409, 433, 434, 458, 466, 493, 495, 500.

CHAPTER TWO

Generally. 6, 13, 42, 43, 47, 89, 90, 129, 231, 257, 356, 363, 374, 392, 393, 394, 417, 437, 477, 488.

Section 1. 21, 56, 92, 153, 196, 204, 441.

Section 2. 21, 40, 56, 71, 72, 83, 92, 155, 163, 188, 196, 240, 260, 285, 403, 405, 406, 441.

Section 3. 21, 22, 74, 86, 119, 153, 196, 201, 204, 285, 286, 325, 376, 408, 410, 441, 453.

CHAPTER THREE

Generally. 13, 42, 43, 47, 86, 106, 231, 299, 333, 334, 356, 374, 392, 393, 394, 417, 468, 477, 488.

Section 1. 11, 21, 22, 59, 71, 77, 114, 139, 150, 154, 157, 161, 194, 196, 197, 204, 209, 213, 220, 232, 243, 258, 259, 281, 285, 288, 339, 346, 349, 352, 355, 363, 399, 429, 431, 439, 452, 456, 478, 479, 491.

CHAPTER FOUR

CHAPTER FIVE

CHAPTER SIX

269, 270, 274, 275, 293, 294, 295, 300, 304, 306, 319, 326, 354, 357, 360, 368, 379, 382, 383, 390, 398, 412, 420, 421, 422, 446, 457, 459, 462, 463, 464, 465, 470, 472, 476, 498.

Section 1. 14, 19, 20, 24, 42, 94, 105, 110, 120, 148, 170, 214, 230, 292, 303, 323, 327, 385.

Section 2. 5, 8, 9, 10, 14, 19, 20, 23, 24, 95, 97, 120, 123, 141, 166, 170, 286, 303, 327, 396, 458, 501.

Section 3. 8, 9, 39, 69, 95, 107, 141, 170, 273, 480.

CHAPTER TEN

Generally. 126.

Section 1. 302, 310, 316, 361, 370, 380, 409, 495, 500.

Section 2. 54, 114, 150, 157, 197, 213, 339, 349, 399, 439, 456.

Section 3. 15, 38, 102, 173, 195, 209, 254, 364, 395, 398, 415, 416, 430, 438, 451, 454, 471.

Section 4. 1, 2, 3, 4, 7, 19, 20, 24, 31, 34, 36, 39, 42, 52, 64, 67, 73, 91, 98, 128, 135, 148, 164, 167, 200, 209, 212, 214, 215, 217, 225, 230, 261, 262, 263, 283, 301, 310, 312, 313, 323, 329, 351, 361, 378, 388, 390, 396, 411, 443, 445, 446, 457, 459, 464, 471, 472.

Section 5. 7, 65, 97, 111, 132, 234, 275, 302, 312, 313, 315, 378, 382, 402, 409, 410, 433, 434, 447, 459.

Index

Page numbers above 468 refer to the Notes.